19 7be 1908

At the beginning of the century sand from the Loire was still hauled by hand before being transported to the port, where it was unloaded by barrow. A sifter then sieved it, using a large wire-mesh sieve.

The winter of 1879–80 was particularly harsh. The Loire was completely iced over. As damage to bridges was feared, the army dynamited the ice flow. Ten years later another bitterly cold spell swept across Touraine, and the Loire remained frozen for twenty-five days. The last memorable winter was that of 1962–3, when the number of days of frost reached a record: the Loire was entirely covered with ice for four weeks.

At the end of the 19th century a large part of the population of the Loire Valley was working in the vineyards or in associated industries. The methods and practices used by the cooper have barely altered over the centuries. He shapes the *douelles* (wooden staves), then assembles them on a "ring". The bending of the *douelles*, a delicate operation that determines the quality and longevity of the barrel, generally takes place over a wood fire.

EVERYMAN GUIDES
PUBLISHED BY DAVID CAMPBELL PUBLISHERS LTD, LONDON

THE LOIRE VALLEY – ISBN 1-85715-877-6

© 1993 David Campbell Publishers Ltd
© 1996 Editions Nouveaux-Loisirs, a subsidiary of Gallimard, Paris

First published 1996

NUMEROUS SPECIALISTS AND ACADEMICS HAVE CONTRIBUTED TO THIS GUIDE.

THE LOIRE VALLEY:
EDITOR: Anne-Josyane Magniant
assisted by Serge Gras, Cécile Gall, Philippe Voyenne (history), Veronika Vollmer (coordination practical information), Sylvie Blanchard and Philippe Yvan (wines of the Loire Valley)
LAYOUT: Olivier Brunot, François Chentrier, Gérard Dumas, Carole Gaborit, Philippe Marchand
PICTURE RESEARCH: Anaïck Bourhis
GRAPHICS: Élisabeth Cohat
THE LOIRE VALLEY (PAGES 12–13): René Maurice
NATURE: Philippe J. Dubois, Frédéric Bony *with* René Chaboud, Alain Perthuis, Gérard Tardivo
HISTORY: Jeanine Labussière
ARTS AND TRADITIONS: François Icher, Denis Le Vraud, Maurice Pommier, Cécile Vuatrin Duflot
ARCHITECTURE: Bruno Lenormand *with* Anne Bourgne
THE LOIRE VALLEY AS SEEN BY PAINTERS: Sylvain Bellanger, Marie-Christine Forest, Yves Mauffrat, Véronique Moreau
THE LOIRE VALLEY AS SEEN BY WRITERS: Lucinda Gane

ITINERARIES:
AMBOISE: Stéphane Gendron, Annie Gros
ANGERS: René Maurice
AZAY-LE-RIDEAU: Marie Latour, Anne-Josyane Magniant
BLOIS: Bruno Guignard, Elisabeth Latrémolière, Florent Tèxnier, Aude de Tocqueville
CHAMBORD: Jean Martin-Démézil, Françoise de Person, Aude de Tocqueville
CHENONCEAUX: Stéphane Gendron
CHINON: Marie Latour
LOCHES: Paul-Jacques Lévêque-Mingam
ORLÉANS: René Maurice
SACHÉ: Bernard Briais
SAUMUR: René Maurice
TOURS: Christian Daumas, Stéphane Gendron, Annie Gros, Jeanine Labussière, Marie Latour, Elizabeth Latrémolière, René Maurice, Andrée Moreau, Danièle Moreau, Véronique Moreau

PRACTICAL INFORMATION:
Alain Bradfer, Christian Daumas, Veronika Vollmer

USEFUL ADDRESSES:
Jean-Claude Ribaut

ILLUSTRATIONS:
NATURE: Anne Bodin, Claire Felloni, Jean Chevallier, Jean Philippe Chabot, Gismonde Curiace, Bernard Duheme, François Desbordes, Gilbert Houbre, Jean-Michel Kacedan, Catherine Lachaud, Jean-Marc Pau, Sylvaine Pérols, Pascal Robin, Frédérique Schwebel
ARCHITECTURE: Philippe Candé, Nicolette Castle, Hugh Dixon, Bill Donohoe, Mick Gillot, Jean-Marie Guillou, Trevor Hill, Roger Hutchins, Tuth Lindsey, Ian Moores, Claude Quiec, Michael Shoebridge, Ed Stuart, Tony Townsend
ITINERARIES: Grégory Baird, Philippe Biard, Jean-Marc Lanusse, Bruno Lenormand, Philippe Lhez, Dominique Mansion, Fabrice Moireau, Jean-Claude Sénée
PRACTICAL INFORMATION: Maurice Pommier
MAPS: Vincent Brunot *with* Atelier de Bayonne, Francine Callède, Dominique Duplantier ; Éric Gillion
COMPUTER GENERATED MAPS: Patrick Alexandre, Édigraphie, Sophie Compagne, Philippe Doussinet, Cyrille Mallié, Patrick Merienne

PHOTOGRAPHY:
Éric Guillemot, Patrick Léger *with* Pierre Aucante, Alain Beignet, Serge Chirol, Alain Doron, Jean-Pierre Gislard, François Joly, Patrick Lavaud, Michel Magat, Jean-Pierre Moreau, Jean-Luc Pechinot, Jean-Philippe Perraguin, Pierre Pitrou, Jean-Noël Thibault

WE WOULD LIKE TO THANK: Jacques Gérard, Jacques Hesse, Pierre Huteau, Nicole Lagravère, Paul-Jacques Lévêque-Mingam, Solange Matheron, Mme de La Morandière, Marc Philippe, Jean-Yves Pinon, Mr de Sainte-Marie, Archives départementales, Galerie La Cymaise (Paris), Bibliothèque départementale (Tours), Bibliothèque Municipale (Tours), Château de Blois, Musée de la Sologne (Romorantin-Lanthenay), Musée des Beaux-Arts (Tours), L'École Nationale d'Équitation, Saumur

TRANSLATED BY GILLES DESMONS AND SUSAN MACKERVOY.
EDITED AND TYPESET BY BOOK CREATION SERVICES, LONDON.
PRINTED IN ITALY BY EDITORIALE LIBRARIA.

EVERYMAN GUIDES
79 Berwick Street
London W1V 3PF

THE LOIRE VALLEY

EVERYMAN GUIDES

Contents

Nature, *15*

Climate, *16*
The Loire, *18*
River banks, *20*
Fish and fishing, *22*
Woodland and forests, *24*
Agriculture and horticulture, *26*
Animal farming and breeding, *28*
Vineyards, *30*
From vine to wine, *32*

History, *33*

From Charles V to Louis XVI, *34*
Chronology, *36*

Arts and traditions, *45*

Boats on the Loire, *46*
Hunting, *52*
Food: fish terrine, *54*
Specialties, *56*

Architecture, *57*

RELIGIOUS ARCHITECTURE:
The Romanesque period, *58*
The Gothic period, *60*
From the Renaissance to classicism, *62*
MILITARY AND RESIDENTIAL ARCHITECTURE:
Castles and keeps, *64*
Fortresses and residences, *66*
The Renaissance château, *68*
CLASSICAL RESIDENTIAL ARCHITECTURE:
The 17th and 18th centuries *70*
URBAN ARCHITECTURE:
Timber-framed houses, *72*
Town houses, *74*
RURAL ARCHITECTURE:
Farmhouses, *76*
Mills and brickyards, *78*
Small farm buildings, *80*

The Loire Valley as seen by painters, *81*

The Loire Valley as seen by writers, *89*

ORLÉANS, *111*

Joan of Arc: "The Maid of Orléans", *116*
Orléans to Gien, *126*
Gien earthenware, *134*
Orléans to Blois, *138*

ORLÉANS

BLOIS, *141*

The assassination of the Duc de Guise, *146*
Chambord to Chaumont
via Cheverny, *156*
Château de Chambord, *158*
The Galerie des Illustres, *168*
The Sologne, *174*

BLOIS

AMBOISE, *179*

Leonardo da Vinci: a universal mind, *186*
Around Amboise, *192*

AMBOISE

TOURS, *193*

The "compagnonnage": craft guilds, *200*
Saint Martin, *206*
Houses on Place Plumereau, *210*
Tours to Valençay via Chenonceau, *216*
Château de Chenonceau, *218*
Tours to Chinon, *234*
Azay-le-Rideau, *236*
Chinon, *242*
The Tavant wall paintings, *252*
Fresco painting, *256*
Tours to Fontevraud, *258*
Louis XI and the silk industry
at Tours, *260*

TOURS

SAUMUR

SAUMUR, 277

The Cadre Noir, *282*
Saumurois: troglodytic dwellings , *286*
Saumur to Angers, *291*

ANGERS

ANGERS, *295*

The Tapestry of the Apocalypse, *300*
Around Angers, *310*

PRACTICAL INFORMATION, *313*

Preparations, *314*
Traveling to the Loire Valley, *316*
Getting around, *317*
Living in the Loire Valley, *318*
Wines of the Loire Valley, *322*
Places of interest, *328*
Useful addresses, *337*

APPENDICES, *347*

Bibliography, *348*
List of illustrations, *350*
Index, *356*

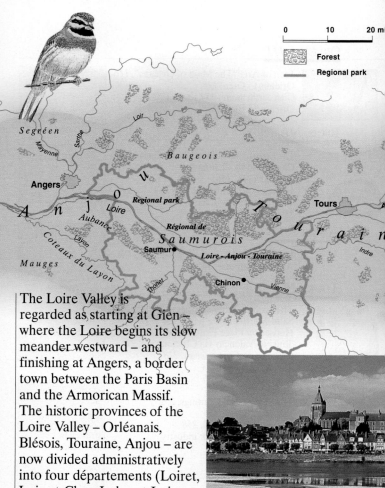

0   10   20 m

Forest

Regional park

The Loire Valley is regarded as starting at Gien – where the Loire begins its slow meander westward – and finishing at Angers, a border town between the Paris Basin and the Armorican Massif. The historic provinces of the Loire Valley – Orléanais, Blésois, Touraine, Anjou – are now divided administratively into four départements (Loiret, Loir-et-Cher, Indre-et-Loire and Maine-et-Loire) and two regions (Centre and Pays de Loire). Nevertheless, the old provinces have retained their geographic characteristics, and the only link between them is provided by the river: by river transport in the past, and by tourism today.

ANJOU ● 37, ▲ 277
More of a historical entity than a geographical one, Anjou is made up of several regions. To the west, bordering the Armorican Massif, the Segré and Mauges regions are known as Anjou Noir, due to their schist and sandstone terrain. To the east the Beaugé plateau and the plain of Saumur make up Anjou Blanc, with its tufa, vines and forests, while around Angers the slopes of the alluvial valley are covered with meadows, vineyards, flower nurseries and market gardens ■ 26.

TOURAINE ● 77, ▲ 193
Nowadays Touraine corresponds to the Département of Indre-et-Loire, which has the well-known university town of Tours as its capital. Spread around the valleys of the Loire and its tributaries, this gentle and luminous region is home to high-quality vineyards ■ 30, which are one of the chief sources of its wealth. As in Anjou troglodyte dwellings ● 76, ▲ 286 are to be found here, dug out in the white tufa.

O r l é a n a i s

Orléans

Loire

Cousson

Gien

Briare

B l é s o i s

S o l o g n e

Blois

Beuvron

ire

Cher

G â t i n e

Valençay

**PAYS
DE LA
LOIRE**

LOIRET

**LOIR-
ET-
CHER**

MAINE-
ET-
LOIRE

**INDRE-
ET-
LOIRE**

CENTRE

**AGRICULTURAL
RESOURCES**
Wine occupies
first place, closely
followed by the
cultivation of fruit,
vegetables and
flowers. Market
gardening ■ 26 has
become an important
addition to the vast
cereal farms of the
northern parts of
Blésois and
Orléanais.

**THE WINES OF
THE LOIRE** ■ 30
The vineyards of the
Loire valley have
been developed along
the river over the
centuries. Touraine
and Anjou (around
Saumur) are the two
most important wine
areas, producing a
variety of well-known
wines that admirably
complement the
varied range of
regional gastronomic
specialities.

*Above: windmill ● 79
at Thouard (Maine-et-
Loire). Center: views
of the towns of Gien
and Blois. Below: the
nuclear power station
at St-Laurent-des-
Eaux ▲ 139.*

ORLÉANAIS ▲ 111
This region stretches
along the curve of the
Loire that reaches its
northernmost point at
Orléans, the capital
of Loiret. Here, more
than anywhere else,
the river unifies the
towns and the land
in a veritable mosaic:
the chalky Beauce
plain in the north is
succeeded to the
south by the sandy
Sologne, and to the
east by the splendid
Forest of Orléans
(c. 90,000 acres), the
clay soils of Gâtinais
and finally the valley
itself. There the river
enters on a sublime
display of landscapes
and châteaux.

BLÉSOIS ● 77, ▲ 141
Blois (above) is the
seat of the prefecture
of Loir-et-Cher. The
poor soils of Sologne
▲ 174, the fertile
plains of Beauce, the
bocage of Perche and
the river valley, with
its great châteaux
such as Chambord
and Cheverny, afford
a remarkable diversity
of landscape.

INDUSTRY
The Loire Valley's
three nuclear power
stations – Avoine-
Chinon (1963),
Saint-Laurent-des-
Eaux (1969) and
Dampierre-en-Burly
(1980) – play a
central role in the
region's economy.

13

HOW TO USE THIS GUIDE
(Sample page shown from the guide to Venice)

The symbols at the top of each page refer to the different parts of the guide.

◼ **NATURAL ENVIRONMENT**

● **KEYS TO UNDERSTANDING**

▲ **ITINERARIES**

◆ **PRACTICAL INFORMATION**

The itinerary map shows the main points of interest along the way and is intended to help you find your bearings.

The mini-map locates the part itinerary within the wider area covered by the guide.

Santa Lucia Station.

The gateway to Venice; after all, is neither the Piazzetta nor the Grand Canal ... churned by propellers, turbulent ... group over a ...
Fernand Braudel, Venice

THE GATEWAY TO VENICE ★

PONTE DELLA LIBERTA. Built by the Austrians 50 years after the Treaty of Campo Formio in 1797 ● *34,* to link Venice with Milan. The bridge ended the thousand-year separation from the mainland and shook the city's economy to its roots as Venice, already in the throes of the industrial revolution, saw its dependence on the mainland grow out of all recognition. **SANTA LUCIA STATION.** The present station dates from 1955, but still bears the name of the Renaissance church demolished in 1861 to make way for it. Opposite is the green dome of the Church of San Simeone Piccolo

▲ Half a day

BRIDGES TO VENICE
The Austrians conceived a project for a railway between Mestre and Venice as early as 1814, but it was not until 1846 that construction of the Ponte della Liberta was finally under way. The span of this new bridge was almost 11,500 feet and it included 222 arches. On April 25, 1933, the Ponte della Littorio was opened. Built to run alongside the rail line than two years by Umberto Fantucci, this bridge was intended for use by motor cars.

● ▲ ◼ ◆
The symbols alongside a title or within the text itself provide cross-references to a theme or place dealt with elsewhere in the guide.

★ The star symbol signifies that a particular site has been singled out by the publishers for its special beauty, atmosphere or cultural interest.

At the beginning of each itinerary, the suggested means of transport to be used and the time it will take to cover the area are indicated:

🚣 By boat
🚶 On foot
🚲 By bicycle
🚗 By car
🕓 Duration

THE GATEWAY TO VENICE ★

PONTE DELLA LIBERTA. Built by the Austrians 50 years after the Treaty of Campo Formio in 1797 ● *34,* to link Venice with Milan. The bridge ended the thousand-year separation from the mainland and shook the city's economy to its roots as Venice, already in the throes of the industrial revolution, saw

🚶 Half a day

BRIDGES TO VENICE

NATURE

CLIMATE, *16*
THE LOIRE, *18*
RIVER BANKS, *20*
FISH AND FISHING, *22*
WOODLAND AND FORESTS, *24*
AGRICULTURE
AND HORTICULTURE , *26*
ANIMAL FARMING
AND BREEDING, *28*
VINEYARDS, *30*
FROM VINE TO WINE, *32*

■ CLIMATE

The Loire in flood at its junction with the Cher.

"Melancholic or radiant according to the season, the skies are never obscured for long", so said Joachim du Bellay (1522–60). The mild and temperate Loire Valley spreads along either side of the river, the natural border between the north and south of France. Near the river the atmosphere seems continuously to hover between sun and clouds; but the frequent morning mists rarely persist, the rain is frequent but never abundant and there is plenty of sunshine, especially on the hillsides overlooking the river. In the north of Loir-et-Cher, toward the Perche hills, the climate becomes more contrasted. In the southeast, the Sologne is characteristically humid because of its numerous forests and ponds.

Orléans
Blois
Angers Tours

Sea breezes
Galerne
Soulaire

The *galerne* is a westerly wind, whereas the *soulaire* or *solaire* blows from the southwest and brings maritime rains.

Heavy snowfalls and intense droughts are unusual in the Loire Valley. The temperate climate and the remarkable light, hardly disturbed by the morning mists, provide a perfect backdrop for its Renaissance buildings.

With its sandbanks and islets, the Loire provides an inviting habitat for migratory birds (ducks, gulls and waders . . .).

After nightfall the ground rapidly loses the heat accumulated during the day and cools down faster than the ambient air. During the night this cooling down process is transmitted progressively to the surrounding air, up to several hundred feet.

After a few hours of sunshine the ground warms up, and so does the surrounding air. The fog rises slowly . . . and clears away.

If the level of humidity in the air is great enough, the vapor condenses into minute drops. This is the phenomenon that creates fog, especially during clear and windless nights.

During the day the earth converts the sun's radiation into heat. The ground, being more conductive than the atmosphere, warms up more quickly. Some of this heat is then transmitted to the surrounding air by radiation from the earth.

17

River   Water meadow   Levee   Poplar plantation

Set in a wide valley since the last glacial period, the majestic
Loire, with its unpredictable floods, is partly constrained
within embankments or levees built in the Middle Ages.
These installations perceptibly altered the Loire landscape,
with its soft hues and restful lines. With the passing of
the seasons and variations of water level, the river is an
extraordinary meeting place of water, sand and light.
It provides an unusual variety of environments: islets,
banks, dry meadows, water meadows and alluvial forests,
which are home to remarkably diverse fauna and flora.

**"THE LAST GREAT
WILD RIVER"**
From its source on
Mont Gerbier-de-
Jonc to its mouth at
St-Nazaire, the Loire
and its tributaries
provide the most
remarkable hydro-
system in western
Europe. When it
floods, it can
double in

volume, turning
into a furious
mass of water. In
the past an important
transportation route
● *46*, remains of
which are still visible
(jetties, ports, quays,
bargees' houses),
it had a great impact
on the local
economy.

AMBOISE. With its mild climate
and pleasant environment,
the Loire Valley made the
perfect setting for
royal houses.

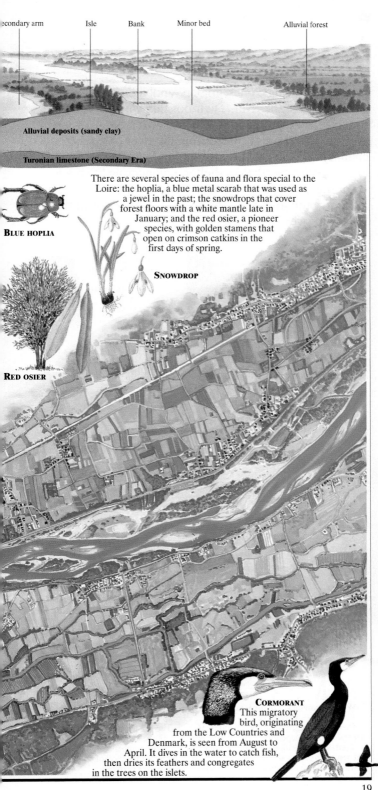

Secondary arm   Isle   Bank   Minor bed   Alluvial forest

Alluvial deposits (sandy clay)

Turonian limestone (Secondary Era)

There are several species of fauna and flora special to the
Loire: the hoplia, a blue metal scarab that was used as
a jewel in the past; the snowdrops that cover
forest floors with a white mantle late in
January; and the red osier, a pioneer
species, with golden stamens that
open on crimson catkins in the
first days of spring.

BLUE HOPLIA

SNOWDROP

RED OSIER

CORMORANT
This migratory
bird, originating
from the Low Countries and
Denmark, is seen from August to
April. It dives in the water to catch fish,
then dries its feathers and congregates
in the trees on the islets.

19

■ RIVER BANKS

WEASEL
This carnivore, partial to rodents, sometimes raids rabbit burrows and readily adds eggs and nestling birds to its diet.

As soon as spring comes, golden sandbanks appear in the shallow bed of the river. Their position varies according to the current, level and flow of the water. Small or large, they are sometimes isolated from the river banks by shallow channels. In spite of the surrounding water, these are arid areas which nevertheless shelter a pioneering life made up of fugacious plants, insects and arenicolous birds. They all contribute to the specific and rich ecosystems of the "last wild river" in France.

The golden banks of the Loire are made up of sand and gravel of varying sizes which originate mostly from erosion of the local rock (flint, chalk, burr) but also from the upstream geology (granite, basalt, gneiss, mica schist).

KINGFISHER
The only member of the kingfisher family found in Europe, this colorful bird nests in the river banks. Highly sensitive to pollution, it is a reliable indicator of water quality.

GRAY WILLOW
Its downy catkins are the first melliferous flowers of spring.

WOOD SANDPIPER, COMMON SANDPIPER, REDSHANK
These long-legged waders work different depths of water, depending on their size, and feed on animalcules found in the mud. The river banks provide these migratory birds with favorable conditions for their halts.

LITTLE RINGED PLOVER
This species nests on the sandy islets in large numbers, whenever the level of the river permits.

WILD RABBITS
The sand provides rabbits with an ideal place to dig their warrens.

SAND MARTIN
Steep, sandy river banks and rockfaces in stone quarries make ideal places for these small sandy-brown birds to excavate their nest burrows.

LITTLE TERN
The Loire is an important site for the preservation of the population of the smallest European tern, which has become an emblem of the river.

CHANGING BIOTOPES
The Loire's traditional landscape has altered significantly. Trees and bushes have been spreading fast, chiefly because of the end of pastoralism and the drop in the water level due to the dredging of the river and eutrophication – excesses in phosphates and nitrates causing algae to proliferate, thus depleting the supply of oxygen.

COMMON TERN
These long-distance migratory birds arrive from Africa late in March to establish their breeding colonies on the emerging sandbanks.

Knot grass

Soapwort

F. Desbordes
Golden cyperus

PALUDINA
A viviparous water snail that feeds on algae and plankton.

CINDELA OR TIGER BEETLE
A carnivorous insect that likes to run across the sand in the sun.

Strapwort

Scirpus michelianus

"GOMPHE SERPENTIN"
A central European dragonfly. The Loire has enabled its spread to the west.

21

FISH AND FISHING

Like the perch, the pike is a redoubtable hunter: it eats three to seven times its own weight in fish per day.

So far as fishing is concerned, the Loire and its tributaries owe their reputation to migratory fish such as salmon, small and allis shad, river and sea lamprey, eels and mullet. In the past a greater number of professionals used to fish the river, but nowadays only a few license holders are authorized to install large nets across the Loire. A decline in the migratory fish population has been brought about by various causes, including the deteriorating quality of the water due to urban, industrial and agricultural pollution and the destruction of spawning grounds due to excessive extraction of sand and gravel.

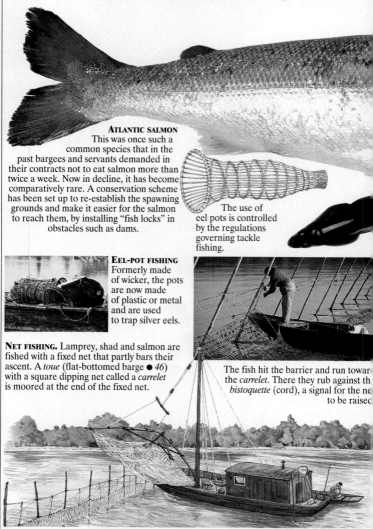

ATLANTIC SALMON
This was once such a common species that in the past bargees and servants demanded in their contracts not to eat salmon more than twice a week. Now in decline, it has become comparatively rare. A conservation scheme has been set up to re-establish the spawning grounds and make it easier for the salmon to reach them, by installing "fish locks" in obstacles such as dams.

The use of eel pots is controlled by the regulations governing tackle fishing.

EEL-POT FISHING
Formerly made of wicker, the pots are now made of plastic or metal and are used to trap silver eels.

NET FISHING. Lamprey, shad and salmon are fished with a fixed net that partly bars their ascent. A *toue* (flat-bottomed barge ● 46) with a square dipping net called a *carrelet* is moored at the end of the fixed net.

The fish hit the barrier and run towar the *carrelet*. There they rub against th *bistoquette* (cord), a signal for the ne to be raised

PIKE
The pike population is diminishing because their preferred spawning grounds, the water meadows, are becoming rarer.

"TROUSSE-CULOTTE" FISHING
This involves tucking up trousers or skirts, standing thigh-deep in the water and stirring up the sand or gravel with one's feet. The resulting sand cloud attracts gudgeon, sparling and bleak.

LIS SHAD. Related to sardines, these migratory fish leave the coastal waters in May and ascend the Loire to lay their eggs.

AKED CARP. They come from eastern and central Europe and are very sensitive to pollution.

GUDGEON
Easily recognizable, this swift, gregarious fish is partial to invertebrates.

EEL. As soon as summer comes, eel go down the Loire for the long journey to the Sargasso Sea.

SPARLING
Small river fish that like sand and gravel.

CATFISH
Originating in North America, they are very small in Europe.

MULLET. These sea fish live in shoals and swim far up the Loire in search of food.

BREAM
They like calm, deep waters and enjoy foraging in muddy river beds to find their food.

RIVER LAMPREY
Primitive migratory fish, with a mouth shaped like a cupping glass. In common with their cousin the sea lamprey, they have now become extremely rare.

The Loire salmon has given rise to numerous local recipes, such as salmon in green sauce and salmon poached in stock with Vouvray wine.

◼ WOODLAND AND FORESTS

SPOTTED SALAMANDER
You are most likely to
encounter this amphibian
on rainy nights.

The middle section of the Loire is surrounded by woods and forests, which are often very dense. Geological influences and human intervention have produced several kinds of landscape. Around Blois, for example, one can find magnificent plantations of sessile and pedunculate oaks; around Orléans Scots pines were introduced 200 years ago to create the largest national forest in France (almost 90,000 acres); and in the Sologne birches and chestnut trees complete the forest tapestry. Toward Anjou maritime pines reign supreme. Among the foliage, rich and diverse fauna and flora thrive in the woodland habitat.

Although perceived as natural landscapes, forests have to a large extent been shaped by human activity.

DEER
In early fall the forests resound with rutting calls. In the rutting season deer stop feeding for several weeks.

EUROPEAN WILD BOA
The mature male (which has a dark, rough coat) leads a solitary life. Matur females lead group consisting of severa generations.

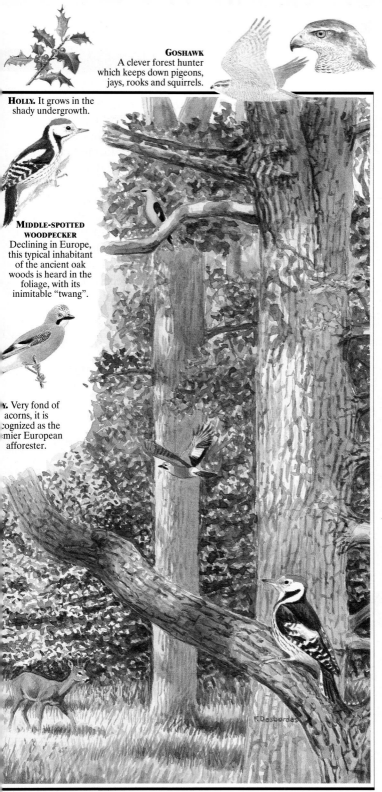

GOSHAWK
A clever forest hunter which keeps down pigeons, jays, rooks and squirrels.

HOLLY. It grows in the shady undergrowth.

MIDDLE-SPOTTED WOODPECKER
Declining in Europe, this typical inhabitant of the ancient oak woods is heard in the foliage, with its inimitable "twang".

y. Very fond of acorns, it is cognized as the mier European afforester.

F. Desbordes

25

AGRICULTURE
AND HORTICULTURE

CUCUMBERS
Grown under glass, like tomatoes.

The quality of the soils in the Loire Valley (light, sandy and rich in silt), together with the mild regional climate, make it ideal for horticulture, market gardening and arboriculture. Large areas of the "Jardin de la France" are farmed (either in the open or under cover), flowers being the dominant crop. Market gardeners in the region specialize in a considerable variety of crops, including white and green asparagus, celery, lettuces, cauliflowers, gherkins and mushrooms. Other crops include soft fruit (strawberries, blackcurrants, raspberries . . .), grain, bulbs, pears and apples. In this way the Orléanais, Blésois, Touraine and Anjou regions contribute to the horticultural and agricultural reputation of the Loire Valley at the European level.

Mushroom caves dug in the chalk can be several hundred yards, or even more than a mile, deep. The mushrooms are grown on a bed of horse manure, straw and fertilizer. From sowing to harvesting takes three months.

CULTIVATED MUSHROOMS
Among the varieties developed from the meadow agaric are *albidus* (white), the most common, and *avelloneus* (blond).

BLACKCURRANTS
These are harvested with grape-picking machines and made into cassis syrup or liqueur.

YAMS
The village of St-Claude-de-Diray is the principal producer of yams in western France.

ROSES
There has been a long tradition of rose-growing in the Loire Valley. Doué-la-Fontaine (Anjou) and Bellegarde (Orléanais) are the two main growers.

HEATHER
Heathers are cultivated on a large scale in Touraine (500,000 pots a year).

CHRYSANTHEMUMS
This flower is popular in France because it is in bloom for All Saints' Day. Anjou and Touraine are large-scale growers.

PELARGONIUMS
Zonal and ivy-leaved pelargoniums are well loved by gardeners. They are a specialty of the Orléans region.

THE "PLATISSOIRE"

A forgotten recipe has been revived in Rivarennes (Touraine) and Turquant (near Saumur): pears or apples are slowly dehydrated in the oven before being flattened and bottled in jars.

STRAWBERRIES
These are grown on mulched sandy soils, like asparagus and vines.

"ALBERGE DE TOURAINE" AND "PRÉCOCE DE SAUMUR"
Two varieties of apricot.

PASSE-CRASSANE, BEURRÉ-HARDY, CONFERENCE
Summer varieties, such as William, and winter varieties (Passe-Crassane) are losing ground to autumn pears such as Conference and Beurré-Hardy.

STE-CATHERINE PLUM
The flowering plum tree of Tours.

GOLDEN DELICIOUS, MELROSE, REINE DES REINETTES, GRANNY SMITH
Arboriculture is important in the Loire Valley. Fruit trees are planted both on hillsides and in the valleys, apples being the most significant in terms of acreage and Golden Delicious the most dominant variety.

Asparagus gouge

Cultivated in France since the 18th century, white asparagus has found ideal conditions in the sandy soils of the Loire Valley.

HARVESTING ASPARAGUS
Plastic mulching (above) has enabled early cropping. Asparagus is harvested from April to June. A special gouge (above, right) is used for cutting the spears.

CAULIFLOWERS
A traditional summer crop in Touraine. Varieties include "Frémont", "Linday" and "Nautilus".

LOLO ROSSA
A recent crop well liked by chefs.

LETTUCE
There can be three successive greenhouse crops.

GREEN ASPARAGUS
Traditionally a southern crop, green asparagus is now being grown in the Loire valley, especially in Loir-et-Cher.

ANIMAL FARMING AND BREEDING

Soil and know-how are the key to becoming a good goat's cheese maker.

Historically, the Loire Valley, from the area around Gien to Anjou, was a region dedicated to animal farming. Unfortunately with the progress of cereal-farming methods and a difficult economic situation, animal farming has been progressively abandoned in favor of corn crops, orchards, market gardening and poplar plantations. Cattle and horses are, however, still to be found in the more humid regions. Poultry, pigs and goats are raised intensively in accordance with the latest quality standards.

THE GÉLINE NOIRE OF TOURAINE
Originating from the French black chicken, its standard characteristics were defined in 1909.

BLACK TURKEY
This bird of American origin is now farmed in the Loire Valley – sometimes with the *label rouge* quality label, as in Touraine.

THE GÂTINAISE
The standard characteristics of this white chicken were defined in 1906. It is specific to the Loiret, and is bred for eating and eggs.

Now replaced by the tractor, the highly efficient draft horse was used for carting sand from the river, as well as for drawing barges along the Loire ● *46* and for ploughing the fields.

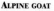

SOLOGNE SHEEP
Until the 19th century this extremely hardy and prolific breed, which is also an excellent walker, grazed in the water meadows beside the Loire and was the basis of a prosperous wool industry. The return of set-aside and rotation may revive it.

ALPINE GOAT
Most Loire herds consist of Saanen and Alpine goats. The small traditional herds are now giving way to the large herds of modern goat farming.

In the Loire Valley,
as everywhere in France, the
white Charolais has become
the reference breed for meat.

WINE AND GOAT'S CHEESE
Goat's cheese can be eaten warm
on a piece of toast or in puff pastry,
or with a salad, or simply for the
cheese course, accompanied
by one of the Loire's excellent
white wines, such as Cheverny,
Saumur or Vouvray.

GOAT'S CHEESE
Much care is needed. Once the milk
has been curdled with the addition
of rennet, it is ladled into cheese
strainers where it is left to
drip and separate from the
whey for twenty-four to
forty-eight hours.

Although a few farms
make cheese from
ewe's milk or cow's milk,
most of the region's
cheesemaking is based
on goat's cheese. Well-
known goat's cheeses
include Selles-sur-Cher
(Loir-et-Cher), the *bûche*
from Ste-Maure (Indre-
et-Loire) and the *pyramide*
from Valençay. The first two
are protected by an AOC.

THE MAINE-ANJOU
This cow is derived
from the Mancelle
breed, which was
crossbred with the
English Durham
and the Shorthorn
in the 19th century,
resulting in the
Durham-Mancelle in
1908. The standard
characteristics of the
Maine-Anjou were
defined in 1925, and
it became established
on the borders of
the Sarthe, Mayenne
and Maine-et-Loire
départements.
Originally a mixed
milk-meat breed, it is
today raised almost
exclusively for its fine
marbled meat, which
enjoys an excellent
reputation. The herds
are mostly in Anjou,
though the largest
ones (numbering
some 85,000 head in
1996) are to be found
in the United States
and Canada.

■ VINEYARDS

Grape picking – a source
of seasonal employment
and also an opportunity to
meet family and friends.

Present since Roman times, vineyards in the Loire Valley were given new life from the 9th to the 12th century thanks to the monasteries, in particular the famous abbeys of St-Benoît in the Orléans region, Marmoutier in Touraine, and Fontevraud in Anjou. The infatuation of the French kings with the Loire Valley contributed to this trend, and the river itself – where barges and lighters plied until the start of the 20th century – encouraged trading. Today the vineyards of the Loire Valley between Sancerre and Angers, covering 150,000 acres, constitute the fourth largest winegrowing area in France. The vines are spread, according to geological and climatic affinities, among some fifty *appellations d'origine contrôlée*, providing a wide choice of dry, sweet, sparkling and *pétillant* white wines, red wines for laying down or immediate drinking, and sweet or dry rosés.

MAIN APPELLATIONS
AOC (Appellation d'origine contrôlée): Anjou, Bonnezeaux, Bourgueil, Cheverny, Chinon, Coteaux-du-Layon, Coteaux-de-l'Aubance, Cour-Cheverny, Mennetou-Salon, Montlouis, Pouilly, Pouilly-Fumé, Quarts-de-Chaume, Quincy, Reuilly, St-Nicolas-de-Bourgueil, Sancerre, Saumur, Saumur-Champigny, Savennières, Touraine, Vouvray.
VDQS (Vin délimité de qualité supérieure): Cheverny, Côtes-de-Gien, Cour-Cheverny, Gris-Meunier de l'Orléanais, Valençay.

Angers

2

1   4

CÔT
This red-grape variety, known as Auxerrois in Cahors, was introduced in Anjou, Touraine and Blésois for making red and rosé Anjou and Touraine wines and also Valençay. It is used with Gamay, Cabernet and Groelleau to produce the finest Anjou rosés.

SAUVIGNON
This early grape variety forms the basis of some lively dry white wines that are spicy and highly aromatic. Its favorite terrain is Sancerrois, the home of Sancerre, Pouilly-Fumé and Mennetou-Salon. Grown in Anjou, Giennois, Blésois and Touraine, it combines well with Chenin Blanc and other grape varieties.

PINEAU-DE-LOIRE (CHENIN BLANC)
Already known in the time of Rabelais, this is the typical Loire-valley grape variety. Used alone, it gives such well-known white wines as Vouvray, Montlouis, Saumur, Savennières, Coteaux-du-Layon, Quarts-de-Chaume and Bonnezeaux. In association with Sauvignon, it contributes to Touraine and Cheverny wines and white Anjous.

GAMAY
Very much in fashion, this red-grape variety with white juice, from Beaujolais, has taken over numerous winegrowing areas, among them Anjou, Touraine and Blésois. It gives full, light, fruity wines and is perfectly adapted to the current vogue for young wines.

CABERNET-FRANC
This grape variety is known as Cabernet-Breton in Touraine and Anjou, because it was brought into these areas via the ports of Brittany. It has earned its reputation in Anjou-Touraine vintages such as Chinon, Bourgueil, St-Nicolas-de-Bourgueil, Saumur and Saumur-Champigny.

LATE HARVESTING
Picking grapes late makes the most of "noble rot" (*Botrytis cinerea*). This is vital for ripening Chenin Blanc, in order to produce smooth amber-colored, honey-scented wines such as Vouvray, Bonnezeaux and Quarts-de-Chaume.

* = VDQS (vin délimité de qualité supérieure)

1 Anjou
2 Savennières
3 Coteaux-de-l'Aubance
4 Quarts-de-Chaume, Bonnezeaux
5 Coteaux-du-Layon
6 Saumur
7 Saumur-Champigny
8 St-Nicolas-de-Bourgueil
9 Bourgueil
10 Chinon
11 Touraine (Azay-Le-Rideau, Amboise, Mesland)
12 Vouvray
13 Montlouis

14 Coteaux-du-Loir, Jasnières
15 Coteaux-du-Vendômois *
16 Cheverny, Cour-Cheverny
17 Valençay *
18 Vins de l'Orléanais (Gris-Meunier) *
19 Coteaux-du-Giennois *
20 Pouilly-Fumé, Pouilly-sur-Loire
21 Sancerre
22 Mennetou-Salon
23 Quincy
24 Reuilly

PINOT-NOIR
Famous in Alsace, Burgundy and Champagne, this grape variety plays a part in the production of the red wines of the Gien, Orléans and Sancerre areas.

ROCHE-AUX-MOINES AND COULÉE-DE-SERRANT (SAVENNIÈRES)
The Chenin Blanc cultivated on 70 acres of steep, picturesque shale slopes on the right bank of the Loire near Angers produces these two exceptionally fine vintages.

■ FROM VINE TO WINE

PRUNING THE VINE
Crucial for both quality and yield, the pruning is done in winter (see the legend of Saint Martin's donkey ● *104*).

BURSTING OF THE BUDS
The leaves burst from the buds in May. Grape picking takes place a hundred days after flowering.

GRAPE PICKING
Whether done by hand or by machine, this takes several weeks, starting in the middle of September.

BOTTLING
The wine undergoes a light filtration process before it is bottled.

PRODUCTION OF RED WINES

After having been hand-picked or machine-harvested, the bunches of grapes are sorted and destalked (**1**), then left in a vat for between five and twenty days (**2**). The juice becomes colored through contact with the grape skins, and the sugars are fermented by the action of the yeasts. The fermented must, or grape juice, that collects at the bottom of the vat is drawn off; this is known as the *vin de goutte* (**3**). Next the *marc* is pressed (**4**), **and** then the *vin de presse* (**5**) **and** the *vin de goutte* (**3**) are mixed together (**6**) and poured into vats (**7**) or casks (**8**) where the wine is left to mature.

PRODUCTION OF WHITE AND ROSÉ WINES

The grapes, either white or black (for rosé), are destalked (**1**), then pressed (**2**) as quickly as possible in order to avoid any harmful oxidation. The juice or must (**3**) is put into a vat for carefully controlled fermentation (**4**). The settling process follows next, during which impurities are eliminated through filtration and racking (syphoning off). The must is then poured into vats (**5**) or casks (**6**) and the settling process continues, concluding with the final racking and clarification just before bottling (**7**). Clarification entails clearing the wine by adding a substance (generally either casein or egg white) that will precipitate any impurities still remaining in it.

SPARKLING AND PÉTILLANT WINES
The Loire's Chenin Blanc grapes are admirably suited to making sparkling and *pétillant* wines. The Crémant-de-Loire *appellation* extends from Angers (downstream) to Cheverny (upstream).

HISTORY

FROM CHARLES V TO LOUIS XVI, *34*
HISTORY, *36*

1. The porcupine, Louis XII's emblem.
2. and **3.** The swan and the ermine, the emblems of Anne de Bretagne and her daughter Claude of France.

4. The salamander, emblem of Francis I.

*CHARLES V (1338–80)

CHARLES VI – Isabel of Bavaria
(1368–1422)   (1371–1435)

CHARLES VII – Marie of Anjou
(1403–61)   (1404–63)

LOUIS XI – Charlotte of Savoy
(1423–83)   (1442–8?)

Anne de Valois – Pierre de Beaujeu   CHARLES VIII – Anne de Bretagne   1. Jeanne de Valois
(1461–1522)   (1438–1503)   (1470–98)   (1476–1514)   (1464–1505)
                                                                 2. Anne de Bretagne
                                                                 (1476–1514)

FRANÇOIS II – Mary Stuart   CHARLES IX – Elisabeth of Austria   HENRI III – Louise of Lorraine
(1544–60)   (1542–87)   (1550–74)   (1554–92)   (1551–89)   (1553–1?)

ANNE DE BRETAGNE. Charles VIII had to stave off the intrigues of François II of Brittany, who wanted to marry his daughter and heiress, Anne, to Maximilian of Austria. Charles forced the young duchess to break off her engagement and dressed himself as a husband in Maximilian's place. Irrevocable commitments were made: if Anne had no male heir, she undertook to marry Charles' successor. And so she did: after Charles' death she married Louis XII, thus making Brittany part of France for ever ▲ 258.

LOUIS XII. The son of Charles d'Orléans ▲ 114, who was a refined man of letters, Louis XII was only three when his father died. Educated by his mother in history, literature and physical education, by the time he ascended the throne he had acquired a taste for socializing and a subtle knowledge of the human character

1.

2.

3.

Jeanne de Bourbon (1338–77)

Louis, Duke of Orléans – Valentine Visconti
(1372–1407)   (1366–1408)

Charles, Duke of Orléans – Marie of Cleves   Jean d'Angoulême – Marguerite de Rohan
(1391–1465)   (1426–87)   (1404–67)   (?–1496)

LOUIS XII
(1462–1515)

Charles d'Angoulême – Louise of Savoy
(1459–96)   (1476–1531)

Claude of France – **FRANÇOIS I**
(1499–1524)   (1494–1547)

Marguerite – Henri d'Albret, King of Navarre
(1493–1549)   (1503–55)

HENRI II – Catherine de Médicis
(1519–59)   (1519–89)

Jeanne d'Albret – Antoine de Bourbon
(1528–72)   (1518–62)

1. Marguerite de Valois –
   (1553–1615)
2. Marie de Médicis – **HENRY IV**
   (1573–1642)   (1553–1610)

LOUIS XIII – Anne of Austria
(1601–43)   (1601–66)

Louis XIV --Maria Theresa of Austria
(1638–1715)   (1638–83)

Louis, the Grand Dauphin – Marie Anne of Bavaria
(1661–1711)   (1660–90)

Louis, Duke of Burgundy – Marie Adelaide of Savoy
(1682–1712)   (1685–1712)

LOUIS XV – Marie Leszczynska
(1710–74)   (1703–68)

Louis of France – Marie Josephe of Saxony
(1729–65)   (1731–67)

LOUIS XVI – Marie Antoinette of Austria
(1754–93)   (1755–93)

*A family tree of reigning kings of France
from Charles V to Louis XVI.*

		2500 BC to 1500 BC Dolmens and menhirs		52 BC Gauls rise against the Romans	
500,000 BC	50,000 BC	10,000 BC	5000 BC	0	40

| 500,000 BC
First human
beings in the
Loire Valley | 80,000 BC TO 35,000 BC
Neanderthal man;
beginning of the last
Ice Age | 7000 BC Farming at Fossé
(near Blois) using wheat
and millet seeds from the
Middle East | 58 BC Start of
the conquest of
Gaul by Julius
Caesar | 258 AD to 260 AD
Penetration by Frank
and Saxons into the
Loire region |

PREHISTORIC AND PROTOHISTORIC

The first human beings in the Loire Valley appear in the Paleolithic era and live by hunting, fishing and gathering. Around 10,000 BC global warming affects their nomadic way of life, causing them to settle down, to start to rear animals and to farm. Between 6000 and 4000 BC, in the Neolithic era, they clear the forests and improve their tool making. Besides flint, they work with wood, horn and bone. From around 2500 BC the countryside is dotted with megaliths for worshipping the dead. Dolmens (collective burial places) are numerous: almost 140 of them have been found in the four départements of the Loire Valley, among them the remarkable Grand Dolmen de Bagneux ▲ 290. The menhirs (monolithic stone blocks) are still shrouded in mystery; although many of them have been destroyed, there are still about 130 of them left. Cremation was practiced too, as evidenced by the field full of earthenware funeral urns discovered near Jargeau ▲ 126. Artefacts from the Bronze Age (around 1500 to 750 BC) are distinguished by their comparative luxury (sword handles and jewelry). From the Iron Age (750 to 50 BC), weapons and jewelry have survived

THE GAULS

THE GAULS

Around 450 BC Celtic tribes from the east settle in the Loire Valley: the Andecavi ▲ 296 in what is now Anjou; the Turones ▲ 196 in Touraine; and the Carnutes ▲ 112 in the Orléans region. They build camps and fortified villages, such as the Châtelliers *oppidum* at Amboise ▲ 182.

THE ARRIVAL OF CHRISTIANITY
It would seem that Christianity developed in the Loire Valley in the 3rd century AD. By the 4th century Angers, Orléans and Tours have their own bishops. Saint Lidoire, first Bishop of Tours (337–70), is succeeded by Saint Martin ▲ 206. Combining his episcopal duties (371–91) with a life of meditation, he establishes a community at Marmoutier, near Tours. This becomes the cradle of the monasticism that would soon spread throughout Europe.

THE CONQUEST OF GAUL

In 58 BC Julius Caesar embarks on the conquest of Gaul. In the Loire Valley his soldiers meet with fierce resistance from the Andecavi and the Carnutes, allies of Vercingetorix. In retaliation, in 52 BC Caesar burns down Cenabum (present-day Orléans), capital of the Carnutes, then the center of Gaul. In the same year the taking of the city of Alesia and surrender of Vercingetorix marks the end of the Gallic Wars.

ROMANIZATION

Rome imprints its administrative and socio-cultural model on Gaul. Cities similar to Roman cities arise from Angers to Orléans. Caesarodunum (Tours) is founded in the year 20 AD. Large farms (*villae*) are set up. Today the imposing aqueduct of a private landowner is still visible in the middle of a field at Luynes ▲ 262. The Romans set up an intricate network of paved roads, sixteen of which radiate from Cenabum.

END OF THE "PAX ROMANA"

In the middle of the 3rd century AD the barbarians, hitherto restrained, cross the frontiers of the Empire. From 258 AD to 260 AD, the Franks and the Saxons ravage the Loire region, which in 274 AD suffers another Frankish invasion. Fortified walls are built to protect towns such as Orléans (in the 3rd century) and Tours (in the 4th century), where splendid ramparts still flank the Quai d'Orléans ▲ 196.

| End of the Western Empire. The barbarians come – and Tours | **751 AD** Start of the Carolingian dynasty: Pepin the Short elected King of the Franks | **Late 8th century to early 9th century** The Carolingian renaissance | **c. 972–1040** Foulques Nerra, Count of Anjou |
| 486 Clovis, King of the Franks | 507 Victory by Clovis over the Visigoths at Vouillé | 732 Charles Martel, mayor of palace, defeats the Spanish Moors at Poitiers | 800 Charlemagne becomes Emperor | 987 Start of the Capetian dynasty; Hugues Capet, Count of Orléans and Étampes, elected King of France |

500   600   700   800   900   1000

THE EARLY MIDDLE AGES

THE BARBARIAN INVASIONS

In the 5th century Germans, Franks, Burgundians and Visigoths overrun Gaul. The population seeks refuge in fortified sites such as Orléans and Tours. In 451 the Huns unsuccessfully lay siege to Orléans; the Saxons are at Angers; and the Visigoths covet Tours. The barbarians carve out kingdoms throughout Roman Gaul.

THE FRANKISH KINGDOM

Franks and Visigoths fight for Touraine. Clovis, by his victory at Vouillé (507) over Alaric II ▲ 190, King of the Visigoths, takes Tours and Aquitaine. On his death his sons indulge in fratricidal fighting, as related in *History of the Frankish Peoples* by Gregory of Tours ▲ 196.

CROSS OF ANJOU

Created for Louis I of Anjou around 1377–9, it serves as the emblem of the Order of the Cross before becoming the Cross of Anjou ▲ 312. In 1431 it takes the name "Cross of Lorraine" when René I inherits the duchy of Lorraine.

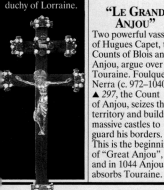

CAROLINGIAN RENAISSANCE

The Merovingian kings are gradually pushed out by the mayors of the palace, who exercise the real power. One of them, Pepin the Short (son of Charles Martel), is elected King of the Franks in 751. His son, Charlemagne (747–814), extends the frontiers of Christianity during his forty-six-year reign. His empire, with Aix-la-Chapelle as its capital, extends for nearly 400,000 square miles. At his bidding, the Basilica of St-Martin in Tours ▲ 204 becomes a royal abbey headed by the erudite Alcuin, who turns Tours into a major religious and intellectual center ▲ 205. Charlemagne entrusts Alcuin and Theodulf ▲ 129, Abbot of St-Benoît-sur-Loire, with the task of reviving the episcopal schools and of creating in each *scriptorium* (scribe's workshop). St-Martin, in Tours, produces remarkable manuscripts during the 9th century.

NEW INVASIONS

The empire, divided and weakened, is threatened by new invaders: the Vikings. On six occasions between 853 and 903 they sail up the Loire from Angers to Orléans, plundering towns, churches and monasteries. The raids only cease when Charles the Simple gives Normandy to the Viking leader Rollo (911), in exchange for his promise to protect the country from invasion. The now much weakened Carolingian dynasty comes to an end in 987 when Hugues Capet is elected king. His realm extends from Compiègne to Orléans. He has constantly to reassert his family's rule over restless feudal lords.

THE ANGEVIN EMPIRE AND THE PLANTAGENÊTS

(1044–1259)

"LE GRAND ANJOU"

Two powerful vassals of Hugues Capet, the Counts of Blois and Anjou, argue over Touraine. Foulques Nerra (c. 972–1040) ▲ 297, the Count of Anjou, seizes the territory and builds massive castles to guard his borders. This is the beginning of "Great Anjou", and in 1044 Anjou absorbs Touraine.

WISE WEDDINGS

The marriage, in 1110, arranged by Foulques V, Count of Anjou (1095–1143), between his son Geoffrey (1113–51) and Matilda, the daughter of King Henry I of England, brings the Angevins the county of Maine. After the marriage has been concluded, in 1129 Foulques V leaves for the Holy Land. Geoffrey, the first member of the Angevins to use the surname Plantagenet, initially a nickname, from the sprig of broom (*genêt*) with which he customarily decorates his cap, takes charge of the county of Anjou. In 1144 Geoffrey conquers the Duchy of Normandy, which he entrusts to his son Henry Plantagenet as early as 1150.

1328 Start of the Valois dynasty

1360 Treaty of Brétigny

1150	1250	1300	1325	1350	13

1154 Henry Plantagenet accedes to the throne of England

1259 Treaty of Paris

1337 Beginning of the Hundred Years' War

1348 The bubonic plague spreads throughout Europe

PLANTAGENETS V. CAPETIANS

On March 21, 1152 the marriage between the King of France, Louis VII (1120–80), and Eleanor of Aquitaine (1122–1204) is dissolved on grounds of "consanguinity". Two months later Eleanor marries the young Henry Plantagenet (1133–89), who in 1154 succeeds to the throne of England as Henry II. The couple are now at the head of a vast state rivaling that of the King of France,

extending from the Scottish border to the Pyrenees, with Anjou at its heart. But in 1189 Henry II is obliged to accept a humiliating defeat near Azay-le-Rideau at the hands of his rebel son Richard the Lionheart (right), in alliance with Philippe-Auguste. He surrenders the crown of England to the former, and backs the territorial conquests of the latter. He dies at Chinon in the same

year. Successive kings of France fight unceasingly to keep the domain of the Plantagenets under French tenure. With the Treaty of Paris (1259) Louis IX puts an end to what has been called the "First Hundred Years' War". He recovers Touraine, Anjou and Maine, and exacts homage from the King of England for Guyenne.

THE PLANTAGENETS' ACHIEVEMENTS

The Plantagenets left a lasting mark on the Loire Valley. They founded several abbeys, among them Fontevraud ▲ 227, which houses their necropolis. The Hôpital St-Jean ▲ 308 in Angers, along with the Chartreuse at Liget ▲ 230, were built by Henry II (below) in atonement for the murder of Thomas Becket. We owe to the Plantagenets the creation of law schools and the origins of the future University of Angers. Angevin vaulting ● 60 – also called Plantagenet vaulting – came into being during their reign, and embankments were raised to protect the Loire Valley from flooding.

THE HUNDRED YEARS' WAR (1337–1453)

THE ACCESSION OF THE VALOIS DYNASTY

In 1328 Philippe de Valois (1293–1350) ▲ 112, nephew of Philip the Fair, succeeds his cousin Charles IV (the last direct Capetian descendant) under the name of Philippe VI. In 1337 Edward III, King of England, who is the vassal of the King of France

for Guyenne, refuses to pay homage to Philippe VI; in return Philippe seizes the domain. In 1340 Edward, who is the grandson of Philip the Fair, claims the French throne. The Anglo-French conflict starts again: it will last 116 years, interrupted by numerous truces.

ARMAGNACS AND BOURGUIGNONS

The conflict starts again in 1337 in the name of the new King of England, Richard II (1367–1400), who is only ten years old. In France Charles VI (1368–1422), also a minor, reigns under the tutelage of his paternal uncles, the Duke of Anjou, the Duke of Berry, the Duke of Burgundy (Philip the Bold) and his maternal uncle, the Duke of Bourbon.

FROM CRÉCY TO THE 1375 TRUCE

In 1346 the English land in large numbers at Calais. Philippe VI and the cream of the French cavalry are decimated on August 26 at Crécy. Ten years later the King of France, Jean the Good (1319–64), son of Philippe VI, is taken prisoner at Maupertuis, near to Poitiers, by the Prince of Wales (the Black Prince) and is held captive in London for eight years. The Dauphin Charles, the future Charles V (1338–80), rules France during the internment of his father. The Treaty of Brétigny (1360) allows Jean to be set

free in return for payment of a ransom. Furthermore, under the same treaty the English king agrees to abandon his claims to Anjou, Aquitaine, Normandy and the throne of France. Nevertheless, the war between England and France is resumed in 1369 when Charles V once again seizes Guyenne. Thanks to Du Guesclin (c. 1320–80), who is appointed High Constable in 1370, the French reconquer almost all their lost territories. The truce of 1375, imposed by the Pope, allows both parties to rebuild their armed strength.

1409 Birth of René I in Angers	**1415** French defeated at Agincourt	**1429** Joan of Arc breaks the siege of Orléans	**1431** Joan of Arc burned at the stake	**1440** Start of a royal presence in the Loire Valley

1400	1410	1420	1430	1440	1450

1407 Assassination of Louis d'Orléans by Jean the Fearless, Duke of Burgundy	**1418** Occupation of Paris by the Burgundians	**1420** Treaty of Troyes	**1429** French victory at Patay	**1453** End of the Hundred Years' War

In 1388, increasingly under the influence of his brother Louis d'Orléans (son-in-law of the Count of Armagnac), Charles VI replaces his uncles with his father's old counselors. In 1392 the king suffers an attack of madness, and his uncles take advantage of his fragile health to regain power. In 1407 the assassination of Louis d'Orléans by the new Duke of Burgundy, Jean the Fearless, stirs up the fight between the Burgundians and the Armagnacs. In 1414 Jean the Fearless forms an alliance with the English against the Armagnacs and the King of France. The English invasion starts in August 1415. After the defeat of the French troops at Agincourt (above) on October 25, 1415, the northern half of the kingdom is occupied by the English and the Burgundians. In May 1418 the Duke of Burgundy takes Paris and captures the king. The Dauphin Charles makes his escape, falling back first to Bourges, then to Chinon. By the Treaty of Troyes (May 25, 1420) Charles VI gives his daughter in marriage to King Henry V of England, whom he acknowledges as his heir, thus barring the "so-called Dauphin" – who stands accused by his mother, Isabel of Bavaria, of being an adulteress – from succeeding to the French crown. On December 1, 1420 the English enter Paris.

THE 1348 PLAGUE
In 1347 a scourge unknown in Europe since the 7th century arrives in Marseilles, brought by boat from the Crimea. The Black Death (bubonic plague) spreads over France during the following year. The Europe of 1349 to 1350 is in mourning. It is estimated that one out of three people in the kingdom has fallen victim.

THE RECONQUEST
In 1422 Charles VII proclaims himself King of France, but remains uncrowned. On October 12, 1428 the English lay siege to Orléans ▲ *116*. Then the unexpected happens – when Joan of Arc (below) leaves Domrémy, is given an audience by her king, on March 6, 1429 at Chinon ▲ *243*, and obtains his agreement to take up arms and go to Orléans. Eight days after her arrival the siege is lifted. After an even more decisive victory at Patay (May 8, 1429), Charles is crowned on July 17 in Reims. On September 21, 1435 he signs the Arras peace accord with the Burgundians, which at last confirms his legitimacy. His reign continues with twenty years of gradual reconquest, beginning in Paris in 1436 and culminating with the taking of Bordeaux in 1453. Thus the Hundred Years' War finally comes to an end, without any peace treaty having been signed.

1498 Louis, Duke of Orléans, King of France

1519 Death of Leonardo da Vinci at Clos-Lucé

1560 Conspiracy of Amboise

1598 Proclamation of the Edict of Nantes

1460   1470   1480   1500   1550   16

1470 Foundation of silk industry in Tours

1491 Marriage of Charles VIII to Anne de Bretagne at Langeais

1523 Calvin at Orléans University

1588 Assassination of the Duke of Guise at Blois

THE GOLDEN AGE: THE 15TH AND 16TH CENTURIES

THE LOIRE, ROYAL RIVER

Starting with Charles VII (1403–61), who is disillusioned with the fickleness of Paris during the Hundred Years' War, the kings of France forsake the capital in favor of the Loire Valley, the itinerant court going from one château to another.

Charles VII sets up successively at Chinon ▲ 244, Loches ▲ 224 and Amboise ▲ 180, before settling near Tours ▲ 196. For eighty years the city becomes the political and religious capital of the kingdom. Louis XI (1423–83) makes Plessis-lès-Tours ▲ 259 (above) his "most visited" residence. Charles VIII (1470–98), husband of Anne de Bretagne ● 34, divides his time between Langeais ● 66, ▲ 268 and

Amboise, where he dies after an accident. Louis XII (1462–1515), who succeeds him, marries his widow and moves the court to Blois ● 67, ▲ 144. François I ● 35 (below) adds a wing to the castle ● 68 and persuades Leonardo da Vinci (opposite, bottom) to come to Amboise. The great man stays at Clos-Lucé ▲ 185 and advises on the design of Chambord ▲ 162. François' son, Henri II (1519–59), finishes the building. He gives Chenonceau ▲ 218 to his mistress, Diane de Poitiers, as a token of his love.

THE RELIGIOUS WARS

Early in the 16th century Luther and then Calvin denounce the privileges of the clergy and demand a reform of the Church. Books, now becoming more widely available thanks to the spread

of printing, and the spoken word help spread the thoughts of Calvin, who has frequently visited the University of Orléans ▲ 121. The Loire Valley is, after Paris, the fulcrum of the Reformation in France. From Gien to Angers, the Huguenots build Protestant churches. The conversion of famous families such as the Bourbons, the Condés and the La Rochefoucaults lends impetus to the formation of a Protestant "party", opposed to the increasingly frequent persecutions. The religious problem soon becomes a political one. Henry II's accidental death during a tournament in 1559 marks the start of a troubled period. His widow, Catherine de Médicis, is prepared to be tolerant, while the powerful Guise family fight for control of the Catholic "party".

In 1560 the Protestant princes attempt to kidnap the young Dauphin François II (1544–60), aged sixteen, to free him from the Guise influence. This is the savagely repressed Amboise conspiracy ▲ 183. The rupture between the Catholics and the Huguenots is now complete. Saint Bartholomew's Day (August 24) in 1572 is followed by the brutal massacre of Protestants in Anger Then in 1588 Henry III (1551–89) has the Duke of Guise assassinated at Blois (below) in an effort t become the sole rule of the Catholics. To escape the anger of the Catholic nobles, Henry III takes refuge at Tours where he gathers his government. His assassination by the monk Jacques Clément in 1589 makes the Protestant Henry de Navarre (1553–1610) his legitimate successor. But the kingdom doe not want a Protestant prince; he therefore agrees to convert to Catholicism and is crowned at Chartres, under the name of Henry IV. In 1598, by the Edict of Nantes, the new king ends forty years of civil war. His accession also marks the end of the royal presence in the Loire Valley.

98 End of the val presence in e Loire Valley	**1648–53** Fronde	**1685** Repeal of the Edict of Nantes	**1709** Hunger riots in France	**1745** Growing influence of Mme de Pompadour on Louis XV	**1774** Louis XVI's reign
1610	**1650**	**1700**	**1725**	**1750**	**1775**
10 Assassination Henry IV by vaillac	**1642** The Loire is linked to the Seine	**17th and 18th centuries** The Loire is a main commercial axis	**1715** Death of Louis XIV		**1774** Looting of boats transporting cereals

PROVINCIAL STAGNATION: THE 17TH AND 18TH CENTURIES

In spite of some disturbances during the early years of Louis XIII's reign (1601–43) and during the Fronde (1648–53), the Loire Valley stays outside the kingdom's political and religious troubles.

Shortly before the Revolution there is, as a general rule, a marked decline in the population of the towns. In a single century Blois has lost some 7,000 to 8,000 inhabitants; and Tours has lost as many as 13,000, as has Angers. Only Orléans has seen some measure of stability.

ARTISTS AND WRITERS

The infatuation of the nobles and the prosperous rading and banking families with the new architecture eads to the building of numerous châteaux and *hôtels particuliers* ● *74* n the Loire Valley. Many of these are decorated by Touraine artists, such as Jean Fouquet ● *88* above, *The Virgin of the Milk*), Jean Bourdichon ▲ *227* nd François Clouet ▲ *220* (1505/10–72). here is also a lively terest in literature. Rabelais mentions his birthplace in *Gargantua* ▲ *250*. Ronsard ▲ *258*, the poet of love, dedicates poems to Cassandra ▲ *140* and Marie, and etires to St-Cosme ▲ *258*. Du Bellay is enthusiastic about the new school of poetry known as the Pléiade.

THE COUNTER-REFORMATION

The Protestants continue to cause unrest. In Saumur, a safe haven for the reformers, colleges and academies are training Protestant clerics. However, the Catholic Church is determined to reduce the influence of the Reformation. From 1614 the Oratorians turn Notre-Dame des Ardilliers ● *63*, ▲ *285*, in Saumur, into an important pilgrimage center; and in 1691 an episcopal seat is created at Blois. But while convents and colleges are being founded, Reformed churches are being closed. As a result, Protestants begin to emigrate ▲ *278*; the repeal of the Edict of Nantes in 1685 by Louis XIV (above) ● *35* accelerates the·surge of emigration.

PROSPERITY AND DECLINE

Orléans has to rely on inland waterways for its trade with the Levant, the Antilles and England, and like Angers is seeking new openings; in the middle of the 17th century the city is linked to the Seine by a new waterway. In the period preceding the Revolution there are some thirty-two distilleries and two hundred vinegar factories ▲ *123* in Orléans, and also manufacturers of painted canvas. Blois has weathered the departure of the royal court (at the end of the 16th century) quite well, thanks to its trade in wine and spirits. However, the "decapitalized" city of Tours vegetates, its silk factories ▲ *260* rivaled by those of Lyon. Convents find the number of vocations is falling.

THE WORK OF THE "INTENDANTS"

The centralization started by the monarchy under Louis XII relies on administrators (*intendants*) with wide-ranging powers. They leave their own mark on the Loire Valley. Du Cluzel, one of the *intendants* in the 18th century, is eager to give Tours the "most beautiful entry in the kingdom", with a stone bridge leading directly to the Rue Nationale. In Orléans another *intendant*, Perrin de Cypierre, opens up the Rue Royale with his famous arcades ▲ *121* that lead to a fine stone bridge. Blois is given a hump-back bridge ▲ *145* around which the life of the town seems to revolve in the 19th century.

41

1810 Talleyrand
buys Valençay

1846 Hunger
riots in Tours

1790   1800   1820   1830   1840   18

1789 Start
of the French
Revolution

1793 Angers
is taken by the
Vendéens

1815 End of the
First Empire

1829 Steamboats
ply between Orléans
and Blois

1849 The railway arrive
at Orléans, Blois, Tours
and Angers

From the Revolution to the Third Republic

REVOLUTION AND EMPIRE (1789–1815)

When Louis XVI (1754–93) convenes the États Généraux (States General) on May 5, 1789, the representative body loses no time in transforming itself into a revolutionary assembly to contest the supremacy of the monarchy. If the inhabitants of towns in the Loire Valley are won over by the arguments being put forward in favor of political and administrative reform (with a legislative assembly and four départements run by elected citizens), the peasant masses feel more and more let down. Religious reforms upset parish life, and the new fiscal regime in no way improves the lot of the peasantry. Discontent continues to grow with the sale of Church property and the requirement that the clergy must swear allegiance to the Constitution.

Finally September 21, 1792 witnesses the proclamation of the Republic, and Louis XVI is beheaded on January 21, 1793. Two months later, in March 1793, the Republic, now at war with the rest of Europe, decrees a mass conscription of the male population. This measure is

deemed provocative by the inhabitants of the Vendée and Anjou who, Royalist at heart, resort to arms. The "Whites" (the monarchists) and the "Blues" (the republicans) clash. Saumur falls, and then Angers. The terrible repression that follows leaves an indelible mark on the collective memory of western France. Napoleon Bonaparte (1769–1821), as First Consul, reacts to the political climate and manages to establish a religious peace, which is extended by the Concordat of 1801. After assuming the title of Emperor in 1804, he attempts to win the support of the monarchist département of Maine-et-Loire, but the renewed threat of conscription alienates the people of Anjou.

UNSTABLE REGIME

The Restoration (1815–30) and Louis-Philippe's "Monarchy of July" (1830–48) are unable to totally erase the advances made by the Revolution and the Empire. In the end Louis-Philippe is definitively ousted by the Revolution of 1848, which sees the birth of the Second Republic (1848–51). In December 1848 Louis-Napoleon Bonaparte, nephew of Napoleon I, is elected President of the Republic by universal franchise. On December 2, 185 a coup d'état ushers in the Second Empire and he is crowned Napoleon III (left). Half-hearted efforts to liberalize his regime come too late to secure the future of the Empire.

1870 Tours serves as temporary seat of French government	1875 Foundation of the Catholic University in Angers	1876–83 Destruction of vineyards by phylloxera

1860   1870   1880   1890   1900   1910

1870-1 Franco-Prussian war: operations by the Loire army	1883 Foundation of the Franciade, France's first agricultural union, in Blois	1902 The end of commercial traffic on the Loire between Orléans and Nantes

THE THIRD REPUBLIC AND WORLD WAR TWO

A RESTRAINED APPROVAL

The Fench defeat at Sedan (September 1, 1870), at the hands of the Prussians, brings about the collapse of the Second Empire. The Third Republic is proclaimed on September 4 and is quickly adopted by the inhabitants of Indre-et-Loire, while those of Loir-et-Cher and Loiret tend to be more restrained. The situation is different in Maine-et-Loire; here the conservatism of the western regions derived from their historical monarchism and clericalism is still very much alive in the rural areas. With the introduction of laws on the secularization of schools and the separation of Church and State (1905), the syndrome of the "Whites" and the "Blues" is given a new lease of life.

THE TOWNS OF THE LOIRE VALLEY IN THE 19TH CENTURY

Angers retains the image of an affluent town, proud of its school of engineering and its numerous private colleges. Its history has been marked by religious and aristocratic influence; this is less true of Tours, where there are numerous civil servants and railway employees. Blois struggles to make its mark, and Orléans experiences only average growth. Manpower from the countryside contributes to the growth of the towns.

INDUSTRIALIZATION AND THE RURAL ECONOMY

Rural depopulation worsens when the phylloxera infestation destroys the region's vineyards between 1876 and 1883. A third of them are not restored, being used for market gardening and as horticultural nurseries instead. The towns increase their activities. In Angers, Tours and Blois companies are founded that acquire a national or even worldwide reputation. Angers is the home of the Bessonneau textile empire and of Cointreau liqueurs ● 56. Tours and Orléans both have pharmaceutical industries, while Blois is renowned for Poulain chocolate ● 56. Loiret welcomes some remarkable foreign companies. The earthenware factory ▲ 134 started in Gien by Thomas Hall in 1821 enjoys its golden age in the second half of the 19th century. An American named Hutchinson brings the rubber industry to Montargis in 1853.

The Prussians in Tours

THE DEFENSE OF THE LOIRE

In 1870 Gambetta escapes by balloon from Paris – which is under siege – to join the Government delegation in Tours, the temporary capital of France. Fighting takes place on the Loire at Orléans and Beaugency ▲ 139. The inhabitants have to contend with requisitions, the cold and epidemics, most notably smallpox.

WORLD WAR TWO (1939–45)

In June 1940 history repeats itself. When the Germans occupy Paris, Tours becomes the capital for three days before the government withdraws to Bordeaux. During the Battle of the Loire, from Gien to Gennes, the cadets of Saumur ▲ 279, ▲ 293 make a heroic stand against enemy forces. Towns with bridges over the Loire are bombarded and suffer considerable damage (more than 40 acres at Orléans). After the Armistice on June 22, 1940, the greater part of the four départements of the Loire Valley is under German occupation, which is completed by 1942. From 1943, and particularly during the spring of 1944, Allied bombs hit airfields and railway junctions, and the towns are hit again. Liberation takes place between August 10 and September 1, thanks to General Patton's 3rd Army, backed up by the French Resistance.

43

1940-4 Bombing of towns in the Loire Valley

1950-70 Postwar reconstruction and emergence of new towns

1986 The Halle aux Grains (grain market) in Blois becom a conference and cultural cen

1920   1950   1960   1970   1980   19

1920 Tours Congress: The French Socialist Party splits, birth of the PCF (French Communist Party)

1940 Tours is the capital of France for three days

1964 Avoine-Chinon nuclear power station starts operations

1972 Creation of the Centre and Pays de la Loire regions

1990 Start of TGV service between Paris and Tours

THE 4TH AND 5TH REPUBLICS: TOWARD THE THIRD MILLENIUM

The era of postwar reconstruction brings urban and industrial renewal accompanied by accelerated rural depopulation. To deal with the influx of people into the cities, new residential and industrial zones are created near the main towns (for example, Orléans purchases the 1,300-acre estate of La Source ▲ 124). There is considerable urban expansion: "Greater Angers" has 215,000 inhabitants; Tours, 282,000; Blois, 65,000; and Orléans, 244,000. Many of the region's older industries disappear, and are replaced by multinationals such as Thomson, Bull, Scania, SKF, Michelin and Matra. One of the most successful enterprises has been the Servier Pharmaceutical Products Laboratory: founded thirty years ago at Gigy with a total staff of nine,

it now employs some four hundred people, with factories in New York and Tokyo and a presence in 130 countries. The power stations beside the Loire ● 13 produce 25 percent of French nuclear electricity. The construction of new highways has made the region more dynamic. Thanks to the high-speed train (*TGV Atlantique*, below), in service since 1990, Tours is now less than an hour from Paris; TAT, the region's first private airline, has its offices in Tours. Universities, long lacking in the four départements, exist today: Orléans, seat of the Orléans-Tours Academy, has had a university since 1966; both Angers and Tours have possessed universities since 1971; and there has been a branch of Tours University in Blois since 1993. The organization of the country into new regions offered an opportunity to create a single entity from the four départements. However, the new administrative division has bought a resurgence of the old antagonisms. Maine-et-Loire has become

part of Pays de la Loire, while the three other départements have been assigned to

the Centre region, with a préfecture and regional council in Orléans ● 12.

Tourism is benefiting from the new means of communication. There are now about a hundred châteaux in the Loire Valley open to the public. After Versailles, Chambord is the most visited historic site in France. The Briare canal bridge ▲ 137 celebrated its centenary in 1996, and the seven Rogny locks (which have survived from the

17th-century canal system) make an impressive staircase of water. Travel on the Loire itself has undergone a revival. The tributaries of the Maine (the Sarthe, Mayenne and Loir) are navigable for part of their length, and Angers makes a good base for cruises on these rivers. The Loiret ▲ 125 offers pleasant walks along its 8 miles.

ARTS AND TRADITIONS

BOATS ON THE LOIRE, *46*
HUNTING, *52*
FOOD: FISH TERRINE, *54*
SPECIALTIES, *56*

● Boats on the Loire

STEAMBOATS
A large number of steamboats were built from 1822 onward. Competition was tough between the differen companies, such as Riverains Paquebots de la Loire and the famous Inexplosibles

The quays and ports of the Loire are reminders of the importance of river transport, which reached its peak around 1860. At a time when the waterways were the principal means of communication, barges or lighters (*chalands*) were used to supply the towns with commodities such as wine, apples, salt, wheat, slates and tufa, and colonial products unloaded in Nantes. Sail navigation, which had adapted to the capricious river over the centuries, finally disappeared around 1900 when the railways arrived in the valley.

THE MERCHANTS' GUILD

From the 16th century onward barges in the area banded together to fight against the excessive tolls imposed by local landlords and to press for necessary maintenance work on the Loire and its tributaries. Delegate from the riverside towns met every four years in Orléans. When the merchants guild died out in 1772, responsibility for buoying, lights and maintenance was taken over by the highways departmen

TRAVELING ON THE LOIRE
A river journey could take any length of time as the weather was so unreliable, and delays could be caused by floods, drought, ice or unfavorable winds. The Briare to Nantes journey, for instance, took around ten days downstream but more than three weeks upstream. On average, the river was navigable for 250 days a year.

THE "TOUE"
Some 50 feet long, this flat-bottomed boat was used as a short distance carrier. Sand dredgers could load it with nearly 10 tons of sand. With a cabin and *carrelet* (square dipping net) it metamorphose into the ideal craft for professional salmon or shad fishermen; floating tanks called *bascules* kept the fish alive until selling time.

THE "SAPINE"
Some 100 feet long, with a very shallow draught, the *sapine* was both carrier and cargo. Built upstream, without mast or sail, it made the journey downriver only once; on arrival it was dismantled, the wood being sold at the same time as its 40-ton cargo goods such as coal and china.

THE "FRAM"

In 1898 a new kind of steamboat was tried out, with a propeller. For ten years the *fram* plied between Nantes and Blois, delivering cocoa to the famous Poulain chocolate factory ▲ 145.

THE "FÛTREAU"

This small 30-foot craft could be rigged or not, depending on use. It became a *chot* for the bargee and ferryman,

and a *galiote* for the fisherman (it was then fitted with a fish tank). *Galiotes* were mostly used for catching perch.

GOING ABOUT

It was not uncommon for the large barges to dismast or haul down the rigging when approaching a bridge. For that purpose a powerful windlass, called a *guindas*, was used. The maneuver was not without danger: eight men were needed either to push (in which case they had to take care in order to avoid breaking the arms of the windlass) or to hang on (at the risk of losing hold).

"Let's sing to the Loire and its fleet, There's nothing like it on earth. On the way, when the sun rises Let's sing to the Loire and its fleet."

Be it a pirogue or a *chaland*, whatever the financial constraints, the Loire people have always made best use of their technical skills to adapt to the demands of the river. The Loire boats all have something in common: a wide, flat bottom raised at the front, a square sail and a large oar, called the *piautre*, for steering.

Clamp

Planking

Knee

Caulking with hemp

Limber hole

Corner peg

Floor timber

Tenon

Keel

HERITAGE OF THE VIKINGS. From the Vikings (who made forays into the lower Loire around the 9th century) came the square sail and techniques such as clinker-building. Certain types of knot have also kept their northern names: *boitas*, *bouline*, *gueurde* . . . square knot, bowline, slipknot.

TOOLS
1. Large saw
2. Beam compass
3. Compass
4. Square
5. Bevel square
6. Tracing iron
7. String and chalk
8. Clamp
9. Marking gauge
10. Brace
11. Auger
12. Planes
13. Large plane
14. Mallet
15. Chisel
16. Gouge
17. Axe
18. Adzes
19. Broad axe

REVIVAL
Fortunately square-sail boats have not entirely disappeared from the Loire landscape. Under the impetus of a few enthusiasts, naval carpenters are yet again building *toues*, *gabares* and *fûtreaux* (different types of flat-bottomed boat).

A FINE TEAM

The upstream barge trains cut a fine figure. At the head, the "mother" ship in full sail, with its *piautre* (steering oar). Behind came the *tirot* and *sous-tirot* with decreasing sails. The smaller *allèges* were not rigged. A crew of ten men could steer such a train of seven or eight barges made fast to one another.

EVOLUTION OF THE LOIRE BOATS

SINGLE-TRUNK PIROGUE

The trunk was dug out with a tool (axe or adze) or using fire. Ribs were left to provide rigidity.

THE ANCENIS PIROGUE

The single-trunk pirogue was split either deliberately or accidentally. The boat was widened with planks, and it was therefore necessary to peg several crosspieces together.

THE LIMOGES BOAT

This was constructed entirely of planks by a carpenter. The use of crosspieces, knees and ribs made it rigid.

VIKING TECHNIQUES AND TOOLS

The Vikings brought clinker-building techniques to France (the planks overlapping one another like slates) and a tool, the *canap* (a large deep-bite clamp), to hold the planks together for pegging.

THE CLASSIC "CHALAND"

Its dimensions were restricted by the length of the tree trunk and the shallowness of the water.

● BARGE FOLK

The Loire bargees led a strange life, forever
at the mercy of the capricious river, but they
maneuvered skillfully. Those of the "lower
country", leading a train of barges upstream,
had to wait for a propitious sea wind, find a
channel and dismast at bridges; those of the "upper country"
had to wait for a rise in the water level in order to rush
downstream on a coal-loaded *sapine* ● 46.

"They also wore gold
or gold-plated
earrings which were
shaped like one-franc
coins adorned with
an anchor in the
middle."
Pierre Mondanel

Tie pin.

FEAST CLOTHES
The bargees' everyday clothes consisted of
a blue smock, corduroy trousers, a scarlet-
flannel belt and a wide-brim felt
hat; on feast days they wore a
white shirt which set off the
brooches bearing the
distinctive signs of their
profession. As for the
cashmere scarf,
it came from India,
via Nantes.

Eyelet

THE "SAINT LOUIS"
In the church in
St-Georges-sur-Cher
there is an unusual
polychrome plaque
depicting a barge.
Made in 1852 by
Eugène Archambault,
the son of a bargee,
it represents the *Saint
Louis*, which plied up
and down the Loire
and the Cher (until
the last century
navigable up to
Vierzon).

Bowlines

Anchor

Poles

Chain plates

"TREMPÉE AU VIN" (DUNKED IN WINE)

Put some stale breadcrumbs in a bowl.
Moisten and sweeten as required. Just before
serving, add a large quantity of cool red wine.
Stir and eat with a spoon.

Salt herrings.

Jug for
walnut oil.

A drop
of cheap
liquor.

WATER NOMADS

Lively and independent, barge people were always on the go. Their
entire fortune was kept in a chest which they decorated themselves.
Jovial drinkers and often bawdy, they would invoke their patron
saints (Saint Clement, Saint Nicholas etc.) when carrying out
a dangerous maneuver or during a sudden storm.

A bargee's
basket.

A two-ring stove
in front of which the
cuit-pomme (apple
tart) was placed.

THE "GUIROUÉ"

Normally an ordinary flag
was enough to tell the
direction of the wind, but
each boat had its own
weather vane for special
occasions. The *guiroué*
was carved during
the long winter
evenings and was the
pride of the crew.

COOKING ON BOARD

Barge crews liked to eat well: cured meat,
meat balls, soup, fish, *matelote* (fish stew),
stuffed carp . . . the whole lot washed
down with some fine wine "borrowed" from
the cargo.

Leach

Food safe.

THE "PIAUTRE"

The large steering
oar, or tiller, is one
of the most original
components of the
Loire *chaland*. It
stands on the stern
and is held firmly
by an array of ropes.
It can be adjusted
according to the
displacement and
depth of the water,
and can be taken
out when the barge
is in a "train".

Strap

Mast stay

Lashing block

Windlass

Tiller

51

Hunting, or venery, is the art of pursuing game with hounds. It has been practiced in France since the 12th century on a regular basis, and in the Loire Valley was the favorite sport of the French kings in the 15th century. Today several thousand lovers of the chase perpetuate a tradition that has become codified by centuries of custom.

HUNTING TERMS
According to the situation, one talks of the *bien-aller* ("tally-ho") – when the *veneur* (Master of the Hounds) sounds the *bien-aller* the hounds are directed either with the voice or the horn – of "starting" the quarry, losing the scent, tracing the drag, changing forests, breaking away, sounding the *mort* (the kill) among others.

"ACCESSOIRES"
In this picture by Henry Koehler (1991) one can see a horn, a whip, a knife, a hat and a belt, all essential items of equipment for the huntsman.

THE "DÉFAUT"
by Karl Reille (1960). A *défaut* means the hounds have lost the scent (*voie*) of the quarry.

BUTTONS AND "BUTTONS"

Each hunt is distinguished from the others by the buttons on the waistcoat (*gilet*) and tunic (the hunter's uniform) – hence the name *boutons* (buttons) sometimes given to the members of the hunt.
Right: the button of the Cheverny Hunt ▲ *172*.

THE PATRON SAINT OF HUNTING

In the 8th century Saint Hubert had a vision of a deer carrying a cross between its antlers.
His saint's day is celebrated on November 3.

"MORT"

by René Princeteau (19th century).
This hunting cry means the animal is at bay.

SMALL OR LARGE GAME

Small-game hunting is for foxes, hares or rabbits.
Large-game hunting is for red deer, roe deer or wild boar.

"HONORS"

It is customary after a kill for one of the followers of the hunt to be "honored" (presented) with a foot or sometimes the antlers.

THE HUNT AND THE HOUNDS

The Master of the Hounds leads the hunt and is helped by the *boutons* (the members of the hunt). The *piqueux* (whippers-in) are responsible for the hounds during the hunt and in the kennels. The pack is made up of about sixty hounds for large-game hunts, and about twenty for small-game hunts. The most sought-after breeds are Anglo-French or English (beagles and harriers). The "followers" (guests) follow the hunt either on horseback or by car.

"In a language difficult to constrain, a style of cooking that is clear, simple and logical, inspired by Rabelais' spirit and Descartes' genius, in a land of gourmets" – that is how the great gastronome Curnonsky described Touraine cuisine. Renowned for its charcuterie, its goat's cheeses, its confectionery and its wines, Touraine is also a land of rivers, so is well endowed with mouthwatering recipes for preparing and cooking fish.

2. Let the stock simmer for 15 minutes, reduce by half and strain.

3. Poach each fish separately in the stock for 8 minutes. Transfer the fish into a large tureen, pour the stock over it and leave to cool.

6. Place the perch fillets in a terracotta dish, then add the chopped egg whites.

8. Add the eel fillets, then cover with the chopped yolks and diced lemon.

9. Leave in a refrigerator overnight and serve with mayonnaise to which some tomato sauce has been added.

INGREDIENTS:

4 lb perch	1 or 2 eggs
3 lb salmon	1 lemon
4 lb eel	Tarragon

STOCK:

Fish bones	1 bouquet garni
and heads	2 large onions
shallots	1 large mushroom
leeks	Half a glass of dry
carrots	white wine
oz butter	Salt and pepper

1. To prepare the stock: chop all the ingredients, put them in a pan, add the wine and cover with water.

Fillet each fish.

5. Hard-boil the eggs, then chop the whites and yolks separately. Peel the lemon and cut it into small cubes.

7. Add the salmon fillets and the tarragon.

● SPECIALTIES

TRADITIONAL VINEGARS FROM ORLÉANS

They say in Orléans that it takes a great wine to make a great vinegar – so it is wine from the greatest vineyards, such as Chinon, and Bourgueil, that fills the 220-litre casks used for the three-week transformation period. The vinegar is then aged for six months in oak tuns.

COTIGNAC D'ORLÉANS

A specialty of St-Ay enjoyed since the 15th century, this quince jelly comes in a box, traditionally made of spruce, with the effigy of the "Maid of Orléans" on it. Benoît Gouchault is the la[s]t maker of this sweet amber-colored delicacy.

REGIONAL PRESS

La Nouvelle Républiq[ue] du Centre-Ouest cove[rs] the news for all the départements of the Loire Valley, while th[e] *Magazine de la Toura[ine]* deals with the histor[y] of the area.

RILLONS AND RILLETTES

Four centuries old, these specialties are made from diced rib and loin pork, simmered over a wood fire. The largest pieces are taken out to make *rillons*; the smaller ones are mashed with a fork to make *rillettes*.

LIQUEURS OF ANGERS

In 1849 the Cointreau brothers, who were confectioners, founded a company to make their celebrated Guignolet using fruits from Anjou. In 1875 Louis, a worthy descendant, created the famous Cointreau liqueur from orange peel.

POULAIN CHOCOLATE

The famous brand, much appreciated by chocolate lovers, is still made in Blois ● *47* and ▲ *145*.

"CHAMPIGNONS DE PARIS"

These have been grown in the Loire Valley since 1895, mainly in the limestone caves around Saumur ▲ *292*.

VALLEY OF VINEYARDS

The region's vineyards ◆ *322* encompass some sixty appellations and about 200,000 acres of vines ■ *30*. You can find very drinkable table wines here as well as noble vintages; consistent, generous, fresh white wines, with a flinty taste and a flowery bouquet; and full-bodied, ruby-colored reds that have a hint of iris, violets or honey.

Architecture

RELIGIOUS ARCHITECTURE
THE ROMANESQUE PERIOD, *58*
THE GOTHIC PERIOD, *60*
FROM THE RENAISSANCE
TO CLASSICISM, *62*
MILITARY AND RESIDENTIAL ARCHITECTURE
CASTLES AND KEEPS, *64*
FORTRESSES AND RESIDENCES, *66*
THE RENAISSANCE CHÂTEAU, *68*
CLASSICAL RESIDENTIAL ARCHITECTURE
THE CHÂTEAU IN THE
17TH AND 18TH CENTURIES, *70*
URBAN ARCHITECTURE
TIMBER-FRAMED HOUSES, *72*
TOWN HOUSES, *74*
RURAL ARCHITECTURE
FARM HOUSES, *76*
MILLS AND BRICKYARDS, *78*
SMALL FARM BUILDINGS, *80*

In the Romanesque period the Loire Valley, particularly Touraine, enjoyed a period of building activity during which a large number of religious edifices were erected. Ecclesiastical architecture was influenced by building methods from Poitou, Aquitaine, Burgundy and Berry: pier-buttressed apses, domes over the transept, doors lacking a tympanum, carvings, etc. The bell towers, however, are original to the region – topped by a spire flanked by pinnacles at the base. Carvings are almost exclusively reserved for capitals, cornice modillions and door arches; murals are relatively common, especially in the crypts.

DOORWAYS
(Church of Chênehutte-les-Tuffaux ▲ 292, 12th century)
The decoration of the main portal was often the most ornate part of the church. The arches are made of a series of voussoirs carved with foliage or geometric motifs.
The absence of a tympanum is typical of the Loire Valley.

FRESCOS
(Below: Church of Tavant, ▲ 251, second quarter of the 12th century)
The Christ in Majesty enthroned in a mandorla (above), which can be seen in the apse of the choir at Tavant, belongs to the so-called *fonds clairs* school (characterized by the use of a light background with a strong vigorous line).

CRYPTS
(Church of Tavant ▲ 251, late 11th century)
Many of the churches of this period have richly decorated crypts. The reason for this was probably the worship of saints and their relics, which the crypt housed or should have housed.
The crypts often had an entrance and an exit in order to regulate the flow of pilgrims.

CHEVETS
(Abbey of St-Benoît-sur-Loire ▲ 129, 1067–80)
A ground plan featuring an ambulatory and radiating chapels is characteristic of churches designed to receive large processions. Most Benedictine churches were built to this design. The plan of St-Benoît-sur-Loire (right) is particularly ambitious, with two of the chapels making a kind of small second transept. The structure of the chevet (apse and ambulatory) is similar to that of St-Étienne-de-Nevers in Burgundy. The chancel was originally flanked by twin bell towers.

ROMANESQUE ELEVATION
(Collegiate Church of St-Aignan ▲ *217*,
late 11th century)
The porch opens onto a nave of four bays
with aisles. The transept is surmounted
by a dome and a bell tower. The ambulatory
opens onto three apsidioles.

**THE SCHOOL
OF AQUITAINE**
(Fontevraud Abbey
▲ *227*, 12th century)
With its single nave
topped by a series
of domes on
pendentives, the
church at Fontevrault
reveals the links
between Aquitaine
and Anjou in
Plantagenet times
● *38*. The transept
and chancel precede
the nave – on the
Benedictine model,
with ambulatory and
radiating chapels.

THE BELL TOWER
(Notre-Dame
de Cunault ▲ *292*,
late 11th century)
This is the prototype
of Romanesque
bell towers in the
Loire Valley. The
first of the three tiers
of windows is blind,
while the alternating
pilasters and columns
of the top one
provide diversity. The
squat polygonal spire
is stabilized by the
surrounding turrets.

Gothic architecture, introduced in France in the 12th century, was characterized by a new treatment of mass and space; stained-glass windows provided a new interplay of light, and décor became less representational. Anjou devised its own style of vaulting, with extra ribs between the main cross ribs and the diagonals. Soaring pillars and high ribbed vaults, from the north (Chartres), stayed in vogue from the 13th to the 15th century. Until the 14th century Gothic architecture was relatively sedate, but the 15th century saw the advent of the Flamboyant style, facilitated by using soft stone, such as tufa.

IN SEARCH OF VERTICALITY
(Chapel of St-Hubert ▲ *184*, Amboise, 1491–6) The chapel's chevet is emphasized by an *avant-corps* (forebuilding) on top of the castle wall. The ornamentation is reminiscent of a Flemish reredos; the Flamboyant style of the north is also manifest in the fine tracery of the windows.

1. Diagonal rib, or ogive
2. Wall rib, or formeret
3. Transverse arch
4. Cell, or web
5. Lierne
6. Keystone
7. Capital

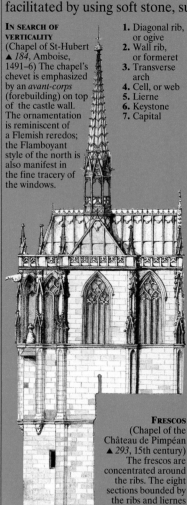

THE ANGEVIN OR PLANTAGENET VAULT
(Church of St-Serge ▲ *307*, Angers) This abbey church is characterized by high convex vaults supported by diagonal ribs (**1**), wall rib (**2**) and transverse arches (**3**), to which extra ribs, the liernes (**5**), were added to strengthen the cell (**4**). The large number of ribs gave rise to the vogue for bosses at the intersections.

FRESCOS
(Chapel of the Château de Pimpéan ▲ *293*, 15th century) The frescos are concentrated around the ribs. The eight sections bounded by the ribs and liernes of the vault illustrate various episodes from the life of Christ.

FLYING BUTTRESSES
(Ste-Croix Cathedral ▲ *114*, Orléans)
During the Gothic period the powerful pier
buttress gave way to the flying buttress,
an arch or half arch that transferred the thrust
of the vault to an outer support or pier.
Pinnacles were placed on top of the slender
buttresses to give them added weight,
which helped to stabilize the structure by
means of the vertical load.

FLAMBOYANT GOTHIC
(St-Gatien Cathedral
▲ *196*, Tours)
The façade was simply
superimposed on the
frame of the old one.
This is a good
illustration of the
Flamboyant style:
the cathedral's three
tall splayed doors,
with their intricate
ornamentation, have
a kind of "miniature
architecture" of
their own.

THE SPIRE
(Ste-Croix Cathedral
▲ *114*, Orléans)
The spire, in the
shape of a slender
pyramid, is the
culminating point of
the bell tower.
This spire, rebuilt in
1858, is a copy of
the one at Amiens
Cathedral.

RELIGIOUS ARCHITECTURE
FROM THE RENAISSANCE TO CLASSICISM

A MIXTURE OF STYLES (capital from the chapel at Ussé ▲ *270*)
The inspiration of this Renaissance capital is classical (Doric),
but the imaginative treatment is clearly medieval.

The chief creations of the Renaissance and of the
classical period were often nothing but an update of
earlier buildings. The churches of the 16th century
were decorated in the Italian style, with basket-handle or
semicircular arches and numerous niches containing statues.
In the 17th century religious architecture became more majestic
with superimposed classical Greek orders, doors surmounted
by pediments, stately domes and grandiose arched doorways
and window frames.

**A NEW
DECORATIVE
ORDER**
(Collegiate Church
of St-Jean-Baptiste
▲ *231*, Montrésor,
1522–41)
To the Gothic
ground plan and
elevation were added
a new decorative
order, visible around
the doors, the tracery
of the windows,
the cornices and
the moldings.
The ornamentation
was inspired
by Antiquity: fluted
pilasters and ornate
Corinthian capitals.
The façade is
similar to that of the
chapel of the
Château d'Ussé
▲ *270*.

FRAMES
(side door of the
Collegiate Church of
St-Jean-Baptiste
▲ *231*) Door and
window frames were
the chosen place for
ornamentation.

TRIUMPHAL COMPOSITION
(Convent Church of the Minimes,
3, rue de la Préfecture, Tours, 1627–35)
This doorway, built like a Roman triumphal
arch, heralded the end of the large Gothic
towers that previously framed church doors.
This style marks the transition between
façades that merely have decorative portals
and fully integrated classical façades such as
that of St-Vincent at Blois (below).

CLASSICISM
(Church of Notre-Dame
des-Ardillers ▲ 285,
Saumur, 17th century)
The classical ground plan
imitated the centered plan with
dome that was a characteristic
of the Italian Renaissance.
Associated with it is the strict
use of the classical orders.
Each of the three façades of
this church has a Doric portico
with four columns, surmounted
by a triangular pediment.
Crowning the edifice is a dome,
roofed with slates, surmounted
by an elegant lantern.

THE COUNTER-
REFORMATION
façade of the Church
of St-Vincent, Blois,
1625–78) Reacting
against the Protestant
reformation and its
emphasis on austerity,
the architects of the
Counter-Reformation
cultivated a grandeur
and flamboyance that
led to the Baroque.
The majesty of the
orders and the basilica
plan were borrowed
from Antiquity. Here
the three main orders
(Doric, Ionic and
Corinthian) are visible,
superimposed one
above the other. The
single nave flanked by
four small chapels is
crowned by a cupola.

Ground plan
of the
Church of
St-Vincent
at Blois.

CASTLES AND KEEPS
11TH TO 14TH CENTURY

MACHICOLATIO
(below, detail of the Porte des Cordelie
at Loches ▲ 229, 15th centu
Machicolations replaced wood
palisades at the level of the wall wa
which were used until the 14th centu
for bombarding attackers belo

In Romanesque times the rectangular or square keep, no doubt based on the wooden structures of the past, was the principal element of the medieval castle. During the Gothic period the keep lost some of its importance, and from the 13th century castles were sometimes built without a keep. After the Crusades progress in offensive techniques meant that defense systems had to be reviewed. Important innovations were introduced; tall stone walls were erected, protected by bastions, watchtowers, wall walks, battlements, machicolations and moats

THE CHÂTEAUX AT CHINON ▲ 244 (5th–15th centuries)

A STRATEGIC SITE

Overlooking the Vienne river and the parallel road, the castles at Chinon were built by the Counts of Blois on a strategic site used since the earliest times. The vast stronghold is spectacular, measuring around 200 x 1,200 feet. It comprises several castles built from the 10th to the 13th century: the Fort du Coudray (**A**), the Château de Milieu (**B**) and the Fort St-Georges (**C**).

1. Tour d'Argenton (late 15th century)
2. Tower from 12th-century rampart
3. Tour des Chiens
4. Bartizan Tower, or Tour de l'Échauguette
5. Tour de l'Horloge
6. Tour du Trésor (built by King Henry II of England)
7. Grande Salle de Charles VII
8. Logis Royaux (Henry II)
9. Tour de Boissy (Philippe-August
10. Tour du Moulin
11. Towers added to 15th-century curtain wall by Henry II
12. Tour du Coudra
13. Priory of Ste-Mélanie

THE KEEP ▲ *228*
(Château de Loches, c. 1030)
The elevation confirms the consistency of floor allocation in medieval keeps. The first floor was used for storing provisions. The third and fourth floors, which were served by narrow stairs built within the wall cavities, housed the feudal hall, the archive room and the seigniorial apartment. For security reasons access was only via the second floor.

BASIC PLAN
(Keep at Beaugency ▲ *139*, 11th century)
This is the archetypal rectangular keep of the Romanesque period, in effect a stone version of the earlier wooden keep. Circulation took place within the thickness of the buttressed walls. Here the base of the keep was set into a motte (mound) to a depth of 20 feet and encircled by two concentric walls.

POLITICAL FIEFS
(Château d'Angers, below)
Unlike forts or keeps intended solely to defend a particular strategic site, this fortress built by Louis IX was a true citadel controlling an entire political area. It was protected by seven massive towers jutting out from the curtain wall and by enormous dry ditches.

ARTIFICIAL MOATS
(left, keep of Château de Sully-sur-Loire ▲ *132*, 1395–1400)
Medieval strongholds in the Loire Valley that were not situated on a promontory or in an elevated position were forced to fall back on the defensive principle of an artificial moat fed by the Loire.

FORTRESSES AND RESIDENCES

The end of the Hundred Years' War (1453) and the popularity of the Loire Valley with the kings of France resulted in a new kind of château design. Although castles built in the second half of the 15th century often still had battlements and the look of medieval fortresses, this arose not so much from a need to exhibit power and strength as from a desire for decoration. Interiors were adapted to a new lifestyle centered on comfort: the residential block became more spacious, the windows were enlarged and reinforced with mullions, and the number of rooms increased. The château had evolved from feudal stronghold to luxury residence.

THE LAST GREAT FORTRESSES
(above, Château de Langeais, ▲ *268*, c. 1465)
A continuous *chemin de ronde* (wall walk) and massive walls are evidence of the military aspect of the Château de Langeais. However, the mullioned windows, installed almost immediately after the completion of the building, show that the château had already lost some of its defensive function. The two *corps de logis* (residential blocks) with high-ceilinged bedrooms overlooking the wall walk are significant of the new emphasis on residential comfort.

THE PREMISE OF A FRENCH RENAISSANC
(below, Château d'Amboise ▲ *184*, c. 1491
Charles VIII had new buildings lookin out over the Loire erected on the site of th ancient fortress, and commissioned the layin out of new gardens. This was in answer to th changing requirements of residential life Nevertheless, the ground plan and elevation remain rooted in th Flamboyant style, as i witnessed by the ta dormer windows and th ornamental elements

POLYCHROME BRICKWORK
(above, Château de Gien ▲ *133*, 1494–1500)
The decorative principle is not based on sculpture,
as in Italy, but on the diamond-pattern diapering
of the polychrome brickwork. A number of
Gothic elements have been retained, notably the
L-shaped ground plan and the elevation.

**PROGRESSIVE
REFURBISHMENT**
(below, Château de
Chaumont ▲ *177*,
1465–1510)
This château was
built in two phases:
the west wing in
1465–75, and the east
and south wings in
1498–1510.
The original medieval
plan was of a square
flanked by towers and
gatehouse. Of the
later modifications,
only the grand
staircase reflected
the burgeoning
influence of the
Italian Renaissance.
Opening the château
onto the Loire was
an 18th-century idea,
in order to offer a
view of the landscape,
as at Valençay ▲ *232*.

**BETWEEN GOTHIC
AND RENAISSANCE**
(Louis XII Wing at
the Château de Blois
▲ *149*, 1498–1515)
Still submitting to the
Gothic rationale, the
architect has shifted
the door of the spiral
staircase to the side.
The Renaissance
influence is clearly
visible in the vertical
alignment of the
centered windows, an
impression reinforced
by the dormer with
gable and pinnacles.
The only obviously
Italianesque feature
is the gallery.

THE RENAISSANCE CHÂTEAU

ROYAL MOTIFS (monogram of François I, Chambord ▲ 158)
Medallions bearing royal monograms, emblems and
heraldic devices invaded the façades and ceilings of the
Renaissance château – serving simultaneously as visible
symbols of power and as decorative motifs.

During the 16th century the military aspect
disappeared and was replaced by a preoccupation
with comfort. The château, at once in harmony with and open
to nature, left the hills and nestled in the valley. Water
was now an essential part of the design. Steeply pitched
roofs covered spacious attics lit by large dormers. A
grand staircase in the center of the façade, with
straight banisters and a coffered ceiling above
it, replaced the corner turret. An elegant Italian-
style gallery opened onto the main courtyard.

THE STAIRCASE
(Château de Blois ▲ 150)
Although staircases with
straight banisters in the
Italian style were beginning
to make their appearance
(as at Azay-le-Rideau), the
spiral staircase set back
from the main edifice was a
French tradition. But the
architects' great innovation
was to multiply its turns and
remove the walls between
the corner posts, so that a
playful aspect was grafted
onto its functional role.
At Blois three stories of
balconies overlook the
courtyard, a design that
reached its apogee at
Chambord ▲ 160.

DORMER WINDOWS
(Château de Chambord ▲ 158, after 1519)
France was still enamored of big roofs.
This handsome dormer has retained its
Gothic structure but has been enriched with
a Renaissance ornamental vocabulary. It is
embellished with geometric motifs in slate,
instead of the Tuscan marble used in Italy.

IN SEARCH OF SYMMETRY (Château de Villesavin ▲ *166*, 1537)
The carefully balanced design echoes the Italian villa and anticipates the so-called classical château. The buildings between the courtyard and the gardens are one story high. Square pavilions have replaced the towers of the past, emphasizing the nobility of the building without compromising its horizontality. The tall dormer windows follow the Loire Valley tradition.

AN ORDERED COMPOSITION
(plan for the Château de Chenonceau ▲ *218*, 1556)
The gallery-bridge acts as an axis of symmetry, reinforcing the perspective. Its original purpose was to provide access to a group of pavilions and gardens on the other side of the Loire.

THE GALLERY
(The Façade des Loges, Château de Blois ▲ *150*, 1515–19)

The Italian influence is clearly evident in this part of the François I Wing. The two tiers of loggias with basket-handle arches could have been inspired by Bramante's Vatican loggias (16th century). Above them is a scalloped cornice; and above that a *promenoir*, or long covered balcony. The decorative motifs were drawn from the classical Italian repertory.

ŒIL-DE-BŒUF (detail from the façade of Cheverny ▲ *170*)
The ornamental possibilities of the dormer were enriched by the introduction of œil-de-bœuf windows.

Abandoned by the court, in the 17th century the Loire Valley ceased to be France's architectural playground. Nevertheless, the aristocracy still enjoyed staying there and built fine châteaux characterized by a rigorously balanced treatment of space. The prevailing classical fashion implied the use of pediments, domes and Greek orders. Châteaux continued to be country houses looking out onto a courtyard and a classic French garden, but in the 18th century parks and secondary buildings, such as orangeries, follies, and other curiosities, were often added, reflecting the naturalist mood of the century of Enlightenment.

LOUIS XIII STYLE
(Château de Cheverny ▲ *170*, c. 1625–9)
The Louis XII style is characterized by a compact plan with juxtaposed pavilions. The Château de Cheverny (above) is one of the finest examples of that style. The main façade is composed of five pavilions, arranged symmetrically around a central pavilion which houses the monumental staircase. Each of the pavilions is roofed individually, a system that gives the building a verticality which is very French. The somewhat severe effect is relieved by the bossed horizontal facing punctuated by niches.

LOUIS XIV STYLE: THE VERSAILLES MODEL
(Château de Valençay ▲ *232*, 1770)
The west wing (below), on the park side, was modified and enlarged the 17th century; on the courtyard side it was faced in the classical style with ionic pilasters in the 18th century. The entrance was embellished with twin pilasters supporting a tympanum with Rocaille ornamentation. The Mansard roof, a newly adopted design (with two distinct slopes, the lower steeper than the upper one), has segmental arches and pediments over the dormer windows, which alternate with œil-de-bœuf windows and urns topped by flames.

THE FRENCH TRADITION
(Château de Blois ▲ *150*, 1635 onward)
Closing the courtyard, the Gaston d'Orléans Wing was
built according to Mansart's plans. It was one of
the first examples of classical architectural principles
applied to a French château. In order to show
off better the central bay and the main entrance, the
avant-corps was raised slightly in relation to the
façades, and curved porticos were installed to lessen
the severity of the outline. Segmental and triangular
pediments punctuate the entablature.

THE VOGUE FOR FOLLIES
During the century of Enlightenment follies
became the fashion. These small allegorical
buildings peppered parks and gardens in a
Rousseau-like vision of an ideal natural
world. At the Château de Menars ▲ *140*
the "Rotunda of Abundance" (above)
was built in 1764 by Jacques Germain
Soufflot (1713–80) to link the château
with the Orangery. The elegant pagoda
at the Château de Chanteloup ▲ *191*,
built from 1773 to 1778, reflects the
infatuation of the time with the exotic,
like its celebrated counterpart in
Kew Gardens, London.

71

GOTHIC STYLE
(Maison d'Adam
▲ *303*, Angers,
c. 1500) Wood is an
ideal medium for
decorative carvings,
be they religious or
secular. This couple,
still medieval in
inspiration, evoke
courtly love.

At the end of the Middle Ages the Loire Valle
experienced a population explosion resulting
mainly from the end of the Hundred Years' Wa
(1453) and the presence of the king and his cou
In towns building plots were becoming smaller
and corbeled timber-frame houses were built o
of necessity. The overhang increased usable sp
sheltered the lower part of the house from rain
and had certain structural advantages. Mercha
premises or craftsmen's workshops often occup
the first floor, while the upper floo
served as living space.

DECORATI
PURSU
(Mais
Rou
▲ 2-
Chin
15th centur
The timberi
arranged i
grid or X-patte
exemplifies t
contempora
search for n
decorative elemen
though the overhangi
truss is as much a part of
construction technique as i
part of a concern with esthetics. T
arch-braced roof has no rid

72

(below, house at 15, rue St-Laud, Angers ▲ *306*) No more corbels, instead carved motifs: foliage and pilasters ornament the façades. However, little change is discernible in terms of building technique.

THE HOUSE OF A WEALTHY BOURGEOIS

(Maison d'Adam ▲ *303*, Angers, c. 1500) This large, handsome corner house witnesses the comfortable lifestyle of its owner. It also shows how versatile timber-frame houses could be: it has three gables on the street side, a double façade, six corbeled tiers, a remarkable corner bartizan and an abundance of richly carved decoration.

THE NOGGINS

Depending on what natural resources were available and the wealth of the owners, the noggings could be made of wattle and daub, lath and plaster, pisé (rammed earth), tufa, ashlar or bricks, and they were sometimes rendered. The bricks could be laid in a pattern (horizontally, vertically, or in a herringbone design) and were often used for a colorful effect. Their essential function, however, was to reinforce the timber structure.

THE END OF THE TIMBER-FRAME HOUSE

At the end of the Hundred Years' War vast deforestation took place to convert land to farming, so there was an ample supply of wood. But in the 17th century, to reduce fire risks, laws were passed banning timber-frame houses.

CREATING DECORATIVE EFFECTS

the half-timbered ouses built during e 15th and 16th enturies the story-gh posts sometimes sted on a stone inth (**16**), and they uld be corbeled 2). The façades ere made to look tremely diverse by using various kinds of noggings, studs (**8**) and braces (**9**): the timbers themselves were arranged in grids, Saint Andrew's crosses or lozenge patterns, and the brick noggings were often used to create decorative patterns.

HE MAISON ROUGE

▲ *246* (Chinon, 15th century)
1. Crown post
2. Collar beam
3. Arched brace
4. Principal rafter
5. Hammerbeam
6. Wall plate
7. Angle brace
8. Studs
9. St Andrew's cross
10. Lower purlin
11. Cross brace
12. Lintel
13. Post
14. Fanlight
15. Cross beam
16. Bay window
17. Running support
18. Wall plinth

CLADDING

(house at 26, rue de la Monaie, Tours, above and right) The noggings of the weather-beaten east and west façades of timber-frame houses were sometimes either rendered or clad with slates to provide protection against bad weather.

TOWN HOUSES

HÔTEL PIERRE DU PUY, TOURS ▲ *209*
With its gabled front facing the street and its central
courtyard, this has the appearance of an ordinary house,
but the fact that it has two separate wings built around a
central staircase and gallery makes it an *hôtel particulier*.

Inspired by the royal residences, from the 15th century onward
the aristocracy and the wealthy bourgeoisie built themselves
magnificent stone mansions known as *hôtel particuliers*. The
design, based on the characteristic layout of the château, set
between front courtyard and gardens, had to be adapted to
the restricted space available in towns. The 17th and 18th
centuries saw the development of town-planning schemes.
Although the austere style known as the "architecture of
the engineers" characterized the first half of the 18th
century, a return to ornamentation marked
the end of the century.

FLEMISH GOTHIC
(Hôtel Pierre du Puy ▲ *209*, Tours, c. 1460–70)
The bricks, the crow-stepped gable and the magnificent spiral
staircase known as the "Vis de St-Gilles" were inspired
by Flemish building styles and are evidence of the commercial
links between the Loire Valley and Flanders. The portico
with rib vaulting and pendant keystones, the corbels of the
dripstones of the windows and the moldings of the ogee arch
over the door are all part of the Flamboyant Gothic style.

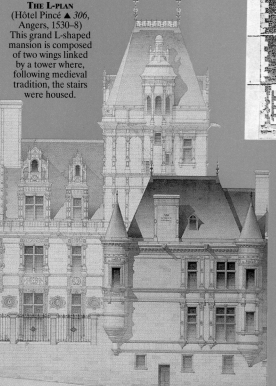

THE L-PLAN
(Hôtel Pincé ▲ *306*,
Angers, 1530–8)
This grand L-shaped
mansion is composed
of two wings linked
by a tower where,
following medieval
tradition, the stairs
were housed.

**EARLY
RENAISSANCE**
(Hôtel Pincé ▲ *306*,
Angers, 1530–8)
The façade (left) is
a brilliant showpiece
exploiting the vast
decorative repertory
of the times. The
concept of profusion,
which was seen as a
virtue, was dear to the
Italian Renaissance.
Human and animal
figures, arabesques,
foliage, shells, friezes
and pilasters enliven
the building's walls.
The overhanging
turrets, supported by
squinches, highlight
the boldness of
the architect,
Jean de L'Espine.

LATE RENAISSANCE
(Hôtel Cabu ▲ *119*,
Orléans,
mid 16th century)
The courtyard façade,
which is attributed
to Jacques Androuet
Du Cerceau (1520 to
c. 1585), presents two
lateral avant-corps
with superimposed
orders. This is one of
the earliest examples
of a Henri II style
building in Orléans.

TOWN PLANNING SCHEMES
(Pavillons d'Escures ▲ *120*, Orléans,
before 1614)
This fine ensemble of four identical houses is
characteristic of the town-planning schemes
of the times. The houses are linked by stone
piers and are not dissimilar to the houses of
the Place des Vosges in Paris. Each has a
courtyard with a gateway to the main street,
and another courtyard with outbuildings and
a porte-cochère at the rear. They are
reminiscent of Du Cerceau's work ▲ *118*.

**THE "ARCHITECTURE
OF THE ENGINEERS"**
(Ancien Évêché
at Blois ▲ *154*,
early 18th century)
On the courtyard side
this rather austere
edifice comprises two
elegant stories.
A large pediment
tops the avant-corps.

MANNERISM
(Hôtel Lefebvre
de Montifray
▲ *214*, c. 1772)
In the center of the
façade two twin
pilasters crowned with
a pediment jut out, in
effect constituting a
false avant-corps. The
windows are profusely
adorned with Rocaille
cartouches and
mascarons – evidence
that ornamentation
was back in vogue.

75

The variety of farm buildings in the Loire
Valley reflects micro-regional differences as
well as the wide range of geological resources
and building materials. Although tufa, in its
various forms, remains the common element,
brick and slate (from Blois to Gien) and schists
(around Angers) add a cheerful dash of color to
farm houses and other agricultural buildings.

THE GATEWAY
In the 16th and 17th
centuries the richer
farmers generally
built walls around
their property. An
arched gateway gave
a farm the look of an
estate. This trait was
sometimes reinforced
(as above) by the
addition of a timber-
framed pigeon loft
with stone noggings.

TROGLODYTE DWELLINGS
Whether on a hillside ▲ 286 or in the plain
▲ 287, troglodyte dwellings were a by-product
of quarrying tufa and falun, and provided
cheap accommodation.

MATERIALS
Tufa and falun ▲ 286
are the principal
building materials in
the Loire Valley, but
schist (in the area
around Angers) and
brick (in Orléanais
and the Sologne)
also contribute to the
appearance of the
buildings. The Loire
and its tributaries
helped to spread
these materials and
give free rein to the
interplay of colors.

BLÉSOIS (the region around Blois)
As in other parts of the Loire Valley, this winegrower's house has a single elongated story. The various windows and doors give an idea of the rooms' uses. The walls of limestone-rubble masonry were usually rendered.

THE SOLOGNE ▲ 174
Builders made good use of the variety of tone and pattern offered by brick. There is an almost infinite range of colors, resulting from the type of earth used in making the bricks and their position in the oven. Bricks were laid in many different ways, the most common design being the Flemish bond (with alternating headers and stretchers).

CHINONNAIS (the Chinon region)
In the 19th century a new prosperity, resulting from agriculture, gave rise to more sophisticated buildings like the one below. The walls were thinner and built of white stone blocks. String courses, moldings and pilasters adorned the façades. The attic roof was covered with slates brought by rail from Anjou.

TOURAINE
Simple buildings like the one shown above are purely functional. The window with the shutter, the door on the left, with the flat stone lintel, and the chimney stack indicate the living quarters. The central door is the entrance to the barn, while the door on the right opens into the cowshed.

The first water mills were established at a very early date. In the 15th century windmills appeared in waterless areas or were added to the existing installations there are several kinds in the Loire Valley, including one type specific to the area, the cave windmill. To the east of Blois there are numerous remains of brickyards and tileries, attesting that these industries were in existence as early as the 12th century and were widespread from the 15th century onward.

WATER MILLS WITH A VERTICAL WHEEL
The mill is said to have either a *roue de dessus* or a *roue de dessous*, depending on the height at which the water flows into the wheel. The side mill wheel (above), with the water level just below the wheel axle, enabled the use of small heads of water.

PIVOT WINDMILL
This type of windmill has a wooden "cage", or cabin, that pivots on a wooden or stone base. Inside the cabin can be found the windshaft and the millstones, in the upper part, and the bolter in the lower part. The millstones have their own axle.

TOWER WINDMILL
The main body of the mill is built in tufa masonry. All the machinery is located under the roof, at the top of the tower. The axis of rotation, which is identical to that of the millstones, enables the miller to set the sails into the wind, thanks to an outside shaft descending from the top of the mill to the ground.

The sails (**1**) drive the windshaft (**2**), on which is mounted the sheave (**3**); this transmits the movement vertically to the millstones (**4**). The whole grain contained in the hopper (**5**) is poured mechanically and ground between the fixed and running millstones. The ground grain is then poured into the bolter (**6**), a large muslin sac where the flour is graded as pure or coarse flour and bran.

CAVE WINDMILL ▲ 286

This unique type of windmill, known as a *moulin-cavier*, is a combination of the tower and the pivot windmill; its origin has never been established. The *cavier* (**1**) is the section, either built in masonry or excavated, on which the pivot, or *massereau* (**2**), stands. The small cabin, called an *hucherolle* (**3**), which contains the windshaft, the sheave and the lantern wheel, rests on the *massereau*, the axle of which differs from that of the millstones. This design offered definite advantages: the spinning mass of the pivot windmill was reduced and the useful volume increased; in addition, the millstones and the bolter were at ground level.

BRICKYARDS

Brickyards were established close to clay veins, near wooded areas that supplied the fuel necessary for baking bricks. A production cycle lasted a year. The earth and faggots were prepared in the fall and winter, then the bricks were molded and dried in the spring and summer. An average of four baking sessions were carried out early in the fall, each batch comprising around 15,000 bricks, which were loaded into the kiln and baked for nearly a week.

1. Vaulted room for storing faggots
2. Furnace (with twin-tunnel hearth)
3. Loading mouth
4. Baking pit
5. Vents

BRICKMAKING

The furnace was lit and heated for two days, after which the roaring fire was kept continuously ablaze for three days. The fire was then smothered, but the bricks continued to bake for another three days. After this, it was necessary to wait two more days before the bricks could be handled.

79

SMALL FARM BUILDINGS

WELLS
The form may vary, but wells are common on the limestone plateaus, where farmers have to dig deep to find water. This well backs onto a troglodytic dwelling cut into a hillside.

Near farms and in the midst of cultivated land one often finds rudimentary buildings either designed to house agricultural equipment or with a utilitarian function, such as wells. The variety of building materials used corresponds to the local resources and sometimes produces remarkable results – such as the large *loges*, or vegetable sheds, found near farm buildings. Dovecotes and winegrowers' cottages are more traditional.

DOVECOTE
▲ *140, 16*
Dovecotes, called *fuyes*, are generally either round or polygonal. Pigeon breeding was a seigniorial right. Pigeons were raised both for food and for their *colombine* (droppings). Within the masonry there are nesting holes, the *boulins*, where the pigeons roost. A ladder, attached by crosspieces to a pivoting central pole, provides access to the nesting holes.

"LOGE DE GÂTINE" ▲ *216*
These vast sheds, found in areas of mixed farming, are used to house farm equipment and sometimes the crops as well. The framework, which starts at ground level, supports the walls and roof. The walls are formed with long rafters, fastened to triangular collar beams to reinforce the structure. The heather thatching is attached on horizontal battens.

A "LUBIT" OR WINEGROWER'S COTTAGE
This was used by winegrowers to house equipment, and sometimes themselves for a few days at a time. These modest buildings were nevertheless often equipped with a fireplace and a well, and were carefully built with hewn stones.

The Loire Valley
as seen by painters

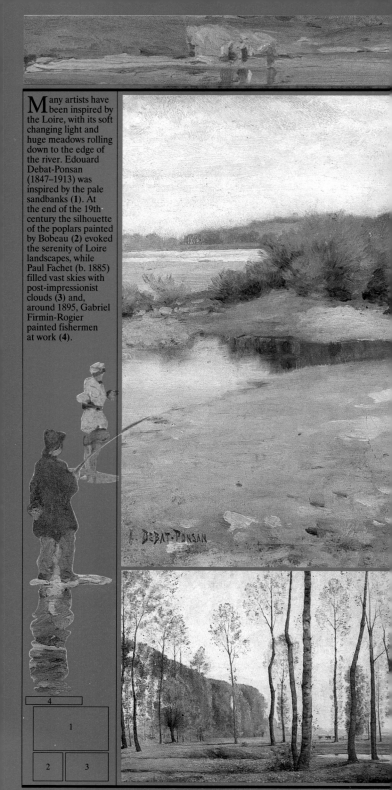

Many artists have been inspired by the Loire, with its soft changing light and huge meadows rolling down to the edge of the river. Edouard Debat-Ponsan (1847–1913) was inspired by the pale sandbanks (1). At the end of the 19th century the silhouette of the poplars painted by Bobeau (2) evoked the serenity of Loire landscapes, while Paul Fachet (b. 1885) filled vast skies with post-impressionist clouds (3) and, around 1895, Gabriel Firmin-Rogier painted fishermen at work (4).

E. DEBAT-PONSAN

4

1

2 3

**"THE LOIRE IS A WOMAN IN LOVE AND IN RAPTURES
BUT SWIFT TO FLEE IN WILD CAPRICES,
HER PERFIDIOUS LANGUOR ASLEEP ON THE RUSSET SANDS,
KISSES THE CURVES OF ITS CHARMED BANKS."**

JULES LEMAITRE

Oliver Debré (born 1920) chose abstraction to express his emotion before the Loire landscapes with which he was familiar. He contrasted the matt ocher of the sand (**1**) with the limpid river (**2**) where a few vigorous brush strokes catch our eye. From his various stays at Huisnes, near Chinon, between 1955 and 1967, Max Ernst kept the remembrance of an indolent province symbolized by his evocatively titled *Le Jardin de la France* (**3**) painted in 1962. A collage enhanced with paint, it is a strong surrealist work, as is shown by the association of incongruous elements.

Dupuis 1853.

> **"ALONG THE ROUNDED HILLS AND THE NOBLE VALES
> THE CHÂTEAUX ARE STREWN LIKE PROCESSIONAL ALTARS . . ."**
>
> CHARLES PÉGUY

Monuments are all-important in the works of artists who came to the Loire Valley, including celebrated landscape painters such as Turner (1775–1851) and Théodore Rousseau (1812–67). Étienne Dupuy (1805–60) moved to Blois around 1849 where he became an art teacher and, in his own words, "a miniature painter". His *Château de Chambord* (**1**) is part of a series of five pictures painted in 1853, depicting Chambord, Blois, Amboise and Chenonceau. One of the great châteaux of the département, partly built during the reign of François I, the Château de Blois enjoyed a tremendous resurrection thanks to the restoration work of Félix Duban between (1797–1870). Several European architects were fascinated by the site, including the architect John Gregory Grace (1809–89) who was responsible for the British rediscovery of the Renaissance. His representation of Blois (**2**, **3**, **4**) in 1600 was inspired more by the famous engraved drawings of Jacques Androuet du Cerceau (c. 1510–c. 1585) kept in London than by the château as it was when he discovered it in 1847. In contrast his compatriot William Burges (1827–81), a disciple and friend of Viollet-le-Duc (1814–79), concentrated on château interiors (**5**).

1

2	3	4	5

"THE FALL OF JERICHO"
This miniature by Jean Fouquet (c. 1415 to c. 1480), from a fine edition of Josephus' *Jewish Antiquities* (c. 1475), is an illustration of the storming of Jericho by the Israelites, from the fourth chapter of Joshua. Seven priests, blowing seven ram's horns, precede the Ark of the Covenant. The blowing of the trumpets causes the immediate collapse of the high walls, thus giving the city over to the Israelites.

Jean Fouquet ▲ 231, a native of Tours, transposes the famous biblical scene from the Jordan Valley to the Loire Valley, easily recognizable by the slate and tile roofs of the Renaissance houses and by the gentle light of the hilly landscape. In the foreground, thanks to the vivid colors and an extremely precise line (used, for example, for the ornaments on the Ark), the seven protagonists stand out against a landscape rendered infinite by soft tones and an

ashen atmosphere. Little is known of the artist's life or training. During his lifetime he was greatly honored (he was the official painter to the courts of Charles VII and Louis XI). Fouquet was then completely forgotten until he was rediscovered in the 19th century and recognized as the greatest French artist of the 15th century. His renewed fame was due to the discovery by Georges Brentano, at the beginning of the 19th century, of forty miniatures from

the *Heures d'Étienne Chevalier*, which led to major scholarly studies of Fouquet's work. The artist was probably influenced by Flemish art, and certainly by Italian art, we know, for instance of his stay in Rome from 1444 onward, where he painted a portrait of Pope Eugenius IV. Among his most famous work are his portrait of Charles VII and the *Virgin of the Milk* (the model for the Madonna being Charles VII's celebrated mistress, Agnès Sorel ▲ 227).

The Loire Valley
as seen by writers

THE GARDEN OF FRANCE

A WELL-TENDED GARDEN

Hippolyte Taine (1828–93), philosopher, historian and literary critic, is perhaps be
known for his influential theories on human thought and development, but his trav
writings both in France and abroad, imbued with his characteristic lucidity, provide th
reader with fascinating, and often charming, insights into the places and peop
he encountered. He visited Touraine in 1863 during a spell as an admissions examin
for the Military School at Saint-Cyr, and was clearly seduced by the landscapes
the Loire.

❝The country is transformed; the wild and succulent verdure ceases. There are
more oaks; the moisture grows less abundant. We pass the Loir, and present
come in sight of the Loire.

There is a wide plain, a stream with no defined course, which is often in floc
and often runs partly dry, amidst eyots of shingle and long banks of sand. Th
sandbanks have a certain vegetation, and there are broad lands covered wi
stunted pines.

But, especially after passing Tours, nothing could be more cheerful, or give bett
indication of comfort and prosperity. There are beautiful meadows, abunda
crops, fruit trees, and rows of poplars, with every now and then a peaceful far
Hemp, corn, various kinds of fruit, are plentiful; there is no more buckwheat, as
Brittany. The sky adds to the pleasantness and cheerfulness of the country. Th
velvet southern sky begins at this point, a radiant blue infused with light, like th
clearest crystal. This lovely colour, sparkling and tender, sheds a glow of happine
over the trees, over the long stretch of fertile fields; the whole landscape resembl
a garden, not the formal, plotted, economised garden of England, but somewh
casually tended, with a suggestion of neglect, though man's light-hearted negligen
robs him of no whit of earth's prodigality. A few white castles, with picturesqu
turrets, perched like pigeons amongst the foliage, raise their blue pointed roofs an
survey the plain from their vantage-ground. They bring to mind the happy life
the Valois, Diana of Poitier and Francis I. and Rabelais, the careless, gallant ways
life, the hunting, the boating-parties on those bright and wayward streams.❞

HIPPOLYTE TAINE, *JOURNEYS THROUGH FRANCE – BEING IMPRESSIONS OF THE PROVINCE*
PUB. T. FISHER, UNWIN, LONDON, 18

A METAPHOR FOR LOVE

Honoré de Balzac (1799–1859) was born in Tours. Set mostly in the valley of the Indr
his novel "The Lily of the Valley" details the intense but unrequited love of a young
man for a chatelaine – a love expressed through the beauty of nature.

❝Nature has certain effects of boundless meaning, rising to the level of th
greatest intellectual ideas. Thus, a blossoming heath covered with diamonds of de
that hang on every leaf sparkling in the sun, a thing of infinite beauty for one sing
eye that may happen to see it. Or a forest nook, shut in by tumbled boulder
broken by willows, carpeted with moss, dotted with juniper shrubs – it scares you
its wild, hurtled, fearful aspect, and the cry of the hawk comes up to you. Or
scorching sandy common with no vegetation; a stony, precipitous plateau, th
horizon reminding you of the desert – but there I found an exquisite and lone
flower, a pulsatilla waving its violet silk pennon in honour of its golden stamens;
pathetic image of my fair idol, alone in her valley! Or again, broad pools over whi
nature flings patches of greenery, a sort of transition between animal and vegetab
being, and in a few days life is there – floating plants and insects, like a world in th
upper air. Or again, a cottage with its cabbage garden, its vineyard, its fence
overhanging a bog, and surrounded by a few meagre fields of rye – emblematic
many a humble life. Or a long forest avenue, like the nave of a cathedral where th
pillars are trees, their branches meeting like the groins of a vault, and at the end
distant glade seen through the foliage, dappled with light and shade, or glowing
the ruddy beams of sunset like the painted glass window of a choir, filled with bird

> ## "THE LOIRE, EMBELLISHED BY OUR PRINCES,
> ## REIGNED ROYAL AMONGST THEM.
> ## SHE WAS THE QUEEN OF OUR KINGS."
>
> RENÉ BENJAMIN

r choristers. Then, as you come out of the grove, a chalky fallow where full-fed
akes wriggle over the hot, crackling moss, and vanish into their holes after raising
eir graceful, proud heads. And over these pictures cast floods of sunshine,
ppling like a nourishing tide, or piles of grey cloud in bars like the furrows on an
d man's brow, or the cool tones of a faintly yellow sky banded with pale light –
d listen! You will hear vague harmonies in the depth of bewildering silence. **

HONORÉ DE BALZAC, *THE LILY OF THE VALLEY*,
TRANS. JAMES WARING, PUB. J.M. DENT & CO., LONDON/NEW YORK, 1897

OLD ROOFS

ss impressed with the local countryside, Edith Wharton (1862–1937) conjures up, in
r travel writings, the sublime views to be enjoyed from the lofty vantage points of
ois.

A short afternoon's run carried us through dullish country from Chartres to
ois, which we reached at the fortunate hour when sunset burnishes the great
rves of the Loire and lays a plum-coloured bloom on the slate roofs overlapping,
ale-like, the slope below the castle. There are few finer roof-views than this from
e wall at Blois: the blue sweep of gables and ridge-lines billowing up here and
ere into a church tower . . . or breaking to let through the glimpse of a carved
çade, or the blossoming depths of a hanging garden; but perhaps only the eye
bdued to tin housetops and iron chimney-pots can feel the full poetry of old
ofs. **

EDITH WHARTON, *ABROAD – SELECTED TRAVEL WRITINGS, 1888–1920*
PUB. ROBERT HALE, LONDON, 1995

NOSTALGIA

aurice Genevoix (1890–1980) was an Orléanais but made frequent visits to friends
ar Brinon-sur-Sauldre in the Sologne region, where he got to know some of the local
achers. His experiences lent an air of authority to his novel "Raboliot", the story of
peasant who has an ambivalent relationship with the animals he kills.

Memories came flooding to him in great waves: all the smells of the woodlands,
e acrid scent of the damp earth covered by fermenting leaves, the light exhalation
f resin, the floury aroma of a mushroom crushed in passing; all the murmuring,
stling and sudden flight in the branches, the noise of birds winging across the
roves or soaring low over the furrows; and the cries of twilight, the grating screech
f the cock-pheasants, the partridges calling to each other, the short chirps of the
ightjars, and at nightfall a grinding sound passing close to
ne's head as the first sparrow-owl flies out hunting . . .

The lagoon of Chanteloup threw up a great
mpid reflection. The surrounding reeds, and a
w still leafless hedgerows, cast their warm tints
f ochre, red and burning russet, against the
olid blue of a pine-grove that closed the
orizon. The sky touched the tops of the
ines, it seemed, to be poised upon them,
eaning there

indefinitely like a globe of green crystal . . . Raboliot breathed slowly, his fles
penetrated by a vegetable well-being, so absolute that he no longer felt his body
He lived only through a few sporadic thoughts, images scattered on the surfaces c
dreams like islets on a lake. It was the fifth evening that he had returned thus to th
edge of the great plain. And as on the other evenings, in front of this familiar space
memories passed through him, visions of the recent past today all gentle, that h
saw slipping onto the shores of his being, soft and slow, barely melancholy . . .

With the month of March, the terrible cold returned from the north, the hars
sleet and the frost nights when the great trees cracked and crackled from top to toe
in the limpid blue air beneath the greenish fires of the stars. During those nights h
went walking, across leagues of countryside. And thus roaming, always towards th
north, he came to the edge of a flat and fertile valley, where the roofs of the house
and the clusters of acacias and poplars were no more than purple and reddis
shapes, blurred behind a veil of fine mist bathed in a gentle light . . . And from the
on, an insidious nostalgia slipped into all his being, slowly penetrating it. He turne
back towards the south, towards the pinewoods and the fields of broom, the copse
of birch and oak where the abundant game was there to nourish anyone who coul
catch it, and where – so long as it had not rained too much – the ditches under th
brushwood offered a warm and dark sanctuary to the fugitive.**99**

Maurice Genevoix, *Raboliot*, Éditions du Seuil, Paris 198

Two turnings

"Le Grand Meaulnes", by Alain-Fournier (1886–1914), is a classic French "coming of-age" novel with chilling descriptions of landscape and character.

66When he had traversed the village, leaving the school-house behind, he had a
choice of two turnings. He hesitated. He knew vaguely that to get to Vierzon on
must bear to the left – but there was no one to ask. So he pushed on at a steady gai
down a road which turned out to be narrow and badly surfaced. For a while he
skirted a wood of firs and at length met a carter to whom he shouted out an
inquiry. But the mare was pulling hard and kept trotting. The carter may not have
understood the question. At any rate he made a vague reply with a gesture no less
vague, and Meaulnes decided to take a chance on the road he was on.

Then once more he was surrounded by a vast frozen plain devoid of landmarks
no living thing in sight but now and then a magpie which rose in alarm and flapped
away to perch on the stump of an elm. Wrapping the heavy blanket around him like

a cape, the traveller now stretched out his legs and, leaning against the side of the carriole, fell into a sleep that must have lasted for some time . . .

. . . When at length, chilled through in spite of the blanket, he came to his senses, the scene was transformed. It was no longer a landscape of distant horizons merging into a boundless white sky, but a patchwork of fields, still green, behind high enclosures. On either side were ditches in which water was flowing beneath the ice. Everything pointed to the proximity of a river. And between the hedgerows the road was now merely a rough narrow lane.

The mare had left off her jog-trot some distance back. Meaulnes used his whip, but nothing would induce her to move faster than a slow walk. Then, leaning forward, his hands on the dashboard, he bent down and discovered that she was limping – something was wrong with one of her hind legs. He drew up and got down in some alarm, muttering to himself:

'We'll never get to Vierzon in time for that train.'

He hardly dared knowledge the most alarming thought of all: that he might have lost his way, that the road he was on might not be the road leading to his destination. **"**

ALAIN-FOURNIER, *THE LOST DOMAIN (LE GRAND MEAULNES)*,
TRANS. FRANK DAVISON, PUB. OXFORD UNIVERSITY PRESS, OXFORD/NEW YORK, 1986

THE LOIRE

A BENEFICENT STREAM

The American-born novelist Henry James (1843–1916) settled in England in 1877 and embraced European culture, in both his life and literary works. He visited France in 1882, and relates his experiences in a charming volume entitled "A little tour in France", of which ten chapters are given to his time spent in Touraine. His account of the Loire Valley and surrounding countryside is scrupulous in contemporary detail, and timeless in its sense of place.

[Touraine] is, moreover, the heart of the old French monarchy; and as that monarchy was splendid and picturesque, a reflection of the splendour still glitters in the current of the Loire. Some of the most striking events of French history have occurred on the banks of that river, and the soil it waters bloomed for a while with the flowering of the Renaissance. The Loire gives a great 'style' to a landscape of which the features are not, as the phrase is, prominent, and carries the eye to distances even more poetic than the green horizons of Touraine. It is a very fitful stream, and is sometimes observed to run thin and expose all the crudities of its channel – a great defect certainly in a river which is so much depended upon to give an air to the places it waters.

But I speak of it as I saw it last; full, tranquil, powerful, bending in large slow curves and sending back half the light of the sky. Nothing can be finer than the view of its course which you get from the battlements and terraces of Amboise. As I looked down on it from that elevation one lovely Sunday morning, through a mild glitter of autumn sunshine, it seemed the very model of a generous, beneficent stream. The most charming part of Tours is naturally the shaded quay that overlooks it, and looks across too at the friendly faubourg of Saint Symphorien and at the terraced heights which rise above this. Indeed, throughout Touraine it is half the charm of the Loire that you can travel beside it. The great dyke which protects, or protects the country from it, from Blois to Angers, is an admirable road; and on the other side as well the highway constantly keeps it company. A wide river, a you follow a wide road, is excellent company; it brightens and shorter the way.**99**

HENRY JAMES, *COLLECTED TRAVEL WRITINGS: THE CONTINEN*
PUB. THE LIBRARIES OF AMERICA, NEW YORK, 199

AN ENCHANTING SIGHT

In an account of her trip to La Charité, Matilda Betham-Edwards (1836–1919) give this description of the magnificent landscape of the Loire.

66Hardly had we reached our rooms in the more than old-fashioned Hôtel d Grand Monarque, than from a side window, we caught sight of the Loire; so nea indeed, lay the bright, blue river, that we could almost have thrown pebbles into its clear depths; quitting the hotel, half a dozen steps, no more were needed, an enchanting scene burst upon view.

Most beautiful is the site of La Charité, built terrace-wise, not on the skirts but on the very hem of the Loire, here no revolutionary torrent, sweeping away whole villages, leaving only church steeples visible above the engulfing waters, as I had once seen it at Nantes, but a broad, smooth, crystal expanse of sky-blue. Over against the handsome stone bridge to-day having its double in the limpid water, we see a little islanded hamlet crowned with picturesque church tower; and, placing ourselves midway betwen the town and its suburban twin, obtain vast and lovely perspectives. Westward, gradually purpling as evening wears on, rises the magnificent height of Sancerre, below, amid low banks bordered with poplar, flowing the Loire. Eastward, looking towards Nevers, our eyes rest on the same broad sheet of blue; before us, straight as an arrow, stretches the French road of a pattern we know so well, an apparently interminable avenue of plane or poplar trees. The river is low at this season, and the velvety brown sands recall the sea-shore when the tide is out. Exquisite, at such an hour, are the reflections, every object having its mirrored self in the transparent waves, the lights and shadows of twilight making lovely effects.**99**

MISS BETHAM-EDWARDS, *EAST OF PARIS*,
PUB. HURST AND BLACKETT, LTD, LONDON, 1902

A MAGNIFICENT PAST

ROMANCE OF A BYGONE ERA

In his verse autobiography "The Prelude – or growth of a poet's mind", Willia Wordsworth (1770–1850) reflects both upon the present and upon a glorious pa: steeped in rich history and legend.

> **66**Along that very Loire, with Festivals
> Resounding at all hours, and innocent yet
> Of civil slaughter was our frequent walk
> Or in wide Forests of the neighbourhood,
> High woods and over-arch'd with open space
> On every side, and footing many a mile,
> In woven roots and moss smooth as the sea,
> A solemn region. Often in such place
> From earnest dialogues I slipp'd in thought
> And let remembrance steal to other times
> When Hermits from their sheds and caves forth stray'd
> Walk'd by themselves, so met in shades like these . . .
>   And when my Friend
> Pointed upon occasion to the Site

Of Romorentin, home of ancient Kings,
To the imperial Edifice of Blois
Or to that rural Castle, name now slipp'd
From my remembrance, where a Lady lodg'd
By the first Francis wooed, and bound to him
In chains of mutual passion; from the Tower,
As a tradition of the Country tells,

Practis'd to commune with her Royal Knight
By cressets and love-beacons, intercourse
'Twixt her high-seated Residence and his
Far off at Chambord on the Plain beneath:
Even here, though less than with the peaceful House
Religious, 'mid these frequent monuments
Of Kings, their vices and their better deeds,
Imagination, potent to enflame
At times with virtuous wrath and noble scorn,
Did also often mitigate the force
Of civic prejudice, the bigotry,
So call it, of a youthful Patriot's mind,
And on these spots with many gleams I look'd
Of chivalrous delight. "

WILLIAM WORDSWORTH, *THE PRELUDE*, *BOOK 9: RESIDENCE IN FRANCE*
PUB. OXFORD UNIVERSITY PRESS, LONDON/NEW YORK, 1970

95

A MAID IN ARMOR

In this passage from Maurice David-Darnac's history of the life of Joan of Arc, Joan receives the gift of a suit of armor and retrieves a holy sword.

❝In Tours Joan was being equipped for battle. The king had a suit of armour made for her. This must have given her much pleasure, as fine arms delighted her throughout her career. In any case the present was a sign of her new status and of the confidence which was now placed in her, as well as marking a definitive separation from the peasant girl she had once been. A full suit of armour, not only because of its connotations, but because it was so expensive, was the thing which most conspicuously set the knight apart from the rest of those who surrounded him. Joan was also offered a sword, but for this she insisted on sending back to Sainte-Cathérine-de-Fierbois. She asked for a weapon which she knew to be concealed at a particular spot within the church:

How did you know this sword was there?
I knew it was there from my voices. I had never seen the man who went to look for it. I wrote to the churchmen of the place to ask for the sword, and they sent it to me. It was not deep in the earth. It was, as I think, behind the altar; but I am not certain whether it was in front of the altar or behind it.

Joan added that, when the sword was found, it was rusty, but 'the clergy rubbed it, and the rust readily fell off'. She also said that she had a great liking for this weapon 'because it had been found in the church of St Catherine, whom she loved well'.❞

MAURICE DAVID-DARNAC, *THE TRUE STORY OF THE MAID OF ORLEANS*,
TRANS. PETER DE POLNAY, PUB. W.H. ALLEN, LONDON, 1969

A MEETING WITH THE DAUPHIN

During her travels Virginia Woolf visited the castle at Chinon, where Joan of Arc first met the Dauphin, later to become King Charles VII of France.

❝Explored castle alone . . . Saw the high unroofed room in wh. Jeanne stood before the King. The very chimney piece perhaps. Walls cut through by thin windows. Suddenly one looks down, down on the roofs. How did the middle ages get through the evenings? A stone crypt in wh. J. lived: people carve their names everywhere. River silken serpentine beneath. Liked the stone roofless rooms; & the angular cut windows. Sat on the steps to hear 2 struck by the clock wh. has rung since the 13th Century: wh. J. heard. Rusty tone. What did she think? Was she mad? a visionary coinciding with the right moment.❞

TRAVELS WITH VIRGINIA WOOLF, ED. JAN MORRIS,
PUB. THE HOGARTH PRESS, LONDON, 1993

GLORIOUS FOOD

RECOLLECTION OF PLEASURES PAST

Vernon Lee was the pseudonym of Violet Paget (1856–1935), the English essayist and novelist who spent most of her life in Italy

❝It is impossible to speak adequately of Touraine, to recall its charm at all adequately (indeed, it was a true instinct which caused me to describe that charm by the word 'flavour') without mentioning things to eat and drink. I confess to not thinking much about my dinner in other countries, save as one of the inevitable bothers of life; but I think about it a great deal, and as a permeating essence of life, in Touraine. It has a right to permeate, because, as I have said, this land has turned it into a poetry. The *déjeuner à la fourchette* at the inn of Saumur was as essential a part of that old town's charm as the discreet Balzac *portes-cochères*, overhung by creepers, and the lovely turreted house built by King René for his daughter. I remember, and shall remember, the beautiful long loaves of bread, like blond ctuses, off which one cut colossal hunks, as well as anything else, at Langeais. ...d as to the Château de St Avry, it sums up all the special poetic prose of the ...ire-side in a draught – a draught out of a silver wine-taster's mug – of ten-year- ...l Vin de Chinon. 99

VERNON LEE, *GENIUS LOCI – NOTES ON PLACES*,
PUB. JOHN LANE, THE BODLEY HEAD/JOHN LANE COMPANY, NEW YORK, 1908

A BITTER AND VIOLENT CONFLICT OVER PANCAKES ("FOUACES")

...e of Touraine's greatest writers, François Rabelais (c. 1494–1553) gives this satirical, ...affectionate portrayal of ordinary folk at their most vulgar and ridiculous

...At that time, which was the season of Vintage, in the beginning of Harvest, when ...e countrey shepherds were set to keep the Vines, and hinder the Starlings from ...ing up the grapes; as some cake-bakers of *Lerne* happened to passe along in the ...oad high way, driving unto the City ten or twelve horses loaded with cakes, the ...d shepherds courteously intreated them to give them some for their money, as ...e price then ruled in the market; for here it is to be remarked, that it is a celestial ...od to eate for breakfast hot fresh cakes with grapes, especially the frail clusters, ...e great red grapes, the muscadine, the verjuice grape and the luskard, for those ...t are costive in their belly; because it will make them gush out, and squirt the ...gth of a Hunters staffe, like the very tap of a barrel; and often-times thinking to ...a squib, they did all-to-besquatter and conskite themselves, whereupon they are ...nmonly called the Vintage-thinkers. The Bunsellers or Cake-makers were in ...thing inclinable to their request; but (which was worse) did injure them most ...tragiously, calling them pratling gablers, lickorous gluttons, freckled bittors, ...ngie rascals, shiteabed scoundrels, drunken roysters, slie knaves, drowsie ...terers, slapsauce fellows, slabberdegullion druggels, lubbardly lowts, cosening ...es, ruffian rogues, paultrie customers, sycophant-varlets, drawlatch hoydons, ...uting milksops, jeering companions, staring clowns, forlorn snakes, ninnie ...cocks, scurvie sneaksbies, fondling fops, base lowns, sawcie coxcombs, idle lusks, ...ffing Braggards, noddie meacocks, blockish grutnols, doddi-pol-jolt-heads, jobernol ...osecaps, foolish loggerheads, slutch calf-lollies, grouthead gnat-snappers, lob-...terels, gaping changelings, codshead loobies, woodcock slangams, ninnie-hammer ...catchers, noddiepeak simpletons; Turdie gut, shitten shepherds, and other such ...e defamatory epithetes, saying further, that it was not for them to eate of these ...nty cakes, but might very well content themselves with the course unraunged ...ead, or to eat of the great brown houshold loaf. To which provoking words, one ...ongst them, called *Forgier*, (an honest fellow of his person, and a notable ...ingal,) made answer very calmly thus: How long is it since you have got homes, ...t you are become so proud? indeed formerly you were wont to give us ...ne freely, and will you not now let us have any for our money? This is not the part of good neighbours, neither do we serve you thus when you come hither to buy our good corn, whereof you

make your cakes and buns: besides that, we would have given you to the barga
some of our grapes, but *by his zounds*, you may chance to repent it, and possib
have the need of us at another time, when we shall use you after the like mann
and therefore remember it. Then *Marquet*, a prime man in the confraternity of t
cake-bakers, said unto him, Yea Sir, thou are pretty well crest-risen this mornin
thou didst eat yesternight too much millet and bolymong, come hither *Sirrah*, con
hither, I will give thee some cakes: whereupon *Forgier* dreading no harm, in a
simplicity went towards him, and drew a sixpence out of his leather sachel, thinki
that *Marquet* would have sold him some of his cakes; but in stead of cakes, he ga
him with his whip such a rude lash overthwart the legs, that the marks of t
whipcord knots were apparent in them; then would have fled away, but *Forgi*
cried out as loud as he could, O murther, murther, help, help, help, and in t
mean time threw a great cudgel after him, which he carried under his arm
wherewith he hit him in the *coronal* joynt of his head, upon the *crotaphick* arterie
the right side thereof, so forcibly, that *Marquet* fell down from his mare, more like
dead then living man. Mean-while the farmers and countrey-swaines, that we
watching their walnuts near to that place, came running with their great poles an
long staves, and laid such load on these cake-bakers, as if they had been to thre
upon green rie. The other shepherds and shepherdesses hearing the lamentab
shout of *Forgier*, came with their slings and slackies following them, and throwin
great stones at them, as thick as if it had been haile. At last they overtook ther
and took from them about foure or five dosen of their cakes; nevertheless th
payed for them the ordinary price, and gave them over and above one hundre
egges, and three baskets of mulberries. Then did the cake-bakers help to get up
his mare *Marquet*, who was most shrewdly wounded, and forthwith returned
Lerne changing the resolution they had to go to *Pareille*, threatning very sharp an
boistrously the cowherds, shepherds, and farmers of *Sevile* and *Sinays*. This don
the shepherds and shepherdesses made merry with these cakes and fine grapes, an
sported themselves together at the sound of the pretty small pipe, scoffing an
laughing at those vain-glorious cake-bakers, who had that day met with a mischi
for the want of crossing themselves with a good hand in the morning. Nor did the
forget to apply to *Forgiers* leg some faire great red medicinal grapes, and s
handsomly drest it and bound it up, that he was quickly cured. **99**

FRANÇOIS RABELAIS, *GARGANTUA AND PANTAGRUE*
TRANS. SIR THOMAS URQUHART AND PIERRE LE MOTTEU
PUB. EVERYMAN'S LIBRARY, LONDON, ALFRED A. KNOPF, NEW YORK, 19•

POUILLY-FUMÉ
*In his book "Bouquet de France" Samuel Chamberlain describes the many culina
delights that France has to offer. Here he praises the Pouilly nectar.*

66Vineyards begin to ribbon the riverbanks near the town of Cosne an
become thicker as one approaches Pouilly. The carefully tended vines a
blue-green with spray. They were growing grapes on these
same chalky slopes a millennium ago, for the archives have
records of a large vineyard which thrived near Pouilly in
the year 859. It takes time to develop a wine as

ductive as Pouilly-Fumé! The town itself is an unpretentious place along the ver, with no particular charm. Every street, every dead-end alley seems to be evoted to wine. Confusion is bound to result from the fact that another fine white ine, this one from the Beaujolais country, carries the name of Pouilly-Fuissé. obody seems to have invented a formula to remember which is which. But you'll ever forget Pouilly-Fumé if you taste it cool from a cellar in Pouilly-sur-Loire! his clean, immensely palatable wine has a rich, fruity bouquet underlying its yness. As a result, it makes a perfectly splendid *apéritif*. It would be unthinkable the Pouilly region to drink anything but white wine of a café terrace. Parisian otorists jam on their brakes and follow a sudden inspiration to enjoy a cool bottle Pouilly-Fumé before proceeding on their journey. No other wine in France ossesses quite the mysterious perfume which a subtle combination of sun and cky soil produces here. The nostril detects the same flinty aroma common to her Loire wines, but there is an added touch of softness, which caresses the roat and rejoices the spirit. The wine of Pouilly *"chaugge le bonhomme,"* as the atives say – fills him with sunshine and then departs, diuretic and beneficial. Why ave a *carete des vins*, they ask, when a single wine suffices for everything? Before, uring, and after your meal – a glistening goblet of Pouilly's lemon-gold glory!

Just to get the record straight, there are two distinct wines from this region. The eat one is Pouilly-Fumé, so-called because of the smoky-blue color of its uvignon grape, or Blanc-Fumé. The mysterious chemistry of the vine produces the ch, golden, liquorous Château d'Yquem from the same plant. How different is pale ouilly-Fumé, the result of the Sauvignon when it grows on a bank of Kimmeridgian alky clay! The wine called Pouilly Blanc comes from another grape, the Chasselas, d is more closely akin to Muscadet, the dry wine which flourishes near the mouth the Loire. It has much the same fresh, faintly flinty bouquet and almost as much esse as the Fumé. Either is an enchantment on a warm summer's day.

SAMUEL CHAMBERLAIN, *BOUQUET DE FRANCE: AN EPICUREAN TOUR OF THE FRENCH PROVINCES*, PUB. HAMISH HAMILTON, LONDON

HÂTEAUX OF THE LOIRE

TALCY

ie châteaux of the Loire are famed for their elegance and beauty. The delightful âteau at Talcy appears to be one that has been undeservedly overlooked.

Talcy is another of the greatly underestimated châteaux, yet it is certainly fit to ke place in the second rank of them, if not in the first. It was built, about 1520, by Florentine, Bernard Salviati, cousin of Catherine de Médicis, at the time when rançois I was busy with the Italianate wing of the château of Blois, when everything alian was the very height of fashion, and the transalpine architects had not yet ssimilated the gentle light and delicate colourings of the Loire valley. Yet, and in is it is almost unique, it is built away from the river in the most unpromising osition of La Beauce, scorning all the natural advantages of the magnificent river tting to be found so few miles away. Built for an Italian, it is as remote from Italy it is from Persia or Cathay. It is, almost alone of its date, uncompromisingly rench. It occupies the site of a small fortress of the twelfth century, from which it herited a certain strength; not enough to make it a fort, but sufficient to make it a anor house easily defended. There is a strong, square tower, surmounted by a corbelled sentry-walk and carrying three turrets with the rather self conscious air of a serious somebody-in-the-city wearing a comic hat to please the children.

Simple, rectangular, unornamented almost, it stands amongst the other châteaux (if the metaphor may be allowed to change sex) like the county lady who, having found a style to suit her, refuses thereafter to pander to the fashion of the day. If the outside is uncompromising, the inner courtyard is soft and feminine to the point of prettiness. In the middle of it is a dome-covered well; the corner of the too-massive keep is rendered surprisingly effeminate by a turret staircase, looking the more delicate for the direct comparison with its heavy neighbour; the main building, lightened by a four-arcaded gallery, severe enough for a monastery, were it not lightened by two fanciful gables. To what extent Bernard Salviati was ruled by his wife, history does not tell, but the evidence of Talcy is that he arranged the exterior to his liking, but his wife asserted her ideas when it came to the courtyards. The second courtyard is difficult to see, so much is it dominated by an immense dovecote, apparently contemporary with the main building, yet still in splendid condition. It has some 1,500 pigeon-holes, if that is the right word in a dovecote; the French *alvéoles* is distinctly more poetic. We know that they were early risers in those days, and well must they have needed to be at Talcy, for the awakening of a thousand doves must have driven all but the dead from their sleep.

Vivian Rowe, *Chateaux of the Loire*, pub. Putnam, London, 195

A reluctant sightseer

In these diary entries the novelist Evelyn Waugh (1903–66) makes it perfectly clear that viewing castles is not his favorite pastime.

❝It continues to be hot, but not intolerable. We are leading a lazy and agreeable life; getting up late, lunching heavily, perhaps going to visit a château, perhaps doing some shopping in Tours and having tea at Massie and going to the cinema at the Café de Commerce, dining heavily and then sleeping heavily. I am reading Richard's *Principles of Literary Criticism* again. My French is making no progress. On Saturday we went to Chenonceaux for luncheon where the *pâté de maison* was excellent. I do not much like seeing over châteaux. We then went to Chaumont and arrived at Amboise just too late to go over the château. Instead we drank some wine at a restaurant to which an importunate little boy directed us. There is little temptation to dine out as the cooking here is so excellent . . . It has rained a good deal in the last few days, bringing all manner of rank smells out of the country. On Monday we did a big round of châteaux, Azay-le-Rideau, Langres, Chinon, Langeais, Ussé. They were less crowded than on Saturday. The chapel at Ussé is very fine. I do not much like seeing châteaux. . . . On Saturday we set out for Blois in the two motor cars, but the Frazer Nash broke its springs. We arranged to spend the night at Blois at an hotel called Angleterre. We saw the château and rested and ate a dreadful dinner and then Julia and I went off in search of a music hall and we found a fair along the Loire where we were photographed. We also saw a patriotic drama and Julia fell in love with a redheaded American girl chewing nuts. When we got back to the hotel we were told that Richard and Elizabeth had gone back to Tours. I may be old-fashioned, but it seemed to me an improper proceeding, particularly as the manageress could only very hardly [?] be persuaded that Julia and I did not want to sleep together. I went for a walk round the town. Next day I went to see a very beautiful church called, as far as I could make out, St Nichole and St Laurent. We lunched at the Angleterre, paid an immense bill, and drove to Chambord – a monstrous building with what the book on Touraine calls 'a dream city' on its roof. Yesterday we pottered about Tours drinking tasteless French beer.❞

Evelyn Waugh, *The Diaries of Evelyn Waugh*, ed. Michael Davie, pub. Book Club Associates, London, 197

People and places

Amboise

The English philosopher John Locke (1632–1704) spent some years traveling through France. His assertion that Amboise was built by Dogabert is thought to be pure legend; as for his warning about the price of good wine . . . it's best to find out for yourself.

THURS. MAY 27. From Tours to Amboise 6 leagues through a sandy valley by the ~~side~~ of the Loire, full of rie and poplar trees: are not 12 ordinary English miles. ~~A~~mboise is a litle, stragleing towne. There is a manifacture of woolen stuffs, an old ~~c~~hasteau, built by Dogabert, which stands high over the towne, wherein is a chappell ~~w~~here are hung up the mighty pair of Stag's hornes, 15 foot high & 7½ broad, the ~~s~~tag, they say, kild in the Forest of Arden in Francis the Ist time, & a round tower ~~t~~here, in a spirall ascent a coach may drive up to the top. In the midle or nave of this ~~wi~~nding ascent is a well, & a cart might goe down the same way to fetch up water. ~~T~~he ascent not very steep, nor the tour very large. A la Corne excellent coole wine, ~~b~~t make your bargain before hand or expect an extraordinary reconing. 99

JOHN LOCKE, *LOCKE'S TRAVELS IN FRANCE, 1675–1679*,
CAMBRIDGE UNIVERSITY PRESS, CAMBRIDGE, 1953

WATCHING THE WEATHER IN SAUMUR

~~H~~onoré de Balzac exercises his aptitude for detailed characterization on the burghers ~~of~~ Saumur, in his novel "Eugénie Grandet" (1833). He exposes their mundane hopes ~~an~~d fears – and, with some irony, their propensity for downright nosiness – with an ~~un~~flinching scrutiny alleviated only a little by a dark vein of humor.

Here, as in Touraine, the whole trade of the district depends upon an ~~at~~mospherical depression. Landowners, vinegrowers, timber merchants, coopers, ~~in~~keepers, and lightermen, one and all are on the watch for a ray of sunlight. Not ~~a~~ man of them but goes to bed in fear and trembling lest he should hear in the ~~m~~orning that there has been a frost in the night. If it is not rain that they dread it is ~~wi~~nd or drought; they must have cloudy weather or heat, and the rainfall and the ~~w~~eather generally all arranged to suit their peculiar notions.

Between the clerk of the weather and the vine-growing interest there is a duel ~~w~~hich never ceases. Faces visibly lengthen or shorten, grow bright or gloomy, with ~~th~~e ups and downs of the barometer. Sometimes you hear from one end to the ~~ot~~her of the old High Street of Saumur the words, 'This is golden weather!' or ~~a~~gain, in language which likewise is no mere figure of speech, 'It is raining gold ~~lo~~uis!' and they all know the exact value of sun or rain at the right moment.

After twelve o'clock or so on a Saturday in the summer time, you will not do a ~~p~~ennyworth of business among the worthy townsmen of Saumur. Each has his little ~~fa~~rm and his bit of vineyard, and goes to spend the 'week end' in the country. As ~~ev~~erybody knows this beforehand, just as everybody knows everybody else's ~~b~~usiness, his goings and comings, his buyings and sellings, and profits to boot, the ~~go~~od folk are free to spend ten hours out of the twelve in making up pleasant little ~~p~~arties, in taking notes and making comments, and keeping a sharp look-out on

their neighbours' affairs. The mistress of a house cannot buy a partridge but th
neighbours will inquire of her husband whether the bird was done to a turn; r
damsel can put her head out of the window without being observed by every grou
of unoccupied observers.

Impenetrable, dark, and silent as the houses may seem, they contain no mysteri
hidden from public scrutiny, and in the same way everyone knows what is passin
in every one else's mind. To begin with, the good folk spend most of their lives o
doors, they sit on the steps of their houses, breafast there and dine there, an
adjust any little family differences in the doorway. Every passer-by is scanned wit
the most minute and diligent attention; hence, any stranger who may happen t
arrive in such a country town has, in a manner, to run the gauntlet, and is severe
quizzed from every doorstep. By dint of perseveranc
in the methods thus indicated
quantity of droll stories may b
collected; and, indeed, th
people of Angers, who are c
an ingenious turn, and quick
repartee, have been nicl
named 'the tattlers' on the
very grounds.**99**

HONORÉ DE BALZA
EUGÉNIE GRANDE
TRANS. ELLEN MARRIAG
PUB. EVERYMAN'S LIBRAR
LONDON, ALFRED A. KNOI
NEW YORK, 19

RECOLLECTIONS OF CHILDHOOD

Sidonie-Gabrielle Colette (1873–1954) was an exotic character who spent her early li
as a music-hall actress. Her bisexuality and risqué dancing won her few friends amor
the staid bourgeoisie, but she became a respected writer in later years. She was admire
for her sensuous prose, and her rich appreciation of mankind and Nature.

66August, in my northern country, was a month for long patience. Like n
deprived of school, the children found the days long. They crowded together durir
their interminable leisure in the shade at the foot of the houses, for they were tire
of the shorn stubble and the silent woods. As the sun rotated they folded up the
dusty legs to shield them from it. They played, we played, at spinning the knif
three pebbles, knuckle-bones. They bit into the first half-green peaches – I dor
write 'we bit' because, as always, I was an expert on the taste of ripe juicy fruit. W
watched the upward growth on the waste land of those thistles, fit for cardin
whose flower, armed overall, takes fire with a violet flame just before the expiratic
of summer. Mulleins also climbed there, all covered – hairy leaves, buff-coloure
flower – with the dustiness of those sultry days. Sated with idleness, listless fro
missing school and from concealing it, we counted the days and lied: 'My wor
doesn't it go quickly!'. . .

Down there the pale, blackhaired women grape-harvesters put on large hat
turn down their sleeves to the wrists, and affect fearfulness: 'Oh, there's a spide
Holy Mother, a snake!' With equal affectation the men shed their coats and thro
off their shirts. While the men go handsomely half-naked, the women laugh free
and sing on the paths. Fine, high voices, which the west wind carries from one ba
to the next . . . The wasps, drunk and defenceless, adhere to the sticky tubs; th
September sun is as good as August's . . .**99**

COLETTE, *LOOKING BACKWARDS*, TRANS. DAVID LEVAY, PUB. PETER OWEN, LONDON, 19

ANOTHER LITERARY FIGURE

The eccentric and perhaps immoral behavior of another French novelist, George Sar
(Amandine-Aurore Lucille Dupin, 1804–76), scandalized bourgeois society and wo
her the distrust and disapproval of her country neighbors.

La Châtre also has a Famous Literary Figure. George Sand (1804–76) did not ve in the town itself but in the pretty, turreted manor house known grandly as her hâteau' two or three miles up the road, at Nohant. It is La Châtre that figures, reet for street, in several of her novels, and the surrounding countryside was the spiration of much of her writing.

In her lifetime many of her country neighbours were wary of her, regarding her an eccentric woman with an immoral personal life and given to dangerous ealistic enthusiasms – an upper-class type that was by then well established. Her ther was an office in Napoleon's Grand Army, her mother had been a camp-llower and was the child of a man who sold birds on the streets of Paris. Her aternal grandmother, who largely brought her up, was herself the child of an egitimate son of the King of Poland. Present-day Anglo-Saxon attempts to set eorge Sand up as as feminist icon, an original rebel against the 'bourgeois orality', are misconceived. But it must be said that the twentieth-century French ndency to canonize her not only as a Great Writer but as *la Bonne Dame de ohant*, as if she had been some kind of country saint ministering to the poor and beloved by all, is equally wide of the mark. In life George Sand had local enemies well as admirers; her numerous novels are variable in quality and hardly qualify 'great'. What matters most about her today is that she was the first person in rance to write about the rural and artisan classes with personal knowledge and sympathy. Unlike her contemporary Balzac, who made his own contribution to the enduring French urban idea of the brutal peasantry, and Zola, who added it later in the century from a position of metropolitan ignorance, George Sand regarded the country people as individuals like herself. Her stories such as *La Mare au Diable*, *François le Champi* and *Le Meunier d'Angibault*, are a fountain of incidental local information concerning the world we have lost – and which was being lost even as she was depicting it. **99**

GILLIAN TINDALL, *CÉLESTINE,*
VOICES FROM A FRENCH VILLAGE,
PUB. SINCLAIR-STEVENSON, LONDON, 1995

AT THE MERCY OF THE PEASANTS OF BERRY
This passage from George Sand's "Le Meunier d'Angibault" shows the difficulty of negotiating the Loire terrain, even for the local people .

66When the sun had set, the darkness came on rapidly in these hollow ways, and the last peasant whom they addressed answered carelessly:
'Go on! go on! you have only a short league more, and the road is all good.'
Now this was the sixth peasant who, within about two hours, had stated that ere was only a short league more, and this good road was such that the horse was chausted, and the travellers at the end of their patience. Marcelle herself began to ar an overturn; for if the patachon and his nag needed all their skill to choose eir passage in broad day, it was impossible that in dark night they should avoid ae false openings which the unequal nature of the ground renders as dangerous as cturesque, and which are liable to sudden terminations, exposing you to a fall of n or twelve perpendicular feet. The lad had never penetrated so far into the lack Valley; he lost patience, and swore furiously every time that he was forced to trace his steps to recover the way; he complained of thirst, of hunger, groaned ver the fatigue of his horse, beating him unmercifully meanwhile, and cursed the vage country and its stupid inhabitants, with all the airs of a little cockney.
More than once, seeing the road steep, but dry, Marcelle and her servants

alighted; but they could not walk five minutes without coming to a hollow where the road narrowed, and was entirely occupied by stagnant springs on the level of the ground, forming a liquid mud impossible for a delicate woman to pass on foot. The Parisian Suzette had rather be overturned, she said, than leave her shoes in these sloughs; and Lapierre, who had passed his life in pumps upon polished floors, was so awkward and confused, that Mmm. de Blanchemont dared not let him carry her son.

The usual answer of the peasant, when asked the way, is, 'Go straight on, always straight on.' This is simply a joke – a sort of pun – which means that you are to walk straight on your legs; for there is not a straight road in the Black Valley. The numerous ravines made by the Indre, the Vauvre, the Couarde, the Gourdon, and a hundred lesser streams which take different names in their course, and have never borne the yoke of any bridge or dike, force you to a thousand turns to find fordable places, so that you are often obliged to turn you back upon the spot you wished to reach.

When they came to an angle of the road surmounted by a cross – a sinister locality always peopled by the peasant imagination with demons, sorcerers, and fantastic animals – our embarrassed travellers addressed themselves to a beggar who, seated upon the death-stone, cried to them in a monotonous voice, 'Charitable souls, have pity on a miserable creature!' **

GEORGE SAND, *THE MILLER OF ANGIBAULT*
PUB. WELDON & CO., LONDON, 184?

A CALL OF NATURE AND A VISIT TO MOULINS

The Swedish chemist John Jakob Berzelius (1779–1848) gives his particular impression of the highs and lows of his trip through France.

**I slept quite well all night long, not waking until we arrived at Nevers, at 8 in the morning. At this point the filthiness of France began to grow indescribable, and it continued in this way southwards. This applies

particularly to the inconvenience of the kind of convenience known in France as *commodit*. Either it is lacking altogether and you are referred to the dunghill, or else it is so decorated that your cleanest and most convenient recourse is to use the floor beside it. 'La méthode est drôle', said one of my fellow passengers, together with whom I had the honour of repaying our debt to nature; but slithering backwards the same instant, he added: 'et mauvaise'. I crave my friends' forgiveness for mentioning these things, but it is impossible to divert attention altogether from subjects which, in every street and courtyard, present themselves in heaps to both eye and foot.

The coach pulled out of Nevers. The country grew increasingly beautiful and fertile. For several miles, ever since the previous day, we had been following the River Loire, which we crossed at Nevers. The road soon brought us to the River Ailler, which debouches into the Loire. We arrived at Moulins, on the shore of the Aillier, at 3 of the afternoon. After taking a dinner which, though mean, was served in three courses, my fellow-passengers went to rest but I, having slept well in the coach, took a guide and went to see the monuments of the town. It is quite a beautiful, well-built town. The most remarkable thing I saw was a tomb of the Duke DE MONTMORENCY in the chapel belonging to le Collège Royal. In accordance with the stage coach timetable, we stayed on until 12 at night, so that after completing my walk I had plenty of time for rest, until we were told that the coach was harnessed.**

CARL GUSTAF BERNHARD, *THROUGH FRANCE WITH BERZELIUS: LIVE SCHOLARS AND DEAD VOLCANOES*, PUB. PERGAMON PRESS, OXFORD, 1989

ITINERARIES
IN THE LOIRE VALLEY

ORLÉANS, *111*
BLOIS, *141*
AMBOISE, *179*
TOURS, *193*
SAUMUR, *277*
ANGERS, *295*

"The river with its endless mottled streams, with its curving lines,

"The lower part of the Loire, torn into strips by its sands and islands,

...ometimes dramatic . . . sometimes indolent in appearance" *Charles Péguy*

...ooked from afar like those silver trails which snails leave across gardens" *René Boylesve*

▲ Château de Chaumont.

▲ The Pagoda at Chanteloup.   Château d'Azay-le-Rideau.

Château de Fougères-sur-Bièvre.

Château de Cheverny.

Château de Beauregard. ▼

▲ Sandbank on the Loire.

▲ The Loire near the Château de Menars.

The Loire in winter.

IN AND AROUND ORLÉANS

ORLÉANS-LA-SOURCE, *124*
OLIVET, *124*
LA FERTÉ-ST-AUBIN, *125*
ST-JEAN-DE-BRAYE, *126*
COMBLEUX, *126*
ST-DENIS-DE-L'HÔTEL, *126*
JARGEAU, *126*
CHÂTEAUNEUF-SUR-LOIRE, *127*
GERMIGNY-DES-PRÉS, *128*
ST-BENOÎT-SUR-LOIRE, *129*
SULLY-SUR-LOIRE, *132*
GIEN, *133*
GIEN EARTHENWARE, *134*
BRIARE, *137*

▲ ORLÉANS

17. CHANCELLERIE
16. HÔTEL EUVERTE-HATTE
15. HÔTEL TOUTIN
14. MAISON DE LA COQUILLE
13. COLLEGIATE CHURCH OF ST-PIERRE-LE-PUELLIER
12. TOUR BLANCHE
11. COLLEGIATE CHURCH OF ST-AIGNAN

On the map: BOULEVARD ALEXANDRE MARTIN · BOULEVARD ROUGEVILLE · PLACE DU MARTROI · 17 · 6 · PLACE DU Gal-DE-GAULLE · 16 · RUE ROYALE · 15 · QUAI CYPIERRE

ORLÉANAIS
From north to south, the loosely defined region of Orléanais stretches from Beauce to the Sologne and (further to the east) from Gâtinais to Gien. It has a very rich historical heritage. In the 10th century the county of Orléans was annexed by the French kingdom by the first Capetians. Their successor, Philippe VI de Valois (above), made the province into a duchy in 1344: the title was traditionally given to the second son of the King of France. This flat region, divided by the Loire and situated between the Forest of Orléans (almost 90,000 acres) ■ *24* and the Sologne ▲ *174*, covers almost exactly the same area as today's département of Loiret ● *12*.

RÉPUBLIQUE FRANÇAISE
LA POSTE 1995
2.80

ORLÉANS
68ᵉ Congrès · Fédération Française des Associations Philatéliques

HISTORY OF THE TOWN

One of the principal towns of the Loire valley, Orléans is located at the apex of the river's bend, at the confluence of two small tributaries (one of them the Loiret). From an early stage the town had a vital strategic function, mainly because it stands at a major crossroads and also possesses a large river port.

CLASSICAL TIMES AND THE MIDDLE AGES. In the 1st century BC Orléans (then named Cenabum) was one of the main strongholds of the Carnutes, a powerful Gallic tribe. Under Roman rule it was renamed Aurelianum. Clovis captured the town in 498 and held the first Council of France here in 511. The coronations of Charles the Bold and Robert the Pious (son of Hugues Capet) took place here in 848 and 987 respectively, reflecting the town's growing political and religious stature. Orléans became an important bishopric and also a renowned intellectual center, with a university that continued the Carolingian academic tradition established by Theodulf ● *129*. The region's growth was underpinned by its rich natural resources: wheat from Beauce, sheep from the Sologne, wood from the Forest of Orléans. Joan of Arc's famous victory of May 8, 1429, when she liberated the town from the English, became an enduring symbol of French resistance to invaders ● *116*.

FROM PROSPERITY TO DECLINE. During the Renaissance phases of growth and construction ▲ 74 alternated with extended periods of turbulence due to the Wars of Religion. In the 17th and 18th centuries Orléans was a flourishing provincial capital and one of the six richest towns in France ▲ 116. However, the revolutionary era and Napoleonist centralism dealt severe blows to this prosperity. The town's fortunes did not revive until the 3rd Republic, when major urban-development projects were undertaken. In June 1940 the center of the old town (around 42 acres) was destroyed by German bombing.

A MODERN CITY. Between 1950 and 1970 Orléans was gradually rebuilt; and in 1959 a new town, Orléans-la-Source, was developed on the south bank of the Loire. Today the city has a population of around 250,000. It has a strong horticultural sector and a lively university, and is active in engineering, electronics and pharmaceuticals.

HIDDEN TREASURES
Here more than elsewhere in the Loire Valley, visitors must be prepared to delve below the surface. Although the charm of Orléans is apparent at first sight, those willing to explore can discover the many historic and artistic treasures hidden away in this old royal city.

The town's first
heroic bishop was
Anianus, later
Saint Aignan. Along
with Saint Euverte,
he played an
instrumental role in
repelling Attila's
Huns in 451.
Later bishops who

contributed to the
region's intellectual
and religious
development included
Theodulf ▲ *128* from
738 to 818, Jonas
from 818 to 843, and
Agius from 843 to
868.

POET PRINCE
Charles d'Orléans
(1394–1465) inherited
the duchy from his
father, Louis
d'Orléans, and
distinguished himself
at the Battle of
Agincourt in 1415.
He was captured by
the English and
imprisoned in
London from 1415 to
1441. To pass the time
he devoted himself to
writing poetry. He left
around one hundred
ballads and laments,
which fell into
oblivion for two
centuries before
being brought to light
by the Abbé Salier in
1734.

THE CATHEDRAL

Construction of Orléans' Cathédrale Ste-Croix took nearly
550 years to complete – from 1287 to 1829 – and yet the resul
lacks neither grandeur nor elegance. The cathedral's unusual
towers are decorated with intricate stonework; its huge
Gothic nave rests on simple, elegant pillars.
DISASTERS. Over the centuries the cathedral suffered a series
of disasters. The first cathedral (4th–5th century) was

destroyed by fire in 989. The second
building, in the Romanesque style
(11th–12th century), partly collapsed in
1278. The Gothic cathedral (late 13th
century, early 16th century) was
destroyed by the Huguenots in 1568. It
was rebuilt under Henri IV from 1599
onward, but the spire of the transept was
demolished in 1691 when it looked likely
to collapse. The cathedral was finally
inaugurated on May 8, 1829.
Unfortunately the vault of the shrine collapsed in 1904,
crushing the altar under tons of masonry.
TOUR OF THE CATHEDRAL. The towers, in the neo-Gothic style
were rebuilt between 1708 and 1829. The present-day central
spire is also neo-Gothic, dating from 1858. Two 16th-century
bays (the third and fourth) survive in the upper nave
(1601–1829), presenting an unusual mixture of Gothic and
classical styles. Stained-glass windows in the right side aisle
(1893–6) depict five episodes from the life of Joan of Arc.
The choir (1605–23) is decorated with splendid 18th-century
wood carvings and carved stalls. The great vault of the apse
was modeled on that of Notre-Dame-de-Cléry ▲ *138*.
Excavations undertaken in
1890 uncovered the pillars
of the Romanesque
building, which can be
seen in the crypt today.
The Tour Ste-Croix
(to the
left of
the

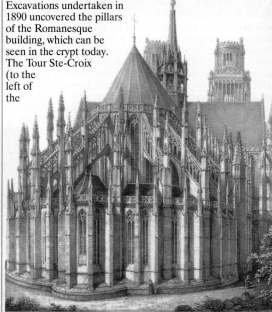

"In short, nothing remained of this great church but the eleven chapels around the end, a few flying buttresses, the last six pillars on either side of the nave, and some ruins of the wings joined to the ten pillars."

ACCOUNT BY A YOUNG CITIZEN OF ORLÉANS, 1567

...thedral entrance) is a fragment of the 4th-century Gallo-...oman wall. Partially demolished and then buried, it was ...discovered in 1980.

...ROUND THE CATHEDRAL

...LACE STE-CROIX. This square first came into being when the ...ue Jeanne d'Arc was built in 1840; it was completed in 1976. ...he cathedral is framed by the Musée des Beaux-Arts and the ...wn hall on one side, and by the regional authority for the ...ntral Loire valley on the other. The buildings opposite have ...eoclassical façades.

...USÉE DES BEAUX-ARTS. The museum was founded in 1823 ...d initially housed in the Hôtel des Créneaux. It moved into ...is contemporary building in 1984. It has an exceptionally ...ch collection, and the displays of paintings, drawings, prints,

...ulptures and objets d'art are changed regularly, presenting ...fairly comprehensive overview of European art from the ...th to the 20th century. Look out for the Cabinet des ...astels (pastels room), the displays of French painting from ...e 17th and 18th centuries (Le Nain, Philippe de ...hampaigne, La Tour, Watteau, Boucher) and the impressive ...ternational collections (Correggio, the Carracci, ...uysdael, and Velásquez's famous *Saint Thomas the ...postle*). The museum is also the proud owner of ...auguin's *Fête Gloanec* (above). One room is dedicated ... the poet Max Jacob ▲ 131.

...NCIEN ÉVÊCHÉ. This private residence (no. 1, rue ...upanloup) was built for Alphonse Elbène, Bishop of ...rléans from 1646 to 1655. In the 19th century a leading ...presentative of the liberal wing of the Church, Bishop ...élix Dupanloup (1802–78), lived here.

...UE DU BOURDON-BLANC. The Collège Jeanne d'Arc (at ...o. 2) occupies the buildings of the former Grand ...éminaire (1705–20), which was built over the ...ollegiate Church of St-Avit. Only the 11th-century ...RYPT of the church survives.

...AMPO-SANTO. Until 1786 this site (in Rue Fernand-Rabier) ...as the main cemetery of Orléans. A corn market was built ...ere in 1824. Today the building with its lovely arcaded ...alleries (15th century) is used for a wide range of events, ...cluding Orléans' extremely popular jazz festival.

THE "BASTARD OF ORLÉANS"
Jean, Comte de Longueville et de Dunois (1403–68) was the natural son of Louis d'Orléans ● 39, hence his nickname. A valiant warrior, he defeated the English at Montargis in 1427, and led the defense of Orléans both before Joan of Arc's arrival and subsequently by her side ▲ 116. He made a vital contribution to France's liberation by taking a number of towns (Chartres in 1432, Paris in 1436, Dieppe in 1443) and through his campaigns in Normandy and Guyenne (1448–53).

THE HISTORICAL MUSEUM ▲ 119
Popular prints made in Orléans showed a highly original

response to the Revolution. Above: Liberty, a print dedicated to the "sans-culottes of Orléans".

The name of Joan of Arc (1412–31) has been linked with Orléans since May 8, 1429, when she rode victorious into the town, which had been besieged by the English since October 12 1428. A humble peasant girl from the Lorraine, only seventeen years old and very religious, she claimed she was guided by the "voices" of Saint Michael, Saint Catherine and Saint Margaret. Orléans has fêted its heroine every year since May 8, 1430. After her martyrdom at Rouen two years later, she became a figurehead for the whole of the nation. The semi-legendary story of how the "Maid of Orléans" miraculously saved the French kingdom is imprinted in the minds of all French people, of whatever political or religious inclination.

THE SIEGE OF ORLÉANS

Ten thousand English soldiers, under the Earl of Salisbury, Lord Talbot, the Earl of Suffolk and William of Glasdale, laid siege to Orléans in October 1428, with the aim of gaining control of the town's river crossing. They erected a number of bastions, cutting the town off from the southern bank of the Loire. The Comte de Dunois (the "Bastard of Orléans" ▲ 139), La Hire, Xaintrailles, th Comte de Clermont and Admiral Louis de Culant led the town's defense.

FROM CHINON TO ORLÉANS ▲ 243, 244, 245

The day after the "Battle of the Herrings", Joan left Vaucouleurs to meet the Dauphin at Chinon ▲ 244. After being interrogated for three weeks she finally left for Tours, where her armor ▲ 199 and standard were made. She then took up position at the head of the army defending Orléans.

"BATTLE OF THE HERRINGS"

On February 12, 1429 an attempt to intercept a convoy of enemy supplies turned to disaster for the inhabitants of Orléans. The fatal "Day of the Herrings" seemed to mark the end of any hope that the Dauphin's armies might save the town ● 39, ▲ 245.

THE LIBERATION OF ORLÉANS

The town was about to succumb to famine when Joan appeared at the head of the royal reinforcements. At nightfall on April 29, 1429 she entered Orléans without meeting any opposition from the English. She stayed in the house of Jacques Boucher ▲ *139*. On April 30 Joan sent a challenge to the English, who replied with insults. On May 4 the French conquered the bastion of St-Loup; and on May 6 the English lost another of their fortifications, at St-Jean-le-Blanc. Close on the heels of this victory, Joan and La Hire recaptured the Augustinian convent; and on May 7, despite having been hit by an arrow, Joan led her companions in an attack on the bastion of Les Tourelles which blocked the bridge to the town. Talbot ordered the English to retreat and Orléans was saved.

AFTER ORLÉANS, THE LOIRE CAMPAIGN
Joan rested for a few days and then, together with the Duc d'Alençon, set off in pursuit of the defeated English armies. During their Loire campaign they captured Jargeau, Meung and Beaugency. On June 18, 1429 the English troops were routed at Patay, thus avenging Agincourt ● *39*.

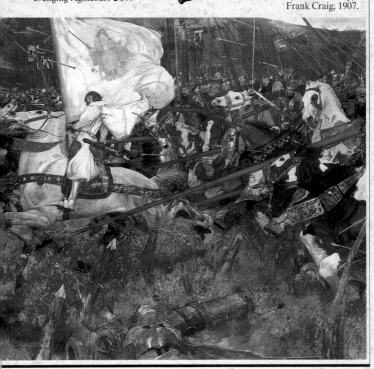

"THE MAID OF ORLÉANS"
(Battle of Patay)
Frank Craig, 1907.

HÔTEL GROSLOT. Since 1790 the town hall has
been housed in this huge red-brick Renaissance
mansion (above), with diamond-pattern diapering and
ornamental window gables, which was restored and
redecorated around 1850. Attributed to Jacques Androuet
Du Cerceau (see left), it was built between 1549 and 1555 for
Jacques Groslot, bailiff of Orléans. The porch of the Chapel
of St-Jacques (late 15th/early 16th century), which once stood
in the Place du Châtelet, now
stands in the small garden; it was
moved here, after being rescued
from demolition, in 1883.

RUE JEANNE-D'ARC. Although this
street was first planned in 1767 by
Monseigneur de Jarente, Bishop of
Orléans, it was not built until 1840, following
plans by François Pagot. The Centre Jeanne
d'Arc is at no. 24, in the former Collège Royal
(1847); its monumental façade does not detract from the
restrained, regular appearance of the
street as a whole. This stylistic austerity
makes an extremely effective backdrop
for the intricate architecture of the
cathedral.

PLACE DU GÉNÉRAL DE GAULLE. The
square has several houses with 16th-
century façades that were either
reconstructed or transferred here after
the bombardments of World War Two.
The façades of nos. 3 and 5 (1539–45)
were moved here from the neighboring
Rue Tabour in 1945. At no. 7 is the
Maison de Jeanne d'Arc, dating from
1425, which was the residence of Jacques
Boucher, treasurer to the Duke of
Orléans; Joan of Arc is said to have
stayed here from April 29 to May 9, 1429.
The house's half-timbered façade ● *72*
was meticulously reconstructed in 1965.

HÔTEL GROSLOT
In the main courtyard
is a statue of Joan
of Arc by Marie
d'Orléans, daughter
of Louis-Philippe
(1773–1850).

THE OLD TOWN

The area between the cathedral and the Loire is the oldest
quarter of the town, with medieval houses and Renaissance
residences.
PLACE ABBÉ-DESNOYERS. The square has noteworthy
houses on two sides, and Rue Ste-Catherine makes up the

ird side. Maison de la Pomme (late 16th
century) presents a lovely façade of brick and
stone; this house, which once stood at no. 43 Rue
Ste-Catherine, was moved when the street was
widened in 1931 and rebuilt on the square. Maison
Sancier (1540–94), which consists of a single
room built over a passageway, was moved here
from Rue du Poirier, also in 1931.

**HÔTEL CABU AND MUSÉE ARCHÉOLOGIQUE ET
HISTORIQUE DE L'ORLÉANAIS ● 75.** The Hôtel
Cabu (right), also known as the Maison de Diane
de Poitiers, dates from 1548. It was built by
Jacques Androuet Du Cerceau for
Philippe Cabu, a lawyer of the town.
Legend has it that Diane de Poitiers,
mistress of Henri II, stayed
here in 1549. The court
façade has two lateral
forebuildings; the one on
the left houses a spiral
staircase. The
archeological
museum was

established here in 1862. Its
prize exhibit is the treasure
discovered at Neuvy-en-
Sullias (between Jargeau and
Sully-sur-Loire) in 1861,
consisting of a collection of Gallo-Roman
bronzes (left, *The Dancer*). Also on show are
sculptures, enamels, ivories and tapestries from
the Middle Ages; and there is a section devoted
to historical displays of local ceramics,
earthenware, porcelain and glass. Do not miss
the gallery showing popular prints of the 18th
and 19th centuries: this genre developed in a
markedly original way in Orléans, especially in
its response to revolutionary events ▲ *115*.

RUE STE-CATHERINE. There is a lovely half-
timbered house at no. 14. However, it is the
HÔTEL DES CRÉNEAUX (1503–13) which
catches the eye, built in a mixture of
Renaissance and Flamboyant styles. The
main wing overlooks Rue Ste-Catherine,
while the rear of the building opens onto
Place de la République. The 17th-century
Passage du Saloir leads from the square
to the street, passing underneath the
building. The Hôtel des Créneaux was
Orléans' town hall until 1790; today it is
an annexe of the Conservatoire de
Musique. Its belfry tower is older: it was
built between 1445 and 1448, over the
remains of the Gallo-Roman wall.

MAISON "DU CERCEAU". One of the
loveliest houses of the old town, no. 6,
rue Du-Cerceau ▲ *120* dates from the
second half of the 16th century. The
three upper stories of this Renaissance

HÔTEL CABU
Section of the façade
overlooking Rue
Charles Sanglier; and
detail of the
courtyard façade.

RÉPUBLIQUE FRANÇAISE
LA POSTE 1996
6,70

TRÉSOR DE NEUVY-EN-SULLIAS
LOIRET · BRONZE GALLO-ROMAIN

**TREASURE OF
NEUVY-EN-SULLIAS**
A quarry worker
discovered the
Neuvy hoard, which
was buried deep in
the ground. This
rare collection of
Gallo-Roman art
includes some
surprisingly stylized
figures of animals
and people – for
example, *The Dancer*
(left). The impressive
statue of the horse-
god Rudiobus
(above) has a
dedication to the
god on the base.

119

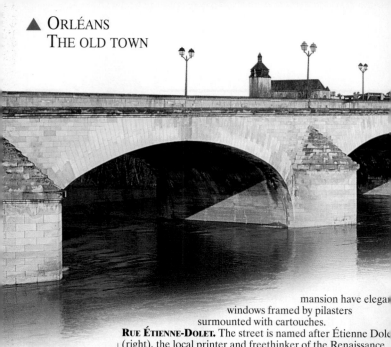

mansion have elega▮
windows framed by pilasters
surmounted with cartouches.

RUE ÉTIENNE-DOLET. The street is named after Étienne Dole▮
(right), the local printer and freethinker of the Renaissance
(1509–46) who was burned for heresy in Paris. At
no. 11 is the Maison des Chevaliers du Guet,
built in 1547 for the widow Marie Brochet;
its decorative brickwork with black
glazed diapering is a relatively late
example of its type ● 67.

RUE DE BOURGOGNE. This street, with
its half-timbered houses (nos. 264, 266,
268 and 270), is one of the oldest in
Orléans. It once ended at the Porte de
Bourgogne, the eastern entry to the
town's fortifications (near the intersections
with Rue du Bourdon-Blanc and Rue de la
Tour-Neuve), where Joan of Arc entered Orléans on April 2▮
1429.

HÔTEL HECTOR-DE-SAUXERRE. This house, on the corner of
Rue de la Poterne, was built between 1543 and 1545. It has a▮
unusual corbeled room on the second story: this was the
library of Hector de Sauxerre, an educated resident of the
town who lived during the reign of François I.

HÔTEL DE LA PRÉFECTURE. The Préfecture of Loiret moved
into a former Benedictine abbey (below) in 1800. The abbey,
Notre-Dame-de-Bonne-Nouvelle, was built in 1653 and
abandoned after the Revolution.

SALLE DES THÈSES. This old library, in Rue Pothier, was buil▮
in the Gothic style between 1411 and 1417; it is all that

ÉTIENNE DOLET
Born in Orléans on
August 3, 1509, the
French humanist
(right) studied first in
Paris then in Padua
and Venice. Highly
quarrelsome, even
with his friends, he
was condemned to
death for his heretical
ideas.

**MAISON
"DU CERCEAU"**
Like Maison Sancier
▲ 119, this house has
a Latin inscription
over the door: *Pax
huic domui* (Peace
to this house).

survives of the medieval university, dissolved in 1793. The university's students included Rabelais, Calvin and Charles Perrault.

COLLEGIATE CHURCH OF ST-AIGNAN. The crypt, in Rue Neuve -Aignan, is all that remains of the 11th-century building. Several kings of France, from Charles I to Louis XII, contributed to the magnificent collegiate church, which was destroyed by Protestants in 1567. Only the transept, the choir and five chapels survived the Revolution.

TOUR BLANCHE. This tower, in Rue Tour-Neuve, was part of the fortifications of the Gallo-Roman town.

COLLEGIATE CHURCH OF ST-PIERRE-LE-PUELLIER. This collegiate church (Rue de l'Université/Rue St-Gilles) was built, from the 12th to the 16th century, near a convent – to which its name, derived from *puella* (the Latin for "girl"), refers. It became national property under the Revolution. Disused since 1958, it has since been restored.

PONT GEORGE-V. Today's bridge, leading from the Quai du Châtelet, was built between 1751 and 1760. It replaced the medieval bridge which played a famous part in the town's liberation in 1429.

RUE ROYALE. This street was built between 1754 and 1760, leading up to Place du Martroi. The Chancellerie was all that survived of the lovely 18th-century arcaded buildings after the bombings of 1940. The façades and arcades (above) have been restored with considerable care.

PLACE DU CHÂTELET. In medieval times a fortress stood here, overlooking a large marketplace.

MAISON "DE LA COQUILLE". The shell (right) on the façade of the 16th-century house at no. 7, rue de la Pierre-Percée is derived from the sign on an earlier house built in 1511.

CHAPELLE NOTRE-DAME-DES-MIRACLES. This chapel, in Rue Saint-Paul, was built in 1629 and restored in 1915. Along with the bell tower (1620–7), it is all that remains of the Church of St-Paul destroyed in June 1940.

RUE ROYALE AND THE "PONT ROYAL"
The Pont George V is 115 feet long, with nine arches. It was built in the 18th century (at the same time as Rue Royale), by the royal engineers under the supervision of Perronet.

MAISON "DE LA COQUILLE" (left, and detail above). The external design of this house is similar to that of the house at no. 6, place du Châtelet known as the Maison de Jean Dallibert.

HÔTEL TOUTIN (1536–40), courtyard.

CHARLES PÉGUY ● 99
Born in Orléans on January 7, 1873, Charles Péguy enrolled as a student at the École Normale Supérieure in Paris in 1894. A socialist and ardent defender of Dreyfus, he founded and published a fortnightly journal, the *Cahiers de la Quinzaine*, despite financial difficulties. He turned to Christianity in 1908 and wrote some important poetic and mystical texts, including the *Mystère de la charité de Jeanne d'Arc* (1910).

JARDIN JACQUES-BOUCHER AND THE PAVILION COLAS-DES-FRANCS. Dating from early in Henri II's reign, the Pavilion Colas-des-Francs was used for storing silverware, money and archives; its ornate interiors have survived.

CHURCH OF NOTRE-DAME-DE-RECOUVRANCE. This church, in Rue Notre-Dame-de-Recouvrance, was built between 1513 and 1519 and badly damaged during the Wars of Religion. Its vaulting was restored in the 17th century, and the choir rebuilt in the troubadour style in the 19th century.

HÔTEL TOUTIN. The house at no. 26, rue Notre-Dame-de-Recouvrance was built between 1536 and 1540 by Guillaume Toutin, who was valet de chambre to Dauphin Henri, son of François I. The building has two wings – one facing the street, the other facing the courtyard (above) – connected by a gallery supported by columns with capitals.

HÔTEL EUVERTE-HATTE, CENTRE CHARLES-PÉGUY. This house, in Rue du Tabour, is one of the city's jewels of François I architecture. It was built between 1524 and 1529 for Orléans merchant Euverte Hatte. From the internal courtyard visitors can admire a magnificent two-story covered gallery. Today the building houses the Centre Charles Péguy, which includes a library and documents relating to the writer's life and works.

THE "VILLE OPULENTE"

In this district 17th-century buildings stand side by side with more recent constructions, reflecting the commercial expansion and prosperity of the town during the 18th century and the first half of the 19th century.

PLACE DU MARTROI. Buildings from several architectural periods, from the 18th century to the modern day, border this square at the heart of the town. With its cafés and brasseries with pavement terraces, the Place du Martroi (above) is a favorite meeting place.

PORTE BANNIER. Remains of the medieval town walls (14th–15th century) were unearthed when a car park was being built beneath Place du Martroi in 1986.

STATUE OF JOAN OF ARC. The bronze equestrian statue at the center of the square was made by sculptor Denis Foyatier in 1855. The bas-reliefs (also 1885) by Vital-Gabriel Dubray around the base recount the life of the heroine of Orléans.

THE CHANCELLERIE AND CHAMBRE DE COMMERCE. The façade of the Chancellerie, dating from 1754, was the only part of the original building to survive the destruction of June 1940. The building was formerly used to house the archives of the Duke of Orléans. The Chamber of Commerce was built in the neoclassical style as a counterpart to the Chancellerie, in 1863.

ANCIEN COUVENT DES MINIMES. The church and cloisters of the former Monastery of the Minims were completed in 1621. The last monks were forced to leave the monastery under the Revolution. Since 1913 the building has housed the Departmental Archives.

PAVILLONS D'ESCURES ● *75.* Rue d'Escures is bordered by private houses dating from the Renaissance and the early 17th century. Next to the Caisse d'Épargne building (in Third Empire style) is a small 16th-century house formerly owned by the Chevaliers de St-Lazare. At nos. 2, 4 and 6 are the Pavillons d'Escures, a group of four private houses built in the 17th century for an eminent local figure, Pierre Fougeu d'Escures (1554–1621), who was mayor of Orléans and a friend of Henri IV. The brick-and-stone buildings, separated by domed pavilions in the Imperial style, are reminiscent of the buildings on Place des Vosges in Paris. They are a rare example of 17th century town planning.

CHURCH OF ST-PIERRE-DU-MARTROI. This church was built in the 16th century during the reign of François I; it is the only religious building in Orléans made of bricks. Rebuilt after the Wars of Religion, it contains a number of old paintings, including those attributed to Jean Restout (1692–1768) on the altarpiece of the high altar (1738).

PLACE DU MARTROI

ORLÉANS VINEGAR ● *56*
Casks of wine commonly turned sour during shipment on the Loire, so the citizens of Orléans decided to turn this to their advantage. High-quality vinegar was manufactured here from 1394 onward, and in the reign of Louis XVI the town had two hundred master "vinaigriers". Maison Desseaux became the leading local vinegar manufacturer in 1826. The famous scientist Louis Pasteur (1822–95), son-in-law of a family of printers in Orléans, often came to the town to study acetic fermentation. Today Orléans still produces half the vinegar consumed in France.

A JEANNE D'ARC
LA VILLE D'ORLÉANS
AVEC LE CONCOURS
DE LA FRANCE ENTIÈRE

123

HÔTEL POMMERET. This sober, harmonious 17th-century residence was owned by the Pommeret family from 1789 to 1978; it was modified under Louis XV and again under the Restoration.

RUE DE LA RÉPUBLIQUE. This semi-pedestrianized street which connects Place du Martroi with Place Albert Ier was built in 1895, to develop the area around the station (built in 1843). The blocks which line the street were erected between 1897 and 1904. The Hôtel Moderne at no. 37 was built for Émile Dindault in 1902, designed by Louis Duthoit in the Art Nouveau style: it is reminiscent of the famous Lavirotte building on Avenue Rapp in Paris.

RUE ALSACE-LORRAINE. The 19th- and early-20th-century buildings create a strikingly unified, harmonious effect.

PLACE ALBERT-Ier. A new shopping center (reached by a flight of steps) has replaced the town's old railway station, which was the terminus of the Paris-Orléans line. To conclude your tour of the city, take a stroll on the tree-lined Boulevard Alexandre-Martin (named after a former mayor).

ORLÉANS-LA-SOURCE

Orléans-la-Source, an extension of Orléans to the south of th Loire, was built in 1959 on a 1700-acre site reclaimed from the Sologne. Features of this "garden suburb" include a remarkable flower park and the new university campus. The latter, opened in 1963 to cater for 10,000 students, covers an area of some 450 acres.

THE PARC FLORAL. During the Orléans flower festival in 196 nearly 2,300,000 visitors discovered the delights of this floral park, created from 86 acres of woodland in 1963. Today visitors can admire some 150,000 rose trees, begonias, dahlia rhododendrons and other plants. Since 1995 new floral and woodland areas have been created within the park, including the Jardin de la Source, the Gloriette aux Papillons (butterfl garden) and an iris garden.

THE SOURCES OF THE LOIRET. This tributary of the Loire has given its name to the whole département, although it is only 8 miles long. It has its source in two springs at the heart of th Parc Floral: the Bouillon (the main spring) and the Grande Source or Abîme.

CHÂTEAU DE LA SOURCE. This building, which now stands in the Parc Floral, was rebuilt in 1622. In 1962 it became the firs wing of the new university.

OLIVET (O2)

Olivet was once a village of fruit-tree nurseries and market gardens. Although

> "NO DAZZLING ATTRACTIONS, NO OSTENTATIOUS GRANDEUR. IT IS
> [N]O MORE THAN A VALLEY . . . WITH THE LOIRE WINDING THROUGH
> [I]T UNDER THE SKY. BUT WHAT GENTLE LIGHT, AND WHAT PURITY
> IN THE LONG TRANQUIL CONTOURS OF THE LANDSCAPE."

MAURICE GENEVOIX

**THE ACADÉMIE
DE LA SOURCE**
Henry St John,
Viscount Bolingbroke
(1678–1751), a friend
of Swift and Voltaire,
became the new
tenant of the château
in the 18th century.
He made it into a
very lively literary
center, which his
friends dubbed the
"Académie de la
Source". Voltaire
read a few verses of
his *Henriade* here in
1722.

A PERFECT MOVIE SET
The Château de La
Ferté-St-Aubin was
used as a movie set
for Jean Renoir's
La Règle du jeu, made
in 1939; a scene from
the movie is shown

[...]is now a residential suburb of Orléans, it has retained
[so]mething of its horticultural character. The Sentier des Prés
[an]d then the Chemin des Moulins (which connects the old
[m]ills of St-Julien, St-Samson, Les Béchets, La Mothe and
[le] Bac) offer a charming countryside walk along the Loiret.

[L]A FERTÉ-ST-AUBIN (P4)

[Al]though this town is on the edge of the
[So]logne, it has been influenced
[ec]onomically and culturally by the nearby
[cit]y of Orléans.

[TH]E CHÂTEAU. The first fortress which
[gu]arded the crossing of the Cosson was
[de]stroyed in 1562 and replaced by a
[se]cond château, built for François de
[St]-Nectaire between 1590 and 1620:
[th]is is the "petit château" which survives
[in] the left-hand section of the present-
[da]y building. St-Nectaire's son Henri,
[ma]réchal de France, instructed
[Th]éodore Lefèvre, architect to the
[D]uke of Orléans, to reorganize and
[ex]tend the château in 1630. The "grand
[lo]gis" (main building), the second level
[of] the terrace and the two pavilions
[fl]anking the entrance, which have
[im]perial-style roofs, are attributed to
[Le]fèvre. The outbuildings of the château
[ap]pear to date from this period, although those on the
[rig]ht are more recent in style and were probably built from
[17]46 onward for the Comte de Loewendal (1700–55),
[m]aréchal de France.

below. The leading
actors were Marcel
Dalio, Julien Carette,
Jean Renoir and
Paulette Dubost.

Houses along the old Orléans Canal at Combleux.

The Val d'Orléans (to the east of the city) extends from the apex of the bend in the Loire back toward the source. Here the Loire, once congested with boats and barges ● *46*, traverses a flat landscape, continuing that of the Sologne ▲ *174*. Beside it runs the Orléans Canal, which linked Orléans with Montargis and the Loing. With their trees and flowers, the banks between the river and the canal make a pleasant place for walking.

ALONGSIDE THE RIVER AND THE CANAL (F

LOCAL WRITER
The writer Maurice Genevoix (1890–1980) lived in Châteauneuf-sur-Loireat at no. 2b, rue St-Nicholas (named after the patron saint of sailors). He was a member of the Académie Française from 1946 and wrote a number of books inspired by the Sologne and the Loire, notably *Raboliot* (winner of the Prix Goncourt, 1925), *La Loire* and *Le Bestiaire enchanté* (1970).

ST-JEAN-DE-BRAYE. This little town perched on the hillside overlooking the Loire is an important historical site. The place known as the Pointe St-Loup was Attila's encampment in 451; it was also the site of an English bastion during the siege of Orléans in 1429 ▲ *116*. The Abbey of St-Loup (14th century) was destroyed by the French army to prevent the English from taking refuge there: only the chapel and a few buildings are still standing.

THE FONDERIE BOLLÉE ★. This is one of the last three bell foundries in France (right). Its museum of campanology is one of the few museums tracing the history of bell founding.

COMBLEUX. Its flowers and its situation beside the Orléans Canal make Combleux a charming town. The towpath from St-Jean-de-Braye to the lock at Combleux offers wide views over the open landscape (above).

ST-DENIS-DE-L'HÔTEL AND JARGEAU (C

These sister-towns stand on either side of the river: their churches have identical square bell towers. At St-Denis-de-l'Hôtel is the MAISON MAURICE GENEVOIX, opened in 1984 and devoted to the author of "romans de la nature" (see left). Jargeau, on the left bank of the river, is famous for its andouilles (sausages). Its collegiate church, St-Vrain (11th–14th century), has a rare wrought-iron pulpit from 1755.

8. SULLY-SUR-LOIRE
9. DAMPIERRE POWER STATION
10. GIEN
11. BRIARE

T he Val d'Or is an expanse of flat countryside traversed
by the Loire, extending from Châteauneuf-sur-Loire to
St-Benoît, across the sands and clays of the
Sologne. Here the Loire, once busy with
river traffic, begins to get wider.

🚗 c. 50 miles
🕐 1½ days

CHÂTEAUNEUF-SUR-LOIRE (G2)

[Fa]mous for its rhododendrons, Châteauneuf-sur-
[Lo]ire was a busy river port until the advent of the railway
[bro]ught about its decline.

[TH]E CHÂTEAU. Although the château
[ori]ginated in the 11th century, it was
[reb]uilt in the 17th century for the Marquis
[Lou]is Phélipeaux de la Vrillière, who was
[Se]cretary of State under Louis XIV. All
[tha]t remains today is a group of
[ou]tbuildings – an attractive architectural
[en]semble consisting of a Mansart-style
[sta]ble block (17th century), an orangery
[(18]th century) and a domed octagonal
[rot]unda which now houses Châteauneuf's
[to]wn hall. The arboretum in the park contributes to the
[to]wn's horticultural reputation.

[M]USÉE DE LA MARINE DE LA LOIRE. This unique museum, in
[th]e former guardroom, was opened to the public in 1962; it
[te]lls the story of navigation on the Loire ● 46.

[P]LADE DES MARINIERS ★. This historical trail starts from the
[m]useum and leads through the old town, showing visitors
[bu]ildings and landmarks which illustrate the life of bargemen
[on] the Loire. The quaysides of the Rampe du Haut-du-Quai
[gi]ve an impression of how this lively port must have looked in
[th]e past. The Colonne des Mariniers on the Place du Port was
[er]ected in 1847 to commemorate the bravery of the bargemen
[du]ring the devastating floods of October 1846.

[CH]URCH OF ST-MARTIAL. This was once the church of the
[ha]mlet of La Ronce (12th century); it was rebuilt several
[tim]es and restored in the 1940's. It houses the tomb of Louis
[Ph]élipeaux de la Vrillière, which is attributed to Dominico
[Gu]idi (1628–1701), a follower of Bernini.

[HA]LLE ST-PIERRE. This building (behind the church) was
[or]iginally a boat house: erected in 1854, it was subsequently
[co]nverted into a corn exchange.

LADY OF THE STAMP
The Musée de la
Fondation Oscar
Roty (1846–1911),
in Jargeau, is named
after the engraver
of La Semeuse
(The Seed-sower),
a famous image
used on French
coins and stamps in
the earlier part of
the 20th century.

(G

THE ARMENIAN INFLUENCE
The churches which most closely resemble the oratory at Germigny in terms of architectural style are those of Armenia – such as the Church of Bagaran and the Cathedral of Edjmiatsin, although both of these have a circular ground plan. Armenian architects like Odo, who built the oratory, were regarded as the best in the world at this time.

VISIGOTHIC ARCHES
The arches at Germigny are of a special type. They are not Romanesque (semicircular), or Arabian (slightly narrower): they are the horseshoe-shaped arches of the Spanish Visigothic style.

ALABASTER FILTERS
The muted light created by the translucent alabaster in the narrow windows of the lantern tower provides the perfect setting for the Carolingian mosaic, which was probably created by a Byzantine artist.

GERMIGNY-DES-PRÉS ★

This Carolingian oratory, set in a tiny village on the right bank of the Loire, is visited by more than 100,000 tourists every year. The Romanesque tiled roof and the cypress trees around the building give it an Italian air.

HISTORY OF THE ORATORY. It was built in 806 for Theodulf, Abbot of Fleury (the original name of the nearby Abbey of St-Benoît-sur-Loire), Bishop of Orléans and one of the *missi dominici* o the Emperor Charlemagne. Originally this private oratory was part of Theodulf's opulent villa, which was destroyed by the Normans; like the oratory of Charlemagne's palace at Aix-la-Chapelle, it was built by Armenia architect Odo (see left). In 1868 the oratory at Germigny wa restored by Juste Lisch, who made major alterations to both the surface and the structure of the building. The two apsidioles of the eastern apse were removed, the western apse was replaced by a long nave, and the lantern tower (belfry) was shortened by 10 feet.

EXTERIOR. The top section of a 16th-century lantern and a 17th-century wrought-iron cock can be seen in the grounds of the oratory. In the

"I, Theodulf, dedicated this temple to the glory of God. All you who come here, remember me"

esbytery is a small 12th-century enameled shrine, which was ade in the workshops of Limoges.

RCHITECTURE OF THE ORATORY. The original church, in the ape of a Greek cross, was built on a square ground plan th three naves and three bays; the addition of apses in the iddle of each side created a quatrefoil design. The contour the demolished western apse is indicated by large floor bs. The original entrance was to the right of the northern se. The pillar piscina with a cable molding dates back to e Carolingian church.

E MOSAIC. The 19th-century alterations were designed to ghlight the superb mosaic in the rounded vault of the stern apse. The apse was iginally framed by two ches: one for the preparation bread and wine, the other r sacred vessels and liturgical stments. It now functions nost like a choir, drawing sitors toward the brightness the mosaic, whose glass bes are the only area of lor in the monochrome urch. The 9th-century osaic is extremely beautiful, d is unique of its kind in France. It is made of 130,000 small uares of glass (blue, purple, white, green, black and gold) d depicts the Ark of the Covenant: two large angels swoop aciously, set against a gilded blue background showing the nd of God. A 16th-century wooden Pietà has been placed low the mosaic: it was carved by a sculptor from the urgundian school.

-BENOÎT-SUR-LOIRE ● 58 (H3)

e town of St-Benoît-sur-Loire was once a port of call for rgemen on the Loire, and old fishermen's houses still line he riverside. However, St-Benoît is chiefly famous for its Benedictine abbey; the town, originally called Fleury, was renamed after the abbey in the 11th century. In the words of the writer Max Jacob (▲ 131), St-Benoît is "a plain leading off into the distance, broken by houses and clumps of trees, a plain for harvest and vegetables. This beautiful landscape is made of more than just contour and color: it is infused with the spirit which reigns over all of St-Benoît, and the source of this spirit is the basilica. . . ."

THEODULF ● 37, 112
Theodulf was born around 760, into a great Spanish Visigothic family. He studied in Aquitaine and stayed at the Abbey of St-Benoît-d'Aniane, not far from St-Guilhem-le-Désert (in the Hérault region). He was appointed Bishop of Orléans in 798 and became abbot of several abbeys, including St-Benoît at Fleury. He was the most important of Charlemagne's *missi dominici* (provincial inspectors) and one of the emperor's advisers. Theodulf was an educated, civilized man, an educational reformer and one of the outstanding figures of the Carolingian Renaissance. In 814, on the death of Charlemagne, he served as a counselor to Charlemagne's successor, Louis the Pious. Falsely accused of conspiracy, he was imprisoned in a monastery in Angers in 818, where he remained until his death in 821.

ABBEY OF ST-BENOÎT-SUR-LOIRE
View of the chevet
● 58.

SUDDEN DEATH
In the 9th century
the abbey was sacked
by the Viking
Rynaldus. The patron
saint of the abbey
punished him with
immediate death.
To commemorate this
event, his snarling
face is carved as a
decorative mask on
the west wall of the
transept.

Belfry porch of the
Abbey of St-Benoît
details of the columns
and carvings.

**THE LIFE OF
SAINT BENEDICT**
The saint was born
around 480 and died
in 543 or 547 at
Monte Cassino in
Italy. In 578 the
monastery there was
destroyed by the
Lombards, and his
tomb buried under
the ruins. His life as a
hermit in Subiaco and
on Monte Cassino is
recounted in the
second book of
Dialogues by Pope
Gregory the Great.
The relics of Saint
Benedict were
brought back from
Italy by the monks of
Fleury around 670–2.

HISTORY OF THE ABBEY OF FLEURY. The abbey was founded i
651 by Leodebold, Abbot of St-Aignan-d'Orléans, and place
under the patronage of Saint Benedict; at this stage it was
called the Abbey of Saint-Benoît-de-Fleury. At the end of th
7th century, after the monk Aigulf was sent from Fleury to
Italy to bring back the relics of Saint Benedict, the abbey too
the name of St-Benoît-sur-Loire.

GOLDEN AGE. The abbey flourished under the rule of
Theodulf ▲ *129*, the builder of Germigny. From the 10th to
the 12th century – under Odon, Abbot of Cluny, Abbon (a
monk from Reims) and Gauzlin (later Archbishop of
Bourges) – St-Benoît's reputation continued to grow,
attracting pilgrims and students to the town. Philippe I,
King of France, was buried here in 1108.

DECLINE. The abbey's decline began in the 13th century,
not long after the basilica was completed (it was dedicated

on October 26, 1218). From 1486
onward the tradition of commendatory
appointments, whereby the abbey's
benefices were granted to a layperson
chosen by the king, produced a series o
conflicts. During the course of one of
these, in 1527, François I had the Tour
Gauzlin knocked down by his troops.
The abbey was sacked by Protestants
during the Wars of Religion. Later
St-Benoît saw a revival in its fortunes
when it was given in commendam to
Richelieu. When religious orders
were suppressed in 1790, the monks
dispersed. Two years later the
monastery was partially destroyed.
RESTORATION AND REVIVAL. In 1865 fo
monks from the Monastery of Pierre-
qui-Vire in Burgundy moved
into the parish, cleared the crypt,
restored the paving of the church and
reconsecrated it. It was not until October 11, 1944, however,
that a monastic community was re-established at St-Benoît.
The monks undertook an extensive programme of
restoration, as a result of which the monastery regained its
former status as an abbey in 1959. Today the Abbey of Fleur
has thirty-five monks, as well as some visiting brothers,
notably from Africa. The monks have a Benedictine library
and meet in the church for services, where Gregorian chants
are sung.

ARCHITECTURE OF ST-BENOÎT

The abbey church stands at the far end of the village square,
on the site of two earlier churches.
BELFRY PORCH (details left) ★. The belfry porch is called the
Tour Gauzlin, after the abbot who built it in the 11th century
It is the oldest surviving section of the abbey, and serves as a
forebuilding to the church. Its sixteen pillars are decorated
with historiated capitals, carved in a striking, expressive style
which incorporates references to Carolingian and classical a
and also to the decorative repertoire of illuminated
manuscripts.

┃OIR AND TRANSEPT. These were built between 1067
┃d 1107. The tall, deep choir is a beautiful example of
┃omanesque architecture. It is the main shrine of the abbey,
┃th its altar dedicated to the Virgin Mary. The columns
┃nd on a platform surmounted by a blind arcature and
┃restory windows; a semicircular vault covers the whole
┃semble. The high, rounded apse over the crypt has four
┃all chapels (two radiating and two aligned, the latter
┃owned by a minuscule Romanesque bell tower). The high
┃ar is surrounded by decorative paving (below), created
┃der Abbot Gauzlin early in the 11th century, which was

┃ncovered during excavations. This is a work of opus sectile –
┃osaic made of relatively large pieces of multicolored marble
┃d out in geometric patterns, with larger discs of different
┃zes to vary the effect.

┃AVE. The vast nave was the last section of the church to
┃ built, probably from 1144 to 1218. It is built in the
┃ansitional Romanesque style, although it looks Gothic at
┃rst sight. It has seven two-story bays and two side aisles with
┃ vaulting. The carved portal (especially the lintel) in the
┃ft side aisle is one of the masterpieces of the period. At the
┃ossing of the nave and the transept is a magnificent group
┃ 15th-century stalls, including a splendid panel depicting
┃e Annunciation.

┃RYPT. The 11th-century crypt is reached by
┃eans of a staircase situated to the east of the
┃de aisles of the choir. Excavated in 1958–9,
┃ extends across the area covered by the small
┃ansept and the apse and ambulatory. Its
┃ructure converges on the central pillar,
┃hich is hollow and contains the relics
┃ Saint Benedict. The relics are kept in a
┃ntemporary shrine designed by
┃. de Laborde, a monk from the
┃bbey of Solesmes. Around it are
┃fteen lamps, symbolizing the
┃ngregations of the Benedictine
┃rder.

┃HAPEL OF ST-MOMMOLE. The
┃outhern end of the crypt leads to
┃is 10th-century chapel; situated
┃nder the sacristy, it predates the
┃st of the church.

**MAX JACOB AT
ST-BENOÎT**
Max Jacob (1876–
1944), a writer and
converted Jew, spent
the last twenty years
of his life at St-Benoît,
seeking to escape the
Montmartre of his
Bohemian youth. He
was arrested by the
Gestapo in 1944 and
taken to the prison
camp at Drancy,
where he died a few
months later. His
works include *Saint
Benoît et l'abbaye de
Fleury* (1938). The
house where the
writer lived is now
the local tourist
office; on the second
story there is a
permanent exhibition
devoted to him.

" In the ever quiet
shades
    Of Sully, this
peaceful place,
    I am a thousand
times happier
    Than the great
prince who has exiled
me. "

Voltaire

**THE ARCHITECT OF
VINCENNES**
Raymond du Temple,
the military architect
who transformed the
royal château at
Vincennes for
Charles V, displayed
his innovative and
progressive talents at
Sully in 1395.

Whereas Vincennes
had square corner
towers, which were
rather old-fashioned,
Du Temple decided
on round towers for
Sully, relying on his
master mason, Colin
des Chapelles, to
execute the design.

**THE BRIDGE OF
SULLY-SUR-LOIRE**
The bridge (right)
built in 1836 was
carried away by the
terrible floods of
1856. It was made
vulnerable by the
access ramps leading
to the suspended
roadway:
unfortunately they
blocked part of the
river bed, which was
very narrow at this
point.

SULLY-SUR-LOIRE   (R

The château of Sully-sur-Loire, a plain-fortress on the left
bank of the river, retains something of its medieval air. It is
surrounded by a moat, which is fed by the small river Sange
and separated from the Loire by a bank of earth and sand.
HISTORY OF THE TOWN. The town flourished from the 10th
century onward as its position allowed it to control both the
river traffic and the road between the royal territories and th
Massif Central. Sully-sur-Loire suffered considerable damag
in the Wars of Religion, then again during the siege of 1563
and the Protestant uprising of 1621. Nearly three-quarters o
the town was destroyed during battles for control of the
bridge in June 1940 and by bombardments in 1944. Apart
from the château and the religious buildings, the only
surviving remnant of the old town is the 16th-century house
at no. 8, rue du Grand-Sully.
THE CHÂTEAU. All that survives of the original château, datin
from 1102, is the layout of the rooms. From 1395 onward a
new château was built at the request of the Trémoille family
by Raymond du Temple, architect of the Château de
Vincennes. Further alterations were made, from 1602 onwar
by the new owner, Maximilien de Béthune, a minister of
Henri IV better known as the Duc de Sully, or simply as Sul
In 1611, a year after the king's assassination,
Sully retired to his estate. Voltaire stayed
here in 1716 and in 1719, when exiled
from Paris by the regent Philippe
d'Orléans (1674–1723).

ARCHITECTURE OF THE CHÂTEAU. The castle consists of two buildings, surrounded by the moat: one from the 14th century, built by Guy VI de la Trémoille, and the other from the 16th century, built by Sully.

THE OLD CHÂTEAU OR KEEP (1395–1400). This impressive rectangular building flanked by four circular towers stands facing the Loire, with Sully's additions between it and the river. The Salle des Gardes, on the ground floor, has enormous stone fireplaces. The annual music festival of Sully-sur-Loire is held here.

THE "PETIT-CHÂTEAU". This comprises the *corps de logis* or residential wing (to the east of the château) added by Sully in the 16th century and fortifications that include the Tour de

Rosny and the large Tour de Béthune. The latter, built by Sully in 1606, looks toward the town, which he regarded as a potential source of trouble.

COLLEGIATE CHURCH OF ST-YTHIER. Despite the damage suffered during World War Two, the church still has important architectural features and furnishings dating from the 16th and 17th centuries, including painted wooden statues and stained-glass windows.

THE DUC DE SULLY
Maximilien de Béthune, Baron of Rosny (1559–1641), was a Protestant whose fortunes were linked with Henri de Navarre's. Serving him in a military capacity, he became his Superintendent of Finances in 1598 and was made Duc de Sully in 1606.

The Val du Giennois traditionally marks the start of the Loire valley for those following the course of the river from its source. In the Middle Ages the first bridge and the first château on this royal route were at Gien. The Val is a border region, set between the Pays Fort and the Sologne on the left bank, and between the Forest of Orléans and Puisaye on the right.

GIEN (S4)

The town (right), which became known for its earthenware ▲ *134* thanks to an Englishman, is best viewed from the left bank of the Loire.

HISTORY OF THE TOWN. Gien stands beside the river, rising in tiers to the château and the Church of Ste-Jeanne-d'Arc. As the ancient Celtic town of Diomagus, it served as a trading place for the Gallic tribes of the Carnutes and the Eduens. In medieval times Gien became the capital of a county annexed to the French kingdom by Philippe-Auguste in 1199.

WORLD WAR TWO
In June 1940 the French armies retreated to the Loire, pursued by German forces. Both soldiers and civilians took refuge in Gien, and from 15 to 17 June enemy aircraft bombarded the town. The old quarters below the château were hit and the center of the town soon became an inferno. The bridge over the Loire was blown up, and the church destroyed. Only a storm saved the château, after its roofs caught fire.

133

▲ GIEN EARTHENWARE

Below: archery trophy (11) with hand-painted decoration, dated 1869.

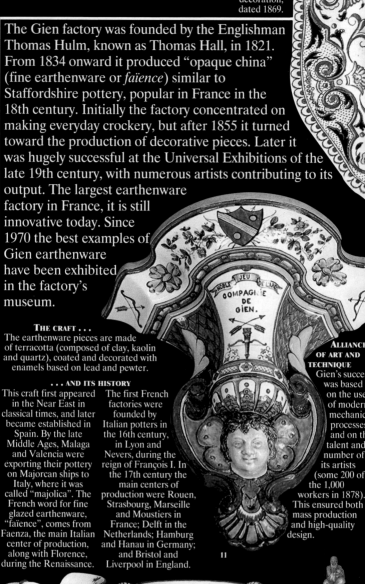

The Gien factory was founded by the Englishman Thomas Hulm, known as Thomas Hall, in 1821. From 1834 onward it produced "opaque china" (fine earthenware or *faïence*) similar to Staffordshire pottery, popular in France in the 18th century. Initially the factory concentrated on making everyday crockery, but after 1855 it turned toward the production of decorative pieces. Later it was hugely successful at the Universal Exhibitions of the late 19th century, with numerous artists contributing to its output. The largest earthenware factory in France, it is still innovative today. Since 1970 the best examples of Gien earthenware have been exhibited in the factory's museum.

THE CRAFT . . .

The earthenware pieces are made of terracotta (composed of clay, kaolin and quartz), coated and decorated with enamels based on lead and pewter.

. . . AND ITS HISTORY

This craft first appeared in the Near East in classical times, and later became established in Spain. By the late Middle Ages, Malaga and Valencia were exporting their pottery on Majorcan ships to Italy, where it was called "majolica". The French word for fine glazed earthenware, "faïence", comes from Faenza, the main Italian center of production, along with Florence, during the Renaissance.

The first French factories were founded by Italian potters in the 16th century, in Lyon and Nevers, during the reign of François I. In the 17th century the main centers of production were Rouen, Strasbourg, Marseille and Moustiers in France; Delft in the Netherlands; Hamburg and Hanau in Germany; and Bristol and Liverpool in England.

ALLIANCE OF ART AND TECHNIQUE

Gien's success was based on the use of modern mechanical processes and on the talent and number of its artists (some 200 of the 1,000 workers in 1878). This ensured both mass production and high-quality design.

11

1

2

3

TRADEMARKS
Gien has used many different
marks, associated with different
collections and factory directors.
Some of them refer to medals won at
the Universal Exhibitions (1849, 1852,
1860, 1875).

**IMITATION,
INTERPRETATION
AND CREATION**
In the 19th
century, with the
rise of the
decorative arts,
Gien founded its
reputation on the
reproduction of a
range of
established shapes
and styles: from
Rouen, Marseille
(1), Italy (2 and 5),
Japan (3), Sèvres,
China and
England . . . Gien also
demonstrated its
creative independence
with Art Nouveau
pieces (6 and 7),
colored
Impressionist
barbotines (8),
heraldic plates
(9 and 10), enamel
ornamentation (4),
and pieces with a dark-
blue background
decorated
with gold
motifs,
known as
"bleu de
Gien".

4   5   6

▲ ORLÉANS TO GIEN
THE VAL DU GIENNOIS

ANNE DE BEAUJEU
Anne de France (1461–1522), the daughter of Louis XI and Charlotte de Savoie, was married at the age of twelve to Pierre II de Beaujeu, Duc de Bourbon, who gave her the county of Gien. Her father appointed her as regent during the minority of her brother Charles VIII: she ruled with a firm hand and succeeded in overcoming a feudal revolt led by the Duc d'Orléans, later Louis XII ● 34. Anne de Beaujeu undertook various projects in Gien from 1481 to 1522: she raised the town wall, restored the bridge, rebuilt the collegiate church, and made attractive modifications to the château.

Joan of Arc passed through Gien nine times in 1429, during her expedition to liberate Orléans ● 116. However, the town's golden age was the era of Anne de Beaujeu, daughter of Louis XI, regent of France and Countess of Gien (right). She altered and enlarged the château; and restored the old stone bridge across the Loire, with its thirteen arches. The young Louis XIV took refuge in Gien for a few days during the Fronde. In the 18th century the town's fortunes revived, boosted by the earthenware industry with which its name is still associated. The bombardments of June 1940 and July 1944 inflicted catastrophic damage on the town; it was rebuilt very tastefully after the war, prompting the writer Jules Romain to call it the "jewel of French reconstruction".

THE CHÂTEAU. The château dominates the town. Its distinctive black-and-red color scheme ● 67 is created by the glazed bricks used to form diamond, checkerboard and herringbone patterns on its walls; light stone frames around the doors and windows accentuate the effect. The only remnant of the feudal fortress is the façade overlooking the river, with its square tower (12th–13th century). The other buildings, set at right angles, were added by Anne de Beaujeu between 1484 and 1500.

MUSÉE DE LA CHASSE. The château was converted into an

international museum of hunting in 1952. The rooms display hundreds of trophies, weapons, paintings and tapestries, all of them relating to hunting.

CHURCH OF STE-JEANNE-D'ARC. The present-day church on Place du Château replaced the 15th-century Collegiate Church of St-Étienne, which was rebuilt by Anne de Beaujeu. The original building was almost completely destroyed in 1940: all that remains is the large square bell tower, around which the new brick-built church was constructed.

The main hall of the Musée de la Chasse has superb exposed beams; it is dedicated to the animal painters François Desportes (1661–1743) and Jean-Baptiste Oudry (1686–1755).

THE BRIDGE. This lovely bridge was built in 1734 to replace the 13th-century bridge, which had suffered severe damage during the floods of May 28, 1733. The present-day bridge has only twelve arches; its predecessor had thirteen.

MUSÉE DE LA FAÏENCERIE. The museum on Place de la Victoire was created to mark the factory's 150th anniversary in 1970. It is housed in one of the factory buildings and displays a magnificent collection of fine earthenware from the early 19th century, as well as large display pieces produced for the Universal Exhibition held in Paris in 1900.

EXCURSION TO BRIARE ★ (T4)

Briare's exceptional location, at the meeting point of the Loire and several canals, makes it a town dominated by water – with no less than two ports, fourteen bridges and seven locks.

THE CANAL-BRIDGE. This bridge over the Loire carries a canal, not a road. It was built to link the Canal Henri IV (or Canal de Briare) with the canal running alongside the Loire. This masterpiece of engineering, which connects the Seine and Saône basins, is an impressive structure of iron and stone: some 725 yards long, including 660 yards spanning the Loire, is the longest metal canal bridge in the world. Built between 1890 and 1894 by the Daydé et Pillé company, it was opened in 1896; Gustave Eiffel's company assisted with the foundations. In many ways the bridge's decoration (right) is reminiscent of the Pont Alexandre III in Paris.

CHURCH OF ST-ÉTIENNE. The church dates from 1895. The Briare enamels on the façade and the interior were intended to demonstrate the skills of the town's craftsmen.

HÔTEL DE VILLE. The town hall is housed in the 17th-century château of the "Seigneurs du Canal" (see right), in a lovely setting surrounded by water. Opposite the town hall is the Musée de la Mosaïque et des Émaux (Museum of Mosaic and Enamels), which traces 150 years of local industrial history.

THE "SEIGNEURS DU CANAL"
This was a group of seventeen (later thirty-three) citizens of Briare who in 1638 decided to complete the Canal de Briare, construction work having come to a halt after the assassination of Henri IV in 1610. The canal was opened in 1642, and was such a success that the untitled members of the group were given noble status. Each of the "Lords of the Canal" was granted use of the château (now the town hall) for a year.

"MODERN LIGHTING"
From the beginning the canal bridge was lit by electricity, using two turbines driven by the water falling into the canal beside the Loire, 26 feet below. The pilasters bear the coats of arms of the towns served by the canal.

The area between Orléans, Blois and the wild landscapes of the Sologne ▲ *174*, is a historical treasure trove, with a rich heritage from its medieval past.

🚗 c. 55 miles
🕐 1 day

CLÉRY-ST-ANDRÉ (C

This village, on the other side of the Loire, almost opposite Meung, at the northern tip of the Sologne has religious origins: a statue of the Virgin found here in 1280 attracted pilgrims for more than two centuries.
BASILICA OF NOTRE-DAME DE CLÉRY. Louis XI built a new church here where another one had been destroyed during the Hundred Years' War, after having dedicated himself to the Virgin of Cléry during the Battle of Dieppe against the English, on August 15, 1443. He made it a royal chapel, so that he could be buried here; destroyed by Protestants, his tomb was rebuilt on the order of Louis XIII. The great square tower to the north is all that remains of the 14th-century building.

MEUNG-SUR-LOIRE (N

JEAN DE MEUNG
Jean Chopinel, known as Jean de Meung (c. 1240–1305), from the Gâtinais region, wrote a sequel to the *Roman de la rose*, the courtly poem composed by another writer from the Loiret, Guillaume de Lorris (c. 1200–10 to c. 1240). The poem was a great success with the aristocracy throughout the Middle Ages. Jean de Meung wrote a second part of some 18,000 lines between 1275 and 1280, adding to the 4,000 lines of the original poem.

This little town dominated by its château has served a variety of purposes – it was a residence for the bishops of Orléans, the headquarters of the English army before they were expelled by Joan of Arc ▲ *116*, one of the places in which the poet François Villon (c. 1431–63) was imprisoned, and the holiday retreat of the famous Inspector Maigret, created by the Belgian writer Georges Simenon.
THE CHÂTEAU. The building has a medieval façade (built in the 12th century by Manassès de Garlande, Bishop of Orléans) and a residential wing dating from the 16th and 17th centuries.
CHURCH OF ST-LYPHARD. The ground plan of this 13th-century church takes the form of a trefoil design, unique in the region. Some Romanesque elements ● *58* survive, along with an 11th-century belfry.
THE TOWN. The Porte d'Amont, a fortified gateway that was altered in the 17th century, opens onto streets lined with stone and half-timbered houses ● *72* and old mills ● *78*.

BEAUGENCY (N3)

ocated on the border of the
épartements of Loir-et-Cher and Loiret,
eaugency (right) is a typical Loire town.
he quayside lined with plane trees, the
d tile and slate roofs, its tall bell towers
d the massive keep combine to make a
ry attractive picture, best viewed from
e left bank of the Loire.

HE BRIDGE. With its irregular arches, this
the only medieval bridge that has
rvived in the middle section of the Loire. Although modified
ver the centuries, it still has several of its Gothic arches and a
rge archway for boats to pass through. The Tour du Diable
n the quayside, downstream from the bridge, was once part of
e fortifications of the Abbey of Notre-Dame.

HURCH OF NOTRE-DAME. Dating from the late 11th century,
is was once the church of an Augustinian abbey that attracted
ilgrims throughout the Middle Ages. The nave and choir
orm a majestic example of Romanesque architecture ● *58*.
adly damaged by the Huguenots in 1567, the church was
eroofed in 1665 using wooden vaulting that slightly distorts its
tended proportions. The abbey buildings, between the
urch and the Loire, date from the 17th century.

HÂTEAU DUNOIS. The château (right) was modernized by the
astard of Orléans ▲ *115* – Jean, Comte de Dunois,

companion in arms of Joan of Arc
▲ *116* – in the second half of the 15th
century, and then by his descendants
in the 16th century. Today it houses a
museum featuring the history,
everyday life and folk art of the
Orléanais region.

HÔTEL DE VILLE. This elegant
building (left) from 1526 is said
to be the work of master mason
Pierre Biart, who built the Hôtel
Hector de Sanxerre ▲ *120* in
Orléans, which would explain
similarities between them.
Displayed in the council chamber
are some splendid 17th-century
tapestries.

BEAUGENCY
The courtyard of the
Château Dunois.

**NUCLEAR POWER
STATION OF
ST-LAURENT-DES-
EAUX** ● *12*
St-Laurent-des-Eaux
was the second
nuclear power station
built by Électricité de
France, following the
one at Chinon (Indre-
et-Loire). It began
operations in 1969.
The site was chosen
for its proximity to
the Loire, since an
abundant supply of
water is needed for
electricity production.

139

LOVE AND POETRY AT TALCY

In the 16th century Cassandra, the

daughter of Bernardo Salviati and Françoise Doulcet, was the first love of the poet Pierre de Ronsard ▲ 258, immortalized in his sonnets *Les Amours de Cassandre*. Later the château witnessed the long and unrequited love of the Huguenot poet Agrippa d'Aubigné ▲ 183 for Cassandra's Catholic niece Diana.

TALCY (M

This charming village halfway between Beaugency and Blois is principally known for its château, which stands between th Loire and the Loir, set slightly off the beaten track in the "petite Beauce".

THE CHÂTEAU OF THE SALVIATI. The lords of Talcy go back to the 13th century, but the château visible today was created by the Florentine banker Bernardo Salviati, who acquired it on November 8, 1517. The Renaissance façade is more ornamental than military, presenting a large square tower above an entrance porch, two hexagonal turrets crowned with machicolations, and a covered walk. The two wings of th building are set at right angles, overlooking a charming courtyard with a well that adds to the tranquil atmosphere of the place. The château has one of the most remarkable dovecotes ● 80 in the region, with 1,500 nesting holes.

THE CHÂTEAU DE MENARS (M

HISTORY OF THE BUILDING. The original château was built around 1646 by Guillaume Charron, a finance minister under Louis XIII; the main building and two pavilions survive today. From 1760 onward the château was altered and enlarged by the Marquise de Pompadour (below), mistress of Louis XV. She added two wings and the buildings around the main courtyard, designed by Ange-Jacques Gabriel (1698–1782), as well as redesigning the gardens and creating sumptuous interiors. Her brother, the Marquis de Marigny, director of the king's buildings, inherited the château in 1764 and appointed Germain Soufflot, the architect of the Panthéon, to add a low forebuilding in front of the central façade. The terraced gardens overlooking the Loire are graced with statues and elegant follies, such as the "Rotunda of Abundance" ● 71 and the Orangery.

"Whatever the weather, from the windows of the château you can let your eyes and mind wander over the water and the great expanse of countryside, where there is always some kind of diversion."
André Félibien

Mme de Pompadour (right) acquired Menars in 1760, but was not to enjoy the château for long, as she died in 1764.

BLOIS

CHAMBORD, *156*
VILLESAVIN, *166*
BEAUREGARD, *167*
CHEVERNY, *170*
TROUSSAY, *172*
ROUJOUX, *173,*
THE SOLOGNE, *174*
FOUGÈRES, *176*
CHAUMONT, *177*

RUE GALLOIS

RUE

5

JEAN- LAIGRET

3

4

1

8

2

QUAI DE L'ABBÉ DE LA

1. Château
2. Church of
   St-Nicolas
3. Anne de Bretagne
   Pavilion
4. Church of
   St-Vincent
5. Hôtel d'Alluye
6. Cathedral of
   St-Louis
7. Garden of the
   Ancien Évêché
8. Place Louis XII
9. Vienne

Hôtel d'Alluye ▼

RUE PORTE - CHARTRAINE

5

PONT JACQUES-GABRIEL

RUE DES MARCHANDS

CHURCH OF ST-NICOLAS ▼

▲ Blois

Bust dating from the 1st century, found at Blois during excavations.

Figures from an anonymous 16th-century painting (right).

Gaston d'Orléans.

Louis XII's signature.

History of the Town (M4,

ORIGINS. The site where Blois now stands was inhabited from the Protohistoric era onward. Archeologists have established that a town was founded between the Loire and the hillside in the 1st century AD. By the early 3rd century the town was well developed, with baths, sewers and a port. It was the capital of a Merovingian *pagus* (district), first mentioned in 584. However, it did not expand significantly until it became the seat of the Counts of Blois-Champagne around 950. From the 10th to the 13th century the town increased in size, as the counts became more powerful and early villages that had grown up around churches were joined together within a single city wall. The first bridge over the Loire was built at the end of the 11th century; and the castle was extended and embellished, symbolizing the town's prosperity and its political and economic status.

CAPITAL OF THE FRENCH KINGDOM. The town was sold to Louis d'Orléans in 1391. The accession of Charles d'Orléans in 1440 marked the start of a new phase of expansion and prosperity through the 15th century. This rise accelerated dramatically when Louis II d'Orléans became king of France, reigning as Louis XII. For a century Blois was a royal residence, which brought many of the king's officers and servants to the region. The town was scarred by the Wars of Religion and was sacked by Huguenots in 1568, leading to the exile of part of the Protestant population. The town retained its allegiance to the kings of France, who stayed here frequently up to the end of the century.

PROVINCIAL EXILE. Gaston d'Orléans, brother of Louis XIII, was exiled to Blois and kept a court in the town; though certainly more modest than the king's, this was large enough to maintain the illusion that Blois was a capital city. During this time a number of convents were founded outside the city walls, a Jesuit college was built, old abbeys were restored and a hospital founded – all reflecting both the prince's generosity and the strength of the Catholic Counter-Reformation. After the prince's death in 1660, Blois lost its dynamism: neither the creation of a bishopric (1698) nor the reconstruction of the bridge (1724) roused the town from its slumbers.

MODERN TIMES. Although the town's architectural heritage suffered considerable damage during the Revolution, at that time Blois became the seat of the préfecture of Loir-et-Cher. Most of the administrative buildings connected with its new civic function were built during the first half of the 19th century, even though this was a time of economic depression. The Préfecture, Palais de Justice, Halle aux Grains, Séminaire and Asile Départemental were all built between 1826 and 1850. The advent of the railway in 1846 brought further changes, and the town's fortunes began to improve significantly under the Second Empire. Mayor Eugène Riffault had roads built to connect the upper and lower town, and Blois' economy benefited greatly from the enterprise of two local industrialists: Auguste Poulain (1825–1918), who founded a chocolate factory, and Louis-Edme Rousset, who mechanized the production of shoes.

BLOIS TODAY. Badly damaged by bombing in June 1940, the center was rebuilt after the war and a new town grew up on the plateau. Today Blois is a medium-sized town, with a rich architectural heritage that has been fully restored. The river flowing through it weaves Blois into the surrounding landscape, making it one of the most attractive towns in the region.

THE BRIDGE ▲ 155
The earlier bridge was washed away in February 1716, when the Loire thawed after a frost. Philippe d'Orléans commissioned the design for a new bridge from the famous architect Jacques Gabriel, the first Royal Engineer of Bridges and Roads.

WATCHMAKING AT BLOIS
Luxury industries like watchmaking grew up here in the 16th and 17th centuries, benefiting from the largesse of royal patrons. In 1640 Blois had forty-six watchmakers, who were renowned throughout Europe for the quality of their work.

The first Poulain chocolate factory ● 57, between the station and the château, opened in 1864.

BY GOD HE'S SO TALL! SO TALL!
HE SEEMS EVEN LARGER DEAD THAN ALIVE.

HENRI
(BEFORE THE CORPSE OF THE DUC DE GUI

Henri III, son of Henri II and Catherine de Médicis, ruled over a France which from 1574 onward was divided by the Wars of Religion. This troubled period was also marked by the slaughter of Protestants in the horrific St Bartholomew's Day massacre. I revealed the power of a man who would do anything to reassert the supremacy of Catholicism in France: the Duc de Guise, commander of the Holy League created in 1576 to oppose the king's concessions toward the Huguenots. The death of the king's brother, the Duc d'Alençon, on June 10, 1584, made Henri de Navarre the heir to the throne. Whereupon a new conflict broke out. The Duc de Guise refused to countenance the possibility of a non-Catholic king, and in the face of an increasingly impotent monarchy he swiftly took control of Paris and prepared to deal his final blow.

THE SECOND ÉTATS GÉNÉRAUX, OCTOBER 1588
Seeking to restore his authority, Henri III convened the second États Généraux (parliament) at Blois. Knowing the Duc de Guise was supported by many of the deputies, the king decided to have him killed, along with his brother the Cardinal de Lorraine.

ASSASSINATION OF THE DUC DE GUISE
Before the murder Henri III declared: "When passion is wounded, finally it turns to fury. Let them not put me to it." The commander of the League did not heed this ominous warning. On the morning of December 23, 1588 the Duc de Guise was summoned by the king and while crossing the royal chamber fell under the blows of Henri's notorious assassins, the "Quarante-Cinq". The king, who had been hiding behind a curtain emerged to witness his rival's death.

CONFRONTATION. The two men met at the Château de Blois a few days before these dramatic events, in a highly charged atmosphere.

HENRI III
The political situation became untenable for the king (on the left). He was driven from Paris by the League in May 1588 and took refuge at Blois.

THE DUC DE GUISE
Lieutenant General of the French kingdom and commander of the Holy League, the duke coveted the French throne and plotted against the king.

THE INSIGNIA OF POWER
Henri III's aim was to reassert the authority of the monarchy in France, where the Catholic League had seized the initiative (with the support of Spain). He joined forces with his cousin Henri de Navarre to lay siege to Paris (July 1589). On August 1, 1589 he was stabbed by the monk Jacques Clément, a member of the League. The following day, as he lay mortally wounded, the French king – who was the last of the Valois line – appointed as his successor Henri de Navarre, head of the House of Bourbon and a direct descendant of Saint Louis. A 16th/17th-century tapestry (left) commemorates the event: the dying king hands over the royal insignia to his successor, who kneels by the bedside. Henri de Navarre became Henri IV of France.

François I staircase.

AUDACIOUS ESCAPE
Marie de Médicis, who had been exiled to Blois, escaped from the castle by sliding down a rope during the night of February 21–2, 1619. Rubens re-created the episode in a painting (right).

Seal of Louis II.

Chapel of St-Calais, in the château.

HISTORY OF THE CHÂTEAU ● 68,

Few buildings enjoy such a rich historical and archite heritage as the Château de Blois. The first reference *castrum* (fort) on this site dates from the 6th centur **THE CASTLE OF THE COUNTS OF BLOIS.** In the 9th century the Counts of Blois built a fortress here, wh was constantly modified over the course of subseque centuries. Today the oldest surviving sections of the château date from the early 13th century. The Salle États, the Tour du Foix and several sections of rampa give some idea of the scale of this early building. **ROYAL RESIDENTS.** When Louis II d'Orléans became king of France in 1498, ruling as Louis XII, he established the political capital of the kingdom at Blois the town where he was born. Taking up residence here he embarked on a complete reconstruction of the castl as well as creating magnificent gardens to the northeast Work was completed with the consecration of the chape in 1508 ● *60*.

François I, who succeeded Louis II, began to rebuild the north wing in 1515. Four phases of building work followed, but construction came to a halt with the death of Claude de France in 1524. After that date François I spent little time at Blois. Henri III convened the États Généraux here in 1576 and 1588. It was during the second session that he had the Duc de Guise assassinated ▲ *146*. After the royal court departed, at the end of the 16th century, the château served as a place of exile for Marie de Médicis and then for Gaston d'Orléans. In 1635 the latter embarked on a reconstruction scheme devised by the famous

architect François Mansart, but this was abandoned thre years later. After the death of Gaston d'Orléans (1660) château fell into oblivion.
CHANGING FORTUNES. The château was scheduled for demolition in 1788; but was saved only by being assig for military use. Regiments of cavalry and engineers occupied the château for eighty years, causing substantial damage to the buildings. In 1842, as a res

> "SPARE THE CHÂTEAU,
> THOUGH DARK AND FEARSOME,
> THOUGH IT IS STAINED WITH BLOOD"
> VICTOR HUGO

the efforts of the Romantic writers, the château was assified as a historical monument. As with many French onuments, Félix Duban was entrusted with its restoration; e aimed to re-create the way it looked at the end of the 15th ntury. Today the château houses a number of museums.

Cul-de-lampe on the façade of the Louis XII wing.

OUIS XII WING ● 67

ROM THE PLACE DU CHÂTEAU. The large gable on the right is that of the Salle des États: it was rebuilt in 1860, following the demolition of the old roof of the château, which provided access to the entrance courtyard. The main portal is surmounted by an equestrian statue of Louis XII made by Seurre in 1858, based on an earlier one destroyed in 1792. The Gothic decoration of the niche contrasts with the setting of the porcupine, the king's emblem, which bears the mark of Renaissance influence. To the left of the portal, two culs-de-lampe framing the first window on the ground floor depict a courtly scene.

THE ORIGINAL EQUESTRIAN STATUE OF LOUIS XII
The original statue showed the king wearing a hat, instead of the crown he bears in the 19th-century replica. Below it was a Latin inscription by Faust Andrelini, which read: "Where Louis was born by the grace of the gods, he holds the royal scepter with a noble hand. Happy the day which shone announcing such a king! Gaul was not worthy of a higher prince."

THE COURTYARD FAÇADE.
On the courtyard side is a gallery supported by square pillars decorated with candelabras. This motif, of Northern Italian inspiration, is typical of the early Renaissance and is the earliest example of its kind in France. By contrast the ornamentation of the windows, and the combination of polychrome brick and stone, is typical of the 15th-century Franco-Flemish tradition.

CHAPEL OF ST-CALAIS. The chapel built by Louis XII has suffered considerable damage over the centuries. The nave was demolished in the days of Gaston d'Orléans. What remains of the choir was divided into three stories during the military occupation. The interior decoration, restored by Félix Duban in the 19th century, was ruined by bombing during World War Two. Today the chapel has a beautiful collection of stained-glass windows (right) created in the workshop of master glassmaker Max Ingrand and dedicated in 1957. The windows depict major events in the château's history, cluding Joan of Arc's visit in 1429.

OUR DU FOIX. The tower's terrace offers a lovely view er the town, the Church of St-Nicholas and the Loire lley. The tower was originally part of the medieval rtress, Gaston d'Orléans had an astronomical servatory installed here. The fountain in the middle the terrace has three marble panels and a marble sin that came from the old gardens of the château.

149

FRANÇOIS I WING

● 6

This wing of the château was constructed scarcely fifteen years after the Louis XII Wing.

THE STAIRCASE. "The famous spiral staircase . . . is a kind of carved cylinder, with large openings which make it effectively an open-air staircase." This is how it was described by Henry James in the 19th century. In addition, it is worth mentioning the decorative detail, which includes buttresses adorned with fine carvings, with motifs such as classical profiles, trophies and candelabras.

THE APARTMENTS. The great staircase leads to the royal apartments on the second story. Their current appearance is the product of Félix Duban's restoration work. In his attempt to re-create the original setting, Duban drew on the few historical remains (pieces of door frames, fragments of painted decorations)

and in particular on manuscript sources. The result is not so much an authentic reproduction of the 16th-century interior as a reflection of 19th-century preoccupations and the Romantic interest in the Renaissance. The most striking features are the painted decorations, probably inspired by late-15th-century manuscripts, and tiling reminiscent of Italian majolica. The carvings on the fireplaces and above doorways reveal an expert knowledge of Renaissance ornamentation. We do not know with certainty what each room was used for in the 16th century. We know only that the rooms overlooking the courtyard had a more public function than those opening onto the Façade des Loges, where the royal residents lived. In the late 16th century the second story was occupied by Catherine de Médicis, while Henri III lived on the third story. Each apartment included an antechamber, a wardrobe, a bedroom, an oratory and a *cabinet* (study). The *cabinet* was where the king or queen worked, but it was also used for exhibiting precious objects, jewelry, medals and exotic curiosities. The famous secret cupboards in Catherine de Médicis' study were in fact used for this purpose. It was many years later, in the 19th century, that Alexandre Dumas *père*, in his novel *La Reine Margot* (1845), depicted them as poison cupboards, giving rise to a remarkably persistent legend.

when he founded the town's first earthenware factory in 1862. The tradition lasted until 1953, when the last factory was closed.

THE FAÇADE DES LOGES
"It has many small galleries, small windows, small balconies and small ornaments, combined without order or regularity: the whole effect is grand, and pleasing." This is how Jean de La Fontaine described the façade, which has been compared with those of Italian palaces.

"BLOIS OFFERS A STRIKING SYNTHESIS OF THREE PERIODS OF FRENCH ARCHITECTURE."

HENRI GUERLIN

⌐E GASTON D'ORLÉANS WING   ● 71

...is part of the château, at the far end of the courtyard, ...s designed by Mansart. This makes it one of the earliest ...ssical châteaux in France. Gustave Flaubert's verdict was ...sty and unjust when he called it "a building of the most ...otic kind . . . [designed] in a detestable manner with its ...lf-baked classicism . . . in execrable taste." In fact this is a ...autifully proportioned and elegantly designed work of ...hitecture. The architect employed a number of devices ...accentuate the central bay and the main entrance of the ...àteau: the forebuilding is slightly higher than the façades, ...d curved colonnades draw the viewer's gaze to the center; ...angular and rounded pediments are used to give emphasis ...to the portico. Inside, the staircase is in the Baroque style. The crowning dome is seen through a semi-cupola halfway up, which accentuates the perspective and increases the majestic effect of the whole. The skillful use of light, a wealth of decorative carvings by the best artists of the time (though these were not completed), and the high quality of the masonry make this one of the masterpieces of French Baroque art.

THE SALLE DES ÉTATS

The tour of the château concludes in a room that survives from the castle of the Counts of Blois. It was constructed at the same time as Chartres Cathedral. The room, one of the oldest feudal halls in France, is divided into two naves by a row of elegant columns.

"One of the fireplaces (in the François I Wing) has as its central motif two medallions containing a salamander and an ermine, each borne aloft by four cherubs. Between the medallions are beautifully crafted candelabras; above them is a frieze composed of scallops alternating with cherubs bearing garlands.**"**
Dr Frédéric Lesueur

HISTORICAL NAME
The Salle des États owes its name to the two sessions of the États Généraux ▲ *148* held here during the reign of Henri III.

The porcupine, royal emblem of Louis XII.

MUSÉE DES BEAUX-ARTS

Housed in the château from the outset, Blois' museum of fine arts has always been somewhat overshadowed by the celebrity of its setting. The restoration of the château in 1845 gave new impetus to the artistic life of the town, prompting the establishment and development of the museum.

MANY ACQUISITIONS. Like so many of the provincial museums that came into being in the mid 19th century, the museum was created by a combination of municipal efforts and donations from local citizens. The French state and the Louvre have also given pictures to the museum, among them *François I Armed by Bayard* (Louis Ducis, 1817) and *The Meeting of Henri III and the Duc de Guise* (Charles Comte, 1855). The museum reflects the importance in the town's history of the Valois family and the assassination of the Duc de Guise ▲ *146*. Paintings on both these subjects have been collected here since the 19th century.

MADELEINE OF SCOTLAND
This portrait of François I's daughter, painted by Corneille de Lyon, has a pale green background, typical of this Dutch artist.

Virgin and Child, detail from a polyptych by Marco d'Oggiono.

THE WORKS. The sculptors Daniel Dupuis, Alfred Jean-Baptiste Halou and Henri Varenne are well represented in the museum's collection of statues, part of which is on display. The museum also has some 16th-century Italian paintings, featuring works by the school of Leonardo including a polyptych by Marco d'Oggiono (detail below) and *Colombine* attributed to Francesco Melzi. French painting of the 16th century is represented by artists such as Antoine Caron, Jean Cousin and Corneille de Lyon. Notable among the extensive 17th-century collections are *Eliazer and Rebecca* by Sébastien Bourdon, *The Visitation* by Michel Corneille and, from schools outside France, *The Death of Adonis* by Maarten De Vos, *Flemish Market* by Anton Polcke and *Hercules and Omphale*, attributed to Antonio Zanchi. From the 18th century there is an outstanding collection of medallions by the sculptor Nini ▲ *177* and *Psyche Receiving the Divine Honors* by François Boucher, along with splendid furniture from the Korewo collection. The 19th-century collections include paintings by Luminais, Bezard, Cormon, Ingres, Compte-Calix and Chassériau. In addition to watches and ceramics from Blois, the museum has large collections of tapestries and ironwork. The very modern arrangement of Louis XII's apartments can still be clearly appreciated by visitors; six rooms (restored by Duban) are served by one of the earliest galleries in France (pre-1501). The recently opened Lapidary Rooms display a splendid collection of sculptures from the 15th and 16th centuries that were removed from the château during the 19th century.

This pavilion, built on a terrace of the gardens in the reign of Louis XII, is one of the oldest garden buildings known in France. To its right is the orangery, a reminder that citrus trees were introduced into the Loire valley at the end of the 15th century, after the Italian campaigns.

AROUND THE CHÂTEAU

In medieval times the Place du Château was the farmyard of the fortress. Later it was bordered by the Collegiate Church of St-Sauveur, where Joan of Arc ▲ 116 had her standard blessed. Some private houses from the 16th century can still be seen. The large house at the eastern end of the square was built in the mid 19th century; from 1997 it will house the Maison de la Magie, featuring a theater for events and performances as well as an exhibition of objects from the collection that belonged to Blois magician Robert-Houdin (see right), including automata and other intriguing devices.

CHURCH OF ST-NICHOLAS ★. The church of the former Benedictine abbey, founded in 924, was built in two phases. The choir, the transept and the first bay of the nave were built in Early Gothic style between 1138 and 1186, whereas the nave and western façade date from the early 13th century and were modeled on Chartres Cathedral. Inside, visitors can trace the development of Gothic style from the chapels of the ambulatory (still clearly influenced by Romanesque) to the Chapelle de la Vierge (mid 14th century), built in the High Gothic style. The transept crossing is surmounted by a pendentives, in a striking design. The nearest to the Loire are still standing; from the 17th or 18th century.

some on abbey buildings most of them date

TOWARD THE château there is a façade of the leads down the Jardin du Roi, façade des cleared below reconstruction had laid out

GARDENS. From Rue des Fossés-du-good view of the impressive external Gaston d'Orléans Wing. A path embankment of the château to the from where you can admire the Loges ▲ 150. In 1992 a space was the Jardin du Roi for a of the gardens that Louis XII here in the early 16th century.

ROBERT-HOUDIN, MAGICIAN OF BLOIS (1805–71)
This suave illusionist was born Jean-Eugène Robert in Rue Porte-Chartraine, once a main street of the city. He was famous for his mechanical inventions and spectacular tricks using electricity. He performed before fashionable Parisian society, at the Théâtre du Palais-Royal, and toured throughout Europe. In 1849 he moved to St-Gervais, near Blois. Escapologist Harry Houdini adopted his name.

BLOIS "GLORIOUS IN FOUNTAINS AND RICH IN AQUEDUCTS"
Eight fountains supplied Blois with water from the 16th century onward. However, by the 18th century the town's needs had outstripped their capacity, and in 1749 a vast cistern, known as Le Gouffre ("the abyss"), was dug out under Place Louis XII to supply the lower town, including the Louis XII fountain (below). The first pumping of water from the Loire began in 1852.

THE UPPER TOWN

This section of the town, set on the hillside, features many charming steep alleyways and streets with steps.

PETITS DEGRÉ DU CHÂTEAU

RUE ST-HONORÉ. The Hôtel d'Alluye ★ at no. 8 (at the top, on the left-hand side) was built for Florimond Robertet, Baron d'Alluye, a powerful man, open to new ideas, who served as treasurer, notary and secretary under three kings: Charles VIII, Louis XII and François I. He had the house built around 1505, and received a Florentine embassy here in 1508. The street façade, which was heavily restored at the end of the 19th century, is similar to the Louis XII façade of the château. The courtyard (which can be visited on weekdays) is better preserved and displays features that were completely new in France at the time: galleries built one above another, uncompromisingly Italianate décor, and terracotta medallions with classical profiles. At the top of the street the Escalier Denis Papin (above) commemorates the inventor of steam power, who was born at Blois in the 17th century. From here there is a wide view over the roofs of the lower town, the château and the ruins of the medieval castle. Rue du Palais, which has lovely 18th-century portals at nos. 3 and 5, leads to Place St-Louis. On this square (at no. 3) is the Maison des Acrobates (late 15th century), decorated with figures dressed in costume of Louis XI's era, whose liveliness and state of preservation is remarkable.

CATHEDRAL OF ST-LOUIS. This complex building is a former collegiate church, founded in the 10th century under the name of St-Solenne. Construction of the façade and the two stories above the bell tower (the base dates from the 12th century) began in 1544: they represent one of the first attempts at classical religious architecture in France.

The nave was destroyed by a hurricane in 1678 and was rebuilt in Gothic style at the end of the 17th century. The building was completed around 1860 with the neo-Gothic Chapelle de la Vierge. The beautifully proportioned interior houses remains of the early 10th-century church, in the crypt under the choir. The organ case was donated by Louis XIV in 1704, the year in which the church became a cathedral.

THE ANCIEN ÉVÊCHÉ. The town hall of Blois was formerly the episcopal palace, built in 1700, following plans by Jacques Gabriel (the comptroller of the king's buildings at Chambord), for Mgr de Bertier, the first bishop of Blois.

he terraced gardens ★ (opposite, center) overlook the Loire
lley and offer a lovely view of the town and the humpback
idge, which was also built by Gabriel.

HE PENTE DU CÔTEAU

etween the cathedral and the Loire is a picturesque quarter
id out in tiers over the hillside. In the 16th century the
ealthy citizens and court dignitaries of Blois lived here; later
remained largely unaffected by changes to the town center.
was renovated between 1970 and 1980, and now gives a
ood idea of how the town looked in the 16th century.
LACE LOUIS XII ★. On Saturday mornings a colorful market
held in this square, which is dominated by the château
alls. Huge steps lead from the square to the Place du
hâteau. The 15th-century Louis XII Fountain (opposite,
ottom left), designed in the Flamboyant style, once stood
gainst a wall. In 1451 Antoine Astesan described it as "a
eautiful stone fountain with bright silvery water that supplies
e whole town". Below this, near to the covered market, is
e former Jacobite convent founded by Jean de Chatillon,
ount of Blois, in the 13th century. It now houses the Musée
Histoire Naturelle (containing local and exotic fauna) and
e Musée Diocésain d'Art Religieux (religious objects,
atues and liturgical ornaments).

IENNE

ienne, on the left bank of the Loire, is a very
d suburb, inhabited since the Roman era.
HURCH OF ST-SATURNIN. An ancient
lgrimage in honor of Notre-Dame des Aydes,
atron saint of Blois, ends at this church.
vidence of this can be seen in the large
umber of *ex votos* in the northern side aisle.
he church was partially rebuilt in the 15th
entury thanks to Anne de Bretagne; however, the project
as left incomplete when she died, in 1514. The church was
urned down by Protestants in 1568 and restored in the 17th
entury; a section of the nave was rebuilt, and a roof added
the bell tower.
LOISTERS OF ST-SATURNIN ★. This is in fact a monumental
emetery, standing opposite the church. It was built in 1516
nd is one of the few to survive in France; today it houses a
apidary Museum.

**PONT
JACQUES-GABRIEL**
Blois had a bridge as
early as the 11th
century. In 1508
Louis XII gave
permission to build
on the bridge "for the
good, profit and use,
decoration and
ornamentation of our
town and of the said
bridge". The present
bridge, designed by
the architect Jacques
Gabriel, was opened
in 1724. The central
arch is surmounted by
a pyramid; the
cartouche bearing the
king's arms at the
base was carved by
Guillaume Coustou,
who sculpted the
famous Marly horses
on Place de la
Concorde in Paris.
Damaged during the
two world wars, the
bridge has been
faithfully restored.

**CLOISTERS OF
ST-SATURNIN**
The stone pillars
of the south gallery
have capitals
depicting funerary
themes, such as
skulls and bones.

🚗 c. 30 miles
⏱ 1½ days

BLACK WOODPECKER
This bird, the largest member of the woodpecker family, has lived in the forests around Chambord and throughout the Sologne for the last thirty years ▲ 174.

THE CHAMBORD ESTATE

The Château de Chambord stands at the heart of dense woodland and is perfectly suited to its natural setting, the Forest of Boulogne. Today the estate (covering 13,500 acres) is the largest enclosed forest park in Europe; the wall that surrounds it is some 20 miles long.

THE NATURE RESERVE.
The park has been a national nature reserve since 1947. Only part of the park (around 1,700 acres) is open to the public; the rest is reserved for the study of wildlife. Around seven hundred red deer and a thousand wild boar (the numbers fluctuate depending on the season), roe deer, mouflon, foxes and other species live here in complete freedom. The bird life is also rich and varied, with one hundred nesting species – including three species of eagle and six species of woodpecker. The forest has been maintained and developed (in 1820 it covered only half the estate) with a view to protecting these animals. Hunting ● 52 is forbidden, although sixteen official hunts are held annually as a means of population control; animals are also captured alive in order to repopulate other territories.

PUBLIC ACCESS TO THE ESTATE. The estate has six entrance gates, each of which is guarded by a forester's cottage crowned by a stag's head (the symbol of Chambord). At each entrance a wide grille over a ditch across the road (similar to a cattle grid) deters the larger animals from leaving the reserve. Visitors can watch the wild animals from observatories in the area open to the public. The deers' rutting season, from mid September to mid October, is an especially interesting time. There are footpaths and bridleways through the estate; and the foresters organize guided tours with commentaries, ranging from a few hours to a whole day. Animal photographers can obtain permission for access to some of the restricted areas between April 1 and July 31.

SAINT-DYÉ, PORT OF CHAMBORD   (D

François I's decision to built a château at Chambord in the early 16th century had a dramatic effect on the fortunes of St-Dyé. The initial intention was to divert a branch of the Loire; however, this project was soon abandoned and

e architects chose the nearest
pint on the river for unloading
pplies, which was the port of
yé. Whole bargeloads of lead,
élazé slate ▲ *312*, and stone from
premont-sur-l'Allier or even from
urré in the Cher valley (which
d to come via Tours) were
lloaded here. From this time
-Dyé's fortunes and activities
ere closely bound with those of
e château. The town flourished
a result: new houses were built
d the church was renovated.
om the 17th century onward
e wine business was another
urce of income: vineyards were
t up around the village, and
rrels of wine were sent along
e river by the hundred to supply
e cafés and restaurants of Paris. Wood was another
nportant cargo. This was the heyday of river transport
the Loire ● *50*, and a new port was built to meet the
mand. The present-day port dates from the second
lf of the 18th century, and the quayside was extended
river in 1806. The whole area was extensively renovated
1984, enhancing the effect of the spacious quaysides
ned with plane trees, running alongside the river for half
mile. The town is a delightful place for a stroll: in its
reets, which run down to the port or across the hillside,
u will come upon old inns and Renaissance buildings
ch as La Salamandre, the Maison du Galet (the love
st of Maréchal de Saxe ▲ *165*) and the Maison de la
ée. Remains of the old ramparts can be seen at various
ints around the town.

**ON THE RIVER
BANKS**
Local tradition has
it that Joan of Arc
stopped in the town
on April 26, 1429,
on her way to
Orléans ● *116*.
After passing along
the right bank of the
Loire, she went up
to the church to
pray at the altar of
the Virgin, then
continued on her
journey, heading
toward St-Laurent-
des-Eaux.

157

It was in the 15th century that the old hunting lodge of the Counts of Blois, set at the heart of a forest full of game, became the property of the French crown. Chambord is more than just a château: it is an architectural jewel, the product of François I's extravagant fantasies. The king intended that its brilliance should enhance the splendor of his reign. Although the building bears the imprint of the French medieval tradition, its dazzling ornamentation and elegant symmetries reflect the influence of the Italian Renaissance. With its 440 rooms, 84 staircases and 365 chimneys, Chambord bears proud testimony to three centuries of French royal history.

THE STAIRCASE
The château is arranged around this masterpiece of French Renaissance architecture. The staircase has two spirals, which allows people to go up and down without meeting; it must have been the scene of many courtly intrigues. This original and elegant design is enhanced by lavish ornamentation: capitals, culs-de-lampe, carved colonnettes, and a ceiling decorated with François I's salamander emblem. Above the terrace the staircase is surmounted by a lantern tower, its tip (177 feet above ground level) itself crowned by a fleur-de-lys carved in stone.

1. Staircase
2. Tour des Cloches (Tour Henri V)
3. Tour Caroline de Berry
4. Tour François I
5. Tour Dieudonné Comte de Chambord
6. Tour de la Chapelle
7. Dauphin's Wing
8. Tour des Princes
9. Porte Royale
10. Tour du Chaudron
11. Outbuildings
12. François I Wing (Orléans Wing)
13. Tour Robert de Parme

THE KEEP

This square building has a ground plan in the shape of a Greek cross, with the great staircase as its central axis. The four great corner towers (left, the Tour des Cloches) still have something of a medieval air, even though they are decorated in the Renaissance style; the same symmetry is observed on the terrace. Around the lantern tower of the central staircase are the roofs of the four pavilions, each housing two stories of apartments. The roofs and decorated chimneys combine to create a landscape of stone and slate. Visitors can walk about the terrace and enjoy the view over the Forest of Chambord.

INTERPRETING THE TEXTS. When French historians began to study Chambord in the mid 19th century, they soon realized how much had been lost: only a small number of documents relating to the building of the château survived. They did establish, however, that François I's decision to build "a beautiful and sumptuous palace at Chambort [*sic*], according to edict and estimation" dated from September 6, 1519. They also discovered the names of some of the key figures: François de Pontbriant, superintendent of the works, Jacques Sourdeau, master mason, Clotet, the treasurer, all of them from the Loire Valley. Pontbriant was old and soon resigned his post; Sourdeau died in 1552. The war against Charles V was resumed, and work on Chambord was suspended from 1524 to 1526; in 1525 the French were defeated at the Battle of

Elevation of the lantern tower of the great staircase.

"I know nothing comparable with this fantasy in stone . . . an incredible profusion of little domes, bell towers and chimneys of all shapes, some covered in mosaics of colored stone."

Prince Pükler-Muskau, *Journal de Voyage*

Pavia, and the king was held captive in Madrid. The old 12th-century castle at Chambord had been built to defend th ford at the bend of the river, and this had to be demolished before work could begin. The 17th-century historians Jean Bernier and André Félibien des Avaux state construction of the château began in 1526, but it is probable that work on the building itself had scarcely begun at this

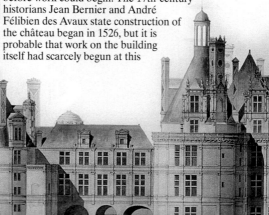

...ne. The king had envisaged a site by the edge of the river, ...hich would be flooded when the water level was high.

...RANÇOIS I – ARCHITECT OF HIS OWN PALACE? In 1526, on his ...turn from captivity, François I stayed at Chambord. We ...ow that he was an impatient man: his workers found this to ...eir cost, except for Antoine de Troyes, ...ppointed comptroller after the death of ...cques Sourdeau (Sourdeau himself was ...cceeded as master mason by Pierre ...inqueau, who held the post until his death in ...38). Charles de Chauvigny was appointed ...perintendent by the king and held the post ...til the 1540's. All the 19th-century ...storians, including Viollet-le-Duc, viewed ...hambord as a thoroughly French work of ...chitecture: they saw it as the last of the great ...ain-fortresses, a younger brother of ...incennes built by the descendants of the ...oire Valley's great master masons, of whom ...ey were proud. François I had whiled away ...e tedium of his long captivity in Madrid by ...ading, and had been captivated by a Spanish ...ivalric novel, *Amadis de Gaule* (a 14th-century ...ork adapted by Garcia Rodriguez de Montalvo). ...hen he returned to France, the king had the novel ...anslated. The hero of the epic lived in the ...hâteau de l'Île Ferme, set in grounds ...habited by a thousand strange creatures, with ...river winding its way through the greenery: ...is must have seemed a fairy-tale version of ...hambord. The name of Chambord's ...chitect, the designer of this grand plan ...mbining French and Italian architectural ...yles, is not mentioned in any of the ...rviving documents. However, the ...le of François I is alluded to repeatedly.

...e decided to have a wall built around the château's grounds ...d personally staked out its course during the winter of ...23–4; at that time the land on the right bank of the Cosson ...d not yet been acquired. The site continued to expand: in January 1530 he again took part in staking it out, and then again, for the last time, in December 1539. François also followed up another project in person: after his return from captivity he appointed an engineer, Pietro Caccia, at Chambord. In July 1529 he

The hundreds of chimneys rising from the summit of the château are crowned and decorated with royal motifs, surmounted by statues and adorned with slate lozenges. Their silhouettes stand out against the backdrop of roofs and domes.

CHARLES V
In December 1539, *en route* from Madrid to Brussels, the Holy Roman Emperor was received by François I at Chambord. He was greeted with ballets in a setting of tapestries and garlands. By this stage only the keep had been finished, with its lantern tower rising into the sky and the French lily at its summit.

The Forest of Chambord was perfect for the traditional sport of kings: hunting.

summoned Caccia to question him regarding "the means necessary to divert part of the Loire river to pass through Chambord". However, the plans were altered repeatedly over the years: the château as it stands today bears the marks of these changes. The idea of diverting the course of the Loire was never carried out; attempts to alter the course of even the smaller Cosson river only succeeded in enlarging the marshes, a problem that was not resolved until the mid 18th century. Perhaps the real architect of Chambord was François himself.

SILENT GENIUS. Acceding to François I's insistent requests, the aging Leonardo da Vinci arrived at Amboise during the winter of 1516–17; the great painter, engineer and architect lived at Clos-Lucé (then called Cloux), which had been renovated for him by the king. François had at first thought of building a palace at Romorantin, where he spent his childhood; sketches for the project survive in Leonardo's notebooks. This idea was later abandoned in favor of the very different plan for Chambord: a hunting château on a centralized ground plan, consisting of four sections of apartments joined by the four corner towers, with intersecting rooms in the shape of a cross at the center of the building. The king had "several plans drawn up before undertaking anything". A wooden model of Chambord, already badly eroded, was discovered in the 17th century: this was preliminary model of Leonardo's design parently made by Dominico da Cortona. Cortona, who had me to Amboise with Charles VIII, produced a whole series architectural models for François I at the beginning of his ign, including this one of Chambord. Leonardo's fragile te of health most probably did not allow him to visit the e; he died in May 1519, and it was not until September of e same year that the building supervisors were appointed.

The king made several visits to Amboise during this time – and may well have had meetings with Cortona and Melzi, Leonardo's companion, in an attempt to discover any further information that might have been left by Leonardo. However, that is purely conjecture.

GASTON D'ORLÉANS. The brother of Louis XIII was exiled to Blois (1634–44) and subsequently, from 1652 until his death in 1660, was wholly isolated from court affairs. He shared François I's passions for architecture and hunting ● 52, and was strongly drawn to Chambord. By this time the waters of the Cosson had eated a marsh in front of the château, which quired urgent attention: three flying ttresses on the lantern tower had llapsed, requiring immediate repair; e terraces of the keep were leaking; d the great casement windows hting the cross-shaped rooms were lling into ruin, as were the arches der the terraces, and the roofs. hese repairs were covered by an timate of 1641–2; the architectural naments on the arches were also to restored to their original state. owever, the work came to a halt due lack of funds; it was eventually mpleted by Louis XIV.

OUIS XIV AT CHAMBORD. Louis IV was also captivated by hambord, visiting a number of nes to enjoy the pleasures of nting and of court life in a rural tting. Molière and Lully presented o comédies-ballets here: *Monsieur Pourceaugnac* (1669) and *Le ourgeois gentilhomme* (1670). 1668 Louis XIV decided the yal apartments of François I ere not grand enough. In a heme that made nonsense of

Sketch of the lantern tower (centre) by Leonardo da Vinci.

❝As for love, it is present everywhere in this labyrinth of turrets and chimneys, designed, it is said, as a setting for amorous encounters, . . . and along the walkways set between heaven and earth.❞

Froberville,
*Guide du Val
de Loire
mystérieux*

163

Louis XIV organized huge hunting parties at Chambord ● 52.

"LE BOURGEOIS GENTILHOMME"
Molière staged the first performance at Chambord in 1670, in the presence of Louis XIV.

the original design, he turned the northern section of the cross-shaped room on the second story into a vestibule; the northeastern apartments were altered, and the tower room adjoining the king's room was reserved for the queen. These apartments were later restored by the architect Jules Hardouin-Mansart. Inelegant stable buildings were put up to the west of the château in 1681 (they were demolished in 1755), and more parts of the interior restored; later the Cosson was canalized. Major excavations in front of the northern façade created large gardens alongside the canalized river, which was diverted to supply moats at the foot of the castle's northern and eastern façades. A royal gateway (the Porte Royale) was built into the southern wing, opening onto a great esplanade flanked by huge outbuildings and stables. The building work finally ceased in 1685, and Louis did not return to Chambord. However, the château was saved from ruin thanks to Colbert reorganization of the Service des Bâtiments du Roi, which was responsible for maintaining royal buildings.

THE 18TH AND 19TH CENTURIES. Residents at Chambord during the 18th century included Stanislas Leszcynski, the deposed king of Poland and father-in-law of Louis XV, who was not happy here, and then Maréchal Maurice de Saxe, who from 1748 until his death in 1750 gave a good deal of attention to managing the forests and carrying out drainage works. The king sent large carved panels from Versailles to Chambord for the former bedchamber of Louis XIV, now occupied by the Maréchal. Enormous earthenware stoves were also sent to heat the rooms of the central cross; one of these survives today. During the Revolution, when all symbols of royalty were earmarked for destruction, this "haunt of vultures" was nearly demolished. The furniture was sold off, and there was some pillaging of paneling from the apartments and lead from the roofs. Napoleon first assigned Chambord to the 15th cohort of the Légion d'Honneur, then in 1806 gave it to Maréchal Berthier (later Prince de Wagram). In 1821, after the death of Berthier, Chambord was acquired by national subscription for Henri de Bourbon, the son of the Duc de Berry. His successors held Austrian nationality; consequently the château was sequestered during World War One. The estate was eventually purchased by the French state in 1930, although the château and park had been classified as a historical monument since 1840.

CHAMBORD THROUGH THE CENTURIES. The château's design, with its massive corner towers and spiral staircases, was already outdated by the conclusion of François I's reign, and variations around the theme of the central keep had done nothing to remedy this. Nevertheless, as the 17th-century historiographer Félibien des Avaux noted: "neither Gothic nor modern", Chambord "can be regarded as one of the most magnificent buildings erected by the kings of France". This remains true of the keep today, with the spirals of its magnificent openwork staircase, its soaring lantern tower, and the matching stylistic features elaborated on the four sections of terracing by Antoine de Troyes. Chambord represented a new phase of architectural development, in which the flamboyant superstructures of the 14th-century châteaux were reworked using the picturesque stylistic language of the early Renaissance.

165

**THE MEDALLIONS
AT VILLESAVIN**
On the wall of the
main court are terracotta
medallions from Bologna,
depicting six Roman emperors.

CHÂTEAU DE VILLESAVIN

● *69 (P5*

**CHÂTEAU DE
VILLESAVIN**
This horseshoe-
shaped château
consists of a single
story, in the style of
Italian villas, and is
crowned by high slate
roofs. Restoration
work has progressed
steadily. The moat
was restored around
ten years ago, and
the bridge rebuilt
using old stone; the
original mullions of
the windows have
also gradually been
restored.

CONVENIENT FOR WORKING AT CHAMBORD. In 1527 Jean Le
Breton, one of the superintendents in charge of work on
Chambord, decided to build himself a relatively modest
residence near the site of the new palace. Le Breton
decorated Villesavin in a simple style, but to the highest
standards of workmanship, using the Florentine sculptors wh
were working on Chambord. The dormer
windows are beautifully carved, some
depicting humorous characters or the
Muses (music, comedy, and so on). A tall
white Carrara marble basin dating from
the 16th century still stands in the main
court. The chapel was decorated with
frescos (1530), which were marked with a
black band, as a sign of mourning, when
Le Breton died. The interior is rustic in
character, with some impressive fireplaces (including a
kitchen fireplace with an enormous roasting jack). At either
end of the château are two charming closed courtyards that
emphasize its intimate atmosphere. In one of them, under th
shade of an old lime tree, there is a collection of horse-draw
carriages, including some intriguing items, among them an
18th-century Central European carriage that was drawn by
eight horses, a Second Empire *coupe de ville* magnificently
lined with Russian leather, and children's donkey carts. With
its sumptuously ornamented dormer windows, its Ionic
pilasters and its carved medallions, the Château de Villesavin
displays a clear kinship with Chambord ▲ *158*. However, this
long, low, Italian-style country villa has its own special charm
which owes a good deal both to its early-Renaissance
architecture and to its romantic and somewhat mysterious
forest setting. Its distinctive, homely atmosphere sets it apart
from the "chateau museums" to be seen elsewhere.

RICHES FROM PIGEON DROPPINGS. The château has a
dovecote ● *80* with a revolving ladder (above), still in perfect
condition. Pigeon droppings were a good source of income at
a time when chemical fertilizers were not available. The
dovecote is made of local stone and has 1,500 nesting holes.
The number of nesting holes was an indicator of a landlord's
wealth, each hole representing an *arpent* (about an acre).
The landlord must therefore have owned some 1,500 acres
here, as well as a further 1,000 acres represented by a second
dovecote on a farm. On the garden side of the château a
wide lawn runs down to the Beuvron river; in the
nearby meadows you can see peaceful Poitou
donkeys, an endangered species which the
proprietor's son is keen to preserve. In the
distance the Forest of Boulogne leads
toward Chambord.

BUST OF FRANÇOIS I
The wall that joins
the left-hand pavilion
of the Château de
Villesavin to the
main building, at the
far end of the main
court, has a gateway
surmounted by a bust
of François I dating
from the late 18th or
early 19th century.

CHÂTEAU DE DE BEAUREGARD (M5)

The Château de Beauregard is set in the peaceful Beuvron valley, hidden way at the heart of the Forest of Russy, on the edge of the winegrowing area of the Sologne. Fields stretch out around it: an unusual sight in the highly populated region around Blois.

AN APPROPRIATE NAME. The château was built in the mid 16th century and extended in the 17th century; it was never intended as a ceremonial palace. It was built by Jean du Thier, Secretary of State to Henri II, who was not aiming to compete with his neighbors at Chaumont or Chambord. He was a man of taste, a friend of the poet Ronsard, and he made this an elegant residence, built in a simple style with refined ornamentation. We do not

The Cabinet des Grelots at Beauregard.

Aerial view of the Château de Beauregard.

know the name of the architect who designed the sober façades and the arcaded gallery of the main building. However, we do know that Niccolo dell'Abbate was responsible for the decorations in the chapel (sadly destroyed in the 19th century), and that the cabinetmaker Scibec de Carpi created the famous Cabinet des Grelots. This small paneled room is named after the *grelots* (bells) that appear as motifs on the coffered ceiling and in between the finely carved wall panels. Bells featured in du Thier's coat of arms, which explains this unusual choice. Paintings illustrate the owner's various pursuits: music, silversmithing, sculpture and games. In the 17th century Beauregard was acquired by the Ardier family, another family of politicians. Paul Ardier retired to this peaceful retreat after serving three kings (Henri III, Henri IV and Louis XIII) and added what is still the showpiece of the château: the gallery of historical portraits ▲ 168.

Part of the numerous collections at Beauregard, this clock can be seen in one of the rooms on the ground floor.

A DELIGHTFUL SETTING. The Château de Beauregard was built on a wooded hill beside the Beuvron, a slow-moving river popular with anglers; it stands in a large, well laid-out park. The current owners, who inhabit part of the building, have planted oaks and cedars. Irises, lupins, foxgloves and other flowering plants have been arranged in the old kitchen garden, delighting visitors with a riot of color. Each spring a plant fair is held in the grounds, which attracts both amateur and professional gardeners. In addition an annual Book Fair is held in the 17th-century outbuildings behind the château, drawing publishers and booksellers from the entire region.

167

The Galerie des Illustres is the showpiece of the Château de Beauregard, and a remarkable example of a genre that was very much in vogue in the 17th century: the gallery of historical portraits. It was devised by Paul Ardier, the state councillor who owned Beauregard at the time, and it contains no less than 327 portraits of people who played an important role in French court or political life over three centuries, from Philippe de Valois to Louis XIII. The three rows of pictures form a pageant of kings, ministers and courtesans, including foreigners who had an influence on the destiny of the French kingdom. There are some amusing surprises: for example, Catherine de Médicis is placed next to François II and Charles IX (she was regent during the latter's minority) and not with her husband Henri II, who is next to his mistress Diane de Poitiers.

A MASTERPIECE REVEALED
It was discovered that the portrait of Paolo di Venetia has Henri de Navarre's eyes. The underlying portrait is to be restored.

RESTORATION OF THE PORTRAITS
Around one hundred portraits in the Galerie des Illustres have already been restored. This demanding, time-consuming project is due to be completed in the year 2000. The restorers aim is to achieve both historical truth and visual quality. Underneath the portrait of the Cour of Fuentes (a mediocre work dating from the 19th century), X-rays have revealed the face of woman who may well be Catherine de Bourbon. Historians have yet to deliver their verdict; s for the time being she remains the "Unknown Lady of Beauregard".

SEBASTIEN · ROY · DE · PORTVGAL ·

CHEVERNY ● *70* (M5

Cheverny's pure Louis XIII architecture is in
contrast to the many Renaissance châteaux of the
Blois region. Completed in 1634, it was built on the
site of a medieval castle at the edge of a somber
forest; its dazzling white, symmetrical façade stands
out boldly against the green carpet of the lawn.
AN UNFORTUNATE JOKE. It was the second wife of
Henri Hurault who supervised the building of the
château: its imposing white mass is relieved by
ornamental niches, balustrades and statues,
creating an impression of
feminine elegance. The son
of Count Philippe Hurault,
he was the governor of
Blois and a faithful servant
of Henri IV. The château
was built following a tragic
episode, recorded by one of
Cheverny's owners in the
18th century. A domineering
character, Hurault had shut
his young wife away in the
old fortified castle at
Cheverny. One day, as a
joke for the amusement of
his courtiers, Henri IV made
the cuckold's sign behind
Hurault's head. Hurault
saw the gesture in a mirror.
Furious, he leapt on his
horse and galloped straight
to Cheverny, where he
discovered his wife in the
arms of a page. He drew his
dagger and killed her lover,
then offered his unfaithful
wife the choice of dying by
poison or the sword. An
hour later she was dead.

The intricate carvings
on the main staircase
(above) feature fruit
and plant motifs.

Detail of the ceiling
in the guardroom
(below).

Henri IV was not at all pleased with this act of rough justice,
and sentenced Hurault to "house arrest" on his estate.
A NEW CHÂTEAU. Hurault's second wife was a more docile
and obedient woman. Doubtless wishing to eradicate the
memory of the unhappy episode, Hurault demolished the
old Cheverny and gave his second wife free rein to build a
new residence in the modern style. The increasing power of
the monarchy had made the old style of fortifications
superfluous. Cheverny was beautifully decorated by the
architect-sculptor Boyer and the famous Blois painter
Jean Mosnier; most of the 17th-century decorations survive
today. The Grande Mademoiselle (daughter of Gaston
d'Orléans ▲ *145*), who was an honored guest here, wrote:
"Nothing is more elegant, more comfortable and more
splendid than the interior." The elegantly decorated main
staircase with straight banisters is reminiscent of the
examples at Chenonceaux ▲ *218* and Azay-le-Rideau ▲ *234*.
Cheverny is exceptional in that the rooms display their

The imposing white façade of
the Château de Cheverny, facing
onto the main court.

iginal furniture: this is highly unusual among the
âteaux of the Loire, which are mainly furnished with
quisitions from museums and later collections. To the
ght of the staircase is the dining hall, hung with Cordoba
ather. This room was restored at the end of the 19th
ntury but has retained most of its original decoration,
rtly produced by Mosnier, who was born in Blois in 1600.
e produced fifteen of the thirty-four painted panels that
corate this room, illustrating fantastic episodes from *Don
uixote* (which Cervantes completed in 1615). The SALLE
ARMES (guardroom) on the second story possesses a
ench-style ceiling made of wooden panels with colored
intings including a variety of motifs (cherubs, mythological
d symbolic subjects). The Chambre du Roi (King's
droom) is even more opulently decorated: the tapestries,
signed by Simon Vouet, illustrate the adventures of
ysses, as do the paintings on the coffered ceiling and the
onumental fireplace; all these works date from the 17th
ntury. Returning to the ground floor, we reach the
RAND SALON with its magnificent furniture and a portrait
the Countess of Cheverny by Nicolas Mignard (1606–68).
e château is beautifully preserved, on both the interior
d the exterior; for this we are largely indebted to the
vner in the early part of this century, who opened the
ilding to the public in 1922. This was a bold idea at the
ne and attracted much criticism, though in later years it
s widely admired.

ODEL FOR MARLINSPIKE. Around forty years ago Hergé, the
eator of Tintin, was on holiday in the region. One day he
ok the road from Contres to Cheverny, formerly the main
proach road to the château, and came across the
ain building without seeing the two corner pavilions,
iich were concealed by trees. Hergé was captivated by
heverny's classical style of architecture and asked
rmission from the owner to make this the model for
arlinspike, the famous castle of Captain Haddock. He
so used Cheverny's great staircase, which the irascible but
teable captain tumbles down so
equently in *The Castafiore Emerald*;
d the guardroom, which figures in
ie *Secret of The Unicorn*
id *Red Rackham's
easure*.

**A GHASTLY
SURPRISE . . .**
Captain Haddock:
"Thundering
typhoons! Am I
dreaming! It's
Marlinspike Hall! . . .
Marlinspike, my
family estate! It's
impossible! . . ."
Tintin: "Well,
captain, it's quite
simple: your family
castle is for sale? . . .
you must buy it
back!"
*Red Rackham's
Treasure*

171

▲ CHÂTEAUX OF THE SOLOGNE WINE REGION

This curious figure is one of many stone carvings to be seen at the Château de Troussay.

En Sologne. — Equipage de Cheverny. — Bois de Cheverny - Le Rendez-vous

The décor of the Chambre du Roi (above); and the Cheverny Hunt.

"I followed the invitation of a little caretaker, neat and proper, who sat with two children taking a breath of fresh air by the door of her cottage; she told me to continue a little further and then to turn to the right. I followed her instructions to the letter and as I turned I saw a house with the charm of an old fairy-tale manor.... A charming and elegant residence overlooked a green lawn, beds of flowers and groups of trees.**"**

Henry James

A FAMILY BUSINESS. Cheverny is unusual among the châteaux of the Loire Valley in that it has belonged to the same family for five centuries. The descendants of the Hurault family, who still live in part of the château, are keenly aware of the importance of their historical heritage and are constantly developing new activities to make Cheverny better known. A highly sophisticated *son et lumière* performance is held at the château each summer, with six hundred actors and many special effects, splendidly re-creating the history of France as seen through the fortunes of the Hurault family.

A REPUTATION FOR HUNTING ● 52. The famous pack of hounds (of the Anglo-Poitevins breed) is still kept in the kennels next to the Salle des Trophées, which holds some two thousand stag's antlers and hunting trophies belonging to the Cheverny Hunt. During the season, hunts are held in the neighboring forests. The Forest of Cheverny is an integral part of the estate and is managed with great professionalism. An 18-hole golf course, complete with copses and lakes, was recently built alongside the forest.

LOCAL WINES ■ 30. The flat countryside of this part of the Sologne is scattered with vineyards, as well as forests. Winegrowers of the twenty-three parishes around Cheverny produce white and red wines that are classified as VDQS (Vins Délimités de Qualité Supérieure). The red wines are light, fruity and pleasant to drink. The whites are highly prized throughout the region; dry and fruity, they are made from Sauvignon, Chardonnay and Romorantin grapes (Romorantin being a local variety).

CHURCH OF ST-ÉTIENNE. This 12th-century church stands opposite the entrance to the château. It is notable for having retained its *caquetoir*, a lovely wooden porch where churchgoers could gather for a chat (*caqueter*) after mass, sheltered from the weather. The porch was also used as a meeting place (for collecting tithes, for auctions, and so on). It is arguably one of the most beautiful porches in France.

CHÂTEAU DE TROUSSAY   (M5)

The elegant Renaissance manor house of Troussay is tucked away among ancient trees, in the midst of vineyards and woodland, two miles from Cheverny. This small château with charming outbuildings gives a good idea of what the small estates of the Sologne must have looked like in the past.

DIMINUTIVE CHATEAU. Troussay has a tall main building, framed by towers with diamond-shaped bricks, and large outbuildings; the superlative quality of its decoration is comparable with the great châteaux of the Loire. Originally a modest 15th-century manor house, it was renovated for the first time in the 16th century. In the 19th century the historian Louis de La Saussaye inherited the house from his uncle Christophe de Réméon; he found it in a very dilapidated state, as it had stood unoccupied since the Revolution. He turned to his friend the architect Jules de la Morandière and then had the idea, not common at that time, of decorating the building (on both the exterior and the interior) with ornaments from historical buildings in the region that were falling into ruins. In this way he was able to save them from destruction and relocate them in an appropriate context. Thus the capital on the left of the entrance from the Château de Bury, and the porcupine on the northern façade from the former residence of Hurault de Cheverny at Blois. The collection of early-16th-century stained-glass windows once adorned the Hôtel Sardini ▲ *141* and the Hôtel de Guise at Blois ▲ *138*. The carved wooden door of the Oratory from the same period, which is the pride of Troussay, came from the Château de Bury. This door was sent to Japan in 1972 for an exhibition on the Loire Valley. Original features of Troussay's decoration that have survived include Louis XII floor tiles on the ground floor and splendid woodcarvings on the doors and windows. The period furniture (16th to 18th century) and old paneling give the château a homely atmosphere. Troussay also benefits from its delightful woodland setting. It is still inhabited, and has changed hands only twice since the 15th century.

RECONSTRUCTION OF TRADITIONAL SOLOGNE LIFE. A little museum of Sologne country life has been set up in the authentic setting of the old outbuildings that were at one time the hub of Troussay's economic activities. Old domestic and agricultural objects are exhibited in the beautiful beamed rooms, some of which are used today for exhibitions and receptions.

CHATEAU DE ROUJOUX. The "magic castle" of Roujoux, situated between Cheverny and Fougères, on the road to Contres, cannot rival its royal neighbors. However, this attractive Louis XIII style residence has been open to visitors since 1986, and makes a pleasant stop, with its park and water-filled moats. The owners have set up a series of historical displays in the rooms, which are almost empty of furniture. Set into the recesses of the library are twenty-seven tapet scenes recounting the history of Roujoux since the arrival of the Vikings.

CHATEAU DE TROUSSAY
Louis de La Saussaye, rector of the Académie de Lyon, brought this old manor house back to life.

DECORATIONS OF THE CHATEAU DE TROUSSAY
The entrance door of the house is framed by two capitals: the capital on the left comes from the former Château de Bury, as does the door of the Oratory.

▲ THE SOLOGNE

For a long time the Sologne region was viewed as a barren land of little commercial value: its acid soils, which were often waterlogged, were ill-suited for agriculture. In the 18th century sheep-rearing became a widespread practice, and the moors used for pasture were extended at the expense of woods and fields. Drainage of the ground was neglected creating unhealthy marshes. The region experienced a recovery under the Second Empire, when drainage, reforestation and the development of agriculture created the basis of its present-day appearance.

THE SOLOGNE AREA
This small region of the old kingdom of France is situated between three départements: Loir-et-Cher, Cher and Loiret. Each of the different areas within it has its own distinctive character: the winegrowing area to the west, lakes in the center, and the Berry district further to the east.

REDEVELOPMENT OF THE SOLOGNE
During the time of the Second Empire Napoleon III did a good deal to revitalize the Sologne. Trees were planted and experimental farms established as part of the rehabilitation program. The emperor's interest in the region attracted wealthy industrialists to come and live here.

THE FOREST ■ *24*
Half of the Sologne is
covered by forest,
which is still the
major feature of the
landscape. It consists
of oaks and birches,
as well as many
varieties of conifer
(including maritime
pines, Scots pine and
larch).

MOORLAND LAKES
These lakes were mostly
created at the instigation
of religious communities,
on marshes left by the
great land-clearing of the
Middle Ages. The
moorland here is
covered with a mixture
of gorse and broom.

SOLOGNE MUTTON ■ *28*
The meat of the region was
once highly prized by Parisian
butchers and was
distinguished by its
own appellation.
Today only a
handful of sheep
farmers
continue to
breed the
local stock.

Legend has it that a lord of Fougères once shut his wife up in one of the towers of the château, before killing her out of jealousy...

CHATEAU DE FOUGÈRES-SUR-BIEVRE. Its charm derives from the picturesque buildings around the main courtyard: towers and turrets, dwellings, the curtain wall, a pavilion and gallery, and a feudal chapel.

RENAISSANCE DECORATION OF FOUGÈRES. The carved decoration of the two Louis XI style accolade doors is of very high quality: on the lintel of the first, Saint Michael and three angels, carved in an elegant, slightly mannered style, guide the visitor through the room toward the chapel; the two warriors on the second represent the defense of the postern guarding the entrance to the staircase. This is the legacy of Pierre de Refuge at Fougères.

FOUGÈRES-SUR-BIÈVRE (LM

It is a surprise on arriving in this small village to discover a massive fortress in the medieval style that is generally overlooked in traditional tours of the châteaux of the Loire. The castle, an archetypal child's image of a fortress, is solidl planted in the middle of the village.

A FORTIFIED CASTLE BUILT IN THE RENAISSANCE ★. Contrary to all appearances, Fougères does not da from medieval times. It was erected on the site of a building destroyed earlier in the 15th century. Around 1475 Pierre de Refuge, treasurer of Louis XI and owner of the estate, obtained permission from the king "to rebuild the Château de Fougères as a fortress". As a result, it is the only Renaissance château of the Loire Valley to have a fortified keep complet with drawbridge, machicolations and loopholes – built some twenty years after the fortifications at the Château de Blois had been replaced with the more cheerful style of decoratio suited to a place of residence. In the 16th century the arrow slits of this little fortress were replaced by windows with carved pediments and the moats were filled in, somewhat softening the austere appearance of the façades. The buildin was converted into a mill in the 19th century, a process whic took years to complete, and the Bièvre was diverted to pass below the chapel. Later Fougères became a hostel for destitute families, before being acquired by the state in 1932 **A SHOWPIECE OF LOCAL BUILDING.** Although from the outsid the château retains its fortresslike appearance, the rounded lines of its interior court give it a distinct charm. A low galle in the Flamboyant style is surmounted by windows with Italianate decoration, which may well have been copied fron the Charles d'Orléans gallery at Blois. The tall slate roofs, th intimate scale of the courtyard and the simplicity of the déco combine to create a charming and authentic impression of rusticity. Local builders and craftsmen were employed for th structural work and the decoration, making Fougères a showpiece of their skills. The rooms are large, bare of furniture, with fine beams. The château fell into oblivion for many years; steps are now being taken to make it better known.

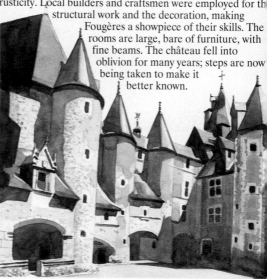

"YES, THIS IS AN ADMIRABLE SIGHT, BUT HOW MUCH
I PREFER MY GUTTER IN THE RUE DU BAC . . ."

MADAME DE STAEL, WHO SPENT THE SUMMER OF 1810
AT CHAUMONT, HAVING BEEN EXILED FROM PARIS BY NAPOLÉON

HAUMONT-SUR-LOIRE ★   ● 67 (L5)

e Counts of Blois built a castle on their
rritory in the 10th century, to ward off
vaders from Anjou. It stood on a steep hill
th a striking view over the Loire.

E CASTLE OF THE AMBOISE FAMILY. The
nboise family acquired the castle through
arriage and kept it for five centuries, during
ich time it suffered many changes of
rtune. In 1465 Louis XI had it razed to the
ound, to punish its owners for having joined
e league of discontented nobles led by
arles the Bold. Pierre and Charles I of
nboise soon returned to favor and began to
build their castle, but they only had time to
-erect the north and west wings. The west
ng still stands today, with a corner tower
ich could serve as a defensive retreat. The
rth wing housed a great hall overlooking
e river. In the late 15th century Charles II (son of Charles I)
anned to complete the building. However, he was called to
ly by the high offices entrusted to him by Louis XII, and
legated supervision of the building work to his uncle, the
tron and minister Georges I of Amboise. The south and
st wings were built at this stage, but sadly they have been
eatly altered since and robbed of their main attraction: the
o great overhanging cornices that ran along the interior
çade of the new building, displaying the full repertoire of
alian decorative motifs. The great cornice of the François I
ing at Blois was a pale reflection of these bold innovations.

E PRICE OF REVENGE. In 1560 Catherine de Médicis forced
ane de Poitiers (formerly the mistress of her husband,
nri II, who had died a year before) to exchange
enonceaux ▲ 218 for Chaumont, which she did not even
gally own yet. And what a pity! The deaths of Georges
Amboise and his nephew, in 1510 and 1511 respectively, had
ft the upper parts of the building unfinished; the task of
storation fell to Diane, who made a brave effort but died in
66 before the work could be completed.

E LE RAY ERA. After a variety of modifications, the château
tered another decisive period when Jacques Donatien Le
ay acquired it in 1750: Le Ray was famous for trading with
e New World and for his business deals with Benjamin
anklin. He had the north wing demolished, along
th the beautiful cornices that joined onto it, in
der to open up the view from the courtyard over
e river valley. He also destroyed the great
aircase, which was doubtless in poor condition, to
it the elevation of the south wing; he completed
e latter by adding a portico and the upper story
at had been missing since the 16th century. The
iling of the chapel was also the work of this prudent
sinessman, who created a small factory for pottery and
ass in the old outbuildings. He hired the services of the
alian artist Giambattista Nini (1717–86) to produce
edallions here. The château fell under threat of demolition
ring the Revolution, and some of the coats of arms were
utilated. After this, peace returned.

DIANE DE POITIERS
Catherine de
Médicis took
her time to
finalize the forced
"exchange" of
Chaumont for
Chenonceaux
and to pay the
death duties due
to the exchequer
at Blois. As a
result, Diane was
not able to take
possession of
her new
home
until
1562.

**NINI'S
MEDALLIONS**
Some of Nini's
terracotta
medallions
depicting famous
figures of the age
can still be seen
at the château.

THE 19TH CENTURY: RESTORATIONS AND GREAT FORTUNES.

Restoration work began in 1833, and took a new turn when Viscount Walsh enlisted the devoted collaboration of the architect La Morandière. The latter, in a first phase of restoration work completed in 1852, rebuilt the great staircase and modified the far end of the west wing in the "troubadour style", to the complete satisfaction of his client. However, the Commission for Historical Monuments was far less happy with his work and Prosper Mérimée, the commission's inspector, had to lay down strict guidelines for the restoration of the south wing. The south wing was altered again after 1875, the year in which the château was acquired by Marie-Charlotte Say, heiress of a huge sugar fortune and later the wife of Prince Amédée de Broglie. This couple entrusted the building to one of the most renowned architects of the era,

Paul-Ernest Sanson. Sanson rebuilt one of the two cornices of the east wing in an inspired neo-Renaissance style, as well as its covered walkway. The château became the setting for extravagant festivities and huge receptions to which the leading figures of the day were invited. There were some surprises: a maharaja, for example, brought an elephant as a gift, a charming if cumbersome creature answering to the name of Miss Peggy. The threat of financial ruin put an end to the festivities, but even cutbacks and economies were not enough to avert disaster.

LATEST DEVELOPMENTS.

In 1938 the state bought the building (by which stage some of the furniture had been sold off), and maintenance work was restarted on a small scale. In 1947 to 1948 several rooms were subjected to "derestoration" work, which had been planned as early as 1943: all or some of the 19th-century decorations were removed in favor of a more austere effect. Sanson's modifications were accorded no better treatment than those of La Morandière: in 1991 his alterations to the ground floor of the east wing were eradicated. An interesting feature, unconnected with the château itself, is the splendid new garden opened in 1992, which is the setting for an international garden festival.

An old well in the châteâu courtyard.

"The château is built on the highest hill of the river bank, surrounding the broad summit with its high walls and its enormous towers; tall slate bell towers rise above them, giving the building that religious air common to all our old châteaux . . . "
Alfred de Vigny,
Cinq-Mars

Paul-Ernest Sanson, an architect popular with the aristocracy and the political and financial élite, was entrusted with the refurbishment of the château at the end of the 19th century: he installed modern conveniences and refurbished both the interior and the exterior, creating magnificent stables and redesigning the castle approaches.

AMBOISE

HISTORY OF THE TOWN, *182*
THE CHÂTEAU, *184*
CLOS-LUCÉ, *185*
LEONARDO DA VINCI, *186*
TOWARD THE
CHURCH OF ST-DENIS, *188*
ÎLE D'OR, *190*
THE CHANTELOUP PAGODA, *191*
AROUND AMBOISE, *192*

▲ Amboise

1. Château
2. Clos-Lucé
3. Hôtel de ville
4. Greniers de César
5. Church of St-Florentin
6. Postal Museum
7. Abbey Church of Saint-Denis
8. Max-Ernst Fountain
9. Île d'Or

DEATH OF CHARLES VIII
Charles VIII hit his head against a door frame. During the evening of the same day, he suddenly fainted, and a few hours later died, at the age of twenty-eight, without leaving a male heir.

EARLY SETTLEMENTS. Amboise was the site of several fortified settlements over the course of the centuries. For over five centuries the Turones (one of the peoples of Gaul) had their capital on the Éperon des Châtelliers, the spur of land on which the château stands today. Their *oppidum* (citadel) was followed by a Merovingian fort, which may have dated from the late Roman Empire (3rd and 4th centuries AD). The first reference to the citadel of Ambatiacum dates from the 6th century, in the writings of Gregory of Tours. This fortress appears to have been destroyed three times during Norman invasions of Touraine, and then rebuilt by Ingelger, Count of Anjou. It was one of the sites fought over by the armies of Blois and Anjou. Foulques Nerra built the Collegiate Church of St-Florentin (demolished in the 19th century) here around 1030.

ROYAL BUILDING PROJECTS. When the Hundred Years' War forced the French kings to leave the banks of the Seine for the Loire, the French court relocated to Amboise. Charles VII confiscated the fortress from Louis d'Amboise in 1434, extended it and added the St-Michel Chapel to the Church of St-Florentin in 1446. He gave the town special privileges and exemptions. Louis XI moved his family to Amboise and rebuilt the château, adding a new wing to the south. He was particularly fond of this place, of which he said: "The estate of Amboise is large and beautiful, in a beautiful and fertile region." Charles VIII, born at Amboise in 1470, built the château's two enormous feudal towers: the Tour des Minimes and the Tour Hurtault. He brought back a score of Humanists from his Italian campaigns, including artists and craftsmen such as Pacello di Mercogliano ▲ *188*, who designed terraced gardens for him between the palace and the dry moat.

THE SALAMANDER
This was the emblem of Charles VIII and of his cousin Charles d'Angoulême, who passed it on to his

son, François I. Only their mottos, which generally accompanied the emblem, differed.

THE EARLY RENAISSANCE. When Charles VIII died, Louis XII moved his cousin Louise de Savoie to Amboise along with her children: François d'Angoulême (later François I) and his sister (later Marguerite de Navarre), who was one of the most learned women of her time. Building work continued on the north wings and the Tour Hurtault, and the gardens were extended. François I was especially fond of this place, where he had grown up: "We lived and were raised for most of the time at Amboise, a place for which we have always had particular love and affection." After 1530, when his mother died, he gradually deserted Amboise in favor of Chambord and Fontainebleau.

> **"WE AND OUR PREDECESSORS HAVE HAD PLEASURE AND AMUSEMENT AT THE MAGNIFICENT CASTLE BUILT IN THIS TOWN."**
>
> FRANÇOIS I

THE AMBOISE CONSPIRACY. Henri and Catherine de Médicis, who moved into the château in 1551, sought to restore the French court to its former splendor and make it a center for all the arts. In 1560, during the brief reign of their son, the young François II (below, as a child), Amboise was the setting for a tragic episode. A Protestant gentleman named La Renaudie in the pay of the Prince de Condé gathered together a group of Reformers. They planned to demand the freedom to practice their faith from the king (then staying at Blois) and probably also to neutralize the Duc de Guise, their most virulent adversary. The plot was betrayed; the king took refuge at Amboise (a castle that was easier to defend) and organized its repression. The conspirators were killed as they arrived – either decapitated, drowned, or hanged from the balcony of the château. These tragic events cast a shadow over Amboise's prestige.

DECLINE. Louis XIII converted the château into a royal prison after confiscating it from his brother, the unruly Gaston d'Orléans ▲ *145*. The financier Nicolas Fouquet and the libertine Duc de Lauzun were held prisoner here under Louis XIV. Later Napoleon gave the château to Senator Pierre-Roger Ducos, who had most of it demolished between 1806 and 1810 since no funds were provided for its maintenance. The future Louis-Philippe inherited Amboise in 1821, and made modifications to turn it into a summer residence. After the 1848 revolution the estate was confiscated again. The first serious restoration work (though carried out with some license) was started at the end of the 19th century by Victor and Gabriel Ruprich-Robert, the official architects responsible for historical monuments.

TODAY. Since 1974 the château has been managed by the Fondation St-Louis, whose president is the Comte de Paris; it is visited by many tourists. The town is pursuing a development strategy to make the most of its historical heritage and attract new businesses to the area.

TERRIBLE REPRESSION
The violence of the punishment exacted on the Amboise conspirators had a profound effect on contemporaries. Agrippa d'Aubigné (1552–1630) was scarred for life by the memory. He was traveling to Paris with his father, from his home of Saintonge, and arrived in Amboise the day after the tragedy. His horrified father made him swear to avenge the Huguenots who had been massacred.

ABD-EL-KADER (1808–83)
This Arab Emir led the resistance to France's invasion of Algeria between 1832 and 1847. After many defeats, he yielded in 1847. He and his followers were held at Amboise from 1848 to 1852, when Napoleon III released him (below).

THE CHÂTEAU

The best view of the château is from the Île d'Or ▲ *190*. The entrance is approached via a covered ramp to the southwest of the rampart.

TOUR DES MINIMES. This enormous circular tower to the north of the château was built at the end of the 15th century. It was named after the Minims' convent that stood between the tower and the Loire. The tower has a ramp for horses and carriages, which winds around its central core leading up to the terraces.

TOUR HURTAULT. This has survived intact, without restoration. It is surmounted by a walkway and a conical roof, and has an entrance ramp. The interior decorations are clearly Italianate.

CHARLES VIII WING. The façade of this wing facing the Loire has a great gallery with seven arcades, seven high windows and a roof with dormer windows, which have been restored. The building stands above a basement of defenses which were freely "improved" by 19th-century architects. The carvings in the Salle des États were completely revamped by the Ruprich Roberts, in Gothic style with early-Renaissance features. It is in this room that judgment was passed on the Protestants who took part in the Amboise conspiracy.

LOUIS XII/FRANÇOIS I WING. This wing has four stories facing the courtyard and three facing the garden. Its elegant early-Renaissance décor is typical of the first part of François I's reign.

CHAPEL OF ST-HUBERT ● *60*. The chapel originally opened on to the galleries of a building that has now disappeared. Built between 1491 and 1496 (the date of Charles VIII's return from Italy), it stands on a forebuilding, which gives its chevet particular prominence, and has magnificent lacework stone ornamentation on two levels. The lintel is decorated with bas-reliefs depicting the legend of Saint Christopher patron saint of travelers) and Saint Hubert (patron saint of hunters). Leonardo da Vinci ▲ *162* is now buried here.

THE PORTE DES LIONS. This gate stands at the eastern end of the gardens; its name was taken from an earlier one surmounted by two statues of lions, probably alluding to the menagerie which Charles VIII kept in the dry moat.

CLOS-LUCÉ

This manor house was known as the Château de Cloux until the 17th century. Built of brick and stone, in 1477, it consists of two main buildings standing at right angles to each other on either side of an octagonal tower.

LEONARDO DA VINCI AT CLOS-LUCÉ. The Italian genius moved to the Château de Cloux in the spring of 1516, at the invitation of François I, and spent the last three years of his life here. The king made extensive funds available to him, "so that he can achieve all that his genius is capable of producing". Despite suffering from malaria, Leonardo continued to work hard, took part in organizing court festivities and devoted himself to projects relating to the region's hydrography (connecting the royal residences by water, diverting the course of the Loire and draining the marshes of the Sologne). He advised on a royal residence that was to be built at Romorantin, and the initial ideas for Chambord have been attributed to him. He died at Clos-Lucé on May 2, 1519 at the age of sixty-seven and was buried in the château's Collegiate Church of St-Florentin. After the Revolution the manor house became a carpet factory, and another wing was added. Today it houses a museum devoted to Leonardo.

CHÂTEAU-GAILLARD. This house, below Clos-Lucé, was built in the 15th century for Pacello di Mercogliano, who introduced Italian garden design to France. Charles VIII required flowers for his terraces and fruit for his table – and Mercogliano created a special garden and greenhouses for the purpose. The first orange trees in France are said to have been planted here.

View of the château from the west.

THE LEONARDO DA VINCI MUSEUM Clos-Lucé is now a museum displaying models of some forty machines ▲ *186* designed by Leonardo. There is a video presentation on his life and work; and his bedroom, with its lovely hooded fireplace, has been restored to its original state. The walls of the chapel, which was Anne de Bretagne's oratory, still have traces of frescos painted by Leonardo or one of his pupils.

185

Leonardo produced a series of sketches and studies of war machines – among them firearms with several barrels (left), projectiles, grapeshot missiles, huge crossbows, and canons with multiple openings – anticipating the designs and devices that make up the war arsenal of our own time.

"Leonardo was truly admirable and divine . . . Nature had favored him to such a degree that he achieved excellence in all the areas to which he directed his mind, his thought and his soul. To everything he did he gave a mark of sensitivity, brilliance, goodness, beauty and grace as has never been equalled."

Giorgio Vasari

THE BURNING DESIRE TO FLY
Models of a parachute plane and helical screw produced by IBM from Da Vinci's many drawings.

THE LAST HOURS OF A GENIUS "MUCH PRAISED AND MUCH CRITICIZED"
Leonardo's amazing ideas, which had not found favor in Rome, fascinated François I and his court. "Vasari has him say, in that famous description of his glorious death tenderly watched over by the king (below), that it pains him to have 'offended God and men by not working in art as he should have done'. When you look for the artist you find a scientist, a 'thinker'; when you look for the painter you find an architect, a sculptor, an engineer; and when you finally do find the painter he is held back by the ideas and experiments of the theorist."

André Chastel

LEONARDO'S "SERENE AND SEVERE FEATURES"
This red pencil drawing, universally attributed to Leonardo, is most probably a self-portrait. Da Vinci was sixty years old at the time of the drawing, which dates from 1512.

PROJECT FOR AN "AERIAL SCREW", ANCESTOR OF THE HELICOPTER. "I thought that it was possible . . . to build a screw that would lift itself into the air as it turned . . . but how to keep this flying spinning top fixed to its support, and to the mechanism below?"
Ralph Steadman

Mary Magdalene, in the
Church of St-Denis.

This view from the
château (below)
illustrates Flaubert's
description: "The
Château d'Amboise
dominates the town,
which seems to be
thrown at its feet like
small pebbles around
the base of a rock . . ."

TOWARD THE CHURCH OF ST-DENIS

TOUR DE L'HORLOGE. The narrow Rue Mably with its old
stone markers leads to the Tour de l'Horloge, formerly the
Porte de l'Amasse, one of six gateways in the medieval
rampart which protected the town. The early wooden portal
was demolished under Louis XI, then replaced in 1497 by the
present stone clock tower. It has two stories, with mullioned
windows on one side, and is crowned with a lantern. In a
niche under the porch
stood a 14th-century
Virgin and Child in
colored terracotta, now in
the Musée de l'Hôtel
de Ville (opposite, right).

MUSÉE DE LA POSTE. This
museum is housed in the
Hôtel Joyeuse, once the
home of the Italian artist
Fra Giovanni Giocondo,
who was brought to
Amboise by Charles VIII.
Both the house and the
street bear his name,
Giocondo being translated into French as "Joyeuse". The
house, which has two small Louis XIII pavilions, features a
beautiful carved cornice from the 15th century. The garden,
laid out on three terraces, was restored in 1900: it aims to
reproduce the garden designed for the house by Pacello di
Mercogliano ▲ 182. At the center water pours into an
ornamental lake from an Italian-style basin. The museum
retraces the history of the postal service from its beginnings,
with models of inn signs, stagecoaches, old trunks, uniforms
and coachmen's gear.

**THE DROWNED
WOMAN OF THE
CHURCH OF ST-DENIS**
This recumbent
figure of a woman's
naked and decaying
corpse is strikingly
realistic: some say it
depicts Marie Babou,
the mistress of
François I who
drowned herself in
the Loire.

MAISON ENCHANTÉE. Around two hundred animated figures
are used here to create some twenty tableaux, including
historical scenes, comic ones and fantasy.

ABBEY CHURCH OF ST-DENIS ★. This church was begun in
1107, apparently to replace one founded by Saint Martin ▲ 206
on the site of a former pagan temple. The choir, which has a
polygonal chevet, and the transept both date from this time;
the nave and two side aisles were added thirty years later.
The two vaults between the bays of the nave are

A 19th-century
lithograph of a view
from the main road
between Blois and
Tours.

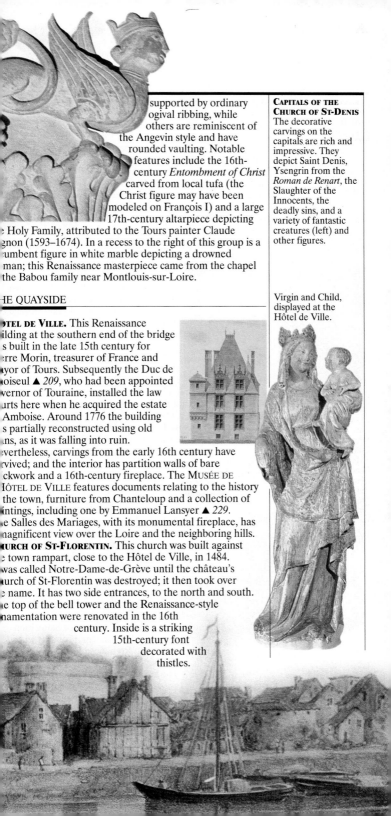

supported by ordinary ogival ribbing, while others are reminiscent of the Angevin style and have rounded vaulting. Notable features include the 16th-century *Entombment of Christ* carved from local tufa (the Christ figure may have been modeled on François I) and a large 17th-century altarpiece depicting

e Holy Family, attributed to the Tours painter Claude gnon (1593–1674). In a recess to the right of this group is a umbent figure in white marble depicting a drowned man; this Renaissance masterpiece came from the chapel the Babou family near Montlouis-sur-Loire.

HE QUAYSIDE

TEL DE VILLE. This Renaissance ilding at the southern end of the bridge s built in the late 15th century for rre Morin, treasurer of France and yor of Tours. Subsequently the Duc de oiseul ▲ *209*, who had been appointed vernor of Touraine, installed the law urts here when he acquired the estate Amboise. Around 1776 the building s partially reconstructed using old ins, as it was falling into ruin. vertheless, carvings from the early 16th century have rvived; and the interior has partition walls of bare ckwork and a 16th-century fireplace. The MUSÉE DE IÔTEL DE VILLE features documents relating to the history the town, furniture from Chanteloup and a collection of intings, including one by Emmanuel Lansyer ▲ *229*. e Salles des Mariages, with its monumental fireplace, has magnificent view over the Loire and the neighboring hills. IURCH OF **ST-FLORENTIN**. This church was built against e town rampart, close to the Hôtel de Ville, in 1484. was called Notre-Dame-de-Grève until the château's urch of St-Florentin was destroyed; it then took over e name. It has two side entrances, to the north and south. e top of the bell tower and the Renaissance-style namentation were renovated in the 16th century. Inside is a striking 15th-century font decorated with thistles.

Virgin and Child, displayed at the Hôtel de Ville.

LEONARDO DA VINCI ON THE ÎLE D'OR
This bronze statue depicting Leonardo da Vinci was produced by an anonymous artist a short time before World War Two. In the 1970's the city of Paris donated it to Amboise, the great man's final home.

THE DUC DE CHOISEUL (1719–85)
A favorite of Louis XV, Choiseul became a minister thanks to the support of Madame de Pompadour. He directed France's foreign policy for twelve years (1758–70).

MAX ERNST FOUNTAIN ● 83. (Quai du Général-de-Gaulle.) Michel Debré, mayor of Amboise, asked Max Ernst (1891–1976) to produce a fountain for the town in 1968. Painter, sculptor, etcher and writer, Ernst took up residence in Touraine, near Huismes, in 1955. A prominent member of the Surrealist movement in Paris from 1921 onward, he experimented with a variety of art forms and invented new techniques of painting involving collage, frottage and transfers.

GRENIERS DE CÉSAR ★. Behind the Hôtel Choiseul there is an unusual construction: a dozen or so caves cut into the tufa rockface. The first of these is now used for exhibitions. Beyond it are the huge and mysterious brick silos known as Caesar's Granaries. The silos do indeed recall methods of grain storage that were used in early antiquity: when a silo was filled with grain it produced carbon dioxide, which prevented fermentation and killed off pests. The sheer size of the complex suggested that only the Romans could have been capable of creating it. However, recent research has shown that the silos have nothing to do with Caesar: they probably date from the 16th century.

MAISON DES PAGES DE CHARLES VII. This half-timbered house below the castle is built of brick and stone; it has two stories and a staircase turret. Carvings can be seen on the façade.

ÎLE D'OR

The Île d'Or (also known as Île St-Jean) divides the Loire into two. It was here, around 504–5, that Clovis and Alaric II ● 37 met to define their territories. The view over the château and the town is magnificent. The island has various leisure facilities, including a picnic area.

CHAPEL OF ST-JEAN. This chapel was built in the 12th century, at which stage it belonged to the Order of Saint John of Jerusalem. From the outside you can see a Romanesque window and the chevet with three irregular openings. The keystones, in the Angevin style, are carved and painted. There was a second chapel on the island: the Chapel of St-Sauveur, which housed poor people suffering from contagious diseases. It was completely destroyed by flooding in the 18th century.

CHURCH OF NOTRE-DAME-DU-BOUT-DES-PONTS (right bank). This was built under François I to provide a parish church for the

burb, which was separated from the Church of St-Denis
the Loire. The single nave has five bays with ogival
ulting; to the south it is flanked by a square staircase
rret. The façades of the old houses around the church
tain their original carvings, including a 16th-century
s-relief depicting a knight giving alms.

HE CHANTELOUP PAGODA ★ ● 71 (K6)

The Loire at the
Île d'Or.

1713 Jean d'Aubiny, Master of the Waters and Forests of
mboise, had a château built at Chanteloup, an estate to the
uth of the town. The architect was Robert de Cotte,
other-in-law of Mansart. The Duc de Choiseul (opposite)
quired Chanteloup in 1761 and added it to his estate at

mboise. He extended the château and surrounded it with
rmal gardens designed by Le Camus. In his 10,000 acres
forest he created a network of intersecting avenues,
cluding seven broad avenues converging in front of the
âteau. A few years later the original gardens were
placed by ones landscaped in the English style, with
inding paths, an artificial grotto, a river with waterfall,
xotic trees and orange trees. The famous pagoda in the
nglo-Chinese style is Choiseul's crowning achievement;
was "built by the Duke in commemoration of the persons
ho visited him in his exile" (Arthur Young, *Travels in
rance in 1787, 1788 and 1789*). Similar to the pagoda in
ondon's Kew Gardens, it was erected between 1773 and
778, following plans drawn up by Le Camus. It was
flected in a vast semicircular lake covering more than
8 acres, connected to the Étangs de Jumeaux by a canal
miles long. This is all that remains of the magnificent
state, the setting for a brilliant court that attracted the
mous and fashionable from Paris, London, Vienna and

"The apartments
of the château are
arranged in a
comfortable and
splendid manner;
those on the
ground floor
have been so
well gilded that
they are brighter
than those created
in our own time.
The château is
decorated with
beautiful
colonnades on
either side."

Élisabeth
Vigée-Lebrun,
Souvenirs

Right and below: details of the pagoda.

Berlin. The château itself was demolished between 1823 and 1825. T▮ pagoda, which is 130 feet high and 50 feet wide, has seven stories; each is smaller than the one below and contai▮ a domed octagonal room. Although exotic motifs can be seen on the balustrades and the geometric designs some windows, the greater part of the ornamentation is in Louis XVI style.

THE PAGODA, A PROTEST AGAINST THE KING'S FICKLENESS
The exiled Duc de Choiseul was very popular, and the pagoda features testimonies to his friends. It has a dedication by the Abbé Barthélemy (1716–95), author of *Voyage du jeune Anacharsis en Grèce*

(1788), and Chinese inscriptions meaning "gratitude" and friendship".

AROUND AMBOISE

CHARGÉ. The MUSÉE DE LA BATAILLE DE LOIRE ET DE LA RÉSISTANCE, opened in 1986, records the events of the Battle of Chargé (June 17–20, 1940).

POCÉ-SUR-CISSE. This town, arranged around the 16th-century Church of St-Adrien (below), has a number of châteaux and manor houses.

LIMERAY. The base of the square bell tower is the oldest section of the Church of St-Saturnin (11th century). Two styles can be seen side by side here: the rounded vaulting of the apse is Romanesque, whereas the vault of the choir is Plantaganet. A curious narthex was recently added to the 16th-century nave – consisting of six marble colonnettes from Amboise and a Romanesque capital from the Abbey of Moncé. A 19th-centu▮ abbot virtually turned the church into a museu▮ collecting fragments of columns, capitals and twenty or so statues from the 15th and 16th centuries. The town's bridge over the Cisse still has its ogival arches dating from the 14th century.

ÇANGEY. The simple gable and the nave of the CHURCH OF ST-MARTIN date from the 11th and 12th centuries. Inside there are historiated capitals, and stained-glass windows made around 1540.

TOURS

CATHEDRAL OF ST-GATIEN, *196*
MUSÉE DES BEAUX-ARTS, *198*
CHATEAU DE TOURS, *198*
CHURCH OF ST-JULIEN, *199*
MUSÉE DU COMPAGNONNAGE, *199*
THE "COMPAGNONNAGE", *200*
RUE DE LA SCELLERIE, *202*
RUE JULES-FAVRE, *202*
RUE NATIONALE, *203*
PLACE ANATOLE-FRANCE, *203*
PONT WILSON, *203*
BASILICA OF ST-MARTIN, *204*
SAINT MARTIN, *206*
PLACE PLUMEREAU, *208*
AROUND PLACE PLUMEREAU, *208*
HOUSES ON
PLACE PLUMEREAU, *210*
PLACE JEAN-JAURES, *214*
AROUND BOULEVARD
HEURTELOUP, *214*
AROUND BOULEVARD
BÉRANGER, *214*
PARKS AND GARDENS, *215*

BOULEVARD BERANGER

PLACE
PLUMEREA

1. CATHEDRAL OF ST-GATIEN
2. MUSÉE DES BEAUX-ARTS
3. CHÂTEAU DE TOURS
4. FOOTBRIDGE
5. CHURCH OF ST-JULIEN
6. LIBRARY
7. PONT WILSON
8. HÔTEL GOUIN
9. PLACE PLUMEREAU

Basilica of St-Martin
Les Halles (market)
Chapel of St-Éloi

13. Hôtel de ville
14. Palais de justice
15. Railway station

16. Palais des Congrès
17. Jardin des
    Prébendes d'Oé

▲ Tours

The town's coat of arms.

HISTORY OF THE TOWN (H

GREGORY OF TOURS
Gregory was Bishop of Tours from 573 to 594. He produced his *History of the Frankish Peoples* and *Books of Miracles* with the aim of glorifying Saint Martin; without them two centuries of western history would be virtually unknown today.

TOMB OF THE CHILDREN OF ANNE DE BRETAGNE AND CHARLES VIII
Formerly located in the Collegiate Church of St-Martin, the tomb was transferred to the Cathedral of St-Gatien in 1810. The recumbent figures of the princes Charles and Charles-Orland were carved in the Gothic style in the early 16th century by Guillaume Regnault, a pupil of Michel Colombe. The tomb itself, which is in the Italian Renaissance style, has been attributed to the Italian sculptor Girolamo da Fiesole. Scenes showing Samson and Hercules decorate the base.

BEGINNINGS. In the 1st century AD, the former capital of the Turones stretched over a plateau between the Loire and the Cher; its name at that time was Caesarodunum.

TWO TOWNS. At the end of the 3rd century, threatened by invaders, the town retreated behind a rampart protecting its administrative and economic center, which lay to the east; it was here that Saint Lidoire built the first church in Tours, on the site of today's cathedral. To the west, in the 5th century, Saint Perpet built a basilica over the tomb of Saint Martin ▲ 207. This is how the town arrived at its double structure, which lasted for the next thousand years. After Viking raids, fortifications were built at the end of the 10th century, encompassing the Basilica of St-Martin and creating the new district of Châteauneuf. In 1368 a rampart was built joining the two sectors, with the Abbey of St-Julien between them.

TOWN OF BISHOPS. The town's bishops dominated its history. Saint Martin (371–97) founded a monastery at Marmoutier, and in medieval times his tomb attracted pilgrims from all over Europe. In the 6th century Gregory of Tours confirmed the town's role as a religious center, and Alcuin made it an intellectual and artistic center in the early 9th century.

CAPITAL OF THE KINGDOM. The French court settled here at the end of the 15th century. Louis XI, who lived at Plessis-lès-Tours, introduced the silk industry to the town ▲ 260. Large private residences were built, especially in Châteauneuf. In later centuries Tours declined: in 1785 the town had only 21,600 inhabitants. However, tourists were attracted by the climate, the valley and the new railway; the town's economy prospered as a result, and the population almost quadrupled between 1789 and 1911. The congress of the Socialist Party (the SFIO) held in Tours from December 25 to 30, 1920 marked the split between the various Socialist factions that led to the formation of the French Communist Party. Tours suffered bomb damage throughout the summer of 1944. Since the 1960's it has become established as the capital of the region.

CATHÉDRALE ST-GATIEN ● 61

The Cathedral of St-Gatien stands on the site of the first settlement, Caesarodunum. The Romans built their public buildings on this slight hill: the governor's palace, arenas, baths and temples. In the Merovingian and Carolingian eras this remained the focus of the town's administrative and religious life, while the economic center moved toward Châteauneuf. The cathedral was originally named after Saint Maurice, but since the 14th century it has been named after Saint Gatien, who may have been the first Bishop of Tours. The first building, dating from the 4th century,

196

...as altered in the 12th and 13th centuries. The choir was also built in the 13th century; the transept in the 14th century; the nave in the 14th and 15th centuries; the façade in the [1]th century; and the towers in the 16th century.

THE FAÇADE. On the lower section, ornamentation in the [Fl]amboyant style has been applied over the façade of the [1]2th-century building. The niches of the portal used to hold [st]atues of saints. These were partially restored in the 19th [ce]ntury. The wooden statue in the pier of the central portal [m]ay show Saint Gatien; it is a copy of a 15th-century work.

THE TOWERS. They are crowned with cupolas, probably [a]mong the earliest examples from the French Renaissance [a]long with the dome of the tower at St-Antoine de Loches). [T]he north tower, in the Flamboyant style, has a spiral [st]aircase leading to the huge dome. Henri IV admired this [m]asterpiece of the late Middle Ages: "Its towers are twin [je]wels set in the Garden of France."

THE NAVE. The nave reaches a height of 95 feet under the arches: its narrow width and the unbroken lines of its columns soaring to the tip of the ogival vaulting make it seem much higher than this.

THE TRANSEPT. The master builder Simon du Mans began rebuilding the transept and the first two bays of the nave in the early 14th century. The north transept is built over a crypt (not open to visitors). Soon after it was completed it had to be strengthened with two flying buttresses and a stone reinforcement for the rose window. The stunning rose window presents a circle within a square with four openwork corners (as compared with only two at Notre-Dame in Paris). The south transept houses the organ, which has 16th-century woodcarvings.

THE CHOIR. The superb Gothic chevet (right) can be admired from Place Grégoire-de-Tours. It has five semicircular chapels fanning out from the choir, with 13th-century stained-glass windows.

THE PSALETTE CLOISTERS. The cloisters consist of three galleries. The gallery to the west and the first bay of the north gallery, in the Flamboyant style, date from the 15th century; the other two galleries were built in the early Renaissance. In the northeast corner is a spiral staircase, a miniature replica of the François I staircase at Blois ▲ *148, 150.*

▲ *148, 150.*

LA PSALETTE
The second story of the eastern gallery of the cloisters used to house the Chapter Library, which had one of the richest collections in France during the Middle Ages.

FROM THE TOP OF THE CATHEDRAL
On the official guided tours, visitors can climb to the top of the south tower (on the right). Arthur Young did so in the late 18th century, as described in his *Travels in France in 1787, 1788 and 1789*: "From the tower of the cathedral there is an extensive view of the adjacent country; but the Loire, for so considerable a river, and for being boasted as the most beautiful in Europe, exhibits such a breadth of shoals and sands as to be almost subversive of beauty."

Abraham Bosse (1602–76)
This Calvinist artist, born in Tours, produced more than

Musée des Beaux-Arts

The museum is housed in the former episcopal palace, built in the 17th and 18th centuries over the foundations of the Gallo-Roman rampart. One of the towers of the rampart can still be seen, well preserved, beyond the portal (built for Louis XIV in 1668 and placed here in 1775). The curved terraces follow the outline of the Gallo-Roman arenas, which are open to the public on certain evenings during July. Napoleon spent the night of August 12–13, 1808 here on his journey back from Spain. In 1870 the museum, along with the Préfecture, was the headquarters of the Défense Nationale (provisional government), which had taken refuge at Tours.

1,500 etchings and engravings, many of them satirical. His works provide a detailed record of 17th-century French society; furniture, décor and buildings are depicted with minute accuracy.

From Verona to Tours
Christ in the Garden of Olives (below) and *The Resurrection* by Andrea Mantegna (1431–1506) were originally part of the altarpiece of San Zeno in Verona. Napoleon brought them back from his Italian campaigns.

Château de Tours

The powerful medieval fortress built by Philip the Bold at the end of the 13th century consisted of a quadrilateral keep with four great corner towers, only two of which survive. The height of the taller of the two, the Tour de Guise, was increased in the 15th century; it owes its name to the young Duc de Guise, who was imprisoned here for three years after the assassination of his father ▲ *146* and escaped on August 15, 1591. Between the two towers is the Logis de Mars, rebuilt in the late 18th century, which houses the Historial de Touraine (a museum of waxwork tableaux of the region's history) and a tropical aquarium. The 16th-century Logis du Gouverneur, built on top of the Gallo-Roman wall, houses an exhibition tracing the development of Tours through archeological excavations. The marriages of the future Charles VII with Marie d'Anjou (1413) and of the future Louis XII with Margaret of Scotland (1436) were both celebrated at the château.

HE FOOTBRIDGE (above). This was built in the 19th century ... the site of the first bridge at Tours; locals call it the "Pont ... Fil" (string bridge).

CHURCH OF ST-JULIEN

... the 6th century Gregory of Tours founded an abbey to ...use the relics of Saint Julian of Brioude. This was replaced ...a succession of later buildings between the 9th and 11th ...turies. In the 13th century a hurricane destroyed part of ... church, which was rebuilt in the Gothic style (the belfry ...rch being all that remains of the Romanesque basilica ...day). In the 16th century two small chapels were added at ... ends of the side aisles of the choir. Behind the organ are ...gments of frescos illustrating the story of Moses, taken ...m an Italian manuscript in the municipal library. ...e church is at a lower level than the Rue Nationale, ...cause the quaysides were raised at the end of the ...h century as a protection against flooding.

CLOISTER. The 12th-century chapter house and a monks' ...rmitory on the second story are the only remnants of the ...onastery buildings. The cloister was rebuilt in the 16th ...ntury and now houses the Musée du Compagnonnage ...uilds Museum). The cellar opposite this, dating from the ...cond half of the 12th century, has been turned into a wine ...seum. Two wine presses stand in the middle of the ...ister: the first dates from the Gallo-Roman era, and the ...cond from the 16th century.

MUSÉE DES VINS DE TOURAINE. The museum, in a large ...ulted room, presents items illustrating historical, ...ciological, oenological and artistic aspects of winegrowing ... the Touraine region.

MUSÉE DU COMPAGNONNAGE. This unique museum combines ... a single display items relating to the history and work of a ...riety of craft guilds.

RUE COLBERT

...ong with Rue Albert-Thomas, this street formed the ...iginal *decumanus* (main east–west axis) of the Roman ...wn. Originally called the Grand-Rue, it still has many ...lf-timbered houses from the 15th and 16th centuries.

MAISON DE LA PUCELLE ARMÉE (no. 39). This 16th-century ...lf-timbered house is said to have been the home of the ...aftsman Colas de Montbazon, who made Joan of Arc's ...mor.

PASSAGE DU CŒUR-NAVRÉ (no. 66). Some houses here ...ve collapsed, closing off the top end of this old alleyway ...ening onto Place Foire-le-Roi. The alley ...ed to have a sign depicting a heart ...erced with a sword – *cœur navré* being ... old French expression meaning ...wounded heart".

PLACE FOIRE-LE-ROI. In 1355 letters of patent from ...ng John the Good established a fair in honor of Saint ...ristopher on this little square. The taxes levied on the ...nts and on the goods sold were used in part to provide ...nance for a new city wall, incorporating Châteauneuf, the ...d town and the area in between. These letters of patent

CHURCH OF ST-JULIEN
The church was virtually in ruins after being used as a coaching inn during the Revolution. It was saved by Prosper Mérimée (1803–70), author of *Carmen*, who was inspector of historical monuments. Restored by Gustave Guérin, it became a place of worship again in 1859.

MUSÉE DU COMPAGNONNAGE
This presents the history, costumes and skills of the *compagnons* (craft guild members) ▲ 200, with exhibits including their masterpieces, tools, accessories and other items .

PLACE FOIRE-LE-ROI
Mystery plays, on religious subjects, were performed in the square in the Middle Ages. Legend has it that in the time of François I a pillory stood here and counterfeiters were boiled in a huge pot.

PLACE FOIRE LE ROI

France's craft guilds came into being during the Middle Ages, in the era of the great cathedrals and pilgrimages. The first of these craftsmen's associations, known as *devoirs*, were formed a a time when the traditional corporations had become inflexible and inaccessible. Their journeymen members traveled all over France to perfect their knowledge and skills in their chosen trade; the guilds have survived through the centuries and today continue to train young people by means of the *"tour de France"*.

"CHEF-D'ŒUVRE"
Journeymen made a masterpiece to display the skills they had acquired on the *tour*. Even today a *chef-d'œuvre* must be produced to obtain the title "Compagnon du Tour de France". The finished piece is presented before the *compagnons* and appraised. Right: masterpiece known in Tours as "La Clef des Cœurs" (Key of Hearts), produced by master wheelwright Philippe Leroux in 1887.

INSIGNIA
At the end of the tour, on the day of their initiation, the *compagnons* received the colors of their corporation and a staff with a metal pommel, decorated with two tassels.

A master blacksmith of the 19th century, dressed in full regalia.

Colors of a *gavot* (highland official),
presented in 1859 to Auguste
Gouttes, master cabinetmaker
of the Devoir de Liberté.

LEGENDS

Legend has it that the origins of the guilds date back to
the building of the Temple in Jerusalem (around 965 BC).
King Solomon and two of his architects, "Master Jacques" and
"Father Soubise", are regarded as the three mythical founders
(below) of the "Ordre des Compagnons".

"COMPAGNONNAGE" AT TOURS

In the old days, the *tour de France* was accomplished on foot. When a journeyman left
one town to head for the next, his fellow craftsmen organized a special ceremony called
the *conduite*: they accompanied the departing apprentice as far as the town gates, where
songs, toasts and rituals were performed in his honor.

THE JOURNEYMEN'S "MOTHERS"

The *mères* or "mothers"
play a key role in the
organization of the guilds.
In the past they were
innkeepers; nowadays
they manage the *cayennes*,
or lodges, which house the
young apprentices on their
tour de France. The "mothers"
are entitled to wear the
colors of the guild.
Right: the "mother" of
the master cabinetmakers
and locksmiths of the
Devoir de Liberté.

POMMEL OF THE STAFF

This was as good as
a passport, bearing
the name of the
compagnon and his
guild, along with
the date and place
of his admission
to membership.

were renewed by Louis XI and then by François I in 1547. This is how the square became known as the "square of the King's fair", although it was used for other markets and fairs, too. The Hôtel Babou de la Bourdaisière (no. 8) was the home of Philibert Babou de la Bourdaisière, a financier who became François I's treasurer in 1520. The entrance portal has magnificent carved doors (left), renovated in the Renaissance style under Louis XIV, and wrought-iron balconies from the 18th century.

PASSAGE DES JACOBINS. The lovely 16th-century house at no. 12 is known as the Maison de Ronsard because the staircase turret in the courtyard bears a coat of arms similar to that of the poet Pierre de Ronsard (1524–85). The windows are decorated with pilasters.

RUE DE LA SCELLERIE

Printers and booksellers set up business here during the Renaissance; today this quarter still has a number of bookstores, along with most of the town's antique stores.

THE THEATER ● 89. The theater (no. 34) was built on the site of the former Cordelier monastery, one of whose doors can still be seen on Rue Voltaire. The monastery was sold as a "national property" under the Revolution, and its chapel was converted into a theater in 1796. The first municipal theater was built here in 1875. All but the façade was destroyed by fire on August 15, 1883; the theater reopened in 1890.

"LE MOLIÈRE". The café next door to the theater has ceilings decorated with oil paintings by Grandin, dating from 1882. One of the paintings shows Molière crowned with laurels and surrounded by cherubs.

RUE DU CYGNE. In the Middle Ages the prison stood on this street, which owes its name to a sign showing a white swan surmounted by a cross. This sign exhorted passers-by to make the sign of the cross, to ward off the ill fortune that might one day make them inmates of the prison.

RUE JULES-FAVRE

HÔTEL DU COMMERCE A paragon of 18th-century architecture (right), it was built for the merchants of Tours. Construction began in 1757. At the far end of the courtyard is a double-flighted staircase with wrought-iron banisters. In the right wing on the ground floor is the old cloth market, with two vaulted halls.

HÔTEL DE BEAUNE-SEMBLANÇAY. Opposite the Hôtel du Commerce is a small garden with the remains of a Renaissance house built by Jacques de Beaune, Baron de Semblançay, finance minister to Louis XII and François I. Most of the house was destroyed in June 1940, but part of the façade survives – with finely carved capitals, and pilasters decorated with diamond motifs and slate (in imitation of marble) – and a gallery with a chapel above.

Rue Nationale
early this century.

UE NATIONALE

his street, which was originally called Rue Royale, is the
ain north–south axis of the town center; it is nearly half a
ile long. It was created in 1765 as part of a project to
large the town; Tours, like Orléans and Blois, had grown up
ong the river and could not expand further in an east–west
rection. This change of axis was vital, even though it cut into
he fabric of the medieval town.

PLACE ANATOLE-FRANCE

Anatole France lived at St-Cyr-sur-Loire, to the
north of Tours. Statues of Rabelais and
Descartes (both local figures) stand on the
square, on either side of the Rue Nationale.

**BIBILIOTHÈQUE
MUNICIPALE.** The
municipal library was built
in 1954–7 by Pierre Patout

d Jean and Charles Dorian. A matching building was
riginally planned for the other side of the bridge. The
pper-roofed library houses a fine collection of old books.

Fountain built by the
United States to
commemorate the
American presence in
Tours during World
War One.

ONT WILSON

nown locally as the "Pont de Pierre" (stone bridge), the
ont Wilson is 1,400 feet long and 48 feet wide; it is supported
fifteen basket-handle arches, each spanning 82 feet. Its
onstruction was supervised by Mathieu Bayeux (the General
spector of Bridges and Roads) from 1764 to 1774, then
mpleted by Jean de Voglie, the architect of the bridge at
aumur. Built on piles, because there is no hard rock on the
ed of the Loire at this point, it has collapsed several times:
1789, 1940 and 1978. In 1983 the second arch, which had
ot been reinforced in the 19th century, was replaced with
 identical structure made of concrete faced with stone.
/hile this project was under way, workers discovered an
unexploded 1,000-pound bomb from World War Two.

AN ILL-FATED BRIDGE
The bridge had barely
been completed, in
1789, when four of its
arches collapsed.
On June 18, 1940
engineers from the
French army blew up
one of the arches as
they retreated. The
blast sent stones and
pieces of cast iron
flying into the town,
causing damage to
roofs and windows
(notably those of the
Church of St-Julien);
one 400-pound block
reached as far as Rue
Corneille. Finally, the
second arch of the
bridge collapsed on
April 9, 1978, at
around 9pm.

THE ORIGINAL BASILICA OF ST-MARTIN

From the 5th century onward pilgrims came from all over Gaul to pray at the tomb of Saint Martin ▲ *207*. The Basilica of St-Martin (above) remained the religious center of France until the end of the Middle Ages. The sanctuary was sacked by the Normans and destroyed several times by fire. Rebuilt in 997, the Romanesque basilica was 360 feet long, with five naves. The vaults were rebuilt in the 12th century, and in the 13th century the choir was rebuilt on the model of Bourges Cathedral. Louis XI had a silver grille built around the shrine of Saint Martin in 1479. During the Revolution the basilica was used as stabling. In 1802, by then in a state of ruin, the basilica was razed to make way for the Rue des Halles. The only sections still standing are the Tour Charlemagne (the tower of the north transept) and the Tour de l'Horloge (the southern tower of the west façade). The best place to stand to imagine the scale of the original building is on Rue des Halles, in front of the Tour Charlemagne.

TOUR CHARLEMAGNE. The tower derives its name from the fact that it was built over the tomb of Luitgarde, the third wife of Charlemagne, who died at Tours in 800. Only the north façade, facing Place de Châteauneuf, remains intact. The south façade was rebuilt after it collapsed in 1928; it was restored in 1963 and now features a bas-relief depicting Saint Martin sharing his cloak. This tower was built over the remains of the 11th-century Romanesque basilica: capital from this early church, depicting Daniel in the lion's den, can still be seen (from Rue des Halles). In the 19th century a foundry for lead shot was installed here; later the building was converted into a water tower, ruining the first story vaulting.

The Tour Charlemagne, seen from the south side; and the Tour de l'Horloge (clock tower), whose structure and decorations reflect the dominance of Gothic style in the late 12th century.

Nineteenth-century lithograph of the Tour Charlemagne.

e original Basilica
St-Martin (left),
t before it was
stroyed.

OUR DE L'HORLOGE. The clock tower dates from the
te 12th century. The clock is wound every
rtnight: a hazardous undertaking, as the tower
s been more or less taken over by pigeons!

HE NEW BASILICA OF ST-MARTIN

int Martin's tomb was discovered in 1860,
inging about a revival in the saint's cult and
ovoking a fierce debate between the Catholic
urch (which wanted the basilica rebuilt on the
iginal plan) and the civic authorities (who did
t want to see this quarter completely disrupted).
compromise solution was found, in the shape of a small
silica, built on a north–south axis, with its sanctuary over
e saint's tomb. The Tours architect Victor Laloux ▲ *214* was
pointed for the project. The new basilica was built between
86 and 1902. From the outside the building has a rather
elegant, stacked-up appearance. The interior, by contrast,
ems surprisingly spacious, an effect created by the basilical
ound plan: three naves separated by monolithic columns of
sges granite, ending in semicircular apses. The capitals are
the Byzantine style and the naves are roofed with beams.
e crypt with the tomb of Saint Martin is beneath the choir,
huge space divided into five bays separated by pink-granite
lumns. A statue of Cardinal Meignan, sculpted by François
card in 1900, stands between two flights of stairs. The walls
the apse are covered with *ex votos*, some brought by famous
gures who came here to pray to Saint Martin, among them
aréchal Foch and the future Pope John XXIII. The square
front of the church was designed by Maurice Boille
llowing preliminary plans by Victor Laloux. The calvary
picting Saint Martin, Saint Perpet and Saint Gregory was
oduced by Henri Varenne.

LOISTER OF ST-MARTIN. Built by Bastien François in the
rly 16th century, the cloister now stands in the courtyard of
private building (no. 5, Rue Descartes). It is a fine, though
complete, example of Tours' early-Renaissance architecture.
USÉE ST-MARTIN. This museum is in the Chapel of St-Jean
t no. 3, rue Rapin). Built in the 13th century, the chapel
used the relics of Saint Martin on several occasions, and
e canons barricaded themselves here when the basilica was
cked by Protestants in 1552. It has some original stained-
ass windows in the chevet, which were altered by Lobin in
88. The museum displays some remains of the old basilica,
well as a striking model of the building.

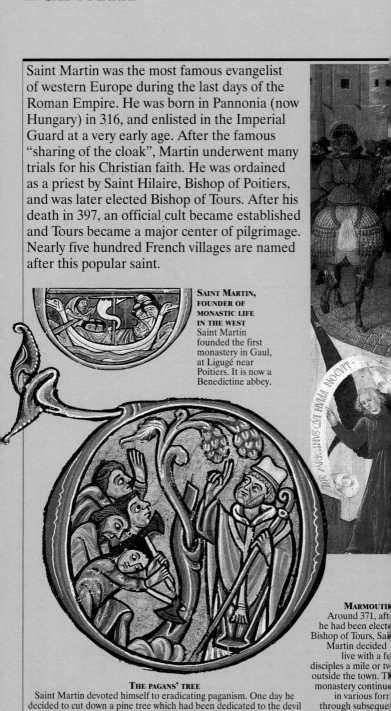

Saint Martin was the most famous evangelist of western Europe during the last days of the Roman Empire. He was born in Pannonia (now Hungary) in 316, and enlisted in the Imperial Guard at a very early age. After the famous "sharing of the cloak", Martin underwent many trials for his Christian faith. He was ordained as a priest by Saint Hilaire, Bishop of Poitiers, and was later elected Bishop of Tours. After his death in 397, an official cult became established and Tours became a major center of pilgrimage. Nearly five hundred French villages are named after this popular saint.

SAINT MARTIN, FOUNDER OF MONASTIC LIFE IN THE WEST
Saint Martin founded the first monastery in Gaul, at Ligugé near Poitiers. It is now a Benedictine abbey.

THE PAGANS' TREE
Saint Martin devoted himself to eradicating paganism. One day he decided to cut down a pine tree which had been dedicated to the devil by heathens. The heathens tied Saint Martin to the tree, on the side to which the tree was supposed to fall. A hurricane then blew up and the tree fell to the other side. When the villagers saw this they converted to Christianity. Saint Martin produced many miracles in his lifetime.

MARMOUTIE
Around 371, after he had been elected Bishop of Tours, Saint Martin decided to live with a few disciples a mile or two outside the town. The monastery continued in various forms through subsequent centuries and still stands today. At first it consisted of simple troglodytic cel

206

MARTIN'S SUMMER"
...Martin died, in
...ber, all the plants
...es on the banks of
...re burst into flower.
...t's day is celebrated
...ember 11.

DIVISION OF THE CLOAK
While he was quartered at
Amiens with the emperor,
Martin tore his cloak in two and
gave half to a beggar. The next
night Christ appeared to him in
a vision, wearing the half he had
given away. As a result, Martin
was baptized and began his long
mission as an evangelist.

The Tours painter André
Bauchant depicted Saint Martin
preaching in the forests of
Touraine (below).

THE LAST BASILICA
Initially a chapel was built
over Saint Martin's tomb, in
Tours. This was followed by a
collegiate church, which was
modified repeatedly over the
centuries. The
present-day
basilica ▲ 205
was built at the
end of the 19th
century by
Victor Laloux.

207

A RENAISSANCE HOUSE
The three forebuildings of the Hôtel Gouin (right, and detail below) were added to a 15th-century façade and richly decorated in Italian Renaissance style, with fluted pilasters, ovum friezes and large foliage scrolls. Most of the house was destroyed by fire in June 1940: only the main façade was saved. The sections that were lost have been rebuilt in their original early-Renaissance style.

PLACE PLUMEREAU

This is the most picturesque and lively part of Tours, the old *carroi aux chapeaux* (hat market). Until the 19th century part of the square was covered over with buildings, including the residence of Charles Plumereau, town councillor of Tours. It is bordered by half-timbered houses from the 15th and 16th centuries ● *73*.

AROUND PLACE PLUMEREAU

HÔTEL GOUIN. This 15th-century house (no. 25, rue du Commerce) was modified in the early 16th century, with additions in early-Renaissance style. It is the oldest Renaissance building in Tours, and the most original. The house's name refers to the Gouin family, a wealthy family of bankers from Brittany who acquired it in the 18th century. It now houses the ARCHEOLOGICAL MUSEUM.

RUE CONSTANTINE. This street marks the border of the area destroyed in the war. On one side is the medieval quarter, while the buildings on the other side date from the 1950's. This street was the home of the silk workers ▲ *260* brought to Tours by Louis XI in 1470. The house on the corner of Rue de Maillé is thought to have been Balzac's model for the silk dyer's home in his *Contes drolatiques*.

"One might also spend some very pleasant hours with the gabled houses on Place Plumereau; every one of these good old houses has a tale to tell. If you could worm their secrets out of them, you would find out some pretty things about the ladies who lived here at the time of Rabelais."
Maurice Bedel,
La Touraine

RUE P. L. COURIER

RUE PAUL-LOUIS-COURIER. At no. 5, in an 18th-century residence, is the CAYENNE DES COMPAGNONS DU DEVOIR (lodge for journeymen ▲ *200*). The wooden dormer window

PLACE ES CARMES

JARDIN SAINT-PIERRE LE PVELLIER

RUE DES TROIS PUCELLES

the courtyard is a masterpiece produced by a carpenter for
mission to the guild. At no. 10 is HÔTEL BINET, which was
ilt in the 15th century; at no. 15 is HÔTEL ROBIN-QUANTIN
rivate), built for the wealthy silk merchant Charles Robin
d his wife Marie Quantin in 1590. The HÔTEL DE JUSTE
o. 17) is said to have belonged to the family of the Italian
ulptors Antonio and Giovanni Giusti, who created the
mous tomb of Louis XII in the Basilica of St-Denis, on
e outskirts of Paris.

UE LITTRÉ. The Church of St-Saturnin, built in the 15th
ntury, was once the chapel of a Carmelite convent; it was
ld off as "national property" under the Revolution. The
mily who repurchased the church renamed it St-Saturnin –
ter another church, in Rue du Commerce, which had been
estroyed during the Revolution.

LACE HENRI-DE-SEGOGNE. During restoration work on the
d town some of the houses were demolished to bring light
d air into the close-knit web of medieval streets. However,
number of chimneys were preserved, so the past would not
e forgotten: they can be seen beside the façades of the
uses left standing. Small squares have been created on the
aces that were cleared.

UE DE LA PAIX. This was formerly the Rue de l'Écorcherie,
med after the abattoir that stood at the far end. The house
no. 21, with half-timbering at street level, was a canon's
use in the 15th century. Near the door is a well: those who
ed it had to pay a fee to the owner. The door leads to the
urtyard called the Jardin des Chanoines (Canons' Garden).

RDIN DE ST-PIERRE-LE-PUELLIER. This garden is reached
rough the Jardin des Chanoines (see above) or from no. 17,
ace Plumereau. It stands on the site of a convent founded
Saint Clotilda, wife of Clovis, in 512. The Church of St-
erre-le-Puellier was built in the 12th century, extended in
e 15th century, and partially destroyed in the 19th century.
oday there is a café in the main section that survived, and
e upper story has been turned into a private apartment.

UE BRIÇONNET. Jean Briçonnet was the first Mayor of Tours,
the end of the 15th century. The MAISON DE TRISTAN (or
ôtel Pierre du Puy ● 74) at no. 16 was built for Tristan
lermite, Great Chamberlain of Louis XI, but by 1495 it
elonged to Pierre du Puy, a wealthy citizen of Tours. This
use and the Château du Plessis-lès-Tours ▲ 259 are the
ly brick-and-stone buildings in Tours. Opposite (at no. 21)
the HÔTEL CHOISEUL: this building is
metimes attributed to the
uc de Choiseul ▲ 190, who
as exiled to the region in
e 18th century, but in
ct he only rented it.
he house at no. 31 is
ne of the oldest in
urs: its façade dates
om the 13th century.
he sculpture studio at
. 4 occupies another
rt of St-Pierre-le-
uellier that escaped
estruction: a bay of a
de aisle.

● 74 ▲ 259 ▲ 190

STAIRCASE OF THE MAISON DE TRISTAN
Inside the house
visitors can admire
the magnificent spiral
staircase with
brickwork vaulting.
It is sometimes called
the "Escalier à la
Rihour", because
there is a similar but
older staircase in the
Palais de Rihour in
Lille; it is also
known as the "Vis de
St-Gilles" (spiral
staircase of St-Gilles).

Garden of
St-Pierre-le-Puellier;
Maison de Tristan
(above).

▲ HOUSES ON PLACE PLUMEREAU

Detail of the house at no. 12.

NOS. 11 AND 12. The house at no. 12 is covered with slate. Its woodcarvings convey the vitality of the town in the Middle Ages: they depict pilgrims in their robes, clutching sticks and purses, kings and queens coming to pray at the tomb of Saint Martin ▲ *207*, and royal moneychangers.

HISTORICAL CENTER
This quarter was spared destruction during the bombardments of World War Two. The buildings, which had become very dilapidated, were restored under a program initiated in 1966. To inject new life into the quarter, the university's new Faculty of Literature was built nearby; the streets were made into a pedestrian zone, and the square (once a parking lot) has become a popular meeting place bordered with cafés and restaurants.

Details of a wrought-iron balcony at no. 10 (right) and of a half-timbered façade (left).

Nos. 8–10. No. 10 stands out among this group of houses on the west ...de of the square. It is built in neo-Renaissance style ...d bears the date 1845 on the third ...ory (above the right-hand ...pital); it also has lovely ...ought-iron balconies.

At no. 9 is the Café du Vieux Mûrier, a typically atmospheric café of the old town. Opposite the café stands a mulberry tree: a reminder that for many years Tours derived its prosperity from the silk industry ▲ *260*.

Nos. 1–7. These houses from the 15th and 16th centuries (no. 2 has an 18th-century stone façade) were built on narrow, deep plots of land. The ground floors were built of stone and housed shops; at the rear a spiral staircase in a tower served the upper stories.

Details of the house at no. 11.

Place du Grand-Marché.

"GEMMAIL"
This is a very thick type of stained glass, usually made in a contemporary design. The *gemmiste* arranges thick fragments of colored glass in layers; the completed work is fired in a kiln. The finished *gemmail* is illuminated from behind to display its full range of colors. The first *gemmiste* in Tours was Roger Malherbe-Navarre, who came here in the 1960's.

RUE DU POIRIER.
The house at no. 2, on the corner of Rue Briçonnet, is said to be the oldest building in Tours. The façade, which dates from the 12th century, has been restored with exceptional care.

RUE DU MÛRIER. At no. 7 is the Hôtel Étienne Raimbault, built in 1825 over the remains of houses from the 12th and 15th centuries. In this building is the MUSÉE DU GEMMAIL (see left), a unique museum with a workshop for demonstrations.

RUE DES CERISIERS. The name of this street refers to the Serisiers, a family of silk manufacturers who lived here in the 18th century. At no. 7 is a small 15th-century house: in the 19th century it was a boarding house for young ladies, described by Balzac in the opening pages of *Père Goriot*.

RUE DES ORFÈVRES. At no. 4 is a house built around 1696 by Pierre Taffu, councillor of Louis XIV. On the upper story the windows are decorated with red-colored heads. A little further on is the Rue du Petit-Soleil, named after an inn that once stood here.

RUE DU PRÉSIDENT-MERVILLE. The street marks the western border of the area destroyed during World War Two. The town hall and law courts stood here in the 15th century. No. 3 now houses the Musée d'Histoire Naturelle.

RUE DU CHANGE. The name refers to the fact that in the 6th century Clovis granted the monks of St-Martin the right to mint coins, and this street was the traditional haunt of moneychangers. The façade of the former Church of St-Denis can be seen at the far end of the alley, between nos. 14 and 16. The house with a corbeled turret (at no. 11, on the corner of Rue de Châteauneuf) once belonged to Jean Briçonnet ▲ *209*.

PLACE DE CHÂTEAUNEUF. This was once the vegetable market. At no. 15 stands Hôtel de la Croix Blanche, also known as Hôtel des Ducs de Touraine, dating from the 15th century. In its courtyard (once the parish cemetery) is the Church of St-Denis, whose main entrance is on Rue du Change (it is not open to visitors).

RUE DE CHÂTEAUNEUF. The former Church of Ste-Croix stands behind no. 17 (near Hôtel Briçonnet, which has a 19th-century neo-Renaissance façade) and no. 19. The remains of the church can be seen from the square on Rue Royer. The nearby Rue du Panier-Fleuri was called Rue de la Pisserie in the Middle Ages, when it was a haunt of prostitutes.

RUE DE LA RÔTISSERIE. This street follows the northern outline of the Châteauneuf rampart. The 15th-century Maison de l'Architecte (no. 3) has a mask with a bow tie, symbolizing architecture, added by Albert Archambault in 1972. To the right of no. 3(b) is a magnificent wooden staircase with balustrades dating from the 16th century, which has been moved for restoration work. A vine was planted here some years back; the harvest is celebrated by the "Entonneurs Rabelaisiens" and the grapes are made into jam.

PLACE DU GRAND-MARCHÉ. This was once the herb market, and also the site of a pillory. Lovely half-timbered houses stand on the west side of the square. On the east side, between nos. 54 and 56, is the Hôtel du Trésor de St-Martin, which has a large 15th-century portal.

RUE BRETONNEAU. This street was formerly called Rue de la Foule-Peinte: it was once inhabited by craftsmen belonging to the varnishers' and furniture polishers' guilds.

RUE DE LA SERPE. The house standing at no. 3 is said to have belonged to Jean Bourdichon, a 15th-century painter and illuminator who worked for Louis XI, Charles XII and François I. Between the ground floor and the upper stories are moldings supported by culs-de-lampe and carved figures.

RUE DE LA GROSSE-TOUR. A number of masterpieces are on display in the window of the guild of architectural craftsmen, at no. 22.

RUE DU PETIT-ST-MARTIN. The Chapel of Petit-St-Martin is at no. 22. It was built in the 14th century, supposedly to replace an oratory that marked the place where Saint Martin's body rested after it had been brought by boat from Candes ▲ 270. Today the chapel houses a school for sculpture restoration and is not open to visitors.

THE GARLIC AND BASIL FAIR
On the feast-day of Saint Anne, when this fair is held, the Place de Châteauneuf is as lively as it ever was; the fair spills over into the surrounding streets.

THE "LIVRE TOURNOIS"
Coins were minted in Tours from 1493 to 1772. However, the Tours *livre* was not a coin but a counting unit used by traders: it was divided into twelve *sous*, and each sou comprised twelve *deniers*. Due to an edict in 1667, the Tours *livre* was the last unit of currency in France before the present system was introduced.

213

VICTOR LALOUX
(1850–1937)
Among the
many buildings
designed by this
Tours architect
were the town hall,
the new Basilica
of St-Martin and
the railway station
in Tours; the Gare
d'Orsay in Paris;
and the town hall
in Lille.

FLOWER MARKET
The flower market
on Boulevard
Béranger, which
is held on
Wednesdays and
Saturdays, presents
a magnificent
display of colors
and heady perfumes.
It is the second-
largest flower
market in France,
after the one held
in Nice.

PLACE JEAN-JAURES

In the 18th century this square was known as Place
des Portes-de-Fer, because it was enclosed by iron
railings with three gates. At that time it was the
southernmost entrance into the town.
PALAIS DE JUSTICE. Built in 1840–3, the grand
Doric colonnade of the law courts exhibits the
classical style in favor at the time.
HÔTEL DE VILLE. The town hall was designed by Victor
Laloux (left) and opened in 1904. The balcony is
supported by four atlantes created by the sculptor François
Sicard (1862–1934). The river gods on either side of the
clock are by Antoine Injalbert (1845–1933). The sculptures
on the pediments represent Strength and Courage, on the
left, matched by Education and Vigilance on the right.
The façade, like the staircase inside and the decoration of
the building, was designed to glorify the Republic.
BRASSERIE DE L'UNIVERS. This brasserie has a colorful
19th-century glass partition showing festive scenes.

AROUND BOULEVARD HEURTELOUP

The boulevards were created from 1843 onward. Originally
lined with elms, today they contain plane trees and maples.
THE RAILWAY STATION. The station was built in 1894–8,
following designs by Bonnaudet for the building and
Victor Laloux for the façade. The two stone wings support
its huge metal framework.
PALAIS DES CONGRES LÉONARD-DE-VINCI (above, right).
This modern building near the station was created by Jean
Nouvel, the architect of the Institut du Monde Arabe and
the Fondation Cartier in Paris and the Opéra in Lyon.
HÔTEL MAME. This house (nos. 17–19, rue Émile-Zola)
is also known as Hôtel Lefebvre de Montifray ● 75, after
the 18th-century Tours merchant who built it. The Mame
family ▲ 215 lived here for many years. Its façade and
rich 18th-century ornamentation can be seen from
the street.

AROUND BOULEVARD BÉRANGER

This boulevard was the favorite place for a stroll in the
19th century.
PRIORY OF ST-ÉLOI. The priory (at the western end of the
boulevard) now houses the municipal archives. Founded in

ALFRED MAME
(1811–93)
Alfred Mame
inherited the family

e 10th century as the Priory of L'Orme-Robert, it was
dedicated to Saint Éloi (councillor and
easurer of the Merovingian king Dagobert)
the 12th century. Legend has it that Éloi
mself made the shrine of Saint Martin here.

TÉ ALFRED-MAME. This workers' estate was
eated by Alfred Mame, in the second half of
e 19th century. It is arranged around a
quare. The corners and window frames are
ade of brick and stone (right). Each of the
ocks has a central forebuilding.

ARKS AND GARDENS

vo hundred gardeners are employed to maintain the
wn's 800 acres of parkland, including the banks of the
her. The largest parks are the Jardin Botanique and the
ırdin des Prébendes d'Oé.

ARDIN DES PRÉBENDES D'OÉ. The Prébendes quarter
as originally a marsh. In the Middle Ages this was the
arket-gardening district: the gardeners had to pay
eir *prébendes* (tithes) to the Provost of Oé, a canon of
-Martin. This superb landscaped park, covering 10 acres,
as designed by the Buhler brothers in 1872 (they also
esigned the Parc du Thabor in Rennes, and the Parc de la
ête d'Or in Lyon).

ARDIN BOTANIQUE. The botanical gardens opened in
343. The main entrance is on Boulevard Tonnelé.
:an-Anthyme Margueron started the gardens in
338 on a 12-acre site, on what was once the bed of the
uau Ste-Anne (a canal created by Louis XI and named
ter his daughter Anne de Beaujeu). Part of the park is
:served for the study of plants by pharmacology
udents. An arboretum
ntains about two
undred trees, including
pyramidal hornbeam
early 150 years old. A wide
venue divides the gardens;
n one side are heathers
nd rock plants, on the
her a garden showing the
evelopment of the various
lant families. The avenue
:ads to a hothouse and
n orangery.

printing firm in
1833 and injected
new life into
the business,
especially on the
publishing side.
The printing
works in Tours
were destroyed
during World
War Two and
rebuilt outside
the town. Today
the Mame
publishing house
specializes in
religious works, art
books and picture
books for children;
its offices are now
in Paris.

**ARBORETUM OF
THE JARDIN
BOTANIQUE**
This section
of the park
includes a
miniature zoo
that contains deer,
sheep, pigs, an
aviary, chickens,
turtles, kangaroos,
and even some bears.

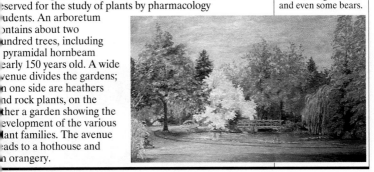

1. TOURS 2. CORMERY 3. THE LOIRE 4. CHANTELOUP PAGODA 5. AMBOISE 6. CHENONCEAU 7. LOCHES 8. BEAULIEU-LÈS-LOCHES 9. CHAPEL OF ST-JEAN-DU-...

c. 100 miles
🕐 1 day

Le Cher

"The Cher – indolent, even lazy – ran in a leisurely manner along its spacious river bed, among meadows bordered with acacias, willows and poplars. It passed from the sand of the Sologne to the clay of Valençay, and on to the limestone near Montrichard, getting ready to don its courtly splendor when it reached Chenonceaux."
Robert Sabatier

CHÂTEAU DE MONTPOUPON
A fortress occupied this site from the 13th century onward, guarding the road to Aquitaine. After the Hundred Years' War the quadrangular stronghold was converted into a residential palace in early-Renaissance style ● 68. Today the château houses a museum of hunting.

BETWEEN THE CHER AND THE INDRE

To the east of Tours, set between the Cher and Indre rivers, is an undulating landscape scattered with woods. In the past this area was split between the provinces of Touraine and Berry; today it is divided between the départements of Indre-et-Loire and Indre. In geological terms it forms a single unit characterized by areas known locally as *gâtines*, which have clay soils that are relatively infertile. In terms of history and architecture the area is an integral part of the Loire valley.

"GATINES", WOODS AND FORESTS. Because this is poor farmland, much of it is covered with forest: the tip of the Forest of Amboise at Chenonceaux; the vast Forest of Loches, which begins right outside the walls of the old town; the Brouard Forest overlooking Montrésor ▲ 231; the Bois du Biard around Montpoupon (below); the Bois de Luçay near Nouans-les-Fontaine ▲ 231; and finally the *gâtine* forest around Valençay ▲ 232, which completes the unbroken chain of woodland stretching from the Champeigne of Touraine to the Champeigne of Berry.

ᴅEFENSE. Over the centuries paths and clearings were created in the forests, marshes drained, and towns and fortresses built. The medieval towns of Loches ▲ *224* and Montrésor ▲ *231*, the Château de Montpoupon and the impressive ruins of the impregnable keep at Montrichard bear witness to the days when defense was the priority.

ᴘRAYER. To thank God for his protection man erected buildings to his glory such as the Chartreuse du Liget ▲ *230* and the Collegiate Church of St-Aignan ● *59*: the latter a beautiful Romanesque church with a crypt containing fine mural paintings (detail below) dating from the 12th, 14th and 15th centuries. The town of St-Aignan (above) is best seen from the Chaussée des Ponts: the white silhouette of the collegiate church and the imposing mass of the Renaissance château stand out on the left bank of the Cher; houses huddle around them, covering the slope down to the green river banks.

ᴘLEASURE. In later, more peaceful, times architecture could reflect the pursuit of pleasure and beauty, as exemplified by the châteaux of Valençay and Chenonceaux. The latter inspired Alfred McMahon to write in his *Chronicles of Touraine*: "Like a classical nymph, Chenonceau dips its bare feet into the clear waters of the Cher, turning its dreamy face to the sunset . . ."

Collegiate church and château, St-Aignan.

ᴘARC ᴅE ᴮEAUVAL (1 mile south of St-Aignan). This ornithological and zoological park was founded at Beauval in 1981. It covers over 20 acres and has some 2,000 birds, as well as monkeys and other species. However, the stars of the zoo are the bears from Jean-Jacques Annaud's movie *The Bear*, and the only pair of white tigers in France.

217

Catherine de Médicis'
Room and Study

Five Queens' Room

Chapel and Gallery

Guardroom

Tour des Marques

Salon Louis XIV
(above the kitchens)

Louise de Lorraine's Room

Access to the
left bank

César de Vendôme's Room

Gallery

Gabrielle d'Estrées'
Room

First story
Second story
Third story

"DIANA'S BATH"
This oil painting on wood (above) by François Clouet (c. 1510–72) celebrates the triumph of the new Diana: Mary Stuart, later Mary Queen of Scots. Her first husband, François II, is often identified as the horseman in the picture, while the seated woman is said to be Catherine de Médicis.

THE SIX CHATELAINES OF CHENONCEAU
Chenonceau was largely created by women: in this it is unique among the châteaux of France. The six women who supervised the construction, conservation and renovation of this masterpiece of Renaissance architecture were: Katherine Briçonnet from 1513 to 1526, Diane de Poitiers from 1547 to 1559, Catherine de Médicis from 1559 to 1589, Louise de Lorraine from 1589 to 1600, Madame Dupin from 1733 to 1799, and Madame Pelouze from 1863 to 1875. The four shown here are Diane de Poitiers (on the left), Louise de Lorraine (top), Catherine de Médicis (bottom), and Madame Dupin (on the right).

HISTORY OF CHENONCEAU (K

This elegant palace bridging the Cher is delightful in every respect. Its exceptionally beautiful setting, its original design and its sumptuous ornamentation make Chenonceau one of the jewels of French Renaissance architecture.

PAYING OFF DEBTS. Around 1230 Chenonceau was just a modest manor house belonging to the Marques famil Subsequently it was demolished (in 1411) and rebuilt by Jea Marques in 1432. A huge burden of debt forced his son Pier to sell the château to Thomas Bohier, a tax collector who came originally from Tours. Bohier took possession of Chenonceau on February 8, 1513; of the earlier castle he retained only the keep, known as the Tour des Marques, and the foundations of a mill which were used as the basis for his new palace on the Cher. Building work started in 1515. When Bohier departed to fight for François I in Northern Italy, he left his wife Katherine Briçonnet to supervise the work at Chenonceau. Later their son, like Pierre Marques, was forced to give up the château: he handed it over to the crown to pay off debts to the treasury and avoid the fate suffered by Jacques de Beaune-Semblançay ▲ *202*.

DIANE'S HOME. The Connétable de Montmorency took possession of the château in the king's name in 1535. By this stage Chenonceau was already sufficiently splendid to be shown to Charles V during his visit to France in 1539 ▲ *162*. When Henri II came to the throne in 1547, he gave the château to his mistress Diane de Poitiers. Diane, who was very fond of Chenonceau, decided to build a bridge joining the Bohier castle to the other bank of the Cher. Philibert de l'Orme was entrusted with the commission in 1556 and supervised the work for the next three years.

CATHERINE'S FESTIVITIES. After the death of Henri II in 1559 his mistress fell from favor and Chenonceau passed into the hands of Catherine de Médicis. Catherine's son, the new king François II, was very young; courtly intrigues were rife, and

View of the château before the gardens and the terrace of the Tour des Marques were modified.

first conflicts between Catholics and Protestants had begun. Catherine responded by making Chenonceau a place of pleasure and intrigue. She held splendid festivities here, known as the "Triomphes de Chenonceau"; and her flying squad of young ladies-in-waiting, drawn from the leading families of the aristocracy, was empowered to seduce and spy on the most powerful lords of the kingdom. Among all these intrigues Catherine did not forget Chenonceau itself. She had a two-story gallery built over Diane's bridge (1570–6); altered the north façade of the main building; and added a small building to the east between the chapel and the library, as well as outbuildings in the courtyard (1580–5). She also planned a new wing at the end of the gallery, on the right bank of the Cher: however, this was never built.

THE WHITE QUEEN. In 1589, shortly before her death, Catherine de Médicis bequeathed Chenonceau to Louise de Lorraine, the wife of Henri III. A few months after Henri's assassination Louise retired to the château: here she led the life of a recluse, dressed always in white, the royal color of mourning. Chenonceau stood empty for a century after her death.

AGE OF PHILOSOPHERS. In 1730 the tax collector Claude Dupin acquired Chenonceau and restored it to its former splendor. His wife, the natural daughter of Samuel Bernard (a wealthy Protestant financier under Louis XIV), organized grand receptions here, inviting the famous philosophers and intellectuals of the age: Rousseau, Voltaire, Fontenelle, Buffon, Condillac, Montesquieu and Madame du Deffand. The château escaped destruction under the Revolution because it was the only bridge over the Cher between Montrichard ▲ 217 and Bléré.

RENOVATION. Madame Dupin died at Chenonceau in 1799 at the age of 93, and one of her nephews, the Comte de Villeneuve, inherited the château. When he died in 1863, Chenonceau was acquired by Madame Pelouze: she appointed Félix Roguet, architect of the Church of Ste-Clotilde in Paris, to restore the château, following plans by Du Cerceau. Roguet began work in 1865; the project took ten years to complete. Most of his efforts were directed toward the northern façades and the Bohier building. Nearly all the interior decorations were restored at this time. Today the château is owned by the Meniers (the family of chocolate manufacturers), who acquired it in 1913.

DIFFERENT SPELLINGS. Although the Château de Chenonceau can be spelled with or without an "x", the name of the village is usually spelled with one.

ROUSSEAU AT CHENONCEAU
The philosopher Jean-Jacques Rousseau (1712–78) came to the château as the tutor of Madame Dupin's son. It was here that he gave the first performance of his operetta *Le Devin de village*. He later wrote in his *Confessions*: "In 1747 we went to spend the autumn in Touraine, at the Château de Chenonceau . . . We had a very enjoyable time in this beautiful place; we were very well fed and I became as fat as a monk."

221

❝The Château
de Chenonceau
exudes a special
sweetness and an
aristocratic serenity.
It stands at the end
of a great avenue
of trees, some way
from the village
which observes a
respectful distance;
it is built on water,
surrounded by
woods, and set in a
huge park with
lovely lawns, with
its turrets and square
chimneys rising into
the air.❞
Gustave Flaubert,
*Par les champs
et par les grèves*

TOUR OF THE CHÂTEAU

Seen from the banks of the Cher, this castle built out
over the water presents a majestic, dreamlike spectacle.
Moreover, its scale can be fully appreciated, as can the
contrast between its length and the different heights of its
three constituent parts: the Tour des Marques, the Bohier
castle and the gallery.

TOUR DES MARQUES. The old keep is separated from the
rest of the château by a bridge; the Bohiers retained it to
give the site a historical flavor. The tower has preserved its
medieval appearance, with machicolations and a walkway.
However, the east section was embellished in the 16th
century, when an elegant turret was added, along with
flamboyant carvings in tufa to match the
architectural style of the new palace.

THE BOHIER CHÂTEAU. This building looks as
if it has simply been placed on top of
the arches of the old mill. Its Renaissance
architecture is delightful: the building is
highly regular in design, with the same
measurements, or multiples of them,
repeated throughout. Four corner towers
emphasize this regularity, which is interrupted only
by two annexes built over the piers on the east side: the
chapel on the right, and
the library on the left.

Below: the Tour des Marques (left) and chapel (right).

ST FLOOR. This story is arranged and a gallery paved with enameled s, which opens onto the larger rooms, uding the rooms of François I and of is XIII, the last king to come to the eau. The Salle des Gardes ardroom), modified in the 18th tury, leads into the small chapel, ch has a triangular apse. The two ls, Diane de Poitiers and Catherine Médicis, both left their mark on enonceau. A room decorated with gnificent 16th-century Flanders estries is named after the former; the inet Vert (Green Study) is where the er worked – its name refers to the fact t she had the walls covered entirely in en velvet. Do not forget to visit the hens, which are inside the piers on river: this arrangement allowed for direct delivery of goods transported oat ● 46.

DLE FLOOR. The second story is reached by a remarkable rcase in the Italian style, with straight banisters and carved stones: it is one of the château's most striking features. vestibule, named after Katherine Briçonnet, opens onto r rooms. On the west side are the rooms named after César de Vendôme (the natural son of Henri IV) and his mother, the beautiful Gabrielle d'Estrée. Opposite these is Catherine de Médicis' Room, richly decorated with Italian Renaissance paintings. The final room of this group is the Five Queens' Room, probably named after the two daughters and three daughters-in-law of Catherine de Médicis.

P FLOOR. The third story has only one room, presenting a creation of Louise de Lorraine's sepulchral surroundings, h funerary motifs and silver tears on a black background.

E GALLERY ● 69. The gallery is built in a classical style, set r the five arches of the bridge across the Cher. Originally vas intended as a ballroom: it is nearly 200 feet long, with a place at each end. Visitors can walk through the gallery to ch the left bank of the river, where there is a breathtaking w of the château. Alternatively you can take a boat trip, sing under the arches of the gallery and landing on the nd in the middle of the Cher – a magical experience.

E GARDENS. The château is flanked by two formal dens. The larger one was created by Diane de Poitiers, l the smaller one designed for Catherine de Médicis. rther to the north is a landscaped garden, the Jardin Vert. the woods between the gardens and the entrance to the unds stands a portico decorated with four caryatids, ich was added to the Bohier tle by Catherine de Médicis l removed in the 19th century. e outbuildings house a xwork museum tracing the tory of Chenonceau.

THE GALLERY IN WARTIME
A plaque commemorates the fact that Gaston Menier converted the château into a hospital during World War One. Between 1940 and 1942 the gallery (above) spanned an important borderline: the southern door opened onto the Free Territories, while the château itself stood in the occupied zone.

THE VILLAGE
The village's 12th-century church was renovated when the Bohiers built their castle. The house known as the Maison des Pages de François I dates from the same period: it has a polygonal staircase turret and mullioned windows.

PUBLIC PARK — PORTE DES CORDELIERS — TOUR ST-ANTOINE — LOGIS ROYAL — CHURCH OF ST-OURS — POR

RUE

PLACE DE LA MARNE

AVENUE DE LA GAÎTE

The Tour St-Antoine and Porte des Cordeliers, in Loches.

HISTORY OF THE TOWN

● 65 (

Loches stands at the junction of two Roman roads, overlooking the Indre: this strategic site, with a view over all the surrounding area, enabled the town to oversee movements of troops and merchandise. With its keep, its collegiate church, its royal residence and its old houses, it is one of the most complete medieval towns to have survive to the present day.

A STRATEGIC SITE. Saint Ours, a monk, founded a monaster in the Roman *oppidum* (fortified town) in the 5th century. Charles the Bald (823–77) built a castle which he gave to on of his vassals, whose descendants passed it by marriage to Foulques le Roux, Count of Anjou (the grandfather of Foulques Nerra). This stronghold was a vital asset for the Angevins in their battle against the Counts of Blois. The formidable keep was built at the southern end of the spur in the late

th century. The Plantaganets
pt Loches until 1205, when
ilippe Auguste captured it and
ve it to one of his officers.
ROWN PROPERTY. Louis IX was
nscious of the town's strategic
portance and repurchased it in
49. The fortress belonged to the
ngs of France for the next six centuries. Early in this period
mparts and towers were built all around the spur. Later,
om the time of Charles VII, the emphasis was on pleasure
ther than defense. Nevertheless, Charles took comfort from
e town's defensive strength, as his kingdom was under
reat from the English.

THE KEEP BECOMES A PRISON. The town was abandoned
by Louis XI, who wanted to escape the memories of a
childhood spent within its forbidding walls.

PRISON ART
The keep and its
annexes housed
a wide range of
prisoners.
Ludovico Sforza,
the scheming
Duke of Milan
(1452–1508) and
patron of Leonardo
da Vinci, was
imprisoned at
Loches by Louis XII
from 1500 until
his death. To
pass the time, he
decorated his cell
with stars, guns
and mottos. On
the wall of
another cell,
two ecclesiastical
prisoners carved
an altar and the
fourteen Stations
of the Cross.

The town of Loches,
19th-century
lithograph.

FANCIFUL RESTORATION
These elevations (above) of the Cité Royale and Logis Royal were created during the course of 19th-century restoration work. The monumental staircase guarded by stone dogs, leading to the interior of the château, was also built at this time. The same is true of the bartizans, the wall walk and other ornamental additions to the turrets and façades of the building. Only the Tour d'Agnès Sorel retains its original simplicity of style.

THE "FILLETTES"
It is said that Louis XI invented the *fillettes* – cruel iron-and-wood cages barely large enough to hold a man – to punish Cardinal Balue (c. 1421–91), a trusted adviser who had betrayed him.

He moved to Tours ▲ *196*, and the keep then became a state prison: the soldiers and courtiers of the royal stronghold were replaced by those imprisoned for treason or as enemies of state. Louis XIV incarcerated Protestant leaders here after the Revocation of the Edict of Nantes. During the Revolution it was used as a prison for aristocrats and bourgeois from Loches and the surrounding area. The fortress remained a municipal prison until the start of this century, which had the advantage of ensuring that the buildings were maintained.

EVOLUTION OF THE TOWN. The Cité Royale (royal stronghold) was permanently inhabited, which encouraged the development of a small town to the west of the fortress; the other side was flooded by the Indre and its tributaries every winter. Later a second fortified rampart was built, with entrances at either end and in the middle, guarded by huge posterns with portcullises and crenelations. In the 19th century the town outgrew its fortifications and spread over the surrounding fields (where the Palais de Justice was built).

THE CITÉ ROYALE

THE PORTE ROYALE. This is now the only way of entering the Cité Royale; in the past there was also a drawbridge to the south, across the old dry moat (now Boulevard Philippe-Auguste). This fortified gateway was rebuilt in the early 15th century and defended by two drawbridges. Visitors can climb up to the top of the gateway (through the museum to enjoy the splendid view.

THE LOGIS ROYAL (royal residence). This little château overlooks the courtyard and a small park to the west; on the eastern side is a terrace above a sheer drop to the banks of the Indre and the houses alongside the river. The southern part of the building dates from the late 14th century; the northern section was completed a century later.

TOUR OF THE ROYAL RESIDENCE. The first room is the RETRAIT DU ROI, the king's bedroom: here visitors can see the remains of a fireplace removed in the 19th century, the walled-up passage to the tower and the remains of a Renaissance tapestry discovered under the paneling of the nearby presbytery. The GRANDE SALLE (Great Hall) was higher in the early 15th century: its beams were visible and inted in bright colors. This hall is also known as the SALLE ANNE D'ARC, because of the meeting here after the victory Orléans ▲ 116 when Joan of Arc persuaded the Dauphin be crowned, as Charles VII, in Reims Cathedral. The room ntains a group of Audenarde (Flanders) tapestries and the lls of a staircase that led to the kitchens and servants' oms. A richly carved door leads to the later part of the âteau, built by Louis XII. In a room with a fireplace om a nearby farm is a superb triptych by Jean urdichon, a painter and miniaturist from Tours . 1457–1521). This work belonged to the artreuse du Liget ▲ 230.

GNES SOREL: THE FIRST OFFICIAL ROYAL ISTRESS. One room in the château is dedicated to gnès Sorel. Opposite her recumbent statue is one nel of the diptych by Jean Fouquet ● 88, ▲ 231, 242 lled the *Virgin of the Milk* (the original is in Antwerp), which ows the Virgin with the face of Agnès Sorel. This portrait is gnificant because Jean Fouquet, Charles VII's official

painter, definitely knew Agnès Sorel; all other portraits of her are posthumous, and based on this work. Agnès Sorel was born in Picardy; her date of birth is not known, so we cannot be sure if she was in her twenties or thirties when she died on February 11,

150 (she may have been poisoned). A lady-in-waiting to abelle de Lorraine, the wife of René d'Anjou and sister-in-w of the king, she met Charles VII at Saumur around 1444 nd became his mistress. During the course of the five years e spent with the king she bore him three daughters, who ere legitimated and married according to their royal rank.

OLLEGIATE CHURCH OF ST-OURS ★ ▲ 228. André allays, a traveler at the start of the 20th century, nthusiastically exclaimed: "The Collegiate Church of -Ours is the wonder of Loches, and one of the onders of our religious architecture." The church ormerly the Collegiate Church of Notre-Dame) has vo bell towers: one from the 11th century, the other a elfry porch built a century later. In 1165 the roof ining the two towers collapsed and was replaced by vo *dubes* (hollow pyramids), which may have been ased on the kitchen of Fontevraud Abbey ▲ 272. riginally conical, they acquired their present ctagonal form during 19th-century restoration work. he church is entered through a narthex (added to the urch at the same time as the *dubes*), which has

AGNES SOREL
The mistress of Charles VII scandalized the court and the French people with her low necklines, her high bonnets and her diamonds. Her royal lover gave her the Château de Beauté-sur-Marne and with it the title of Dame de Beauté (with its double meaning, Lady of Beauté/Lady of Beauty). She used her influence to place valuable counsellors around the king, like Jacques Cœur and Étienne Chevalier, who in turn gave her their protection. The medallions depicting Charles VII (above) and his coat of arms are from the château's stained-glass windows.

ORATORY OF ANNE DE BRETAGNE
The oratory has a rich heraldic decoration of ermines, as well as Anne de Bretagne's motto "Rather death than dishonor", and knotted ropes alluding to her association with the Franciscan Order.

ALFRED DE VIGNY
(1797–1863)
The statue of
the writer on Place
de Verdun, by
Tours sculptor
François Sicard,
commemorates the
fact that Vigny was
born in Loches on
March 27, 1797.

The Church of
St-Ours (below).
Detail of the portal
(above).

protected the magnificent early-12th-
century polychrome portal so the colors
retain their original brightness. The
southern side aisle was built in the 12th
century; the northern side aisle, with
ogival vaulting, dates from the 15th
century. An avenue of lime trees, flanked
by old houses, leads from the church to
the keep.

THE KEEP AND ITS FORTIFICATIONS ★
● 65. The imposing rectangular keep
stands at the far southern tip of the rocky
spur; it is reached by a barbican and a
drawbridge. The keep was built by the
Counts of Anjou around 1070; it
measures approximately 80 by 50 feet and
stands 120 feet high. Further ramparts
were built to reinforce the defenses over
the course of subsequent centuries. In the
13th century three pointed towers were
added to complete the southern defenses of the site. Then
from the mid 15th century onward, as military architecture
evolved, three new buildings were added: the barbican, the
TOUR NEUVE (or TOUR RONDE), at the junction of the town'
ramparts and the keep, and the fearful MARTELET, a hulk of
masonry housing three stories of underground prison cells.

TWO LITTLE-KNOWN MUSEUMS. The MUSÉE DU TERROIR is
housed in the vaulted rooms of the Porte Royale. Founded b
Tours ethnographer Jacques-Marie Rougé (1873–1956), it
contains items relating to the life of the local peasants in
the 19th century. Next door, in a 19th-century bourgeois
residence, is the MUSÉE LANSYER, which displays the work o
Emmanuel Lansyer (1835–93) ▲ 229, a pupil of Gustave
Courbet. The collection also includes engravings by Piranesi,
Canaletto and Doré, and wash drawings by Victor Hugo.

WALK THROUGH THE TOWN

Like the Cité Royale, the old center of the town is surrounde
by ramparts, which are more than half a mile long.
Leaving the fortress by the Porte Royale, at the end
of the Mail de la Poterie you will come to the hous
where Louis Delaporte (1842–1925) was born,
which stands in the street named after him. This
explorer revealed the importance and interest o
the ruins at Angkor and assembled a collection
of Indo-Chinese art that formed the basis of the
Musée Guimet in Paris.

RUE DU CHÂTEAU ★. From the Porte Royale, the Rue du Château leads back down toward the town. The house at no. 19 is known as the MAISON D'AGNÈS SOREL because of the bust over the entrance. The 16th-century house at no. 10, the MAISON DU CENTAURE, owes its name to the bas-relief on the façade (above). The MAISON DE LA CHANCELLERIE (no. 8) is decorated in the Italian style and bears the date 1551 on a cartouche, along with the monogram of Henri II. This house became known as the chancellery from its two inscriptions: *Prudentia nutrisco* ("I am nourished by prudence") and *Justicia regno* ("I govern by justice"). But Loches did not in fact have a chancellery in the 16th century. Finally at no. 1 is a 15th-century house (recently restored) that has a neo-Gothic façade with rather heavy-looking sculptures.

THE TOWN GATES ★. The PORTE PICOIS (left), the northwestern entrance to the town, was built into the rampart, like the Porte des Cordeliers to the northeast and the Porte Poitevine (no longer standing) to the southwest. Porte Picois was built in the 15th century as a fortified gateway, with machicolations and a wall walk: the latter bears the marks of missiles from the Wars of Religion.

T. Bardon, Editor.

HÔTEL DE VILLE ★. The town hall is a perfect example of Renaissance architecture. François I authorized its construction, beside the Porte Picois, in 1519; but the work did not begin until 1535.

AROUND THE TOUR ST-ANTOINE. The TOUR ST-ANTOINE was built between 1529 and 1575 to serve as a bell tower for the adjacent chapel. At no. 3 on PLACE DU MARCHÉ-AUX-LÉGUMES is a late-15th-century turret. At no. 5, rue St-Antoine stands Hôtel Nau, with loggias on three stories, dating from the mid 16th century. On the Grand-Rue is the oldest pharmacy in the town, which has been in business for nearly three hundred years.

ALONG THE RAMPARTS. The steep walls of the collegiate church and the château overhang the picturesque Rue St-Ours. At nos. 13 and 15 are the lovely façades of the MAISON DE L'ÉCUYER DU ROI; then at no. 21 the Renaissance turret of

**ABBEY OF
STE-TRINITÉ**
The abbey church
and its magnificent
bell tower date
mainly from the
11th century, with
15th-century
additions and
embellishments.

A ROUND CHAPEL
The circular design
of the Chapelle du
Liget is most unusual
for a medieval
building. Constructed
from tufa, it dates
from the mid 12th
century.

the MAISON DE L'ARGENTIER DU ROI; and at no. 10 the
entrance of the former priory. After this continue along
Boulevard Philippe-Auguste, which follows the course of
the old dry moat.

BEAULIEU-LÈS-LOCHES

To the left of the road leading to Beaulieu-lès-Loches from
the Porte des Cordeliers stand the imposing 17th-century
hospital and then the Sous-Préfecture, which was once the
Hôtel d'Armaillé. On the right-hand side of the road is the
manor house of Sansac, built during the reign of François I
(a terracotta bust of the king can be seen on the forebuilding
ABBEY OF STE-TRINITÉ ★. The old village of Beaulieu, with i
15th- and 16th-century houses, grew up around the famous
Abbey of Ste-Trinité, founded by Foulques Nerra ● *37* in 100
His son Geoffroy Martel extended the church in the mid 11t
century and buried his father here. It is one of the
largest surviving buildings of this era in France.
The abbey's long period of prosperity ended
during the Hundred Years' War,
when it was ransacked by the
English. It never entirely
recovered its former glory, and
was sold off as national
property under the Revolution.

CHARTREUSE DU LIGET ★

The road through the Forest of
Loches via the Pyramide des
Chartreux leads to the
Carthusian monastery at Liget.
THE MONASTERY. In 1178
Henry Plantaganet ● *38*
acquired an area of wood with a spring and gave it to the
Carthusians to found a monastery – no doubt hoping to
make amends for the assassination of Thomas à Becket, the
Archbishop of Canterbury who had refused to submit to his
will. Further donations were made by King John of England
twenty years later, and a donation by Louis XI in 1234
established a tradition of liberality toward the Carthusians o
the part of the French monarchy. A series of portals and gate
lead the visitor down toward the monastery buildings. The
monumental 18th-century ENTRANCE PORTAL has carved bas-
reliefs on the pediment depicting Saint Bruno (who founded
the Carthusian order in 1084) and
Saint John the Baptist, who was the
monastery's patron saint.
**CHAPEL OF ST-JEAN-BAPTISTE
OF LIGET.** A forest path leads
along the side of the
monastery to this small
Romanesque chapel. It is
famous for its late-12th-
century mural painting
which are among the
most beautiful of the
Middle Ages.

MONTRÉSOR ★

Montrésor was a stronghold under Foulques Nerra, and in the
12th century belonged to Henry II of England until it was
captured by Philippe Auguste in 1188. It was later owned by a
number of famous families, most notably the Bastarnay family
in the 16th century, who founded the collegiate church. In
1849 the château was bought by the Polish Count Branicki,
whose descendants still live here. Branicki, a friend of
Napoleon III, was one of the great financiers of his age.
THE CHÂTEAU. The château is entered through the ruins of a
12th-century building whose arches are protected by splendid
neo-Gothic ironwork. The building was converted into a
comfortable residence in the early 16th century, under Imbert
de Bastarnay (1438–1523); it is surrounded by a double
curtain wall with large round towers from the 12th century.
Inside, little has changed since the 19th century: velvets and
plaids provide a setting for Polish objets d'art, Napoleon III
furniture, and paintings by the Italian school, Winterhalter
and Élisabeth Vigée-Lebrun.
COLLEGIATE CHURCH OF ST-JEAN-BAPTISTE. (1520 and 1541)
The chapel is built on a Gothic ground plan, with beautiful
Renaissance decorations. In a side chapel is an *Annunciation*
painted by Philippe de Champaigne (1602-74).

NOUANS-LES-FONTAINES

The village church is dedicated to Saint Martin. The
celebrated Pietà in the choir is attributed to Jean Fouquet.
This artist from Tours, who lived from c. 1420 to c. 1480,
became famous as a portraitist and miniaturist. He is regarded
as one of the most important of the early French painters.

**THE CARDERS OF
MONTRÉSOR**
Until the 19th
century wool from
the local sheep was
carded, spun and
woven in Montrésor.
The 17th-century
wooden market halls
in the town – the
Halle des Cardeux
(carders' market)
and Halle aux Laines
(wool market) – owe
their names to this
traditional craft.

**THE "PIETÀ" OF
NOUANS**
The painter Jean
Fouquet spent a
considerable time in
Italy, after which he
was appointed
official court painter
under Charles VII
and then under
Louis XI. The
somber colors, the
beautifully rendered
drapery, and the
reserved and serious
expressions of the
faces make this panel
painting one of the
masterpieces of
French art.

The "pyramide de Valençay",
a famous goat's cheese ● 29,
and Valençay wine

nickname "Diable
Boiteux" ("limping
devil").

. . . AND THE DIPLOMAT
Talleyrand started
out in the priesthood
and in 1789 became
the clergy's
representative on
the États Généraux.
As the head of the
constitutional
clergy he was
excommunicated by
the Pope and had to
leave the Church.
His diplomatic
career began under
the Assemblée
Législative. However,
accused of conspiring
with Britain on behalf
of the Duke of
Orléans, he was
forced to
emigrate
in 1792.

HISTORY OF THE TOWN

Strictly speaking, Valençay is located in the Berry
region: however, it merits inclusion in the Loire
valley because of its impressive château, similar in
many respects to those on the Loire itself. The
town grew up on a hillside overlooking the Nahon river, as an
important staging post between Touraine and Berry,
consisting of three distinct settlements: the old town, the
Bourg-de-l'Église and the Bas-Bourg. Over the years the
history of the town became intertwined with that of the
château, which underwent many alterations. The Valençay
estate is now one of the largest in France, stretching over
some 50,000 acres. Under the Empire the estate was owned
by Talleyrand, Napoleon's celebrated minister, whose lavish
royal receptions and political intrigues added sparkle and
interest to the life of the town.

HISTORY OF THE CHÂTEAU ★

The oldest part of the château as it stands today dates from
the first half of the 16th century. Later additions were
arranged around the original building in a subtle mix of styles
creating an elegantly structured architectural group. The
first section of the château was built by Louis d'Estampes,
governor of Blois, and Marie Hurault, daughter of the lord of
Cheverny ▲ 170, around 1520. Their son, Jacques
d'Estampes, married the daughter of a rich financier in 1540
and extended the château to its full size. Valençay was to
remain under the ownership of financiers for some time,
belonging successively to several "fermiers généraux"
("farmers-general", or tax collectors), including John Law
(1686–1761), the famous speculator who created the first
paper money in France during the regency of the Duke of
Orléans. In 1747 the château was acquired by the farmer-
general Charles Legendre de Villemorien, whose alterations
gave the building its present shape. The splendid palace was
sold to Talleyrand in 1803, with the
encouragement of Napoleon, who saw this
as a way of keeping his
troublesome minister at a
distance, entrusting him with the
reception of high-level guests
and enforced exiles like the
princes of Spain, including the
future King
Ferdinand
VII.

VALENÇAY ▲

West façade of the main
courtyard of Valençay ● 70.

When Talleyrand's nephew died, in 1898, the estate was split up.

A BLEND OF ARCHITECTURAL STYLES

In the 18th century Legendre de Villemorien demolished the east wing and the arcaded gallery of the south court, opening up a beautiful view over the landscape of the valley, as at Chaumont ▲ 177, ● 67.

NORTH WING. This wing dates from the 16th century, with a round tower (the Vieille Tour) to the west dating from 1520–30. Similar in size to the towers at Chambord ▲ 158, it is surmounted by an Imperial-style dome; its machicolations and wall walk are purely decorative in function ● 68. The entrance pavilion at the center, reminiscent of Chenonceau ▲ 218, was built around fifty years later. It forms a keep flanked by four turrets and is richly ornamented with dormer windows, pilasters and chimneys; its corbeled wall walk and decorative machicolations match those of the Vieille Tour. The Renaissance residential wing facing the courtyard is more elaborate, with an elegant gallery of basket-handle arches (right).

WEST WING. The northern half of the west wing, on the park side of the building, was built at the same time as the Vieille Tour. The southern half was built in the 17th century; its roofs and dormer windows were restored in the 18th century, following the original design. However, this uniformity of style was disrupted through the addition of a new tower, built as a counterpart to the Vieille Tour. The classical façade on the main courtyard is a dazzling Ionic composition reminiscent of some parts of Versailles (top of page).

INTERIOR. Some of the rooms – including the Salon Bleu with its lovely Louis XVI paneling – display magnificent Regency, Louis XVI and Empire furniture along with objets d'art. On the first story is a gallery dedicated to Talleyrand's family. On the second story, beside Talleyrand's bedroom, there are several rooms where famous visitors stayed, including the bedroom reserved for the King of Spain (above) and the one used by the novelist Germaine de Staël (1766–1817).

TALLEYRAND THE INTRIGUER
After Napoleon's coup d'état of 1799 Talleyrand became his foreign minister and was granted the titles of Grand Chambellan de l'Empire, Prince de Bénévent and then Vice-Grand Électeur. An opponent of the emperor's foreign policy, he was disgraced for intrigues in 1809. He became the leader of the provisional government in 1814 and regained his post at the foreign ministry under the first Restoration, negotiating the first Treaty of Paris (1814) and maneuvering to divide the allies during the Treaty of Vienna (1814–15). Under the Second Restoration he was appointed Président du Conseil (1815) and joined the liberal opposition. After being sent to London as French ambassador from 1830 to 1834 he finally returned to Valençay, where he died in 1838.

233

The château and the village around it were named after Hugues Ridel, lord of Azay in the 12th century. From the 15th to the 17th century the town was called Azay-le-Brûlé ("Azay-the-Burnt"), after being destroyed by fire.

c. 50 miles

1 day

PICTORIAL RECORDS
The earliest existing pictures of the château date from the 19th century.

Legend has it that in 1418, in the middle of the Hundred Years' War ● *38*, the future Charles VII was insulted by the Burgundian troops occupying the fortress of Azay, who made disparaging remarks about him. In revenge for the insults, Azay was burnt to the ground and the soldiers were massacred. Afterward the local people rebuilt the town and the ramparts. A few 15th-century buildings still survive: in Rue de l'Abreuvoir there is a simple round tower, built of small stones, the top of which was demolished; and in Rue de la Mairie there is a house (above) with a half-timbered upper story, over a lower story made of stone.

THE CHÂTEAU   (G

The Château d'Azay-le-Rideau was built on a small island in the Indre in the early 16th century, on the site of an earlier fortress. A long avenue of chestnut trees, ending in a semicircular courtyard shaded by lime trees, leads to this "many-faceted diamond set in the Indre,

CHÂTEAU D'AZAY LE RIDEAU
CIRCUITS AUTOMOBILES DE LA Cie
D'ORLÉANS AU DÉPART DE TOURS

mounted on
piles, and masked
by flowers" (Balzac).

THE BUILDERS. Gilles Berthelot, Treasurer of France,
bought the estate of Azay-le-Rideau and the land around
in the 16th century. He demolished the feudal castle,
with the exception of the large tower (which was replaced in
the 19th century). Work on his new castle began in 1518, at
the same time as Thomas Bohier was completing Chenonceau
● 218 and François I was making plans for Chambord.
Gilles Berthelot's wife, Philippe Lesbahy, supervised the
construction work for long periods while her husband's
official duties kept him in Paris.

THE CONSTRUCTION OF THE CHÂTEAU. Some receipts and
accounts of expenditure have survived, providing invaluable
information about the construction of Gilles Berthelot's
château. A large number of laborers, masons and carpenters
worked on the building day and night. They used pumps to
drain the site and huge iron bars to drive in the piles.
They cut and assembled stone from quarries
near the château; harder stone had to be
brought from quarries further off, in
Bourré and St-Aignan, which was
transported to the site by river and on carts.
The accounts do not provide any clear
evidence regarding the name of the architect.
It may have been Étienne Rousseau, who seems
to have been the only master mason in direct contact
with Gilles Berthelot. François I visited the site of the new
château on February 2, 1518. After this the work progressed
rapidly: the staircase was probably finished by 1524, as it
bears two royal emblems: the salamander of François I
and the ermine of his wife, Queen Claude, who died in the
same year.

THE SECRET OF AZAY
"From time
immemorial this
had been the site
of a fortress whose
function was to
defend the crossing
of the Indre on the
road from Tours to
Chinon. The builders
who modernized the
fortress of Azay in
the 16th century did
not forget this, as
can be seen in the
military features
they provided,
nearly all of which
survive today."
Jean-Claude
Le Guillou

"A SINGLE DESIRE"
This was the motto
of Queen Claude,
wife of François I and
daughter of Louis XII
and Anne de
Bretagne ● 34.
The ermine is her
personal emblem.

235

The Château d'Azay-le-Rideau stands by the riverside, between two branches of the Indre. It was built in a single phase, from 1518 to 1524. Consequently, although never completed, it is the archetypal Loire château, incorporating all the typical features of the genre. Here the feudal elements, such as the turrets, wall walk and moat, are purely symbolic in function, their sole purpose being to demonstrate the high rank of the château's owner. Inside, Azay-le-Rideau was thoroughly modern, with a simple, practical layout in which comfort was the prime consideration. The château presents a successful blend of medieval traditions and the new classical Italian influences. It was the most perfect château of its era, reflecting the progressive aspects of early-Renaissance architecture.

ELEVATION, WITH CROSS-SECTION OF THE STAIRCASE
In contrast to the great spiral staircase of the François I wing at Blois, the staircase at Azay is designed on the Italian model with straight flights of stairs. Its design is innovative, as is its inclusion within the main building of the château: the staircase well opens onto both the exterior and the internal courtyard. The prototype of this staircase design was built at the Château de Bury (now destroyed).

THE STAIRCASE
The staircase occupies a wide central bay, protruding from the north façade. Its structure can be seen on the elevation four stories of vaulte twin bays mark the half-landings. Mos of the building's decorative carvings are concentrated here: on the engage columns, pilasters and entablatures, decorated with foliation, shells and medallions. The staircase break up the regularity of the façade, which has vertically aligne windows and horizontal moldings

The dormer windows are heavily ornamented in the Italian style, with shells, candelabras, and so on. The salamander and ermine are homages to François I and Queen Claude.

PILASTER CAPITAL
The Ionic capitals were based on classical models. They support the horizontal entablatures formed by Italian-style moldings.

COFFERED CEILING
The sloping coffered ceiling over the staircase has depressed arches with pendants; it is decorated with roses and classical medallions.

THE GROUND PLAN
The ground plan intended for Azay had been used for many châteaux, from the 15th century onward: a quadrilateral consisting of three main wings, plus a lower wing featuring the entrance portal. However, only the east and north wings were built. The design at Azay was innovative in that it gave the great staircase a prominent position in the main building, making it the pivot of the building's symmetries.

REAR FAÇADE
The façade illustrates the symmetrical design centered on the staircase bay, similar to that of the Château de Bury. A double row of horizontal moldings and pilasters on either side of the windows form a grid pattern: this type of arrangement can also be seen at Gaillon and Blois.

FACADE SUD

PROUD OWNERS ... Armand de Biencourt and his wife Anne de Montmorency added their initials to the doors in the 19th century (below).

DISGRACE. The ambitious project was interrupted by a dramatic course of events. A number of families in the Tours region had grown rich through speculation and lent money to the crown. After his Italian campaigns the king, who owed them a great deal of money, accused them of embezzlement. Jacques de Beaune-Semblançay, his superintendent of finances, was condemned and hanged in 1527 ▲ *202*. Gilles Berthelot did not escape: in 1528 his possessions were confiscated by François I and given to Antoine Raffin, one of the king's companion in arms. Berthelot took refuge at Cambrai, where he died a year later. For several years Philippe Lesbahy tried to hold ont Azay; but she finally lost it in 1535, when Raffin took possession of the estate.

FROM THE 16TH CENTURY TO THE PRESENT DAY. The château remained in the hands of the same family until the Revolution. In 1791 it was acquired by the Marquis de Biencourt, renowned for his revolutionary ideas. His descendants kept it until 1899, and in 1905 it was purchased by the state.

AN EARLY RENAISSANCE MASTERPIECE. In the mid 19th century the Marquis de Biencourt took steps to give the château its present unified appearance: he replaced the great medieval tower with a tower more suited to the style of the building, and replaced a small turret in the troubadour style (dating probably from around 1800) with a turret matching the others on the main façade. Despite these later modifications, the château remains an early-Renaissance building. In its overall appearance it is still faithful to the medieval tradition – with its high roofs and chimneys, corner turrets, and wall walk with machicolations However, the site was chosen for its pleasant situation rather than for a defensive purpose. The influence of the Italian Renaissance is tangible, notably in the structure of the façades, with windows at regular intervals flanked by pilasters, horizontal moldings between the stories, and carved capitals.

THE STAIRCASE. The main entrance of the château is also the entrance to the staircase. The straight staircase, with one flight over another, is highlighted by its central position on the main façade and by its

"YOU WOULD NOT HAVE THOUGHT THAT THIS WAS ONCE A PLACE OF STRATEGIC IMPORTANCE. HOWEVER, IN TIMES GONE BY [AZAY] RESISTED A NUMBER OF SIEGES."

PIGANIOL DE LA FORCE

agnificent decoration of medallions, foliage and shells. The namentation features the initial and the salamander of François I (below), the letter C and e ermine of Queen Claude, and the initials G and P of e builders of the château (Gilles Berthelot and Philippe sbahy).

HE INTERIOR OF THE CHÂTEAU. Rich tapestries and rniture from the 16th, 17th and 18th centuries decorate e apartments, which were refurnished by the national mmission for historical monuments. The kitchen ceiling s splendid surbased vaulting, decorated with cartouches at e springing points of the arches. The huge fireplace, near the well, bears Berthelot's coat of arms: the escutcheon of Philippe Lesbahy must have been painted over it. The great hall, formerly a reception room, occupies the entire western half of the residential wing. As was customary, its ceiling is higher than that of other rooms in the château; the decoration of the fireplace is especially fine.

THE GROUNDS. To view the other sides of the château d the wall walk, take a stroll in the extensive landscaped ounds which replaced the formal gardens in the 19th ntury. Also in the 19th century a dam was built across the dre, in order to transform the moat into a lake. To the west the château is a small Gothic CHAPEL, restored after staining serious damage during World War Two. The view the south includes the MANOIR DE LA RÉMONNIÈRE ormerly "la Romainière"), from the 16th and 17th centuries. nce a hunting lodge belonging to Azay, it was built over the mains of a Gallo-Roman villa (a number of classical ins have been found nearby, notably the base f a Roman temple). Today it is a hotel: sitors can stay here or walk in e grounds while ewing the hâteau.

Above: the southeast façade of the Château d'Azay-le-Rideau. Below: aerial view of the west façade and part of the village.

THE INTERIOR OF AZAY IN THE 19TH CENTURY
Armand de Biencourt and his wife Anne de Montmorency were keen to share the artistic treasures that they had inherited, and enjoyed showing the rooms of the château to visitors interested in art and history. Under the Second Empire their home was considered one of the best museums in France.

DECORATION OF THE CHURCH OF ST-SYMPHORIEN
The lower row of statues was partially destroyed to make way for a window installed at a later period (12th or 13th century).

CHÂTEAU DE SACHÉ
This was built in the 16th century, on the site of an earlier fortress.

CHURCH OF ST-SYMPHORIEN

The unusual historiated façade dates from when the church was built (11th century). It is decorated with miter-shaped arches and two rows of statuettes in rounded niches. The vaulted main nave was built between 1020 and 1040, while the left-hand nave dates from the 12th century. The Chapelle Seigneuriale, which doubled as a funerary chapel, was built in the 17th century by Antoinette Raffin, the mistress of Azay at that time. Its façade and the ornamentation of the doorway can be admired from the château grounds. The master glassmaker Max Ingrand (1908–69) ▲ *149* made the four stained-glass windows of the main nave (depicting Saint Martin, Saint Henry, Saint Barbe and Saint Bernadette) and the one depicting the Assumption in the Chapelle Seigneuriale.
BESIDE THE INDRE. The square adjoining the church leads to the banks of the Indre, which separates the town of Azay from the château. From the bridge there is a fine view of the château and an old mill; on the island, which once belonged to the château, visitors can relax, play boules, or doze off to the gentle lapping of the water.

BALZAC'S BEDROOM
This tiny low-ceilinged room under the eaves was furnished sparsely, so that nothing would distract the writer's attention. Balzac worked here, shut away for whole days "like a monk in a monastery", with an oil-lamp for lighting, "asking ideas from the night and words from the silence".

SACHÉ

SACHÉ AND BALZAC. Saché is known for its connections with the novelist Honoré de Balzac (1799–1850). He seems to be present everywhere in the valley – which may lead visitors to overlook the fact that he only stayed here a few times, coming to this corner of the Touraine to seek refuge from the turbulence of society and the demands of his creditors.
A CHÂTEAU BATHED IN SILENCE. Balzac stayed at the Château de Saché, a "melancholy place full of harmonies too serious for superficial souls, but dear to poets, whose souls are full of sadness". The owner of the château at this time, Monsieur de Margonne, was an old friend of the Balzac family and treated the novelist as if he were his own son. The austere building still has what Balzac described as its "large knotty trees" and an "ineffable air of mystery, seeping across the solitary valley".
MUSÉE BALZAC. The château's main entrance, which has ornamental pilasters with torus moldings, leads to a straight staircase at the top of which stands a bronze statue of Balzac by the Tours sculptor François Sicard (1862–1934) ▲ *214*. Two rooms, the dining room and the drawing room, have been reconstructed in the

le of the period. A museum on
e top floor is dedicated to the
iter's life and work. The place
ere Balzac's presence can be
ost keenly felt is his bedroom
the top of the house. A single
ndow looks over a "calm,
litary valley, a huge fold of and
rdered by two-hundred-year-
d oak trees".

THE VILLAGE
OF SACHÉ
The village has a
number of old
houses; a 12th-
century half-
timbered inn near
to the church (left) is
particularly striking.

HURCH OF ST-MARTIN-DE-
RTOU.
The church (right) is
uated at the center of the town.
lzac used to accompany his
sts here from time to time.
wooden porch stands in front of
e entrance to the main nave (12th and 13th century).
second nave was added on the north side in the 16th
ntury. To the left of the choir is a plaque inscribed in Latin
scribing the virtues of the blessed Marguerite de Rouxellé
608–28), whose tomb became a place of pilgrimage.

ANOTHER FAMOUS RESIDENT OF SACHÉ:
CALDER. The American sculptor
and painter Alexander Calder
(1898–1976), the witty inventor of
"mobiles" and "stabiles", moved
to Saché in 1955. One of his works – a composite
"mobile-stabile" (right) – can be seen in the
square in front of the church, in a striking
juxtaposition of 20th-century art with a
historical setting. Described by his friend
Miró as a "solid-looking man with the soul of
a nightingale", Calder bought an old house on
the hillside on the right bank of the Indre and
dubbed it the "Maison de François I", without any
historical justification for the name. Later he had a
house and huge studio built on a hillside at Le Carroi
(north of Saché), with enormous windows that give it
the air of a cathedral. Today the building houses the
Centre National des Arts Plastiques, which
welcomes young artists from France and abroad.

CALDER'S "STABILES"
This term was
invented by the
sculptor Jean Arp
(1887–1966) to
describe Calder's
massive sculptures
made of sheet metal.
Most of them are
black in color.

241

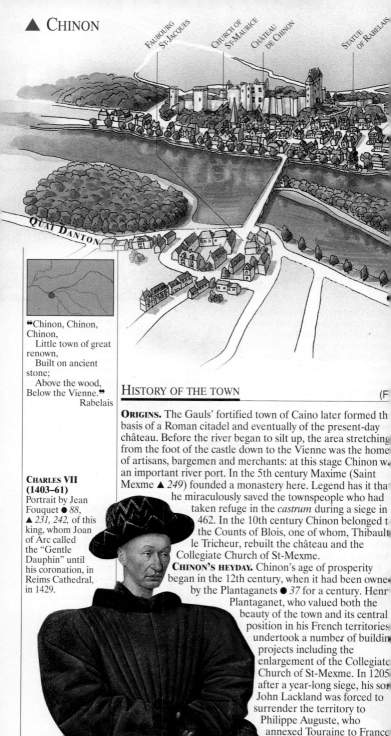

FAUBOURG ST-JACQUES · CHURCH OF ST-MAURICE · CHÂTEAU DE CHINON · STATUE OF RABELAIS

QUAI DANTON

"Chinon, Chinon,
Chinon,
    Little town of great
renown,
    Built on ancient
stone;
    Above the wood,
Below the Vienne."
            Rabelais

**CHARLES VII
(1403–61)**
Portrait by Jean
Fouquet ● 88,
▲ 231, 242, of this
king, whom Joan
of Arc called
the "Gentle
Dauphin" until
his coronation, in
Reims Cathedral,
in 1429.

CHARLES · SEPTIESME · LE LE NOM

HISTORY OF THE TOWN

(F

ORIGINS. The Gauls' fortified town of Caino later formed th
basis of a Roman citadel and eventually of the present-day
château. Before the river began to silt up, the area stretching
from the foot of the castle down to the Vienne was the home
of artisans, bargemen and merchants: at this stage Chinon wa
an important river port. In the 5th century Maxime (Saint
Mexme ▲ 249) founded a monastery here. Legend has that
he miraculously saved the townspeople who had
taken refuge in the *castrum* during a siege in
462. In the 10th century Chinon belonged to
the Counts of Blois, one of whom, Thibault
le Tricheur, rebuilt the château and the
Collegiate Church of St-Mexme.
CHINON'S HEYDAY. Chinon's age of prosperity
began in the 12th century, when it had been owned
by the Plantaganets ● 37 for a century. Henri
Plantaganet, who valued both the
beauty of the town and its central
position in his French territories
undertook a number of buildin
projects including the
enlargement of the Collegiate
Church of St-Mexme. In 1205
after a year-long siege, his son
John Lackland was forced to
surrender the territory to
Philippe Auguste, who
annexed Touraine to France
**ATROCITIES IN THE 14TH
CENTURY.** Philip the Fair
imprisoned the leaders of
the Templars in the castle

'ARC

JOAN OF ARC ESCORTED TO CHINON
This 13-year-old peasant girl from Lorraine heard voices commanding her to liberate France, which at that time was almost entirely occupied by the English. The young girl asked Robert de Baudricourt, the king's captain at Vaucouleurs, for an escort to accompany her to Touraine to see

Chinon in 1314, then had them burned alive in Paris. In 321 his son Philip the Tall exacted the same punishment on 0 Jews of the area, who were charged with poisoning the wn's well. The real motive for this massacre, like that the Templars, was the seizure of their property.

CHINON, CENTER OF THE FRENCH KINGDOM. In the 15th century the Duc de Touraine (the future Charles VII) took fuge behind the town's ramparts. It was here, in 1429, that oan of Arc convinced him to go to the aid of Orléans ▲ 116. hen Louis XI's chamberlain Philippe de Commynes became overnor of the town he strengthened the château's defenses nd undertook major alterations to the Church of St-Étienne. esare Borgia, the son and legate of Pope Alexander VI, met ouis XII at Chinon in the late 15th century: Louis wanted to ave his first marriage annulled so he could marry Anne de retagne, Charles VIII's widow, and thereby annexe Brittany France. At the end of the 15th century, François Rabelais 97 was born not far from here at La Devinière ▲ 250.

Charles VII. Baudricourt, considering the French cause to be more or less beyond rescue, gave way at their second interview, with the words "Go, go! And happen what may!".

243

Sketch of the south elevation (above) and north elevation (below) of the Château de Chinon by Henri Deverni, 1882.

DEFENSES
A wide and deep dry moat, once spanned by a drawbridge,

separates the Château du Milieu and the Fort du Coudray. Underground passages supplemented the fort's defense system. One of these is said to have led to the manor house of Roberdeau (now destroyed), to the north of the château: this was the residence of Charles VII's mistress, Agnès Sorel ▲ 227.

North elevation of the Château de Chinon.

CHINON ABANDONED. The kings abandoned the austere château in the 16th century. After this it passed into the hands of Cardinal Richelieu, who obtained permission from Louis XIII to demolish it. This proved to be too costly an undertaking and was not carried out, but time and neglect eventually destroyed a large part of the building. The town's fortified ramparts were demolished in the late 18th century. Shortly before the Revolution a road was built connecting Chinon and Tours via Azay-le-Rideau. Despite the decline of river transport, Chinon was also preserved from isolation by the advent of the railway in the 19th century. A good deal of renovation work was undertaken around this time: the quaysides were built, streets were widened, and the Place Jeanne d'Arc was created.

CHINON TODAY. The Avoine-Chinon nuclear power station was built in 1964, boosting the economy by creating jobs. Chinon's wine ■ 30 has had its own "Appellation d'origine contrôlée" since 1937, and the town still has extensive vineyards, covering an area of 4,200 acres. Local authorities have been developing tourism and the historical heritage; a medieval market held annually in Chinon, involving two thousand participants in costume and attracting some twenty thousand visitors.

THE CHÂTEAU ● 64

The Château de Chinon is built on a rocky outcrop overlooking the Vienne: its scale is best appreciated from Faubourg St-Jacques on the other side of the bridge. The château, surrounded by a fortified rampart whose oldest section dates from the 10th century, actually consists of three buildings separated by dry moats: from east to west these are the Fort St-Georges, the Château du Milieu and the Fort du Coudray.
FORT ST-GEORGES (private property). Today little remains of this fortress built by Henry Plantaganet. Its name refers to an adjoining chapel, of which only the crypt survives.
CHÂTEAU DU MILIEU. The drawbridge that defended the entrance to the château was replaced by a fixed bridge in the 18th century. Next to the southern rampart are the GRANDE SALLE DE CHARLES VII, of which only the fireplace survives, and the LOGIS ROYAUX (royal residence) built by Henry Plantaganet. It was here, at the end of February 1429, that the first meeting took place between Joan of Arc (statue, above) and Charles VII ▲ 116. The Maid of Orleans had been preceded by rumors:

is young girl was claiming that God had commanded her to
ght the English and expel them from France. To test her, the
ng disguised himself as a page and his cousin took his place
 the throne. Joan of Arc was not deceived: she went
aight up to the "Gentle Dauphin". Contemporaries
ported that the king emerged from the ensuing private
terview with a radiant expression, convinced of Joan's
ssion. He supplied her with a small army, and after the
ctory at Orléans she persuaded him to eradicate all doubts
garding his legitimacy by being crowned, like his ancestors,
in Reims (on July 17, 1429). Joan of Arc was sold to the
English by the Burgundians; she was
declared a heretic after the famous trial
and burned alive at Rouen on May 30,
1431. She was rehabilitated in 1450 and
canonized in 1920. The displays in the
LOGIS ROYAUX include a model of the
château in its heyday and tapestries

om Flanders and Aubusson (16th–17th centuries). The
th-century rampart to the north has three main towers.
e TOUR D'ARGENTON (15th century) is named after its
ilder Philippe Commynes, lord of Argenton; its walls are
er 16 feet thick, with holes for chains reflecting its use as a
ison. The TOUR DES CHIENS, from the 13th century, owes
 name to the fact that it housed the royal hounds; it is of
eat architectural interest, with three stories of rooms with
ival vaulting. THE TOUR DE L'ÉCHAUGUETTE (Bartizan
wer), on the northeast corner, is partly ruined.
RT DU COUDRAY. The fort is bordered to the
st by the oldest curtain wall of the château,
ich dates from the 10th century. It is separated
om the Château du Milieu by a dry ditch, dug out
 the early 13th century, which is over 65 feet wide
d nearly as deep. The ditch served as a quarry for
ilding work on the TOUR DU COUDRAY (Philippe-
uguste's keep), which overlooks it. To one side was
e CHAPEL OF ST-MARTIN (now destroyed) where
an of Arc came to pray. On the southwest corner stands the
agnificent TOUR DE BOISSY built by Philippe Auguste, which
offers a panoramic view over Chinon and the

THE ECHO OF CHINON

❝There is a remarkable echo from the northern wall of the château, close to the car park. If you ask *'Les femmes de Chinon sont-elles fidèles?'*, the echo queries *'Elles?'*. If you retort *'Oui, les femmes de Chinon'*, the echo replies *'Non'*.❞

Guide du Val de Loire mystérieux

THE TOUR DE L'HORLOGE

This late-14th-century tower (left) acts as a monumental gateway to the château. It houses a museum which tells the story of Joan of Arc. Its bell, named "Marie Javel", dates from 1399.

CHINON'S WINE

The local wine is known for its slightly earthy, fruity fragrance ■ *30*.

RVE HAVTE
St MAVRICE

The cellar's name comes from Rabelais' description of the paintings of dancing satyrs on its walls. Like the Caves Vaslins behind it, this cave was once a stone quarry, used when the château was enlarged in the 14th century. It was used for storing wine from the 15th century onward. In *Pantagruel* Rabelais recalls his visits to the Cave-Peincte where he drank "many glasses of chilled wine" while singing *Bonum vinûm laetificat cor hominum* ("Good wine gladdens the heart"). In the cul-de-sac parallel to this is a wine museum, the Musée du Vin et de la Tonnellerie, which has life-size mechanical figures illustrating work in a vineyard.

river valley. The tower served as a place of worship before the Chapel of St-Martin was built, which explains the presence of an apse. The machicolations around the top were added during the Second Empire. The TOUR DU MOULIN (Mill Tower) stands as a lookout post at the tip of the promontory; its name may be derived from the ovens near the gateway. The Angevin vaulting ● 60 on the first story probably dates from when the tower was built, under the Plantaganets.

BELOW THE CHÂTEAU ★

This quarter (opposite), which was once the center of the fortified town, has retained its medieval street pattern. The main road through the old town is the Rue Voltaire, formerly the Rue Haut-St-Maurice, of which René Boylesve said in his book *La Jeune Fille bien élevée*: "Rue St-Maurice in Chinon is so delightfully pretty! . . . The newest houses date from the 17th century; most are from the 15th and 16th centuries, some half-timbered and decorated with simple carvings, others built in the soft local stone, flanked by corner turrets with conical roofs, and pierced with bright mullioned windows."

THE GRAND-CARROI. The Grand-Carroi ("main crossroads") was the center of the town in the Middle Ages. It was here that the Rue Haut-St-Maurice met the streets rising from the Vienne to the château. One of the most beautiful half-timbered houses in the region can be seen here, on the corner of Rue Voltaire.

RUE JEANNE D'ARC. This street gives pedestrian access to the château. On the corner of Rue Voltaire, standing against a slate-covered house, is the coping of a well. According to legend Joan of Arc stepped on it, to dismount, when she arrived in Chinon; since then the well has never dried up. Not far from here is the Hôtel Torterue de Langardière (c. 1760), which has lovely wrought-iron balconies.

MAISON ROUGE. The Maison Rouge (nos. 38–42, Rue Voltaire) dates from the 14th and 15th centuries. Built of brick and wood, it is a typical example of the town's medieval architecture.

MAISON DES ÉTATS-GÉNÉRAUX. This house built of tufa owes its name to the meeting of the États-Généraux convened by Charles VII in 1428, when the English were laying siege to Orléans; it was held in the hall on the second story. On April 6, 1199 Richard Lionheart is said to have died here, from wounds received at Chalus. The collections of the Amis du

"Chinon, like Loches, is a masterpiece of a town. It is crowned with towers, keeps and crenelations, its houses with their pointed roofs are packed in between the rampart and the river, where a line of plane trees affords a perfect riverside promenade: this linear layout has its own special charm. Chinon is a jewel in the crown of Touraine; Chinon, through Joan of Arc, crowned the kingdom of France; Chinon is the glory of our past. How beautiful this town is: so insignificant today and yet in the past so replete with our country's future! Beautiful? Yes, it has the beauty of someone who has accomplished their task and retired from the commotion of the world to live in peaceful retirement. Not that it is overcome with sleepiness, or dozing off gradually at the foot of the hillside; but all that remains of its violent glory are the high ramparts and the empty towers, although something of its past splendors can still be sensed in the Grand-Carroi with its half-timbered houses, in the Carrefour du Puy-des-Bancs, in Rue de la Lamproie and Rue du Grenier-à-Sel, where it is easy to imagine the young Rabelais living a life of reckless pleasure."

Maurice Bedel
La Touraine

Hôtel des Eaux et Forêts (above); and Place du Général-de-Gaulle (below).

Vieux Chinon displayed here feature items relating to river transport and popular traditions. They include a full-length portrait of Rabelais by Delacroix and an 11th-century cope, said to be Saint Mexme's, made of rich oriental fabrics.

PRIVATE HOUSES. Rue Voltaire is lined with private houses from the 15th, 16th and 17th centuries. Don't miss the HÔTEL DU GOUVERNEUR at no. 48. The town's governors lived in this house (built in the 15th and 17th centuries) after the château became inhabitable. The wing at the far end of the courtyard is taken up by a stone staircase with converging flights of stairs. The HÔTEL DU BAILLAGE (no. 71), now the Hostellerie Gargantua, was built in the 15th century: Rabelais' father, a lawyer, used to plead there. At no. 82 on Rue Voltaire, after the Church of St-Maurice, is the 16th-century HÔTEL DES EAUX ET FÔRETS (left), a U-shaped building with a raised courtyard. Opposite this is one of the old gates of the town (17th century), set into the façade of a building dating from the 15th and 16th centuries, which once housed the museum.

CHURCH OF ST-MAURICE. The church was built on the lower side of the street between the 12th and 16th centuries. The main nave has 12th-century Angevin vaulting.

FROM THE HÔTEL DE VILLE TO ST-MEXME

PLACE DU GÉNÉRAL-DE-GAULLE (below). This square used to be called the Place des Halles, because a covered

market stood on the site of the present-day town hall until the 18th century. From the square you can see a bronze statue of Rabelais by Émile Hébert (1882) and the Rue Rabelais, which is a pedestrian shopping street.

RUE DE LA LAMPROIE. The 18th-century house at no. 15 was built over the house of Rabelais' parents ▲ 250. It is said that Rabelais fished from the house when the water level was high – perhaps catching lampreys?

CHURCH OF ST-ÉTIENNE. Tradition has it that the church was built by a butcher, a draper and a baker; be that as it may, construction work began in the 15th century and the building was completed by Philippe de Commynes, governor of Chinon from 1477 to 1483, whose coat of arms can be seen over the portal. The three stained-glass windows of the choir were made by Léon Lobin in the 19th century, depicting the life of Saint Étienne and two historical events that took place in Chinon: the recognition of Charles VII by Joan of Arc and the meeting of John the Recluse with Saint Radegund.

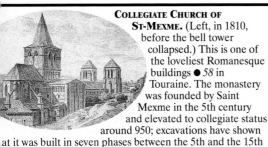

**COLLEGIATE CHURCH OF
ST-MEXME.** (Left, in 1810, before the bell tower collapsed.) This is one of the loveliest Romanesque buildings ● *58* in Touraine. The monastery was founded by Saint Mexme in the 5th century and elevated to collegiate status around 950; excavations have shown at it was built in seven phases between the 5th and the 15th nturies. It was closed down during the Revolution and then uffered serious damage when the central bell tower collapsed 1817, destroying the choir and the transept. The rebuilding, from the early 11th century, is magnificently ecorated with seventy carved slabs illustrating scenes from e life and passion of Christ. Before entering the nave, note e famous bas-relief of the Crucifixion, now damaged. One the towers contains a chapel which was painted in the late 5th century: the Last Judgment (on the north wall) and the ountain of Forgiveness (on the west wall) are still visible.

OTEAU STE-RADEGONDE

he steep path uphill is bordered with caves which ere once used as dwellings (one or two are still habited). From here there is a view over the newer uarters of Chinon and the Vienne.

HAPEL OF STE-RADEGONDE ★. (This can be reached by car, a the Route du Tunnel.) It is said that Saint Radegund *248* (below) came here to ask the English hermit John the ecluse to pray that she would not be forced to return to the urt. When her prayer was answered, she decided to take the eil and founded a convent at Poitiers. John the Recluse oved here in the 6th century, after having prayed at the mb of Saint Mexme. The Chapel of Ste-Radegonde was uilt in the 11th century on a north–south axis, around the ave where the hermit had lived: his mb, which was plundered uring the Revolution, can ill be seen inside. On the ault of the small semicircular pse is the early-13th-century ural known as *La Chasse Royale* Royal Hunt). Behind the chapel is small museum of popular rts and traditions.

"LA CHASSE ROYALE"
There are at least three interpretations of this 13th-century mural (detail below). It may depict a subject taken from a chivalric novel, or the legend of Saint Gilles. According to the legend, Charlemagne had committed incest with his half-sister and no one, from his personal confessor to the pope, was willing to absolve him from the sin, until he encountered the hermit Saint Gilles during a hunt. The hermit heaped reproaches on him and commanded him to pray. The emperor and the saint then implored God's pardon together and a hand appeared, which symbolized divine absolution. However, the most generally accepted hypothesis is that the painting depicts the hunt during which John Lackland, accompanied by his mother Eleanor of Aquitaine, met his future wife Isabelle d'Angoulême.

RABELAIS COUNTRY

RABELAIS AS SEEN BY PAINTERS
Since all portraits of Rabelais are posthumous, we do not know what he really looked like (above, anonymous 17th-century portrait). In view of this, the very sober-looking image (below) created by Matisse for La Devinière in 1951 is all the more surprising. Matisse opted for the more refined of the two faces of Rabelais described by La Bruyère: "When he is bad, he goes far

beyond the very worst and acquires the charm of the rabble; when he is good, he aspires to the exquisite and the excellent, and can be the most refined of writers."

François Rabelais (1494–1553) is one of the four famous French writers born in the "Garden of France"; the others are Pierre de Ronsard ▲ 258, the philosopher René Descartes (1596–1650) and Honoré de Balzac ● 90, ▲ 240. Between them the works of these four authors illustrate almost every aspect of the French character. Only Descartes – who was born in La Haye, now called Descartes, in southern Touraine – appears not to have been inspired by his native region. Nevertheless, the rigorous style of his philosophical works doubtless had its origin in this area, where the purest French is spoken. The region, especially the area around Chinon, had a strong influence on Rabelais.

LA DEVINIÈRE. This house, Rabelais' birthplace, is located at the heart of Rabelaisia, where the Picrocholine War (an important episode in *Gargantua*) is set. The world view of the Middle Ages had been based on a strict hierarchy ruled over by God; the Renaissance, with its new scientific, technical and intellectual discoveries, overthrew the old order, giving birth to new thoughts and ideals. This new age generated a hunger for knowledge and an unbounded enthusiasm for progress, which were given symbolic expression in the insatiable appetite of Rabelais' giants. La Devinière dates from the 15th century and was probably a winegrower's house.

It contains a collection of documents relating to the life and works of Rabelais, along with local furniture from the 16th and 17th centuries. The troglodyte caves in the basement are open to visitors. In the garden is a map created by the ceramist Jean Luneau in 1989, featuring characters, themes and locations from Rabelais' works.

CHÂTEAU DU RIVAU. Rabelais immortalized the name of Rivau in *Gargantua*, Chapter 49: Grandgousier, Gargantua's father, gives a great feast in honor of the Gargantuist captains who had won the Picrocholine War and showers them with gifts: "And what is more he gave to each of them on permanent lease (unless they died without heirs) his adjoining castles and estates, to suit each of them: to ꞉nocrates he gave La Roche-Clermault, . . . Le Rivau to ꞉lmere." The three cylindrical towers, the moat and the ꞉çade behind the main building are remnants of the 13th-꞉ntury feudal castle. Pierre de Beauvau, the château's owner ꞉ the 15th century, obtained permission from Charles VII to ꞉rtify it. The outbuildings, now separate from the château ꞉elf, date from the early 16th century. The great cylindrical pigeon loft has more than two thousand nesting holes.

ABBEY OF ST-PIERRE-DE-SEUILLY.

Rabelais began his education at this 12th-century Benedictine abbey. He later set a scene of the Picrocholine War here (*Gargantua*, Chapter 27: "How a monk of Seuilly saved the abbey precinct from sacking by the enemy"). It was here that Frère Jean of the Entommeures – "who had a great big gob and was well provided in the nose department, who could rush through the hours and rattle through the mass" – attacked the troops of Picrochole, king of Lerné. The abbey now houses a center for environmental education.

CHÂTEAU DE LA ROCHE-CLERMAULT (private property).

The château replaced a fortress used by Rabelais as a model in *Gargantua* (Chapter 28: "How Picrochole captured La Roche-Clermault"). Building ꞉ork came to a sudden halt in 1638, leaving one of the side ꞉ings unbuilt. The castle has vast underground passages (said ꞉ be the most extensive in the region), with mysterious ꞉arvings on the walls. The road to Lerné is lined with ꞉oglodyte houses ● *80*.

꞉N THE BANKS OF THE VIENNE, TAVANT

꞉HURCH OF ST-NICHOLAS ★. This church, dating from the ꞉arly 12th century, has a raised choir above a semi-꞉nderground crypt. The wall ꞉aintings in the crypt have ꞉ade the church famous ▲ *252*, *54*. The carved entrance portal ꞉ flanked by two blind arches. ꞉he capitals are decorated with ꞉otifs, such as sirens and fish, ꞉luding to Tavant's riverside ꞉ocation. In the choir is a ꞉ainting of Christ in Majesty ꞉urrounded by the symbols of ꞉ne four Evangelists, and a cycle ꞉epicting Christ's childhood.

GREAT HUMOR AND SATIRE
Rabelais studied philosophy and Greek before becoming interested in medicine, which he practiced throughout his life. Regarded as the father of French prose, he was a linguistic craftsman and creator of words, expressions and images. His humanist philosophy expresses both the joys of knowledge and the pleasures of the flesh – celebrating food and wine, language, erudition and the spirit of tolerance – all conveyed by satire and parody.

FOUACES ● 97
It was these delicious pancakes (cooked in the oven or under the ashes, then filled with either *rillettes* or cheese) that sparked off the Picrocholine War, the bitter conflict between Grandgousier, Gargantua's father, and the king of the village of Lerné (below).

1. Figure fighting with a lion. King David? Samson?

2. Saint holding a flowering stem.

9. Man with outstretched arms, carrying a beam. He faces figure **12**.

3. Figure seated on a throne. Saul listening to King David (**7**)?

4. Man with raised arms. David dancing?

Plan of the crypt ● *58*

A UNIQUE CYCLE OF
ROMANESQUE ● *58* PAINTINGS

The Comte de Galembert revealed the paintings' existence at the Archeological Congress of Caen in 1862, in a paper entitled *The Frescos of Touraine*. They were then forgotten again, until a short study by the American Melville Webber appeared in *Art Studies* in 1925. However, it was only through the writings of art historian Henri Focillon (1881–1943) and restoration work undertaken in 1942–5, by a team from the Beaux-Arts directed by Suzanne Flandrin, that this treasure of religious art became widely known. In Focillon's words this is "an art full of poetry and immediacy, life and movement. The figures themselves vibrate with life, their energy intensified by the speed with which they were produced." A reconstruction of the wall paintings can be seen in the Musée des Monuments Français in Paris.

6. Two men walking. Representing months or seasons?

7. King David playing the harp.

8. Angel carrying a candleholder, as in figure **5** (left).

5.

18. Christ in Majesty, at the far end of the crypt.

10. Figure in armor fighting a monster. The battle between Good and Evil?

11. Adam delving and Eve spinning.

SUBTLE COLORING ▲ *257*
Unfortunately only some of the paintings in the narrow crypt still survive. The color range consists of ochers, green earth, white and black. Blue was not used: this color featured only rarely in Western paintings of the time as it was obtained from lapis lazuli, an expensive gemstone.

SYMBOLISM. The significance of some scenes remains obscure. For example, there are two scenes that may depict the allegorical battle between Good and Evil (**10**).

12. Atlas (cf. figure **9**).

13. Centaur.

16. Dishevelled woman. Various interpretations have been proposed. Perhaps she represents Lust, with bare breasts, attacked by serpents? Or Anger, piercing her own breast, as suggested by the Latin inscription *ira* (anger), which is no longer visible? Or even Lust and Anger combined?

17. Descent to Purgatory: Christ seizes Adam and Eve, God's hand holds back the devil.

4. The Virgin of Sorrows, with her arms outstretched.

15. The Deposition.

The ancient technique of fresco painting was used in the region from the Middle Ages onward. After 1450, when an increasing number of "gigantic" murals were produced, the painters began to use different grounds, pigments and preparatory methods.

"A FRESCO" PAINTING

In the *a fresco* painting technique the pigments are diluted with water and applied to a ground that is still wet (*fresco* = fresh). This means the artist has to work very quickly: the ground dries in less than a day.

"A SECCO" PAINTING

To overcome this difficulty painters adopted the *fresco secco* technique: the paint was applied to a dry ground of lime and plaster which they saturated with water before painting. This soaking technique, originally used by fresco artists to retouch their works, became the dominant technique in Europe after 1450. It gave the painter greater freedom, though at the expense of durability (fresco paintings are generally better preserved).

RESTORATION

Restorers sometimes retouch frescos discovered beneath whitewash by using watercolors then protecting the paintings with a removable fixative.

THE WALL. For fresco painting the wall is painted with an undercoat about half an inch thick, made of one part lime mixed with three parts of coarse sand. This coating produces a rough surface which helps bond the second layer (the *arricciato*), a finer mixture about a quarter of an inch thick. The third layer (the *intonaco*) is made of lime-rich plaster; the painting is done while the surface is still wet.

Pigments of mineral origin were ground, then diluted in water. They were applied with thick bristle brushes.

CARTOON TECHNIQUE
The artist marked out the composition by making perforations along the lines of the drawing. The cartoon was applied to the wall and dabbed with charcoal powder to reproduce the image. After 1450 this method gradually replaced the *sinopia* technique (in which a red pigment was used to draw the design on the *arricciato*).

FINISHING
The painted surface was smoothed with a trowel coated with a wax-based solution, and then polished. Sometimes it was varnished with wax.

IE PIGMENTS. Frescos are painted on an alkaline surface, 'ich produces variations in the color and luminosity of the int as it dries. The best pigments are those of mineral or ganic origin with a good resistance to lime. For retouching, e pigments were ground in a binding medium such as egg, milk or limewater.

PRIORY OF ST-COSME ★   (H6

🚗 c. 50 miles
⏱ 2 days

HISTORY OF THE PRIORY. In 1092 the Basilica of St-Martin in Tours founded a priory for five canons on the former island in the Loire where the Chapel of St-Cosme had been built a century earlier. A huge church was built in the Poitevin Romanesque style, and a large refectory was added in the 12th century. The priory benefited from the proximity of the royal residence at Plessis-lès-Tours ▲ 259: Louis XI financed the rebuilding of the church and the prior's house. The priory was closed in 1742 and then stood empty until it was sold in 1791. Most of the buildings were destroyed in 1944.

RONSARD AT ST-COSME. The poet first came to St-Cosme at the invitation of his brother Charles, who had been given the priory by King Henri II. The leader of the Pléiade was captivated by the place and obtained it from his brother in March 1565, in exchange for a priory in the diocese of Rouen; he remained prior of St-Cosme until his death. Ronsard liked to stay at St-Cosme when he did not have to be at court, and wrote four cantos of his *Franciade* epic here as well as two books of poems.

PIERRE DE RONSARD (1524–85) Ronsard was born in the Vendôme, the son of a minor aristocratic family. At the age of sixteen he became partially deaf and gave up his military career to become a monk. Although he had taken a vow of celibacy, Ronsard devoted the rest of his life to the delights of poetry and the celebration of love. In 1553 he produced the *Amours de Cassandre* which brought him the title of official poet to the king (1559). He was one of the leading figures in the Pléiade, the group of writers that helped to establish French literature. Like all Renaissance artists, they imitated classical models.

…e is buried in the choir of the church (his cenotaph can … seen at the museum in Blois).

…UR. All that survives of the priory buildings today is the …lendid refectory, the *hôtelier* (guest house), the *régulier* …onks' house), the prior's residence (with reconstructions … Ronsard's bedroom and study) and some ruins of the …urch (the ambulatory and two apsidioles).

…HÂTEAU DU PLESSIS-LES-TOURS   (H6)

…UILT BY LOUIS XI. Plessis-lès-Tours is mentioned in …th-century documents, under the name of Chastel des …ontils or Plessis-du-Parc-lez-Tours. At that time it was …wned by the Maillé family. Louis XI bought the estate in …64 and built a sober château of brick with stone piers. …e château gradually became the king's favorite place of …sidence, and thus the center of the French kingdom. **…OYAL RESIDENCE.** Plessis was not deserted by the royal family …ter Louis XI's death: they stayed here frequently, …d work on the château continued for nearly a hundred …ars. Drawings of the château from the 17th century show …at at that time it was considerably larger. It was probably …essis that made this type of brick building fashionable …om the end of the 15th century onward. Near the château …as a large park, which served both as a rabbit warren and …menagerie: this was one of the favorite attractions of the …ng and his guests.

SAINT COSMAS AND SAINT DAMIAN
The priory, like the early chapel, is dedicated to Saint Cosmas; it is probable that the chapel housed the saint's relics. Cosmas and Damian were Syrian doctors who were martyred in the early 4th century. Their cult was very popular in Touraine. The central apsidiole of the Church of St-Cosme has copies of 15th-century statues of the two saints, bearing the tools of their trade; the originals can be seen at the Hôtel Gouin in Tours ▲ 208.

FAMOUS EPITAPH
Ronsard's tomb bears the following inscription: "Pay heed, passer-by! This ground is sacred. Ronsard lies here. The Muses were born with him and died with him, and were buried in the same tomb."

259

▲ LOUIS XI AND THE SILK INDUSTRY AT TOURS

fondée en 1830

This emblem can still be seen on the pediment over the door of the Le Manach factory.

Today the silk industry of Tours, which was started by Louis XI, employs no more than forty or so people; but in the late 16th century it sustained one third of the town's active population. For many years Tours rivaled Lyon in terms of the volume and quality of silk produced; since then the industry has gradually fallen into oblivion.

THE FIRST FACTORIES
In 1470 Louis XI decided to found a silk factory near to his château at Montils-lès-Tours and brought workers for it from Lyon. The trade gradually became established, and guilds with strict regulations were founded. At this time Tours was the capital of the kingdom:

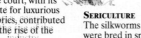

the court, with its taste for luxurious fabrics, contributed to the rise of the new industry.

SERICULTURE
The silkworms were bred in special farms known locally as *verreries* or *verries*. Only the white mulberry (above) provides the right conditions for the larvae of *Bombyx mori*, the white moth that produces silk thread.

SILKWORMS
The worm lives for only six days. It makes its cocoon by spinning a continuous thread of silk that can be up

HEYDAY AND DECLINE
In 1550 the town had 85,000 inhabitants (as many as in 1939) and the silk industry supported nearly 40,000 of them: weavers, dyers, haberdashers, ribbon makers, embroiderers and merchants. The fabrics produced included taffeta, velvet, damask and sumptuous brocades. Later the Tours silk industry was eclipsed by its competitors, mainly Protestant manufacturers who left France after the revocation of the Edict of Nantes and settled in England and Holland. By 1689 only 120 looms were in operation.

to 1,600 yards long. The cocoons are collected before they can be shed; the chrysalises are destroyed. Only pupae destined for breeding are allowed to become moths.

> "THE PANNES [VELVETS] THEY MAKE IN TOURS ARE SO GOOD THAT THEY ARE SENT TO SPAIN, ITALY AND OTHER FOREIGN LANDS."
>
> CARDINAL DE RICHELIEU

RENAISSANCE

Tours' silk industry revived in the early 18th century, and the local designers were widely reputed. A decree issued by the Conseil d'État in 1787 protected their patterns for fifteen years. Fabrics from Tours won the top prizes at the universal exhibitions of 1867 and 1878. Today only the Roze and

Le Manach factories continue the tradition of making silk in Tours.

Louis XI having mulberry trees planted (A. Bauchant, 1943)

Charles d'Albert, originally from Tuscany, was the head of Louis XIII's government. He left his mark on the Château de Maillé, giving both the castle and the village the new name of Luynes.

PLESSIS AFTER THE ROYAL ERA. In the mid 18th century the château was converted into private houses, and the grounds were used as a nursery for mulberry trees. Later it became a paupers' prison. In the following century the buildings were converted into a factory for lead shot, then into a farm, and even into an immunological institute. The old royal castle was altered beyond recognition.
A four-hundred-year-old mulberry can still be seen in the grounds – one of the trees planted by Henri IV, following the tradition established by Louis XI ▲ 260.

"A HOUSE IN THE COUNTRY"
This is what Louis XI wanted his château to be. It was made of brick with stone piers, like the houses that the nobility and wealthy citizens were building by the Loire at this time. Toward the end of

LUYNES

The Château de Luynes belonged to the same Maillé family ▲ 259 that sold Plessis to Louis XI. In 1619 it was acquired by Charles d'Albert (1578–1621), proprietor of an estate at Luynes in Provence.
CHÂTEAU DE LUYNES. This imposing foursquare fortress with circular towers stands on a rocky outcrop overlooking the Loire. Built in the 13th century, it was altered in the 15th and 17th centuries. A dry moat separates it from the hillside to the north and the east. To the west is a brick building with stone piers, reminiscent of Plessis-lès-Tours. The Chapel of the Canonesses, in the Flamboyant style, dates from 1486. The château has come through the centuries intact and has been owned by the same family for three hundred years. Now at last it has opened its doors to visitors, who can admire its gardens and its rich interior decoration. It is an unusually harmonious place, a living illustration of historical continuity. At the foot of the château a number of 15th-century half-timbered houses can be seen around the picturesque marketplace.

SAVONNIÈRES ★

Savonnières (below) is reached by the D88, a small road that runs between the Loire and the Cher, offering a pretty view of one of the most picturesque villages in Touraine.
THE GROTTES PÉTRIFIANTES. These caves were first mentioned by the ceramist Bernard Palissy (c.1510–90) in 1547; they are old quarries which were used in the

his life Louis XI became obsessively fearful of assassins and had the château made impregnable, with iron railings, grilles and spikes. These extreme security measures led Walter Scott (1771–1832) in *Quentin Durward*, and after him the Romantic writers, to depict Plessis as a fortress.

5th century for mining the white chalk, known as *pierre de tuffeau*, employed for building the Château de Villandry. Water oozing out of the cave walls leaves a deposit of calcite (as much as half an inch during the course of a year), so objects left there become petrified.

VILLANDRY

THE CHÂTEAU. The Château de Villandry was built by Jean Le Breton, secretary of state under François I, who also created Villesavin ▲ *166*. It was built between 1532 and 1540 on a platform surrounded by a moat, with a design that was typical of the period ● *69*: a main building at the far end of a paved courtyard, with two side wings set at right angles to it. However, at Villandry the wings are not exactly the same length, and they do not form an exact right angle with the main building. These irregularities came about because the château was built over the foundations of an earlier construction, the Château de Colombier. A fourth wing closing off the courtyard was demolished in the 18th century. The façades are surmounted by square mullioned dormer windows, crowned by ornate protruding pediments. There are galleries with porticos, at ground level, around the main courtyard. The elegant façades feature a grid-like arrangement of horizontal and vertical lines. The château was acquired by the Marquis de Castellane in 1754. He made significant alterations to the old Renaissance building, adapting the façades to the classical style. Early this century Dr Joachim Carvallo restored Villandry's 16th-century appearance and re-created the gardens ▲ *264* in Renaissance style. In the east wing of the château is a gallery with a collection of paintings by Spanish masters and sculptures, including a Virgin and Child from the 11th century. From the gardens there is a lovely view over the chevet of the Church of St-Étienne, which dates from the 11th and 12th centuries.

TWO ARCHITECTURAL TRENDS
Villandry stands at the crossroads of two architectural styles. On the one hand, it reflects the style in which the châteaux of the Loire valley had been built for the two previous decades. On the other, it bears the mark of the architectural style fashionable in the Île-de-France region around 1530: this can be seen in the square pavilions that take the place of corner towers.

"SAPONARIA"
The name Savonnières comes from *saponaria*, Latin for soapwort, a plant that was used in fulling cloth.

Early this century Joachim Carvallo undertook to re-create the gardens of Villandry as they would have been during the Renaissance. From the 16th century onward there were two main sources of influence on French garden design: the monasteries with their kitchen garden tradition, and the ornamental gardens of Italy, with their fountains and arbors. One of the first Italian-style gardens was created at Amboise ▲ *188* under Charles VIII, using Italian gardeners.

JOACHIM CARVALLO (1869–1936), CREATOR OF THE GARDENS
Carvallo was born in Spain, to a family of modest means. He studied medicine in Madrid then joined the physiology laboratory in Paris of Professor Charles Richet (Nobel Prize, 1913). Here he met Ann Coleman, a wealthy American whom he married in 1899. While looking for a house in the country they came upon Villandry ▲ *263* and fell under its spell. Carvallo gave up his medical work and devoted his life to the château. First he removed architectural features of the 18th and 19th centuries, and then started his restoration project for the gardens, a unique undertaking in France. The gardens he created are maintained by his descendants today.

SOURCES OF INSPIRATION
There were no documents relating to the gardens of Villandry in the 16th century. Joachim Carvallo drew his inspiration from two reference works on Renaissance art: the *Monasticon Gallicanum* produced by the congregation of St-Mau in 1694, and *Les Plus Excellents Bastiments de France* by Jacques Androuet du Cerceau.

N TO VEGETABLES. Nicolas de Bonnecamp, a 17th-century doctor and described kitchen gardens in the following words: "The asparagus and tichoke, the piquant celery/ The beetroot, the cauliflower, and spicy y/ The royal lettuce and the all too tender afange/ With scornful city take the place of flowers./ Their size, their tenderness and their Reveal to gourmets the goodness within them./ Thus in these gardens and delight/ Join together, to feast the eyes and the dinner table."

"ENGLISH" GARDENS
The 19th-century Romantics preferred landscaped gardens in the English style, with their curved contours and their wild appearance. They rejected the formal style of garden, of which Lord Byron said "such symmetry is not suited to solitude". This engraving shows Villandry and its gardens as Joachim Carvallo found them at the start of the century.

PLAN OF THE GARDENS AT VILLANDRY
They cover 17 acres, on three levels: the KITCHEN GARDEN is at the center, framed to the south and the east by ORNAMENTAL GARDENS and to the west by the HERB GARDEN. In the southern part of the grounds is the WATER GARDEN, with a huge lake. The ornamental gardens, which have box and yew hedges planted around the flowerbeds, are divided into three separate sections or "salons": the GARDEN OF LOVE, the GARDEN OF CROSSES and the GARDEN OF MUSIC.

▲ THE GARDENS OF VILLANDRY

Below: view of the kitchen garden.

A GARDEN FOR ALL SEASONS
Gardening plans are drawn up during November and December. They have to take into account both horticultural considerations (including flowering times and the need to rotate plants to maintain soil fertility) and esthetic ones, as well as color schemes and the provision of a year-round display. Villandry has a team of full-time gardeners to take care of this work, including the vast task of pruning the trees and rose bushes during the winter. From March onward vegetables and flowering plants are planted; they are tended and replaced according to the garden plan through to November.

A square of the kitchen garden (right).

THE GARDEN OF LOVE. The designs of the four squares of the garden symbolize four aspects of love: hearts (left) and flames for romantic love, swords and daggers for tragic love, horns and fans for adulterous love, and broken hearts for passionate love.

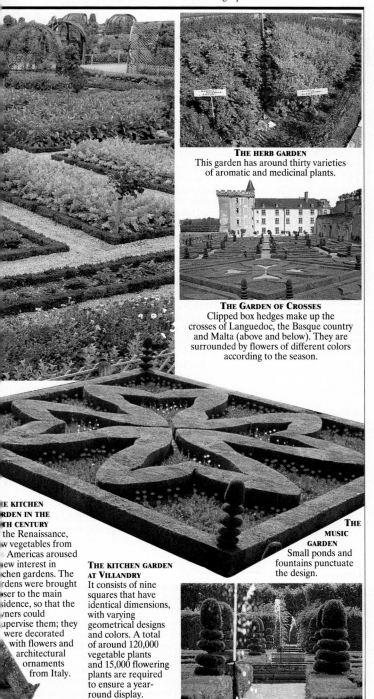

THE SYMBOLIC MEANINGS OF CERTAIN VEGETABLES

EGGPLANTS can signify pleasure – but also symbolize poison.
CABBAGES, with their tightly packed leaves, represent happiness and prosperity.
BROAD BEANS are supposed to house the souls of the dead.
PEPPERS symbolize fire, one of the four elements of which the world is made.
PARSLEY is considered to be a magic plant.

THE HERB GARDEN
This garden has around thirty varieties of aromatic and medicinal plants.

THE GARDEN OF CROSSES
Clipped box hedges make up the crosses of Languedoc, the Basque country and Malta (above and below). They are surrounded by flowers of different colors according to the season.

THE KITCHEN GARDEN IN THE 16TH CENTURY
the Renaissance, new vegetables from the Americas aroused new interest in kitchen gardens. The gardens were brought closer to the main residence, so that the owners could supervise them; they were decorated with flowers and architectural ornaments from Italy.

THE KITCHEN GARDEN AT VILLANDRY
It consists of nine squares that have identical dimensions, with varying geometrical designs and colors. A total of around 120,000 vegetable plants and 15,000 flowering plants are required to ensure a year-round display.

THE MUSIC GARDEN
Small ponds and fountains punctuate the design.

CHEMIN DE FER DE PARIS À ORLÉA

LA LOIRE & SES CHÂTEAUX

LANGEAIS

CHÂTEAU DE LANGEAIS ● *66.*
Louis XI had this château built by
Jean Bourré in 1462, to protect the
western entrance of Tours against an
attack by François II of Brittany. Langeais is a good example
of 15th-century military architecture. From the outside it
looks like a fortress: it has a drawbridge over the moat,
towers, and a continuous wall walk with machicolations.
However, once past the drawbridge (the entrance slope was
replaced by stairs in the 19th century), visitors come upon the
elegant façades of a royal residence opening onto the
courtyard, with three staircase turrets and high dormer
windows. The interior is worth particular attention. The
rooms are decorated with a collection of 15th- and 16th-
century tapestries of very high quality, along with furniture
from the 15th, 16th and 17th centuries and some copies of
period furniture. There is a striking reliquary shrine in
gilded wood from the 13th century depicting the Foolish
Virgins and the Wise Virgins. The château as it is today
conveys a good impression of the setting in which the
marriage of Charles VIII and Anne de Bretagne ● *268* was
sumptuously celebrated in 1491. It is well worth walking
round the wall walk, which runs around the entire building.
From here there is a view over the rooftops to the Loire.
Opposite: views of the Loire near Langeais.
THE OLDEST STONE KEEP IN FRANCE. In the château garden
stand the east and south walls of a keep built before the year
1000 by Foulques Nerra, the powerful Count of Anjou
known as the Black Falcon ▲ *278, 297.*
THE TOWN. Opposite the drawbridge as you leave the château
is a Renaissance house known as the House of Rabelais,
where the writer is said to have lived. The CHURCH OF ST-
JEAN-BAPTISTE, beyond the small bridge, is striking for its
large transept and its juxtaposition of diverse architectural
styles. The square porch tower with buttresses dates from the
12th century, while the transept was added in 1869; a
photograph of the church before the addition of the transept
can be seen in the 16th-century vaulted porch. In the choir
is a frieze showing two lions facing each other, separated by
a palm leaf, probably from the Carolingian period. On
Rue Foulques-Nerra is the former CHURCH OF ST-LAURENT
from the 12th century: it now houses the MUSÉE DE
L'ARTISANAT, which displays a vast collection of 19th-century
tools and brings to life all sorts of forgotten crafts and trades.

RIGNY-USSÉ

**CHÂTEAU D'USSÉ, FROM THE MIDDLE AGES TO THE
RENAISSANCE.** Gildin de Saumur, the rival of Foulques Nerra,
was the first to settle here: he built a fortress to command the
Loire valley. A passage from inside the castle leads to an
underground refuge – a telling reminder of that turbulent
time. In the mid 15th century Antoine de Bueil, whose wife
Jeanne was the daughter of Agnès Sorel ▲ *227, 244* and
Charles VII, decided to build a château in contemporary
style. A drawbridge gave access to the quadrangular inner
courtyard, which was surrounded by buildings and curtain

**ANNE DE BRETAGNE
AND CHARLES VIII**
The crown of Brittany
was a major stake in
the conflict between
the Capetians and the
Plantaganets. The
marriages of Anne de
Bretagne (1477–1514)
with Charles VIII
(1470–98) and then
with Louis XII
(1462–1515) annexed
the Duchy of Brittany
to the French
kingdom. However,
the two territories
were not officially
united until the États
de Vannes of 1532.

**LANGEAIS
EARTHENWARE**
Charles de
Boissimont
(1817–79) made it
famous throughout
Europe: his factory
produced pieces in
unusual shapes,
decorated with
platinum (which
was cheaper than
gold or silver).

THE BRIDGE AT LANGEAIS (1950)
This bridge has been rebuilt
four times and still plays a vital
role: it is the only bridge across
the Loire between Tours ▲ *193*
and Bourgueil, which are
28 miles apart.

Dormer window
of the Château
d'Ussé.

CHEMIN DE FER D'ORLÉANS

TOURAINE
CIRCUITS AUTOMOBILES

CHÂTEAU D'USSÉ
With its terraced
gardens, an orangery
(recently restored),
and furniture
collected by the
owners since the
17th century, this
château has a
fairy-tale air about
it. Perrault is said
to have used it as
his model for the
castle in Sleeping
Beauty; Alexis de
Tocqueville called
it "a symbol of the
Old France".

walls. The château stands
above a sheer rockface
overlooking the Indre; it is
protected on the forest side
by a deep dry moat and
defended to the west by a
high keep which had a view
over the hill. A century later
the wall facing the valley was
demolished, and the château's doors
and windows were ornamented in the Italian
Renaissance style. A lovely chapel on the hillside
reflects the high status of Ussé's owners, who
founded it as a collegiate church.

FROM THE 17TH CENTURY TO THE PRESENT DAY.
In the 17th century, for the marriage of Maréchal
de Vauban's daughter, the glacis on which the château stands
was transformed into a series of terraces, slopes and steps
decorated with flowers and orange trees. The old keep was
partly hidden by an Italian-style wing with more comfortable
rooms. In the 19th century the Duchesse de Duras bought
the estate and all its furniture; the poet Chateaubriand
visited her and wrote part of his *Mémoires d'outre-tombe*
here. The duchess left the château to her daughter, who
added a façade in the troubadour style and built a gallery
decorated with stained-glass windows on the west façade
(the gallery connected the far end of the château with the
Vauban wing, bypassing the public rooms). After this the
château passed to the Duc de Blacas, a minister of
Louis XVIII; his descendants are the current owners.

CANDES-ST-MARTIN   (E

This is one of France's loveliest villages, located halfway
between Chinon and Saumur. Its name derives from the
Gallic word *condate* (confluence): the Vienne river meets
the Loire at this point.

BEFORE CANDES BECAME CANDES-ST-MARTIN. The history
of Candes begins with the Roman occupation, when
fortifications were built around the town. At the end of the
19th century archeologists discovered the remains of a
pagan temple: it had been demolished by Saint Martin, who
came to Candes around 387 to convert the inhabitants and
found the fourth or fifth parish of France. In 397 Martin
returned to Candes to settle differences that
had arisen between the monks, and died here
after completing this task. Candes
immediately became a major
pilgrimage center and a stage
on the pilgrims' route to
Santiago de

LOCAL DISPUTE
When Saint Martin
died at Candes, his
remains became the
object of a dispute
between the monks
of Poitou and
Touraine. The
Poitevins claimed
the body, but the
Tourangeaux stole
it by night and
brought it back to
Tours by boat.
A solemn procession
was held at Tours,
where the saint
was buried.

PORTAL OF THE COLLEGIATE CHURCH OF ST-MARTIN
The niches around the doorway contain decapitated statues, carved into the stone of the façade.

At the foot of the statues are crowned heads, as well as interlacing foliage, dragons and sirens.

THE DEATH OF SAINT MARTIN
Detail from a stained-glass window depicting the saint's burial ▲ 270 and the last years of his life ▲ 206. The window, which measures approximately 23 feet by 5 feet, comes from the choir of the Cathedral of St-Gatien at Tours ▲ 196. It was made around 1300.

Compostela. Several kings of France stayed here: Charles the Bald, Philippe Auguste, Charles VII, Louis XI and Charles VIII.

COLLEGIATE CHURCH OF ST-MARTIN. The house where Saint Martin died was beginning to fall into ruin at the start of the 12th century, and the canons built a church in the saint's name around it: this is the present-day CHAPEL OF ST-MARTIN (to the left of the main altar of the collegiate church). The collegiate church itself was built later, from 1175 to 1225: the short time span explains its unity of style. As one war followed another, the church was fortified for self-defense and to shelter the local population from invaders: inside the church is a well, and there are bread ovens in the lofts. The ENTRANCE PORCH to the south is unique and worth a close look. The vaulting, whose ribs resemble the branches of a palm tree, springs from a light monolithic column at the center, which appears to bear the entire weight of the structure. Above the porch, one of the windows of the CHAPEL OF ST-MICHEL looks directly onto the vaults of the collegiate church. The west façade is dominated by a stone cross situated at the junction of two staircases leading to the top of the two square defensive towers. The great portal to the west is surmounted by thirteen empty niches which may have held statues of Christ and the twelve apostles. The church's north façade is remarkable for its synthesis of religious and military architecture, and for its two towers with crenelations and machicolations.

THE INTERIOR OF THE CHURCH. The main nave of the church is very striking, with its pure soaring vaults in the Plantaganet style ● 60. The choir and the apse, with their rounded vaults, date from the late Romanesque era. The vaulting of all three naves, which are of equal height, has intersecting ribs springing from decorative culs-de-lampe. The carvings vary greatly in style, and there are even some rough blocks of unworked stone in the church and on the façades. No doubt a limited budget meant that artists of varying abilities were employed, and that the decorations could not be completed as planned.

THE VILLAGE. In the Middle Ages the town's Roman defenses were reinforced with solid walls surrounded by a dry moat. At

INTERIOR DECORATION OF THE CHURCH
The culs-de-lampe of the nave are carved with plants and figures. Some of the original colored paintwork can still be seen on statues of the apostles, Old Testament prophets and kings, and Saint Martin himself.

The Grand-Moutier
Cloisters at
Fontevraud (below).

Plan of t[he]
abbey (righ[t])

**ROBERT D'ARBRISSEL
AT FONTEVRAUD**
D'Arbrissel
(right) founded
five priories in
1101, each
providing for a
different religious
community:
STE-MARIE or the

GRAND-MOUTIER
for nuns; LA
MADELEINE for
repentant prostitutes;
ST-JEAN-DE-L'HABIT
for monks;
ST-LAZARE for lepers
and the nuns who
tended them; and
ST-BENOÎT (which
later became a
hospital) for the sick
and infirm.

THE KITCHEN
This was restored by
Magne in the early
20th century. He
reproduced the
original appearance
of the roofs of the
apsidioles, but added
lantern chimneytops.

this stage Candes was ruled by the archbisho[p]
of Tours, who used the castle as a summer
residence. The original CASTLE was ruined
during the Hundred Years' War and
was rebuilt in 1485. In 1682 the
bishop found it uncomfortable
and built another RESIDENCE
near to the 15th-century
Tour de l'Enfant on the
ramparts. Opposite the church was a
MAISON-DIEU, which took in the sick and
also poor pilgrims. Some lovely old houses
can be seen in the picturesque little
streets of the village.

ROYAL ABBEY OF FONTEVRAUD (E8)

The Abbey of Fontevraud was
built in the 12th century on
the Benedictine model and covers
an area of 35 acres, making it the
largest monastic complex in western
Christendom. Work on the
buildings began in 1101 and
continued until 1789: as a result the abbey
displays a range of architectural styles.
The buildings reflect the taste, techniques
and artistic aims of the various periods in
which they were built.
BEGINNINGS. The end of the 11th century
was an unsettled time, when the Gregorian
reforms were slowly beginning to bring order
into the life of the clergy, condemning practices such as the
sale of ecclesiastical benefits and indulgences. Robert
d'Arbrissel (c. 1047–1117) was a priest from Brittany who
attempted to implement these reforms, without success.
As a consequence he decided to live as a hermit. Soon he wa[s]
surrounded by disciples and founded his first abbey, situated
on the borders of Brittany, Normandy and Anjou. Pope
Urban II appointed D'Arbrissel an apostolic
preacher and he left his community to take
up an itinerant life. Again he gathered a
group of men and women from all walks
of life and settled on a site in the middle
of a forest, near to a spring and the
Loire river, on the borders of three
bishoprics: Anjou, Touraine and Poitou.
This was to become Fontevraud.
D'Arbrissel decided that the Order
of Fontevraud would include both
men and women, and follow the
Benedictine rule; he also decreed
that it should be directed by a
woman. This tradition remained
unbroken: Fontevraud had a total
of thirty-six abbesses from its
foundation until the Revolution
(half of them of royal blood).

NTIL THE REVOLUTION. The abbey attracted large donations om the start. More priories were founded, and at its height e Order had priories all over France (123 in all) and also in ain and England. Fontevraud flourished under the otection of the Plantaganets, who made it their al mausoleum ▲ *183*. Their decline affected the abbey's prosperity, which only recovered in the 17th century, thanks to the influence of abbesses from the House of Bourbon. Gabrielle de Rochechouart (left), the thirty-second abbess and a very learned woman, was the sister of Madame de Montespan, Louis XIV's mistress: under her rule Fontevraud became a cultural center, where literature and philosophy were discussed. Louis XV entrusted the education of his four youngest daughters to Abbess Louise Françoise de Rochechouart, whom he made a duchess. Under the Revolution all the monks and nuns were expelled, the abbey's furniture was designated national property and sold off, and two of the priories were demolished and used as sources of stone.

THE PRISON ERA. In 1804 Napoleon converted the abbey into a penitentiary for women, men and children. Its intended capacity was seven hundred people, but it actually housed as many as eighteen hundred. Under the Restoration it became a central

ANGUISH
"Of all the central prisons in France, Fontevraud is the most disturbing. This is the one which gave me the strongest impression of anguish and desolation." These words of Jean Genet (1910–86), describe the abbey in his novel *Miracle de la Rose* (1946). He was never imprisoned at Fontevraud himself, but was familiar with prisons from having passed three years in jail as a youth and frequently visited a friend detained at Fontevraud.

The lovely 17th-century spiral staircase at the Priory of St-Lazare.

THE CHAPTER HOUSE
It was here that the chapter of nuns took decisions relating to the life of the abbey. It was built between 1543 and 1562, with a richly worked portal opening onto the main cloister.

prison for nineteen départements; the buildings were partitioned, divided or demolished, and the prisoners worked more than twelve hours a day in various workshops and factories. Later it was used as a prison for member of the Resistance during World War Two, then for collaborators in 1945.

ARCHITECTURAL DIVERSITY. The ABBEY CHURCH, the main place of worship, was built in the 12th century. It is impressive for its generous dimension (300 feet by 50 feet), for the ethereal architecture of the choir, and its Romanesque nave with Byzantine cupolas. In architectural terms the Romanesque KITCHEN is Fontevraud's most famous feature. This round building, 100 feet high with eight apsidal hearths, is built entirely of stone (including the roof, which has a fish-scale pattern). Its unusual appearance has prompted questions regarding its purpose. Was it originally the refuge of the brigand Evraud, who according to legend was converted by Robert d'Arbrissel? Or a funerary chapel? Nevertheless, its seems probable that it was indeed a kitchen used for curing food and preparing meals for the abbey's three thousand inhabitants. The CHAPEL OF ST-BENOIT has

The walls are covered with scenes from the New Testament (above), painted by the Anjou artist Thomas Pot around 1560. If you look closely at the paintings, you will see that some figures are incomplete. It was a tradition that each Abbess of Fontevraud should be represented in the chapter house, and some of the figures had to be erased to make space for new ones.

Plantaganet-style vaulting, as does the CHAPEL OF THE PRIORY OF ST-LAZARE. Many of the abbey's buildings, including the MAIN CLOISTER and the GRAND-MOUTIER CLOISTERS, were rebuilt or extended in the 16th, 17th and 18th centuries.

TODAY. The abbey was handed over to the Ministry of Cultur in 1963. Until 1985 one of the priories continued to house around thirty detainees whose job was to eradicate the most obvious reminders of the prison era. Intensive restoration work has been under way since 1975. Be sure to take a walk in the village. The charming CHURCH OF ST-MICHEL, with its rich interior decoration, stands at one end of a pleasant avenue of lime trees; nearby is the FUNERARY CHAPEL OF STE-CATHERINE.

ROYAL MAUSOLEUM

ROYAL MAUSOLEUM
In the abbey church
are the colored
recumbent effigies
of Henry II (left),
the first of the
Plantaganet kings
of England ● *38*,
his wife Eleanor of
Aquitaine (bottom),
their son Richard
the Lionheart
(above) and Isabelle
of Angoulême (left),
wife of their other
son, John Lackland
(King John). The
history of the
House of Anjou is
closely interwoven
with that of
Fontevraud. Henry
II's grandfather gave
many donations to
Robert d'Arbrissel;
and his daughter,
Mathilde d'Anjou,
became the second
abbess of Fontevraud.
Henry II stayed
here with his aunt
in 1154 before
setting off to
pursue his claim to
the English crown.
Eleanor made
substantial donations
to Fontevraud after
1170: on her
husband's behalf
she was seeking to
stir up the nobility
of western France,
and wanted to
ensure the support
of this powerful
abbey. She retired
here in 1194, when
over seventy years
old, while continuing
to support her sons in
the struggle against
Philippe Auguste.

ALEXANDRE DUMAS AND HISTORY
Charles de Chambes, Count of Montsoreau, married Françoise de Maridor in 1576. She was wooed by Louis de Bussy d'Amboise, who boasted of his success.

The husband was informed of the affair by Henri III, and he had Bussy assassinated at the manor house of Coutancière (on the other side of the Loire) on August 18, 1579. The couple were reconciled: they lived for another forty years and had nine children. Alexandre Dumas (1802–70), author of the *Three Musketeers*, had a passion for reworking historical subjects and gave his own version of these events in his novel *The Lady of Montsoreau*, published in 1845.

MONTSOREAU (E

The Château de Montsoreau stands at the foot of a tufa rockface that stretches along the river. It was the earliest fortress in southern Anjou ▲ 12, a stronghold built in the Middle Ages to defend the territory against Touraine and Poitou. It overlooks the beautiful, serene landscape around the Loire and Vienne rivers. The old town on the hillside is so close to the village of Candes ▲ 270 that Rabelais' words are still quoted: "Between Candes and Montsoreau grazes neither cow nor calf."

THE CHÂTEAU. From the 11th century onward the castle commanded the river route between Saumur and Chinon, serving as both fortress and tollhouse. At this time the town consisted of the port of Rest-sous-Montsoreau, beside the river, and the town of Montsoreau on the hillside. Today's château was built in three phases between 1445 and the end of the 15th century, by Jean de Cambes, counsellor of King Charles VII. Its contrasting styles of architecture illustrate the transition between feudal fortress and Renaissance palace ● 67.

Two towers of military appearance, with crenelations, loopholes and machicolations, overlook the river. The main building was erected between these two towers from 1510 onward, in a delightful early-Renaissance style with mullioned windows and two small adjoining wings. The right-hand wing contains an impressive staircase, added between 1520 and 1530. The rooms of the second story now house the Museum of Moroccan Goums (the Goums were cavalry units administered by the French army during the colonial period and World War Two). The museum was transferred here from Rabat at the suggestion of the château's owner, the Marquis de Geoffre, in 1956 at the end of the French Protectorate.

THE OLD TOWN. The path up to the old town leads through streets with houses dating from the 15th, 16th and 17th centuries (Ruelle des Trois Pigeons, Place des Diligences, Passage du Marquis de Geoffre, Haute-Rue, Chemin du Coteau). From here there is a lovely view of the château courtyard and the Loire. Take Rue Françoise de Maridor to return downhill.

SAUMUR

CHÂTEAU DE BOUMOIS, *285*
HILLSIDE DWELLINGS, *286*
PLAIN DWELLINGS, *287*
DOUÉ-LA-FONTAINE, *288*
BAGNEUX, *289*
LE COUDRAY-MACOUARD, *289*
ABBEY OF ASNIÈRES, *290*
LE PUY-NOTRE-DAME, *290*
MONTREUIL-BELLAY, *290*
ST-HILAIRE-
ST-FLORENT, *291*
CHÊNEHUTTE-
LES-TUFFEAUX, *292*
TRÈVES, *292*
GENNES-SUR-LOIRE, *293*
CHÂTEAU DE PIMPÉAN, *293*
BRISSAC-QUINCÉ, *294*
LES PONTS-DE-CÉ, *294*

TUFA, HORSES AND WINE
These are the three symbols of Saumur. Tufa ▲ 286, the white local limestone that can be seen on many

of the town's medieval and Renaissance houses, gives the town its bright, distinctive appearance. Saumur is the capital of French equestrianism ▲ 282. Wine ● 30 makes a vital contribution to the region's gastronomic reputation ● 13; it is made from vines grown in terraced rows on the hillsides overlooking the Loire and matured in cellars dug into the tufa.

HISTORY OF THE TOWN

The old province of Anjou ● 12 embraced most of today's département of Maine-et-Loire; the beautiful town of Saumur stands at its far eastern end. Saumur itself, on the south bank of the Loire at its confluence with the Thouet, is the capital of a varied, verdant region known as the Saumurois. The town was once a Carolingian villa. Fortified by Thibault, Count of Blois, in the 10th century, it was conquered by Foulques Nerra ▲ 297, Count of Anjou, in 1026. His successors, the Plantagenets, lost the province in their struggle with Capetian France ● 38, and Philippe-Auguste annexed it to the French kingdom.

ENLIGHTENED PROTESTANTISM. Saumur's enlightened Protestant governor Philippe Duplessis-Mornay (1549–1623) ▲ 281 left his imprint on the town, which had become a

fuge for the Huguenots in 1589. Because of the Protestant
...iversity he founded, the town became known as the
...'rench Geneva" and for around a century Saumur served
... an intellectual and religious center for the whole of
...otestant Europe, reaching heights of prosperity that were
...ver equalled after the revocation of the Edict of Nantes
...d the emigration of the town's Protestant population ● *41*.
...ie Catholic Church responded by
...ganizing major pilgrimages here
...*285*, which spawned a flourishing
...ade in rosaries and religious jewelry.
...OWN OF THE HORSE. In the mid 18th
...ntury the town saw a revival, when
...e École de Cavalerie (Cavalry
...hool) was established here.
...aumur became the
...ichallenged equestrian
...pital of France, owing its
...tional reputation to the
...adre Noir ▲ *282*, an élite
...rps of trainers,
...structors and riders which
...pholds the French equestrian
...adition.
...AUMUR TODAY. Food (mushrooms,
...arkling wine and canned vegetables)
...akes a major contribution to the
...wn's economy, as does the
...owing tourist trade.

**THE HEROIC SAUMUR
"CADETS"**
When Germany
invaded France in
June 1940, the
officers and eight
hundred pupils of the
École de Cavalerie
posted themselves
along the Loire ● *43*
between Gennes and
Montsoreau to the
enemy from
crossing the
river. From 19 to
21 June this small,
poorly equipped
group put up a heroic
resistance to the
much larger German
force, which attacked
them from the ground
and the air.
General Weygand,
Commander-in-Chief
of the French army,
decorated the École
de Cavalerie with the
Ordre de l'Armée,
commenting that it
had "written in
the annals of
equestrianism a
page worthy of all
its glorious past".

279

"GOOD KING RENÉ"
Duke René I of
Anjou (1409–80) was
the son of Yolande
d'Aragon and Louis II
of Anjou; he also held
the titles of
Duc de Bar, Duc de
Lorraine, King of
Sicily and Jerusalem,
and Comte de
Provence. His second
wife was Jeanne de
Laval. Known as
"the Last of the
Troubadours", he was
a disciple of the poet
Charles d'Orléans
▲ 114 and wrote
chivalric romances
which he illuminated
himself, among them
the *Livre du coeur
d'amour épris* (1457).
He was also a
prodigious creator
of buildings in the
Angevin ▲ 298 and
Provençal styles, such
as the châteaux of
Tarascon and Saumur.

HISTORY OF THE CHÂTEAU

No matter how you approach Saumur, it is the château that
you see first, rising above the town on a limestone outcrop.
After the fortress fell under French rule it was rebuilt by Saint
Louis ▲ 296, from 1227 onward. Louis I of Anjou, brother of
King Charles V, carried out major alterations between 1367
and 1376. New polygonal towers were built over the base of
the old round towers, and the keep and a vast residential wing
were added. René I of Anjou (see left) renovated the east
tower (known as the Tour de la Chapelle) and refurbished the
château as a whole. In the 16th century the town's governor
Philippe Duplessis-Mornay ▲ 281 commissioned the Italian
engineer Bartolomeo to fortify the castle. Bartolomeo built a
star-shaped enclosure – anticipating those later designed by
Vauban – with bastions and curtain walls. Between the reigns
of Louis XIV and Napoleon I the château was used as a
prison; subsequently it became a military storehouse. In 1906
the municipal authorities acquired it from the state in grave
disrepair. Restoration work is still in progress.

TOUR OF THE CHÂTEAU ★

Despite its robust fortifications, the Château de Saumur
belongs to the great architectural tradition of Loire châteaux.
The 14th-century keep has two corner bartizans and a
gatehouse; it leads into the Great Court, with a grand
staircase (14th century) decorated in the Flamboyant style.
The belvedere terrace has a magnificent view over the river
and the town.
MUSÉE DES ARTS DÉCORATIFS. This is one of the most
delightful museums in France outside Paris. Located on the
middle floor of the château, it houses the collection of rare
pieces, such as 13th-century Limoges enamels and a large
collection of 16th- and 18th-century French earthenware,
tapestries (left) and woodcarvings (below), left by Count
Charles Lair, a wealthy scholar of Saumur, in 1919.
MUSÉE DU CHEVAL. This museum is housed in the top story of
the château, which has splendid curved beams shaped like
those of a ship's hull. It traces the
history of horses and riding in the
world, from antiquity until today.

TOUR OF THE TOWN

There are two ways up to the château
from the old town. The MONTÉE DU
PETIT GENÈVE runs alongside the
former Protestant cemetery and
leads to the panoramic terrace,
while the MONTÉE DU FORT, a
steep street with half-timbered
houses ● 72, leads from PLACE
ST-PIERRE directly to the
entrance.
CHURCH OF ST-PIERRE. This
church shows a mixture of
architectural styles. The choir
and transept date from the

"We caught sight of the keep and the white houses of Saumur, a beautiful view in the distance . . .
This town has a grandiose air about it;
it stands at the top of a lovely hill."

Stendhal

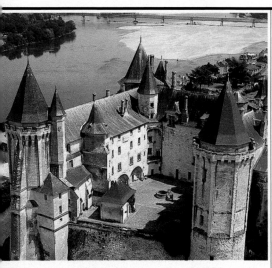

...e 12th century, while the nave dates from the 13th century ...d the façade is built in the Jesuit style. Inside there are ...autiful 16th-century tapestries depicting the lives of Saint ...ter and Saint Florent, both popular local saints, and ...markable stalls which follow the curving outline of the apse.
...UAI MAYAUD. From the 17th to the 19th century the ...mmercial importance of river traffic led to the construction ...mansions and other substantial buildings beside the Loire.
...ÔTEL DE VILLE. The town hall, on Place de la République, ...tes from the 16th and the 19th centuries.

...HE EQUESTRIAN AND MILITARY QUARTER

...ilitary and equestrian establishments were traditionally ...cated in this part of town. Some of the riding schools ...d stables are still used by the École Nationale de ...avalerie, others have now been converted for other uses.
...ANÈGE DES ÉCUYERS. This riding school was built in 1863 ...t today's Place Charles-de-Foucault; it was the setting for ...splays by the Cadre Noir, Saumur's celebrated corps of ...ding instructors ▲ 282. On the right-hand side of the square ...e the old stable buildings, dating from the 19th century.
...LACE DU CHARDONNET. For a long time this was the exercise ...ound for the equestrian establishments grouped around it. ...he first carrousel (equestrian display) by the Cadre Noir was ...ld here in 1828, in honor of the Duchesse de Berry. The ...adition of the carrousel is still very much alive: it is held on ...e Place du Chardonnet every year at the end of July, ...esented by the pupils of the École d'application de l'arme ...indée et de la cavalerie and those of the Cadre Noir.
...COLE D'APPLICATION DE L'ARME BLINDÉE ET DE LA CAVALERIE. ...he academy of the armored corps and cavalry stands near ...ace du Chardonnet, on Avenue du Maréchal-Foch. The ...uilding, in the classical style, was erected between 1767 and ...69. From 1825 to 1969 it was home of the École de ...avalerie, led by the Cadre Noir. It was given its present ...me in 1945.

RENÉ I'S "CHÂTEAU D'AMOUR"
In the middle ages this Château was so famous that it was depicted in the illuminated manuscript of the *Très Riches Heures du Duc de Berry*, kept at the Château de Chantilly (illustration for September, the month of harvesting, ▲ 277).

A GREAT PROTESTANT LEADER
Philippe de Mornay (1549–1623), lord of Plessis-Marly, is better known as Philippe Duplessis-Mornay ▲ 278. Nicknamed "the Pope of the Huguenots", he acted as a lawyer and diplomat in the service of the Huguenot party before becoming chief finance minister to Henri de Navarre (later Henri IV of

France). Duplessis-Mornay took a moderate political line. After he was appointed governor of Saumur, he fortified the castle and the outskirts of the town and created a Protestant university. Together with Hubert Languet he wrote the *Vindiciae contra tyrannos* (1579), one of the most important political treatises of the Wars of Religion, which sought to limit royal power.

Saumur's Cadre Noir is a group of trainers and riders whose aim is to uphold the French equestrian tradition, which dates back to the 16th century, when governor Duplessis-Mornay ▲ *281* founded a riding academy as part of his Protestant university. In 1763 Louis XV entrusted the Duc de Choiseul with the complete reorganization of the French cavalry, and the "best riding school in the world" was built on Place du Chardonnet to house the officers of the cavalry regiments. The cavalry school operated until 1788, and was re-established in 1824. At the first carrousel, held in 1828, the officers presented an impressive display of dressage and jumps which resulted in the foundation of the Cadre Noir, consisting of the school's riding instructors. In 1972 the École Nationale d'Équitation (National Riding School) was founded around the Cadre Noir, whose specialty is the study and teaching of *haute école*, the most elaborate form of dressage. Today the Cadre Noir includes both military and civilian members.

EQUESTRIAN CELEBRITIES
The world of academic equestrianism has i own celebrities. There was Pluvinel (1550–1620), under Louis XIII, and La Guérinière (1688–1751) under Louis XV. After the academic riding school was founded, there was Monsieur Corder, the fi *écuyer en chef* (principal rider) of the Cadr Noir; and later Général L'Hotte (left), who gave the French tradition its own distinctiv style. A strict hierarchy indicates the level o achievement reached by the riders: *élève-écuyer* (pupil rider), *sous-écuyer* (under-rider *écuyer* (rider), *écuyer de première classe* (first-class rider) and *écuyer en chef* (principal rider).

THE "REPRISE"
This is a display of the dressage movements performed in high-level competitions. The aim of academic dressage is to restore to the mounted horse all the animal's natural grace of attitude and movement. Right: the passage.

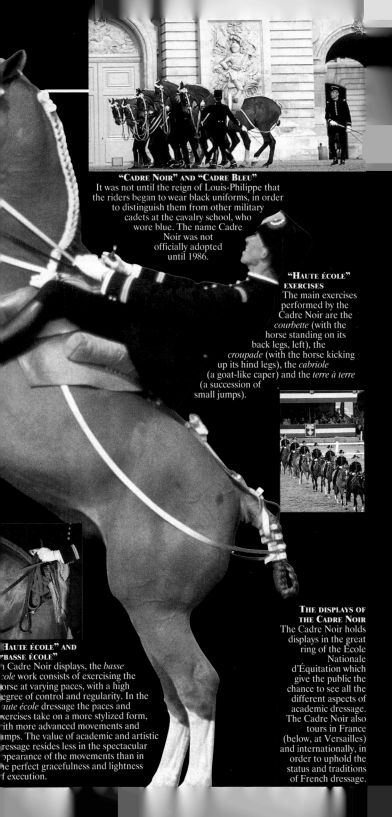

"CADRE NOIR" AND "CADRE BLEU"

It was not until the reign of Louis-Philippe that the riders began to wear black uniforms, in order to distinguish them from other military cadets at the cavalry school, who wore blue. The name Cadre Noir was not officially adopted until 1986.

"HAUTE ÉCOLE" EXERCISES

The main exercises performed by the Cadre Noir are the *courbette* (with the horse standing on its back legs, left), the *croupade* (with the horse kicking up its hind legs), the *cabriole* (a goat-like caper) and the *terre à terre* (a succession of small jumps).

"HAUTE ÉCOLE" AND "BASSE ÉCOLE"

In Cadre Noir displays, the *basse école* work consists of exercising the horse at varying paces, with a high degree of control and regularity. In the *haute école* dressage the paces and exercises take on a more stylized form, with more advanced movements and jumps. The value of academic and artistic dressage resides less in the spectacular appearance of the movements than in the perfect gracefulness and lightness of execution.

THE DISPLAYS OF THE CADRE NOIR

The Cadre Noir holds displays in the great ring of the École Nationale d'Équitation which give the public the chance to see all the different aspects of academic dressage. The Cadre Noir also tours in France (below, at Versailles) and internationally, in order to uphold the status and traditions of French dressage.

**THE BIRTH OF
COCO CHANEL**
Gabrielle Bonheur
(1883–1971) was born
in a train; when the
train arrived at
Saumur she was taken
to no. 27, rue St-Jean,
where she grew up.
Later she moved to
Paris and, under the
name of Coco
Chanel, founded an
haute couture house
where she created a
new style in women's
fashions that made
her famous
throughout the world.

ÉCOLE NATIONALE D'ÉQUITATION. France's national riding
school was founded in 1969 at Saumur-Terrefort (3 miles from
Saumur), with an extension at Verrie. The school is dedicated
to dressage training, and is also the national training center
for French cavalry officers. Training is carried out by the
Cadre Noir ▲ *282*, which now includes women in its ranks
(left).

L'ÎLE D'OFFARD

From Place de Bilange – where Saumur's market has been
held for the last nine centuries – the Pont Cessart (above),
completed in 1768, extends across the river to the Île d'Offard.
MAISON DE LA REINE DE SICILE. This is the most striking
building on the island: an elegant residence on Rue Montcel,
dating from the first half of the 15th century, built of tufa with
mullioned windows and two staircase turrets. The house is
named after Yolande d'Aragon, Queen of Sicily and mother
of René I of Anjou ▲ *280*. She is said to have died here,
probably in 1442.

NOTRE-DAME DE NANTILLY ★

This is the oldest of Saumur's four churches. Situated in
the southern part of the town, it was built by the monks of
St-Florent early in the 12th century in the Romanesque style.
The transept was rebuilt in the 14th century, and a century
later Louis XI doubled the size of the nave, adding a huge
side aisle in the Flamboyant style. The shrine was restored,
starting in 1851, by the architect Joly-Leterme, a follower
of Viollet-le-Duc. The church has a Romanesque façade
influenced by the Aquitaine style, with four high
buttresses surmounted by a cornice and a set of
blind arcatures.
INTERIOR. The southern apsidiole, which dates from the
12th century, contains a colored sculpture of the Virgin
and Child from the same period; known as the Notre-
Dame de Nantilly, it is worshiped for its miraculous
powers. The spectacular vaulting of the Romanesque
nave, 40 feet across, and the highly developed style of
the historiated capitals make this a unique example of
Angevin Romanesque architecture ● *58*. The church
also has a remarkable collection of tapestries from the
16th and 17th centuries.

> **"THIS IS ONE OF THOSE CORNERS OF FRANCE
> WHERE FRANCE IS AT ITS MOST FRENCH."**
>
> GEORGE CLEMENCEAU

NOTRE-DAME DES ARDILLIERS ★

This impressive building, in the eastern part of Saumur,
can be spotted from a distance by its monumental rotunda
crowned by a dome similar to that of Les Invalides in Paris.
The first church, in the Flamboyant style, was built on the site
between 1534 and 1553, marking the spot where a peasant

had found a statue of the Virgin in 1454. In the 17th century
Notre-Dame des Ardilliers became a major center for
pilgrimages, and two side chapels were added in the classical
style ● 63. The church was dedicated as
a royal chapel in 1614 and given to the
Oratorians, making it a visible symbol
of Catholicism in a town dedicated to the
Protestant cause. The central rotunda,
which serves as a vestibule to the shrine,
was built between 1655 and 1693 by the
architects Biardeau and Gondoin.

CHÂTEAU DE BOUMOIS

This château was built early in the
16th century on the right bank of the
Loire, about 4 miles northwest of
Saumur. With its tufa stonework and
two massive machicolated towers it looks
like a plain fortress, but concealed within
its feudal exterior is an elegant residence
built in the Gothic style with Renaissance
decorations. The door to the staircase
leading up to it has a remarkable
wrought-iron lock bearing the arms of
René de Thory, the first lord of Boumois.

**MUSEUM OF
ARMORED VEHICLES**
The Musée des
Blindés and Centre
de documentation sur
les engins blindés
(CDEB) were
established in 1982,
in a former riding
school. The museum's
three halls, which are
named after three
generals (Estienne,
Patton and Rommel),
display exhibits from
the world's largest
collection of 20th-
century armored
vehicles and artillery.
The CDEB is at once
an information
center, a training
center, and a
technical center for
engineers, technicians
and specialists (both
military and civilian).

CHÂTEAU DE BOUMOIS
Details of the tufa
stonework.

285

▲ SAUMUROIS TROGLODYTIC DWELLINGS

TUFA AND FALUN
Tufa (*tuffeau*) ● 76 is a chalky, white limestone rock from the Turonian level of the lower Cretaceous period (Secondary Era). In the Saumurois region ▲ 278 the rock stratum is sometimes as much as 160 feet deep. Tufa is easy to work, with a tendency to disintegrate under the dissolving action of rainwater. Faluns are conchiferous (shell marl) deposits formed in the Tertiary Era. The thickest stratum, 74 feet deep, is at Doué-la-Fontaine.

Since very early times the inhabitants of the Saumurois region ● 12 have cut into their limestone hills and plains, either to mine stone for building houses or to make their homes in the rock itself. Over the course of the centuries this has produced a whole subterranean troglodyte world, including *champignonnières* (mushroom caves, ▲ 292) wine cellars, caverns, workshops, hamlets, and even chapels and manor houses. The Saumurois region is unique in possessing two types of troglodyte habitations: both hillside and plain dwellings.

HILLSIDE DWELLINGS (E7)

Troglodyte dwellings are carved into the cliff faces on either side of Saumur (D7), between Montsoreau and Gennes. The tufa rocks provide the white stone that gives the châteaux and houses of the Loire valley their distinctive appearance. Some of the hillside (or "horizontal") troglodytic habitations were formerly quarries. Now rarely occupied as homes, they are mainly used by craftworkers, winegrowers and mushroom farmers.

Falun was extracted vertically, working from ground level – not by tunneling, as for tufa. Houses were built into the walls of the ditches created by quarrying the stone.

VAL-HULIN (E7). Some of the most interesting hillside dwellings are at Val-Hulin (below), near Turquant, between Montsoreau and Saumur. Above this small semi-troglodytic hamlet is a splendid moulin-cavier (cave mill) ● 79, ▲ 294, which has been restored.

…A
…RANDE
…IGNOLE (E7).
…his small troglodytic
…anor house (opposite) was
…ilt in the 15th century by Jean de
…ignole, president of the Chamber of Accounts of Anjou
…d a liegeman of René I ▲ *280*. It was modified in the 16th
…ntury, then again in the 19th century. René's daughter,
…arguerite d'Anjou (1429–82), is said to have died here. This
…xtraordinary building is regarded as one of the most
…markable troglodytic dwellings in the whole of Europe.

…LAIN DWELLINGS (C7, D7)

Troglodytic plain dwellings – made in
holes or ditches dug into the falun – can be
found within an area of approximately
150 square miles to the south of Saumur,
mainly around Doué-la-Fontaine. Falun, a
tertiary limestone rock composed of organic
debris, contains a great variety of fossils (left,
fossilized tooth of a carcarodon, a formidable
shark that lived in the ancient Falun Sea). For
…nturies "vertical" troglodytic dwellings were the main form
…f habitation for poor farmers in this area (they only had to
…ig a hole to make their home), and a distinctive lifestyle
…volved around them. As recently as a hundred years ago
…ere were still only a few houses above ground level in each
…llage. Today these troglodytic habitations are considered an
…nportant part of the region's heritage; there has been a great
…vival of interest in them, and many unusual sites have been
…pened to the public.

🚗 c. 80 miles
🕐 2 days

**TROGLODYTIC FARM
AT MARSON** ▲ *288*
The ditch produced
by vertical quarrying
(see opposite) served
as the farmyard.
Rooms were carved
out from the rock.
On the surface the
falun was covered
with earth, providing
a kitchen garden for
the underground
farm.

287

INFORMATION CENTER
La Boutinière, a former troglodytic farm to the south of Dénezé, has been turned into an information center on troglodyte dwellings in the region and throughout France. It has a permanent exhibition devoted to the troglodytic world.

ROU MARSON. This romantic, verdant spot is part of a group of three parishes: Rou, Riou and Marson. The Château de Marson – built in Renaissance style, although it dates from 1850 – stands at the foot of troglodytic rocks. Beside the small road leading to the villages of Riou and Les Ulmes there are *caves demeurantes* – troglodyte caves that are still inhabited.

LA FOSSE. This impressive site consists entirely of inhabited caves and their annexes. Dating from the 17th century, it is a typical hamlet of troglodytic plain dwellings. The underground farm is arranged around a courtyard known as the *carré* (square); the slope leading down to the house is called the *courdouère*. The kitchen garden and the orchard were

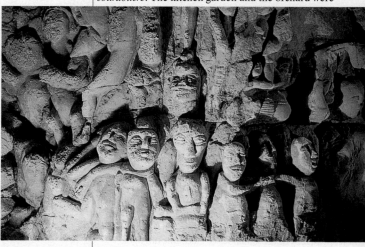

MUSÉE PAYSAN, ROCHEMENIER
This museum, in two disused underground farms, includes houses, stables, storerooms, ovens and sheds, with original décor and everyday items from the late 19th and early 20th century.

traditionally located over the roof of the farm, the produce being harvested through holes in the roof called *jittes*.

DÉNEZÉ-SOUS-DOUÉ. This carved cavern (16th century) is a strange and fascinating place. Four hundred figures, carved in a simple style, stand out from the wall; hundreds more have been destroyed. The carvings show the initiation rites of stonecutters and record their protests against the royal edict of Villers-Cotterêts (1539), which outlawed certain associations of craftworkers. Near to Dénezé are the troglodyte hamlets of Mousseaux and Saugré.

ROCHEMENIER. This troglodyte village was founded in the 10th century on a falun deposit and consisted of around 250 caves, belonging to forty farms. The village covered an underground area two or three times the size of what could be seen on the surface; today it is completely abandoned.

DOUÉ-LA-FONTAINE
The troglodytic Rue des Perrières.

DOUÉ-LA-FONTAINE   (C7, C8)

The town, built entirely on a bank of falun deposits, has been inhabited since prehistoric times. The site was once occupied by a Gallic tribe; in 796 it became one of the four winter residences of Louis the Pious; and at the end of the 10th century Foulques Nerra, the famous Count of Anjou ▲ *297*, built a castle here. The town was modernized from 1765 onward by Joseph-François Foulon (1715–89), later a finance minister. The development of the rose-growing industry

MUSÉE DES ANCIENS COMMERCES AT DOUÉ-LA-FONTAINE
This museum presents a history of retailing (1850 to 1950), from peddling to storekeeping.

...osted its economy. Known as the "City of Roses", it ...roduces more than eight million rose bushes every year.

...OSERAIE DU PARC FOULON. More than five thousand rose ...shes grow in this public park, presenting a multicolored, ...veet-smelling display of the roses produced locally.

...RÈNES DE DOUCES. This "amphitheater" is in fact an old ...uarry – tiers were cut into it in the 15th century. Rabelais *250* may have been thinking of it when, in *Pantagruel*, he ...lks about the "games of Doué".

...UE DES PERRIÈRES. This street (opposite page, bottom) is ...ned with troglodyte houses cut into the old falun quarries. ...ne unusual architecture is accentuated by the honey-colored ...one and the half-darkness illuminated by shafts of light.

...A SABLIÈRE. This former quarry gallery, embellished with ...eautiful vaulting, is now a rosewater distillery.

...AISON CAROLINGIENNE. This is part of the oldest rectangular ...eep in France, dating from the late 10th century and ...scovered by chance in 1966. It is believed to have formed ...art of a residence belonging to Robert I, Count of Anjou.

...OULIN DE LA FOURCHETTE. Also known as the Moulin ...artier, this was the last windmill built in Anjou – a rare *...oulin-tour* (tower mill) ● *78*, ▲ *294*.

Montreuil-Bellay, to the southeast of Saumur, is another region of hills, forests and vineyards. Many of the larger ...wns are perched on hilltops: from the dawn of the Middle ...ges onward they acted as defensive outposts, protecting the ...rder of Poitou from Anjou.

...AGNEUX (D7)

...his suburb of Saumur has a number of interesting Neolithic ...mains. The Grand Dolmen de Bagneux is the largest ...olmen in France, and one of the largest in Europe. It ...onsists of fifteen sandstone slabs and is a typical Angevin ...olmen, similar in form to the one at La Bajoulière (C6). ...he elongated chamber covers an area of 970 square feet; it is ...5 feet long, 25 feet wide, and 11 feet high. A smaller dolmen ...23 feet long) can be seen near the cemetery.

...E COUDRAY-MACOUARD (D7)

...he charming winding streets of this picturesque village, ...erched on a hilltop, are lined with houses built between the ...5th and 18th centuries.

...HURCH. This was once the chapel of the 12th-century ...hâteau (now destroyed). It was rebuilt in the 18th century. ...he retable of the high altar, ...epicting the Assumption of the ...irgin, dates from the same ...eriod.

...AGNANERIE. The Impasse ...el-air – a group of troglodyte ...uildings devoted to silkworm ...reeding ▲ *260* – includes the *...agnanerie*, where the *magnans* ...outhern French for silkworms) ...ere bred, and an exhibition ...elating to silk weaving.

PARC ZOOLOGIQUE DES MINIÈRES
This zoo in a former conchiferous-stone quarry has around five hundred animals, kept in an admirably natural environment. The number of animals born here testify to its success. The zoo has some rare species, such as the snow panther, Sumatran tiger and red panda.

DOLMENS ANGEVINS ANGEVIN DOLMENS
The dolmens ● *36* of Anjou were built between 4000 and 2000 BC; most of them are located around Saumur and Baugé, and many are still completely or nearly intact. Most of the dolmens in Anjou have a low, narrow entrance opening onto a large rectangular chamber. Below: the Dolmen de la Madeleine, near Gennes ▲ *293*.

A RELIC FROM JERUSALEM IN ANJOU
The Holy Girdle of the Virgin, made of linen and oriental silk, is said to have been brought back from a crusade by Guillaume IX of Aquitaine, as a gift from the

ABBEY OF ASNIÈRES (D8

Impressive ruins are all that remains of this imposing Benedictine abbey, founded in 1114 by Bernard Thiron, a follower of Robert d'Arbrissel ● *272*. The lords of Montreuil made it into a prosperous abbey and their place of burial. The abbey fell into decline after being sacked by the Huguenots in 1500, and was closed in 1746. The square tower of the transept crossing, dating from the 13th century, was restored in the 17th century. The 17th-century dovecote was recently restored: its seven-sided design is unique in Anjou.

LE PUY-NOTRE-DAME (D8

The town is perched on a vine-covered hill of tufa, 340 feet high, called the Montagne de Marie. In medieval times pilgrims flocked here to worship a relic of the Virgin – a girdle brought from Jerusalem (see left), which was greatly revered by Louis XI.

Patriarch of Jerusalem. The two rock crystals were donated by Anne of Austria, who wore the girdle for the birth of Louis XIV. The gold endpieces (above), made by goldsmith Mathieu Dupond, date from 1537.

COLLEGIATE CHURCH OF NOTRE-DAME. The Holy Girdle of the Virgin (above) is displayed in the treasury of the church (12th–13th century). The nave, which has six bays and side aisles, is built in the Poitevin style, while the rounded vaults are in the Angevin Gothic style ● *60*. In the choir, the oak stalls carved with human figures date from the 16th century.

MONTREUIL-BELLAY, THE WALLED TOWN ★ (D8

This magnificent medieval town is perched on a steep rocky spur by the Thouet, a tributary of the Loire. It is the only one of the thirty-two walled towns of Anjou to have preserved its ramparts and its four monumental gates. It is best to enter the town through the Porte du Moulin (16th century), just beyond the bridge over the river. From here you can see the white silhouette of the town through the trees – with a lovely view over the water mill, which was destroyed by fire in 1896 and rebuilt in the Renaissance style.
HISTORY. Montreuil-Bellay was an independent barony for many years. When the Saumur region was annexed to Anjou by Foulques Nerra ▲ *297* in 1026, it became a border town. To the south the 13th-century wall around the Porte St-Jean faces toward Poitou. To the north is the Porte Nouvelle, looking toward Anjou. To the west the Porte du Boëlle, on the Thouet, controlled shipping and tolls.

MONTREUIL-BELLAY
The Tour St-Jean (15th century) is decorated with bosses, a popular form of ornamentation.

ANJOU ▲
SAUMUR TO ANGERS

HE CHÂTEAU. The present appearance of
he château is the result of alterations
undertaken by the Harcourt family. It has
hree sections: the CHÂTEAU-VIEUX
(15th century), with a defensive structure
n front of it with a round barbican from
he 13th century; the LOGIS DES
CHANOINES DE LA COLLÉGIALE (Canons'
wing) from the late 15th century; and the
CHÂTEAU-NEUF (15th–16th century),
restored in the late 19th century. The Flamboyant oratory is
decorated with magnificent mural paintings. The Collegiate
Church of Notre-Dame (1472 and 1484, restored in 1865) was
riginally the castle chapel; it became a parish church in 1810.
HE TOWN. This is a pleasant place for a stroll, with houses
uilt between the 15th and 18th centuries. From Boulevard de
Ardenne there is a spectacular view of the valley.

Heading toward Angers along the Loire, the landscape is
scattered with patches of greenery. This area has a
umber of important classical and prehistoric sites, which
rovide evidence of early human occupation. Over the
centuries the towns crowning the hilltops to the south of
the Loire have gradually spread downhill toward the
river.

ST-HILAIRE-ST-FLORENT   (D7)

This suburb, west of Saumur, encompasses the
old town of St-Hilaire-les-Grottes and the area
around the Abbey of St-Florent. It stretches along
the left bank of the Thouet, over a hillside dotted
with caves used for maturing wine ■ *30* and growing
ushrooms ■ *26*. The dolmens ▲ *289* of St-Hilaire and Bois-
e-Feu can be seen here.
BBEY OF ST-FLORENT. This Benedictine abbey was famous
nd powerful from the 11th to the 16th centuries; its decline
as hastened by the Revolution, and it fell into ruins after
805. All that remains today is the base of the choir of the
bbey church, above a remarkable crypt (11th–12th century)
ith Romanesque capitals. The narthex (late 12th century) is
perfect example of the Angevin Gothic style ● *60*.
HURCH OF ST-BARTHÉLEMY. The church has two naves in the
ngevin Gothic style (late 12th and 14th century). On the
orth wall of the church is a plaque commemorating Joan of
rc's visit to St-Florent in 1429.

**JEANNE D'ARC
IN ST-FLORENT**
Joan of Arc ▲ *116*
came to the Abbey of
St-Florent on March
17, 1429. Marie de
Bretagne, mother of
the Duc d'Alençon,
and Jeanne
d'Orléans, the duke's
wife, were staying
here at the time.
Joan of Arc hoped to
convince the duke,
who was a prisoner
on parole after three
years of captivity, to
take up arms again
at her side. Her
mission was a
complete success:
the duke sold his
possessions to pay
his ransom and
resumed the fight
against the English.

**THREE HOMES
FOR THE ABBEY**
The monks built their
first abbey to house
the relics of Saint
Florent at
Montglonne, near
St-Florent-le-Vieil,
to the east of
Ancenis. In the 9th
century Norman
invasions forced them
to flee, and they
retreated to Saumur.
When Foulques
Nerra ▲ *297*, Count
of Anjou, captured
the town in 1026, the
monks moved their
monastery again, this
time settling at a
place called St-
Florent-le-Jeune,
near the Thouet,
where the great abbey
prospered in peace.

Château de Pimpéan.

TROGLODYTE CAVES. At the Musée du Champignon, in the caves to the west of St-Hilaire-St-Florent, you can sample different kinds of mushroom and view a collection of fossils and ammonites. Sparkling Saumur wine is also produced in these caves, using the technique introduced in 1811 by Jean Ackerman (1788–1866), son of a banker from Antwerp.

CHÊNEHUTTE-LES-TUFFEAUX (D?

The small towns of Chênehutte-les-Tuffeaux and Trèves-Cunault, which merged in 1974, present an exceptional group of historical sites and monuments.
THE PLATEAU. This area was inhabited from the bronze and iron ages onward. A Gallic *oppidum* and then a Roman fortification were located here, followed in turn by a Carolingian villa and, finally, by the Abbey of St-Florent. An archeological trail and an exhibition display the wealth of remains that have survived from these times, including sections of wall, tombs, coins and pottery.
THE TOWN. In the town itself, at the foot of the plateau, is the Church of Notre-Dame (12th century), which has a Romanesque ● *58* portal, ornamented with acanthus and foliage motifs, and a bell tower with paired windows.

TRÈVES ● *59* (D?

The village stands amid green countryside, facing a large island in the Loire. It is dominated by the 15th-century keep, 100 feet high and surrounded by magnificent yew trees. This is all that remains of the fortress, demolished in 1747, built by Robert le Maczon (or le Maçon), Baron de Trèves, chancellor of Charles VII and companion in arms of Joan of Arc.
CHURCH OF ST-AUBIN. This delightful 12th-century building has a 13th-century bell tower and a 15th-century spire. In the nave is a 12th-century baptismal font with four 11th-century masks.
THE VILLAGE. There are a number of 15th- and 16th-century houses. The Logis de la Cour-Condé (early 17th century) has a square corner watchtower.

CUNAULT ★ (D?

Notre-Dame de Cunault ● *59* was founded by monks from the Île de Noirmoutier who had fled from the Norman invasions of the 9th century. A new collegiate church was built between the 11th and the 13th centuries. One of the loveliest Romanesque buildings in Anjou, it has

Elevation of Notre-Dame de Cunault, a splendid example of Romanesque architecture.

23 capitals and a famous square bell tower (11th century).
he entrance on the west façade is built in typical Poitevin
yle, with a portal (13th century) framed by five archivolts.
INTERIOR. The church has three naves of equal height. The
hoir is surrounded by an ambulatory whose chapels contain a
olored stone Pietà from the 15th century and the shrine of
aint Maxenceul (13th century) made of painted carved
alnut. Opposite the church is the house of a prior, Pierre
ottereau, which dates from the reign of François I.

GENNES-SUR-LOIRE (D6)

he Angevin-type dolmens of La Madeleine, La Forêt, La
our d'Avort and La Pagerie show that this site has been
habited since the Neolithic era. Not far from here stand the
enhirs of Bois-Gilbert and Le Bouchet. Roman remains
clude the site of Gallo-Roman baths, which were supplied
y an aqueduct that can still be seen, and the ruins of an
mphitheater where excavations have been under way since
985. The disused Church of St-Eusèbe, perched on the
lltop, still has its square 12th-century bell tower. Next to the
uins of the nave stands a memorial to the cadets of Saumur,
ommemorating the battles of June 1940 ▲ 279. The Logis de
ardron is a beautiful 15th-century house.
CHURCH OF ST-VÉTÉRIN. The church was built in the 12th and
5th centuries. It has a number of features from the
arolingian period and contains several Merovingian tombs.
WATER MILL OF SARRÉ. This 16th-century mill is one of the
w in the region with its water wheel ● 78 still in use.

he Pays de l'Aubance begins immediately after Gennes.
The road follows the winding course of the Aubance river,
assing from the bright limestone of the Saumur region to the
ark schists of Anjou, through a landscape of vines and
opses. Finally, to the south of Angers, the
ountryside opens onto the famous
neyards of the Coteaux du Layon.

CHÂTEAU DE PIMPÉAN (C6)

he château with its four square corner
owers stands on a hill in an undulating
ndscape of forests and vines, overlooking
e town of Grézillé. It was built in the 15th
entury by Bernard de Beauvau, seneschal
f Anjou and friend of King René I ▲ 280;
was modified in the 17th century. A restoration program
undertaken by the current owners is still
in progress.

CHAPEL ★. The chapel stands in the
internal courtyard of the château.
The building, which dates from the
15th century, is perfectly preserved,
with murals that are among the best
in Anjou. Particularly striking is the
fresco ▲ 256 of angels holding the
instruments of the Passion, produced
by Coppin Delft of the Flemish
school.

**"HÉLICE TERRESTRE
DE L'ORBIÈRE"**
Downriver, near
St-Georges-des-
Sept-Voies (C6),
is a monumental
sculpture in two
parts: one hollowed
out of the rock, the
other freestanding.
This troglodyte
group is the studio
of sculptor Jacques
Warminski, whose
drawings can also be
seen at the Château
de Pimpéan; one
room is devoted to
troglodyte
architecture.

**FESTIVAL OF WINE
AND MUSIC**
The Pimpéan music
festival is held
annually in the
magical setting of the
castle chapel, with
recitals held every
afternoon from
July 31 to August 31.
The recitals are
followed by tastings
of wines produced by
the vineyards around
the château.

WINDMILLS ● 78
Anjou is said to have had some two thousand mills in the 17th century. Several different types of windmill can still be seen. Tower windmills (*moulins-tours*) with a stone tower have several stories, crowned by a roof that pivots to change the direction of the sails. Cave windmills (*moulins-caviers*), like the Moulin du Pavé (below), have a conical stone tower with a pivoting wooden cabin on top; "Turkish windmills" (*moulins-turquois*) have a cylindrical stone tower.

BRISSAC-QUINCÉ (B6)

This is one of the most extraordinary châteaux in Anjou. Pierre de Brezé, a counselor to Charles VII and Louis XI, built a feudal castle here in the 15th century, on the foundations of an older castl built by Foulques Nerra ▲ *297*. It was acquired by René de Cossé, Duc de Brissac, in 1502. His grandson Charles, Maréchal de France and governor of Paris, began building a elegant new residence in 1600, but work came to a halt at his death in 1621. The new building was still incomplete when th feudal castle was partly demolished. This led the present (twelfth) Duc de Brissac to describe it as a "half-finished new château built in a half-ruined old château": the 17th-century residence, for example, is flanked by two medieval towers, dating from the 15th century.

INTERIOR. The 203 rooms, including the huge Salle des Gardes, the portrait gallery, the Salle des Chasses and the bedchamber of Louis XIII, are richly decorated with splendid Flemish tapestries from the 16th century. A beautifu Louis XIII style staircase serves the five upper stories of the pavilion.

CHAPEL. The 15th-century chapel has a funeral stele carved b David d'Angers ▲ *304*.

LES PONTS-DE-CÉ (B6

Providing access to Angers across three branches of the Loire the Canal d'Authion and the Louet river, this town has been of strategic importance for centuries. It straddles three islands. One of them has a pentagonal keep – all that remain of the château, which was rebuilt in the 13th century.

THE KEEPS. The machicolated keep stands on a curious spur of land, which enhances its impressive appearance. Inside is a museum of Angevin headdresses.

CHURCH OF ST-AUBIN. This church was built in 1003 and extended several times; it has a lovely Romanesque nave.

CHURCH OF ST-MAURILLE. Although built in 1840, this churc has lovely carved stalls from the 16th century – including one depicting Saint Babille with a padlock on her mouth.

"As for the Ponts-de-Cé, this is no longer the old group of bridges it was in the past, which probably went back to Caesar's time, crossing the wide streams of the Loire with 109 arches of all shapes, widths and ages, often knocked down and carried away by the torrents of the river at times of flooding ... Those old Ponts-de-Cé, which were modified and rebuilt again and again, have now been replaced by a large modern bridge.**"**
Albert Robida

IN AND AROUND ANGERS

SERRANT, *310*
LE PLESSIS-MACÉ, *310*
LE PLESSIS-BOURRÉ, *311*
BAUGÉ, *312*
MONTGEOFFROY, *312*
TRÉLAZÉ, *312*

▲ ANGERS

1. CHÂTEAU
2. RUE DONADIEU-
   DE-PUYCHARIC
3. RUE ST-AIGNAN
4. MONTÉE
   ST-MAURICE
5. CATHÉDRALE
   ST-MAURICE
6. MAISON D'ADAM
7. GALERIE DAVID-
   D'ANGERS
8. LOGIS BARRAULT
9. ABBEY OF
   ST-AUBIN
10. CHURCH OF
    NOTRE-DAME
11. HÔTEL PINCÉ
12. LA DOUTRE :
 – HÔPITAL ST-JEAN
 – MUSÉE
   JEAN-LURÇAT
 – THE RONCERAY
 – ÉGLISE DE
   LA TRINITÉ

PRINCELY TITLE
In 1246 Charles, the
younger brother of
King Louis IX
(below), was given

the cadet title of
Count of Anjou. His
descendants reigned
over Naples, Sicily,
Hungary and Poland.

THE ANDECAVI
The Gauls who
inhabited the site of
Angers were called
the Andes by Julius
Caesar and the
Andecavi by Pliny,
Tacitus and Ptolemy;
the name may have
meant "peace-
loving". Domnacus,
chief of the Andecavi,
resisted the Romans
during their conquest
of Gaul, but was
defeated in 51 BC.

HISTORY OF THE TOWN   (B5, B

Built on the banks of the Maine, a small tributary of the
Loire, this former stronghold of the Dukes of Anjou, with its
formidable castle, became famous for its tapestries.
INGELGERIANS AND PLANTAGENETS. Angers was once the hom
of a Celtic tribe, the Andecavi. At the end of the 9th century
became the capital of the county of Anjou. After the era of
invasions the town prospered under the Ingelgerian dynasty,
whose most famous representative was the fearsome
conqueror Foulques Nerra (see opposite). His successors, th
Plantaganets, made Angers the keystone of their new Anglo-
Angevin empire (Normandy, Aquitaine, Touraine and
England), built through alliances and conquests ● 37.
CAPETIANS. After fifty years of resistance Angers fell into the
hands of the Capetians, and Louis IX (1214–70) – the future
Saint Louis – fortified the town. In 1360 Anjou was raised
to the status of duchy and annexed to the French kingdom.
Under René I ▲ 280, the last representative of the House
of Anjou, Angers became a flourishing city.
"THE ATHENS OF THE WEST". During the
Renaissance the town saw another golden
age, both culturally and intellectually
(with the development of universities and
colleges) and in terms of architecture
(with the construction of many fine
private residences, ▲ 302–7).
It became known as the
"Athens of the West".
DECLINE AND REVIVAL. Growth
in the 17th and 18th centuries
centered on the manufacture of
sailcloth and rigging. After this
came a long period of decline.

Since the 1960's Angers has compensated by actively encouraging the development of new industries. Today the town has more than 200,000 inhabitants and a very progressive outlook – particularly in the computer sector (represented by Bull, Thomson and Packard-Bell) and with the development of PLANT BIOTECHNOLOGY at the Institut National de Recherches Agronomiques and HORTICULTURE at the Centre National de l'Industrie Horticole.

THE CHÂTEAU

With its tall, somber towers, the fortress has an imposing, powerful presence. Its medieval military architecture ● 64 offers a striking contrast to the delicate patterns of the formal gardens surrounding it.

CENTRE INTERNATIONAL DE LA TAPISSERIE. The museum, established in 1951, displays an unrivaled collection of tapestries dating from the 14th to the 16th centuries. The most famous of them is the Tapestry of the Apocalypse ▲ 300.

"BLACK FALCON" OF ANJOU (c. 972–1040) In 987 Foulques III, known as Foulques Nerra, inherited the weak county of Anjou.

He was a fierce warrior and rapidly expanded his territory at the expense of his feudal neighbors, including the powerful Count of Blois. He built fortresses (Loches ▲ 224, Langeais ▲ 268), fortified Saumur and Angers, built various châteaux (Montreuil-Bellay, Baugé ▲ 312) and, by way of expiation, founded religious buildings, such as the Abbey of Beaulieu-lès-Loches, which houses his tomb ▲ 230. His descendants continued his work expanding the lands of "Grand Anjou" ● 37.

297

HISTORY OF THE CHÂTEAU

From the 6th to the 9th centuries the residence of the bishop of Angers occupied the site of the present-day château. Foulques Nerra ▲ 297 built a fortress here in the 9th century only a wall from the great hall survives today.

Cul-de-lampe bartizan on one of the two towers forming the Porte de Ville (13th century).

CAPETIANS. Between 1230 and 1240 King Louis IX erected one of the greatest fortresses of his day on the site of Foulques Nerra's castle. Louis II of Anjou and Yolande d'Aragon added the new chapel and the Logis Royal in the early 15th century. In 1442 their son René I ▲ 280 (below) extended the royal residence and built the Châtelet to close off the main courtyard.

THE WARS OF RELIGION. Under pressure from the Angevin rebels ● 40, Henri III authorized the demolition of the château in 1585. However, the governor Donadieu de Puycharic seized the opportunity to improve its defense system by reducing the height of the towers to that of the curtain walls, thus making it possible for artillery to move around the whole circumference of the building.

PIERRE DONADIEU DE PUYCHARIC
Donadieu was appointed governor of Angers in 1585 and modernized the

château's defense system. When Henri III ordered the destruction of the château, Donadieu bided his time, simply removing the top stories of the towers while waiting for the order to be reversed. The funerary statue (above) is in the Chapel of St-Jean-Baptiste, adjoining the Logis Royal. It was produced by Jacques Sarrazin, one of the greatest French sculptors of the court of Louis XIII, who also created the tomb of Cardinal de Bérulle now in the Louvre.

THE ANCIEN RÉGIME. In the 17th century the château became a state prison. But in 1793, when Angers declared itself a republican town, the château once again played a military role, by halting the advance of the Vendéen army.

MODERN TIMES. In 1951 the national fine-arts commission took over the building, which had been badly damaged during the bombardments of 1944, and began a program of restoration. Transformed into a museum and public park, it remains a place of great historic and artistic interest.

TOUR OF THE CHÂTEAU

The château stands on a sandstone and granite outcrop, above a deep dry moat. It is built in an irregular pentagonal shape, flanked by seventeen cylindrical towers which are nearly 130 feet high and 60 feet in diameter. The towers, built of dark schist with bands of light sandstone, were formerly one or two stories higher and had pepperpot roofs. In the 13th century arrow slits protected the castle; canon holes were added three centuries later. Originally there were two entrances: the Porte de Ville (the present-day entrance) to the north, and the Porte des Champs to the south.

REMAINS OF FOULQUES NERRA'S CASTLE. The wall of the feudal hall dates from the 11th century; the great door with cylindrical and ribbon moldings was added in the 12th century. The high mullioned windows date from the 14th and 15th centuries.

"ANGERS IS SLUMBERING, WITH ITS BEAUTIFUL TREES, ITS CHATEAU WITH ROUND TOWERS LIKE CHIMNEYS, ITS ROYAL MEMORIES, ITS AVENUES EMBROIDERED WITH FLORAL MOSAICS."

PAUL NIZAN

CHAPEL OF STE-GENEVIÈVE-ST-LAUD (12th century). The northern part of the chapel is set into the Gallo-Roman ramparts. Only the apse survives today.

THE LOGIS ROYAL AND THE GRANDE CHAPELLE (15th century). Both were built by Louis II of Anjou. In 1453 René I added a gallery with windows to the Logis Royal, prefiguring the galleries of Renaissance châteaux ● *68*. The chapel adjoins the Logis, and has a lovely oratory with a triple arcature where the lord and lady of the château could pray.

THE CHÂTELET. The gatehouse was built by René I ▲ *280* around 1450 to serve as the château's main portal. Its pepperpot towers give it an archaic, medieval appearance.

LOGIS DU GOUVERNEUR. This charming 18th-century residence, built around a 15th-century house, stands against the eastern wall of the château, hidden away in the gardens.

THE MOAT. Never filled with water because it was too far above river level, the moat is now used as a deer park (right).

GALERIE DE L'APOCALYPSE ★. The gallery runs along the south wall, close to the remains of the Chapel of St-Laud. It houses the famous tapestry after which it is named ▲ *300*.

"An almost fairy-tale surprise . . . to see a herd of dappled deer grazing"

J. Gracq

FEUDAL AND ROYAL ARCHITECTURE
Left: views of the Louis IX's fortress, with its massive polychrome walls, including the Grande Chapelle, the Logis Royal and the Châtelet (detail below right).

THE GALERIE DE L'APOCALYPSE
In 1950 the architect Bernard Vitry built a unique gallery (below) to provide an appropriate setting for the Tapestry of the Apocalypse ▲ *300*, allowing visitors to see it as a whole and to admire each of its scenes in detail.

Each of the six groups of pictures has a famous figure introducing the story depicted in the scenes.

In 1373 King Charles V sent his brother Louis I. Duke of Anjou, a richly illuminated manuscript of *The Revelation of St John*, also known as *The Apocalypse* (from *apokalupsis*, the Greek for "revelation"). From it Louis commissioned the leading court painter, Jehan de Bondolf (sometimes called Hennequin de Bruges), to design a tapestry with eighty-four scenes – of which seventy-six have miraculously survived. These have been restored and are now displayed in a special gallery at the Château d'Angers.

THE BOOK OF "THE APOCALYPSE"
The mystical last book of the New Testament describes the Last Judgment and the plagues that are to threaten the "inhabiters of the earth". However, it also prophesies the triumph of the "Lamb of God" and the fall of "the great city of Babylon" (above), a symbol of ungodly societies.

"I JOHN SAW THE HOLY CITY, NEW JERUSALEM . . ."
Saint John is depicted as a witness in almost all the scenes of the tapestry. Here he is shown dazzled by the brilliant vision of the new Jerusalem "descending out of heaven from God" – the ultimate symbol of the revelation, a portent of heavenly bliss.

"An Apocalypse in French, illustrated with figures and scenes . . . the king gave it to Monsieur d'Anjou to make his beautiful tapestry."

INVENTORY OF THE ROYAL LIBRARY

RESCUED AND RESTORED

work was woven in Paris by Nicolas Bataille
d Robert Poisson, using the most advanced
chniques for weaving and fixing pigments.
ring the Revolution it was discarded and cut
to pieces. In 1848 Canon Joubert, the keeper
e treasury of Angers Cathedral, bought back
e pieces for 300 francs and embarked on a
ute restoration, which took fourteen years to
plete. The tapestry has been on display since
1983; it is 350 feet long and 15 feet high.

FABULOUS CREATURES AND ORNAMENTATION

The early scenes have
plain backgrounds
and simple
landscapes. Later
scenes display
luxuriant vegetation
and extraordinary
monsters, with skies
bounded by friezes of
scalloped clouds.

HORSEMEN OF THE APOCALYPSE

The sixth trumpet
of the Apocalypse
summons the
horsemen of hell,
who are to
slaughter one-third
of humanity.
The dark-blue
background
throws into
relief the
movements
and
expressions
of the scene
and highlights
the colors of the
costumes.

BRIGHT COLORS HIDDEN AWAY

In 1981 the lining was
removed for cleaning –
revealing the reverse
of the images, on the
back of the tapestry.
The colors on the
back are dazzlingly
bright, showing how
the tapestry must
have looked
when it was
made (all the
pictures here
are from the
reverse side,
except the
frieze).

Opposite
Cathedral of St-Maurice

"LA CATHO"
When, in 1875,
Bishop Freppel of
Angers (1820–1906)
founded the Facultés
Catholiques de
l'Ouest, his aim
was to create
"a Christian élite"
in the various
professions.
The Catholic
University, known
as "La Catho",
soon established
an impressive
reputation,
especially for its
theological faculty,
which is one of the
most famous
in France.

As well as a
remarkable treasury
(right, a 15th-century
arm reliquary), the
cathedral has an
organ case in the
Rocaille style (above)
and mural paintings
(14th and 15th
century) depicting the
life of Saint Maurille
(below).

THE OLD TOWN ● 72, 7

This is the quarter between the cathedral
and the château, the area originally
covered by the old walled city. Its
narrow, winding streets are lined
with religious buildings and old
houses, many of them half-
timbered, including some fine
examples of architecture from the
late Middle Ages.

PROMENADE DU BOUT-DU-MONDE.
This esplanade created in the 19th century
leads from the château toward the old town. It offers views
over the Maine to the quarter of La Doutre on the other side
of the river.

LOGIS DE L'ESTAIGNIER. In the cobbled Rue St-Aignan, amid
the medieval houses (such as nos. 15 and 17) stands a turreted
building from 1448 which now houses the Musée de l'Étain
(Pewter Museum). The building is also known as the
Maison du Croissant, after the order of knights founded
by René I ▲ 280.

RUE DONADIEU-DE-PUYCHARIC. This street is typical of the
quiet charm of the old town. There are some delightful
buildings, such as the Hôtel St-Martial (17th century), which
was formerly a canon's residence, and the beautiful Hôtel de
Coulanges (16th century), built around a garden that has an
old well and a covered walk.

MONTÉE ST-MAURICE. As you climb up this old flight of steps
from the bank of the Maine, the cathedral at the top gradually
comes into view.

CATHEDRAL OF ST-MAURICE. Construction of the present
cathedral was begun on the orders of Bishop Ulger of Douai
in the early 12th century, and continued by his successors
Normand de Doué and Guillaume de Beaumont.
EXTERIOR. The two 12th-century towers were modified in the
15th century and crowned with stone spires in the
19th century; they stand on either side of the 16th-
century clock pavilion. The façade wall, built around
1180, displays a composite style influenced by the
Aquitaine tradition. The portal (1170–80), with its
four historiated archivolts, is
surmounted by a gallery (which
replaced an earlier gable in 1537)
with eight tall statues of soldiers,
including Saint Maurice.
INTERIOR. The oldest part of the
cathedral is its single nave, which
was built between 1148 and 1153,
featuring the earliest Gothic
arches in the Angevin style ● 60.
As well as the choir, completed in
1274, the church has a large
number of magnificent stained-
glass windows from the 12th and 13th centuries
which give the building its distinctive
luminosity. The large rose windows of the
transept (above, the *Last Judgment*) were
created by André Robin, master glassmaker of

302

RENÉ BAZIN
Born in Angers in 1853, René Bazin studied at the Catholic University from the time of its foundation and in 1875 became its first Doctor of Law. A Catholic and a nationalist, in 1884 he embarked on his career as a journalist and novelist. He wrote twenty novels inspired by the Angers area and by his Christian faith (including *Stephanette*, *La terre qui meurt* and *Le blé qui lève*), as well as travel books (such as *Les croquis italiens*) and numerous essays (including ones on Pius X and Charles de Foucault). He was made a member of the French Academy in 1904, and in 1926 published *Paysages et pays d'Anjou*. He died in 1932.

e cathedral from 1435 to 1465. The high altar with its nopy in red marble was built in 1757–9 by Antoine-Denis ervais, the king's architect, imitating Bernini's *baldacchino* St Peter's in Rome. Of all the churches in Anjou, the thedral has the richest treasury. Among the most striking eces are the silver receptacle which contained the heart of arguerite d'Anjou-Sicile and several reliquaries made of ver, gold and precious stones.

UE DE L'OISELLERIE. There are three merchants' houses os. 5, 7 and 9) with corbeled gables d diamond-pattern timbering. The dest dates from the 16th century.

NCIEN ÉVÊCHÉ. The former iscopal palace (no. 2, rue de Disellerie), completed under Bishop lger, was restored in the 19th century. consists of two wings forming a shape. The bishop received his ssals in the low hall (12th century).

ÔTEL DE LA GODELINE (no. 73, rue antaganêt). This lovely building rved as the town hall from 1484 to 1529. It was restored in 41 and now houses the Maison des Vins and the eadquarters of the Wine Council of Anjou and Saumur.

LACE SAINTE-CROIX. In the Middle Ages this was the ommercial center of the town and one of its liveliest districts. he prosperity of the time is reflected by several of e houses, the most spectacular of which is the Iaison d'Adam (see below).

ÔTEL DE THÉVALLE. This lovely building om the late 16th century has square avilions with large dormers and high ullioned windows. It was owned by the owerful Thévalle family, originally from e Maine region.

IAISON D'ADAM ● 73. Built on the orner of two main roads in the early 5th century; this is considered to be e loveliest old house in Angers. s diamond-timbered façades (right) se up over five corbeled stories, ith a profusion of figures (above) nd Flamboyant ornamentation rved in the wood. Up to the 9th century statues of Adam nd Eve stood on either side of e Tree of Life, below the emarkable corner bartizan. he house's name derives either

DAVID D'ANGERS
Pierre-Jean David (1788–1856), the son of an ornamental sculptor, studied first at an art school housed in the Logis Barrault, and then at the École des Beaux-Arts in Paris. He became known as David d'Angers and won the Grand Prix de Rome in 1811 for his bas-relief *The Death of Epaminondas*, which established his fame. His close friend Victor Hugo praised his "dazzling" monumental masterpieces. David created the pediment of the Panthéon in Paris; his most famous statues are those of Bonchamps (1824), Bernardin de St-Pierre (1851) and Général Drouot (1853).

This female mask from the Middle Ages in gilded copper (right) is one of the rare masterpieces on display in the museum of the Logis Barrault (below).

from these statues or from the name of its owner, Michel Adam, an alderman of Angers, who acquired it in 1714.

RUE SAINT-AUBIN. On this street is the façade of the Hôtel de Cheval-Blanc (no. 12), a private house from the 18th century, which still has a lovely wooden staircase in the courtyard, with its original steps and balustrades.

FORMER ABBEY OF ST-AUBIN (Rue des Lices/Rue St-Aubin). The abbey is said to have been founded around 535 by Saint Germain, Bishop of Paris. It was extended in the 18th century. Today the former abbey buildings house the Conseil Général and Préfecture of Angers. Much of the original abbey was destroyed when the Rue St-Martin was built; surviving sections include the cloister (12th century), the Romanesque arcades (above), the chapter house (12th and 17th century) and the sacristy (17th century). The 18th-century monumental railings outside came from the choir of the abbey church at Fontevraud.

TOUR SAINT-AUBIN (Rue des Lices). This was the belfry (12th century) of the Abbey of St-Aubin; the square tower, nearly 180 feet high, terminates in an octagonal story with four pinnacles.

FORMER COLLEGIATE CHURCH OF ST-MARTIN (Rue St-Martin). This is the oldest church in Angers. A Merovingian oratory was founded here by Saint Loup, Bishop of Angers, in the 7th century. The building was restored by Foulques Nerra ▲ *297* in 1012. Its transept dates from the Carolingian era; the columns are from the 11th century.

médiévale française.

THE LOGIS BARRAULT (MUSÉE DES BEAUX-ARTS) ★. This mansion, in Rue du Musée, is without doubt the most impressive in Angers. It has two wings set at right angles, faced with tufa and decorated in the Flamboyant style, and a corbeled staircase tower. The house was built for Olivier Barrault, treasurer of Brittany and mayor of Angers, in 1487. It was altered in the 17th century and converted into a prison for priests during the Revolution; it was turned into a museum in 1801. The displays of the

e Musée des Beaux-Arts has a painting by
gres (below) depicting the unhappy love of
olo Malatesta and Francesca da Rimini
m Dante's *Inferno*.

Musée des Beaux-Arts consist chiefly of paintings – with some outstanding works by French painters of the 17th century (Philippe de Champaigne, Pierre Mignard) and 18th century (Watteau, Chardin, Fragonard, Boucher, Lancret and Greuze). There is also an impressive collection of sculpture, including works by Houdon, Falconet, Lemoyne and Carpeaux. The

cond story houses displays of local furniture and sculpture
m the Middle Ages and the Renaissance, including a
ded-copper mask (opposite) that is a rare masterpiece of
edieval French metalwork.

UE TOUSSAINT. Substantial remains of the Gallo-Roman
mparts, dating from the 3rd century, can be seen here.
ALERIE DAVID D'ANGERS (no. 33b, rue Toussaint). The
llery is housed in what was once the church of the Abbey of
ussaint (13th century), of which the nave and two side
apels survive. The rectangular choir was added in the early
th century. The church stood in ruins from 1810 until 1984,
en it was restored by Pierre Brunet, chief architect of the
tional commission for historical monuments, who gave it a
lendid glass roof. The municipal authorities decided to use
e building to display the works of the famous sculptor David
Angers (see opposite), giving them the space and
ominence they deserved. The gallery was opened by
esident François Mitterrand (1916–96) in 1984.
ÔTEL DU ROI-DE-POLOGNE. This elegant late-16th-century
sidence at one end of the Pont de la Basse-Chaîne, close
the château, is one of Angers' most popular buildings.
prob᎒ly owes its name to the Duke of Anjou who

briefly became King of Poland in 1573, before being crowned King Henri III of France in 1574

HERVÉ BAZIN
Jean-Pierre-Hervé Bazin, the great-nephew of René Bazin, was born in Angers (in Rue Du-Bellay) in 1911. A novelist and president of the Académie Goncourt, he set some of his stories in Anjou, particularly in the Segréen ▲ *310*. His novels – *Vipère au poing* (1948), *La Mort du petit cheval* (1950), *Qui j'ose aimer* (1956), *Au nom du fils* (1960) and *Madame Ex* (1975) – deal with the theme of oppression within the family and in society.

Natural light from the glass roof highlights the modeling of the splendid sculptures of David d'Angers – such as the plaster casts below.

THE COMMERCIAL QUARTER

This area developed to the east and northeast of the old city in the 17th and 18th centuries; many buildings were erected at this time, including a number of ostentatious private residences. In the 19th century the industrial age contributed its usual quota of neoclassical houses and public buildings.

PLACE DU RALLIEMENT. This square, which stands on the site of a former Christian cemetery (3rd century), has been the focal point of the town since the Third Republic. Its present name dates from the Revolution, when volunteers from all over Anjou gathered here before setting off to join the army. The auditorium of the municipal theater was rebuilt between 1869 and 1871, after a fire; its ceiling displays a large painting donated by the Angers artist Jules-Ernest Lenepveu (1819–98). Lenepveu created the ceiling of the Opéra Garnier in Paris around the same time.

HÔTEL PINCÉ (MUSEÉ TURPIN-DE-CRISSÉ) ★. This elegant turreted Renaissance mansion ● 74, at no. 32b, rue Lenepveu

rivals the attractions of the Logis Barrault ▲ 304. It was built, between 1530 and 1538, for Jean de Pincé, Lieutenant Criminel (crown prosecutor) and mayor of Angers. In 1861 the building was given to the town by the painter Guillaume Bodinier (1795–1872), who converted it into a museum. In it Bodinier displayed the substantial collections of Turpin de Crissé (1782–1859), a painter and former chamberlain to the Empress Joséphine. Later donations brought the museum splendid collections from the Far East.

RUE SAINT-LAUD ● 73. The street looks just as it did two centuries ago, with a number of notable private residences, including Hôtel Ménage (16th century, altered in the 17th century), Hôtel Bardoul de la Bigottière (18th century) and Hôtel Chemellier (18th century), where the sculptor David d'Angers ▲ 304 was born in 1788.

URSULINE CHAPEL (Rue des Ursules). This 17th-century building houses a remarkable Louis XIII altarpiece, attributed to Pierre Corbineau. It is one of the most spectacular examples of Lavallois altarpiece art, which spread from Brittany to Touraine at this time.

MAISON DE LA "BELLE ANGEVINE" (corner of Place du Pilori and Rue Lenepveu). This 16th-century half-timbered house is said to have been that of Renée Corbeau, the beautiful cloth merchant's daughter who was known as "la Belle Angevine".

RUE DU CORNET. This street below the old market district has several striking houses, including Hôtel Ayrault-de-St-Hénis, built for Lieutenant Criminel (crown prosecutor) Pierre Ayrault, and Hôtel de Maquillé (1789), now the headquarters of the town's architectural commission.

PLACE LOUIS-IMBACH. In medieval times this was the town's market square; today it is named after a seed merchant who fought with the Resistance and died during deportation to Mauthausen. The building where the city council was once located was taken over in 1823 by the Court of Appeal.

> **"THE CUISINE OF ANGERS IS STRAIGHTFORWARD, SENSIBLE AND GOOD-NATURED; IT NEVER STRIVES FOR EFFECT . . . ANJOU IS A PARADISE FOR PEACEFUL DIGESTION."**
> CURNONSKY, THE "PRINCE DES GASTRONOMES"

MUSEUM OF PALEONTOLOGY.
(No. 2, Place Louis-Imbach). This museum, in the former courtroom of the Court of Appeal, was founded in the late 19th century. Its collections are mainly of local origin.

HÔTEL DE LANCREAU-DE-BELLEFONDS (no. 14, rue Pocquet-de-Livonnières). This splendid building, which dates from 1789, consists of three wings set around a main court closed off by an Ionic porchway.

NATURAL HISTORY MUSEUM (no. 43, rue Jules-Guitton).

Since 1958 the town's natural history collections have been housed in the Hôtel Valentin (early 19th century). Left: plates by the botanical painter Pierre-Joseph Redouté (1759–1840).

LYCÉE JOACHIM-DU-BELLAY (Avenue Marie-Tallet). The Lycée is housed in the former Abbey of St-Serge, founded in the 7th century. Some of the Benedictine abbey's buildings were restored in the late 17th century and can still be seen today.

CHURCH OF ST-SERGE ★. The former abbey church, flanked by a tower added in 1480, dates from the early 13th century. Its remarkable nave with rounded Angevin vaulting (below) marks the peak of Plantaganet Gothic style.

JARDIN DES PLANTES. The botanical gardens were established in the late 18th century on land belonging to the Church of St-Serge. The former Church of St-Samson is now used for horticultural purposes.

RUE DES ARÈNES. Remains of a 2nd-century amphitheater were unearthed here by local archeologists in 1868, during construction work on the Church of St-Joseph.

JARDIN DU MAIL. These gardens were opened in 1859 alongside an industrial and horticultural exhibition, on the site of a royal-tennis court. The centerpiece is a huge fountain adorned with figures of gods.

HÔTEL DE VILLE. The town hall, opposite the Jardin du Mail, is housed in the classical buildings of the former Collège d'Anjou, built by the Jesuits in 1691. The building was extended in 1823. It was completely renovated in 1981, with the addition of a contemporary extension designed by architect Philippe Morel.

**"LA BOULE DE FORT":
A LOCAL VARIANT
OF BOULES**
This is a very popular game in Anjou, especially between Les Ponts-de-Cé and the Bourgueil area. It is a team game, played on a curving wooden or plastic *piste*, using bowls that are weighted on one side. As in ordinary boules, the aim is to get as close as possible to the jack or *maître*. The origins of the game are uncertain, but its popularity revived in the mid 19th century. It is similar to the British game of bowls, the main differences being that it is played indoors and that the bowls are bound with iron hoops.

CURNONSKY
Maurice-Edmond Sailland, born in Angers in 1872, became a journalist specializing in food and restaurants. He signed his first articles with the pseudonym Curnonsky and became the champion of traditional French food, especially the cuisine of Anjou. Founder of the Académie des Gastronomes, he was feared by restaurant owners throughout France and in 1927 was proclaimed the "Prince des Gastronomes". He died in Paris in 1956.

The Pont de Verdun over the Maine.

QUARTIER DE LA DOUTRE

The La Doutre quarter – from *d'outre Maine* (on the other side of the Maine river) – grew up in the Middle Ages on the right bank of the Maine, around the Abbey of the Ronceray (11th century). It was neglected in the 19th century and has recently undergone a major restoration program.

TOUR DES ANGLAIS. This tower at the end of the Pont de la Haute-Chaîne, which spans the Maine, was once part of the ramparts built by Louis IX in the 13th century.

HÔPITAL SAINT-JEAN ★ (no. boulevard Arago). Built in 1175 by Étienne de Marsay, seneschal to King Henry II of England, this is the oldest hospital in France and a masterpiece of Early Gothic architecture.

MUSÉE JEAN-LURÇAT ★. Since 1967 the museum (below), installed in the former Hôpital St-Jean, has displayed the magnificent tapestry by Jean Lurçat (see opposite) entitled *Le Chant du Monde*, which was to have been some 400 feet long. This work,

created as a tribute to the Tapestry of the Apocalypse ▲ *300*, was woven at Aubusson between 1957 and 1966, when the artist's death brought the project to an end. Ten panels (around 260 feet long) are on display, presenting a pessimistic vision of humanity (*The Great Threat, Man of Hiroshima*) and the prospect of renaissance (*Man in Glory and Peace*).

MUSÉE DE LA TAPISSERIE CONTEMPORAINE. This museum was established in a neighboring building in June 1986 and exhibits the donations of Mme Simone Lurçat as well as tapestries by the contemporary weaver Thomas Gleb and other modern artists.

THE HOSPITAL CHAPEL ★. The chapel was built in the 12th and 13th centuries, with magnificent Angevin vaulting. Its

...ained-glass windows date from the 13th century,
...e Baroque high altar from the 17th century.

...ACE DE LA PAIX. A paupers' cemetery was
...cated here in the Middle Ages. The square as it
...today has a number of imposing buildings, most
...otably Hôtel de Richeteau (17th century) and
...ôtel du Guesclin (1554).

...IE RONCERAY. Founded by Foulques Nerra
297 around 1060, the Abbaye du Ronceray
...mained the only religious institution for women
... Angers. The Romanesque building displays the
...rliest example in Anjou of a high nave with fully
...vaulted side aisles. The abbey was rebuilt in the 17th
...century; since 1815 it has housed the École Nationale
des Arts et Métiers.

ÉGLISE DE LA TRINITÉ
(second half of the 12th
century). This
church stands next to
the Ronceray. Its
single nave has a series
of side chapels
fanning out in a
semicircle. At the
entrance to the nave is
an unusual carved
wooden staircase
from the early
Renaissance, which was
originally part of an organ case.

...ÔTEL DES PÉNITENTES. Initially this building (on Boulevard
...escazeaux), dating from the
...th century, served as a refuge
...r monks from the Abbey of
...-Nicolas. From 1640 it became a
...mmunity for prostitutes and
...her female penitents, founded by
...arguerite Deshaies.

...ORMER ABBEY OF ST-NICOLAS. The
...bey was founded by Foulques
...erra in the 11th century; it was
...built in 1725. The grand southern
...çade, nearly 300 feet long,
...erlooks the lake and the gardens.

JEAN LURÇAT
Jean Lurçat
(1892–1966) was
initially a painter and
engraver, influenced
by Matisse and then
by Surrealism; his
interest in tapestry
began in 1933.
In 1937 he saw the
Tapestry of the
Apocalypse, an
experience which
inspired him to
create his major
work, *Le Chant du
Monde* (*Song of the
World*). He produced
more than 800
tapestries and helped
to give weavers their
own place in the
history of modern art.
Left: *Liberté* (1943),
inspired by a very
beautiful poem by
Paul Éluard.

The exhibitions held
at the Musée de la
Tapisserie display
works by the best
artists from France
and abroad. Left:
Mai (1960) by Mario
Prassinos (1916–85).

Left: *Champagne*
(1959) by Jean
Lurçat. Above: a
postage stamp issued
in his honor.

LE PLESSIS-MA
Right: the fortified keep towering above t
moat. Far right: the tufa balcony of t
château's Renaissance residential wir

Serrant, a stylish and
sumptuous château.

Angers is the undisputed economic and cultural center of
the region, but the neighboring areas of Anjou offer
visitors a great diversity of landscape and architecture ● *12*.

THE VALLEY (A

To the southwest of Angers the landscape around the Loire i
composed of hills standing on either side of the alluvial valley
Here the river has many islands, of which the Île de Chalonn
is the largest. Beyond the river the landscape is still quite wil
though criss-crossed by shady lanes and hedgerows, with a fe
aristocratic residences dotted here and there.

CORNICHE ANGEVINE ★. The winding road which overhangs
the Louet river between Les Ponts-de-Cé and Chalonnes,
downriver from Angers, is one of the loveliest in Anjou. It h,
magnificent views of vineyards, the Loire and the river valley
and villages with turreted buildings and slate roofs.

CHÂTEAU DE SERRANT ★. The château stands in extensive
grounds, surrounded by a deep moat, on the right bank of th
Loire near St-Georges-sur-Loire. It is built of grey schist and
white limestone, in a satisfyingly harmonious style – even
though it took a century and a half to complete. The first
phase of construction started in 1546, directed by Philibert
Delorme, the architect of Fontainebleau; the chapel was bui
later (in 1700–10) by Jules Hardouin-Mansart, architect of tl
chapel at Versailles. The residential wing is flanked by two
round towers, each crowned by a pinnacled dome. The main
façade, like the one at Azay-le-Rideau ▲ *234*, features a
staircase surmounted by a pediment. In the chapel the white
marble mausoleum (1705), carved by Antoine Coysevox, is
dedicated to the Marquis de Vaubrun, who was killed in the
Battle of Altenheim in 1675. The château's apartments
display a magnificent collection of furniture and objets d'art
as well as tapestries from Flanders and Brussels (12th
century), including a series depicting scenes from
Ovid's *Metamorphoses*. The splendid library
contains over 12,000 books.

THE SEGRÉEN (A4, A

This region of hills and hedgerows around th
village of Segré, to the northwest of Angers,
stretches as far as the border
of Brittany, where many
defensive fortresses were bui
CHÂTEAU DU PLESSIS-MACÉ ★
This château, to the west of
Angers, was originally a
fortress built by the feudal
lord, Macé du Plessis, in the
12th century. Three centuries
later it was modified by Louis
de Beaumont, chamberlain of
Louis XI. It is an imposing
sight, with its 12th-century
ramparts and machicolated
rectangular keep (rebuilt in
1445) surrounded by trees a
hundred years old. This

omber effect is offset by the delightful 15th-century
residential wing, with walls of dark schist which contrast with
the white tufa of the elegant carved balcony and windows.
The chapel, also from the 15th century, is dedicated to Saint
Michael; its original altar and a wooden two-story organ loft
have survived.

CHÂTEAU DU PLESSIS-BOURRÉ ★. The château is situated to
the north of Angers, in the town of Écueillé, between the
Sarthe and Mayenne rivers. Jean Bourré, treasurer and
confidant of Louis XI, acquired the estate of Plessis-le-Vent in
1462 and in only four years (1468–72) built this dazzling
creation of tufa limestone, which appears to be floating on
water. It is set in the middle

of a moat so wide that it
looks more like a lake. The
building's fortresslike
appearance is largely due to
the fortified entrance, the
great towers at the four
corners (the southeast tower
has a wall walk with
machicolations) and the ring of low terraces designed to serve
as platforms for artillery. The Renaissance-style residential
wing, less austere in appearance, is set in a vast interior
courtyard. The guardroom (on the second story) has an
astonishing coffered wooden ceiling, decorated with curious
allegorical and satirical pictures, such as *Donkey Singing the
Mass* (above) and the more obscure *Immodest Venus*, many of
them magnificent examples of 15th-century painting.

**WINES FAMOUS SINCE
THE MIDDLE AGES**
■ *30*, ◆ *322*
Although Anjou's
most widely known
wine is Rosé de
Cabernet, the region's
reputation is primarily
due to the quality of
its white wines. To the
south of Angers, on
both sides of the river,
are the Coteaux-de-
Loire which produce
Savennières, the most
celebrated of the dry
white wines, as well as
the famous wines of
La Roche-aux-Moines
and La Coulée-de-
Serrant (one of the
greatest white wines
in France). On the
left bank, the Chenin
Blanc grapes are used
to make Coteaux-du-
Layon-Village wines,
the best of which are
Bonnezeaux and
Quarts-de-Chaume.

**STAUNCH BUILDER
OF CHÂTEAUX**
Jean Bourré (1424–
1506), son of a lawyer
from Château-
Gontier, entered the
service of Louis XI
after studying law. He
became head of the
royal chancellery,
governor of Langeais
and then treasurer of
France. He was made
commander of the
Château d'Angers
under Charles VIII,
and built châteaux at
Vaux, Jarzé and
Plessis-Bourré in the
Maine-et-Loire
region.

The dispensary of the Hôpital St-Joseph at Baugé.

THE BAUGEOIS (D5, E

The area around Baugé, to the east of Angers, is a sandy plateau covered alternately by deep forest and farmland.
BAUGÉ. The town is situated on the right bank of the Couasnon, at the edge of the Forest of Chandelais, on the border of Touraine.
THE CHÂTEAU ★. The first château was built by Foulques Nerra ▲ 297 around the year 1000. In the 15th century Baug was a favorite residence of René I ▲ 280: from 1455 onward he continued the renovation work begun by his mother, Yolande d'Aragon. Above the grand staircase in the north pavilion of the residential wing there is splendid palm-tree vaulting decorated with the arms of Anjou and Sicily. Today the château houses the town hall and a small museum devoted to local history and customs.
HÔPITAL SAINT-JOSEPH ★. The hospital's 17th-century *apothicairerie* (dispensary) displays a rare collection of earthenware pots and jars (left), ranging from the 16th to the 18th century.
CHAPELLE DE LA GIROUARDIÈRE. Since the Revolution the former chapel of the Hospice des Incurables (18th century) has housed the Cross of Anjou ● 37, said to be made from the True Cross.

THE AUTHION VALLEY (D5, D

This long valley to the southeast of Angers was once marshland; today the river banks are lined with fields of flowers and corn. A number of aristocratic residences were built here after the area was drained in the 18th century, adding to the charm of the pretty local towns and villages, with their little windmills and tufa houses.
CHÂTEAU DE MONTGEOFFROY. This neoclassical château ● 70 was built by the architect Nicolas Barré for the Maréchal de Contades in 1772. The impressive 18th-century residential wing is flanked by the chapel and two round towers from a 16th-century manor house. The château has an exhibition of documents signed by Louis XV, Napoleon and Louis XVIII. The small temple in the grounds dates from the 19th century

TRÉLAZÉ (B6)

From the 15th century onward Anjou was famous for its slate, extracted from the schist quarries of Trélazé, for a long time one of the main slate-quarrying towns in the world. However, five of the six mines were forced to close because of the difficult economic climate and competition, notably from Spain. Today Trélazé's slate quarries employ only nine hundred workers, but they still produce 90 percent of the slate used in France.

PRACTICAL INFORMATION

PREPARATIONS, *314*
TRAVELING TO THE LOIRE VALLEY, *316*
GETTING AROUND THE LOIRE VALLEY, *317*
LIVING IN THE LOIRE VALLEY, *318*
ACCOMMODATION, *320*
WINES OF THE LOIRE VALLEY, *322*
PLACES OF INTEREST, *328*
USEFUL ADDRESSES, *337*

Between Gien and Angers, the Loire flows through four départements: Loiret, Loir-et-Cher, Indre-et-Loire and Maine-et-Loire. This majestic river valley is one of France's best-known regions, famous above all for its many magnificent châteaux. The Loire Valley also offers excellent facilities for tourists, especially those who come to see its cultural attractions. It is close to Paris, and easily accessible by road, by TGV (high-speed) trains and by air. Spring, from May onward, and summer are the ideal seasons discover the artistic, historical and gastronomic treasures of the valley of the French kings.

TOURIST INFORMATION

For information regarding accommodation and tourist events, contact the regional tourist boards (for the Centre and Pays-de-Loire regions), the departmental tourist boards, and local tourist offices
◆ *320.*

REGIONAL TOURIST BOARDS (CRTS: COMITÉS RÉGIONAUX DE TOURISME)
◆ Centre
9, rue St-Pierre-Lentin
45041 Orléans cedex 1
Tel. 02 38 54 95 42
Fax 02 38 54 95 46
◆ Pays-de-Loire
2, rue de la Loire
44200 Nantes
Tel. 02 40 89 89 89
Fax 02 40 08 07 10

DEPARTMENTAL TOURIST BOARDS (CDTs: COMITÉS DÉPARTEMENTAUX DE TOURISME)
◆ Indre-et-Loire
18, pl. de la Préfecture
B.P. 3217
37032 Tours cedex
Tel. 02 47 31 42 60
Fax 02 47 31 42 76
◆ Loiret
8, rue d'Escures
45000 Orléans
Tel. 02 38 62 04 88
Fax 02 38 62 98 37
◆ Loir-et-Cher
5, rue de la Voûte du Château
41000 Blois
Tel. 02 54 78 55 50
Fax 02 54 74 81 79
◆ Maine-et-Loire
Place Kennedy
BP 2147
49021 Angers cedex 02
Tel. 02 41 23 51 51
Fax 02 41 88 36 77

A FEW GOOD REASONS FOR VISITING THE LOIRE VALLEY

◆ The vineyards, the wines, the restaurants . . .
◆ One hundred or more châteaux
◆ The Tapestry of the Apocalypse at Angers
◆ The troglodyte dwellings
◆ The windmills of Anjou
◆ The magnificent château gardens, especially Villandry
◆ The Loire itself, the last untamed river of France
◆ The gentle pace life
◆ The great writers from Gregory of Tours, Joachim du Bellay and Rabelai to Balzac, Proust, René and Hervé Bazin . . .
◆ The painters and sculptors: David d'Angers, Leonard da Vinci, François Clouet, Michel Colombe, Jean Bourdichon, Jean Fouquet, Juste, Corneille . . .

HEALTH

Form E111, available from post offices in the UK, allows EC nationals to receive free emergency health care. Other travelers are advised to take out special insurance cover before leaving.
◆ For "son et lumière" displays you are advised to equip yourself with mosquito repellent.

TOURIST PROFILE

The Loire Valley is one of the most popular regions of France, attracting nearly ten million visitors each year. It has 730 hotels, with a capacity of 18,000 beds. The majority of these are two-star hotels (accounting for nearly 70 percent of the total). Other types of accommodation are also available, including rural gîtes and guest houses. The most popular historical building in the region is the Château de Chenonceau, which attracts 900,000 visitors each year, followed by Chambord, with 800,000. The Aquarium de Touraine at Lussault-sur-Loire, which opened in 1994, has already become a major attraction, with nearly 800,000 visitors annually. In recent years the region has successfully developed its varied, delightful countryside as a tourist attraction in its own right.

WHEN TO VISIT

The Loire Valley is known as the "Jardin de la France" ("Garden of France"), a name that takes on its fullest meaning in May and June. Many music and theater festivals are held then, and the monuments and châteaux are not yet overcrowded with visitors. The weather is generally good: there may be the occasional shower cold spell but these never last long. The late fall is also a go time to come: durin this period the "vendanges" (grape harvesting) are the focal point of local life.

DOCUMENTATION

EC nationals arriving in France need only present an identity card or passport. Tourists from other countries will need to present a passpo and in some cases a visa.

FESTIVALS

SPRING

February–March	International 20th-century piano competition, Orléans
March–April	St-Cosme spring music festival (Indre-et-Loire)
April	"Fête des plantes et des jardins de Touraine", Montlouis
April–September	Public display by the Cadre Noir at the Grand Manège of the National Equestrian School, Saumur
Late April	"Acteurs-Acteurs": international drama festival, Tours
April 29–May 1	Joan of Arc festival, Orléans
Late May	"Florilège vocal" (choral music festival), Tours
May–June	Festival of classical music, Sully-sur-Loire (Loiret)
Late June	Rock music festival, Tours
	Music festivals in Touraine, Grange de Meslay, Tours
May–September	Summer music and organ festival, Amboise

★ Wine festivals: Vouvray in February, Chinon and Bourgueil in March, Saumur in April, Amboise at Easter . . .

SUMMER

Late June/early July	"Orléans'Jazz", Orléans.
July	Festival d'Anjou: music and arts in the châteaux of Anjou
	National opera festival for children at the Chapelle-St-Mesmin (Loiret)
	"Les Semaines musicales" music festival, Tours
	Festival of musical theater in Touraine, Loches and Chinon
July–September	International festival of parks and gardens, Chaumont-sur-Loire

The medieval market of Chinon in August: tumblers, puppets, trades of the past, medieval delicacies . . . experience Chinon as it was in the Middle Ages

FALL

Late September	Jazz in Touraine, Montlouis

★ "Le Mondial du Lion": international equestrian competition at the Lion d'Angers

WINTER

January–February	Regional music festival, Montlouis

SON ET LUMIÈRE

May–September: Château d'Azay-le-Rideau

June–August: Château d'Amboise

June–September: Château de Blois and Château de Chenonceau

July–August: Château de Cheverny, Château de Loches, Château du Lude (Sarthe)

CLIMATE

The Loire Valley blessed with especially attractive climate: is close to the sea, and the maritime influence events extremely mild conditions; the same time the continental influence raises summer temperatures. Anjou and the Touraine are more mild than the areas around Blois and Orléans. The higher humidity levels mean that there are more foggy or misty days. Rainfall is regular, but rarely heavy or long-lasting. Summer storms are more common here than by the sea, ensuring a good level of rainfall during the summer months.

The temperature rarely falls below 5°c during the winter. Spring weather is mild, though cold at night. In summer it can be really hot, reaching 30°c. The fall often brings magnificent Indian summers.

BE PREPARED

Rain can come without warning – sometimes with violent storms, especially in summer. It is a good idea to carry an umbrella and a raincoat with you.

PUBLIC HOLIDAYS IN FRANCE

- ◆ January 1
- ◆ Easter Monday
- ◆ May 1
- ◆ May 8
- ◆ Ascension Day
- ◆ Pentecost Monday
- ◆ July 14
- ◆ August 15
- ◆ November 1
- ◆ November 11
- ◆ December 25

BY TRAIN
TGV (HIGH-SPEED) TRAIN
These fast, comfortable trains provide a quick, direct service to the Loire Valley.

RAILWAY STATIONS (SNCF)
There is now a single, central telephone number, for all stations, for train times, fares, reservations and sale of tickets. Tel. 36 35 35 35 or minitel 3615 SNCF

◆ Tours is served by several TGV trains daily, direct from Paris-Montparnasse (1 hr journey time), Lyon-La-Part-Dieu (3½ hrs), Lille (3¼ hrs) and Bordeaux (2½ hrs). The trains stop either at Tours station or at St-Pierre-des-Corps (where there is a regular shuttle service into the town center of Tours).
◆ Several TGV trains run daily from Paris-Montparnasse to Angers (1½ hrs), from Lille to Angers (3¼ hrs) and from Lyon-La-Part-Dieu to Angers (4 hrs).

"CORAIL" TRAINS
These provide a slower but very frequent service. The trains leave Paris nearly every hour for
◆ Orléans (departure from the Gare d'Austerlitz, 1 hr journey time);
◆ Blois (Gare d'Austerlitz, 1½ hrs);
◆ Gien (Gare de Lyon, 1½ hrs).

REDUCTIONS
The SNCF offers a number of reductions: Joker (tickets reserved at least 8 days in advance), Carrissimo (for 12–25 year-olds), Vermeil (for the over-60's), Carte Famille (for families) and Carte Couple (for married or unmarried couples). There are also special rates for different days and journey lengths.

AIR TRAVEL
TO NANTES
Nantes International Airport is 55 miles from Angers and 11 miles from Tours. Flights from this airport serve Paris and many other cities in France and internationally. Both French and international airlines fly from Nantes, offering a range of prices and substantial reductions depending on the date of the flight, the length of stay and the age of the passenger.
◆ Information: Aéroport International de Nantes Tel. 02 40 84 80 00

You can put your bicycle on the train, even on a TGV! It is carried free of charge in the hand-luggage section, or for a charge in the registered luggage section. For information contact railway stations or tour operators.

Freeway
Main roads
TGV

TOURS
The airline company
TAT offers two flights
daily (on Friday and
Saturday) between
Tours and Lyon,
where you can get a
connecting flight for
other destinations in
France or abroad.
◆ TAT (in Tours)
Tel. 02 47 41 23 23
◆ Aéroport Tours-
Symphorion (4 miles
from the town center)
Tel. 02 47 54 19 46

BY CAR
ON THE FREEWAY
All the major towns in
the Loire Valley can
be reached by
freeway. The A10
(Paris-Bordeaux)
serves Orléans, Blois
and Tours. Angers is
on the A11 (the
"Océane", Paris-
Nantes). Traveling
from the Lyons region
or from the southeast
of France, you can
reach Orléans on the
A72 and the A71,
continuing your

journey on the N152
which runs alongside
the Loire between
Orléans and Saumur.

ON THE MAIN ROADS
From the north or the
southwest of France,
take the N10 (Paris-

HALTE
PEAGE

Bordeaux-Hendaye);
from the west or the
southeast, take the
Laval-Bourges-
Moulins road.
◆ Road information
Tel. 08 36 68 20 00
or minitel
3615 ROUTES

ALLOSTOP
An organization
which puts drivers in
touch with would-be
passengers, who
make a financial
contribution
calculated
according to
the length of the
journey.
◆ Reservations:
Tel. 01 53 20 42 42
(from Paris)
01 53 20 42 43
(from outside Paris)

**REGIONAL
TRANSPORT**
The region is
covered by trains
and coaches on
the TER network.
For information
on departure times,
connections and
journey times, see
the "Guide régional
des transports"
(Regional Transport
Guide), available
from railway stations
and tourist offices
◆ 320.

SNCF STATIONS
Information on train
timetables and ticket
prices:
Tel. 36 35 35 35
◆ Orléans
6, rue St-Yves
◆ Blois
Av. Jean-Laigret
◆ Tours
Place du Maréchal-
Leclerc
◆ Angers
Place de la Gare

COACH STATIONS
◆ Orléans
Rue Marcel-Proust
Tel. 02 38 53 94 75
◆ Blois
2, Place Victor-Hugo
Tel. 02 54 78 15 66

◆ Tours
Place du Maréchal-
Leclerc
Tel. 02 47 05 30 49
◆ Angers
Place de la
République
Tel. 02 41 88 59 25

**TRANSPORT FOR
TOURISTS**
The departmental
tourist boards
organize specialist
tours on foot, on
horseback, by
caravan or barouche,
on bicycle or by
canoe: these can
last one or more
days. You can also
travel by boat –
by renting a barge,
for example.

**FLYING OVER
THE LOIRE**
Although expensive,
this is a spectacular
way of traveling
over the region:
by hot-air balloon,
helicopter or plane.
As might be
expected, the views
are stunning,
the river valley
offers a mosaic of
landscapes dotted
with châteaux.
◆ Information at
the "Loisirs Accueil"
services of the
CDTs ◆ 314 or
from tourist offices
◆ 320.

◆ LIVING IN THE LOIRE VALLEY

In the Loire Valley, as in many other tourist regions, prices can vary with the seasons. As summer and the holiday period approach they tend to creep upward. . . . The difference is most noticeable in hotels and restaurants, whereas entrance prices for châteaux and other historical monuments stay the same throughout the year.

METHODS OF PAYMENT

CREDIT CARDS
Credit cards are accepted in almost all hotels, restaurants and stores. You can withdraw up to 2,000F weekly using national and international credit cards affiliated to the Visa, Mastercard or Eurocheque networks; up to 4,000F with a Diners card; and up to 6,000F with an American Express card.
◆ All towns of significant size have at least one auto-teller.

TRAVELERS' CHECKS
Hotel chains and a large number of restaurants and stores accept travelers' checks in French francs. Some display signs to this effect in their windows, though it is always wise to ask in advance. Travelers' checks in foreign currencies are not generally accepted: they should be converted in a bank or bureau de change, which will generally charge a commission on the sum of money exchanged.

EUROCHEQUES
Although this is a common form of payment in some other European countries, Eurocheques are not very well received in France: storekeepers are increasingly reluctant to accept them. However, the EC guarantee card which accompanies Eurocheques can also function as a cash withdrawal card, allowing you to withdraw up to 2,000F in currency each week.

LOSS OR THEFT

IDENTITY PAPERS
Contact the nearest police station; also, contact your consulate or embassy in Paris.
EUROCHEQUES AND EC CARDS
Notify the bank that issued the checks as soon as possible.
CREDIT CARDS
Notify the organization that issued the card instructing them to cancel the card, and send a registered letter to your bank. Allow three weeks for a new card to reach you.
◆ Visa
Tel. 01 42 77 11 90
◆ Eurocard and Mastercard
Tel. 01 45 67 84 84
◆ American Express
Tel. 01 47 77 72 00
◆ Diners Club
Tel. 01 47 62 75 75

RESTAURANTS

The Loire Valley offers a wide range of restaurants, allowing visitors to taste local specialties like *matelote d'anguille*, *rillons de Touraine* and the famous *tarte Tatin*. Prices range from 60F for a decent quality menu to 1,000F for a top-class restaurant, with a full range of options between these two extremes. Away from the immediate vicinity of the river there is an excellent choice of menus offering much better value for money. Nearly all restaurants in the Loire Valley area open at noon; in the evening they generally open at 7pm. In the towns, some restaurants serve meals until midnight, while others remain open all night. In more rural areas restaurants will not generally serve meals after 10.30pm.

BANKS

Banks are generally open from 9am to noon and from 2pm to 5pm (some banks in large towns stay open through the lunch hour). Banks are closed on Sundays, public holidays, and Saturdays or Mondays. Independent bureaux de change have longer opening hours and are often open at the weekend.

PRICE GUIDE

1 bottle of Chinon: 40F

1 hot-air balloon flight: 1,000F per person

1 Kilo of "Champignons de Paris": 14F

1 bottle of traditional wine vinegar (75cl): 20F

1 night in a private château: 350–1,200F for two people

1 entrance fee to a château: 10–40F

1 pot of "rillons de Touraine": 68F

1 entrance ticket for the château and Apocalypse tapestry in Angers: 32F

POST OFFICES

Post offices are open from 8am to 7pm Monday to Friday, and from 8am to noon on Saturdays. The normal rate for France and EC countries is 3F for a letter or card weighing up to 20g. Stamps can be purchased from post offices or at a "tabac".

MARKETS

Open-air markets are held in the squares of towns and villages once or twice a week. These are the best places to buy fresh produce: fish, meat, cheese, local vegetables, seasonal fruit and typical local delicacies.

EMERGENCY NUMBERS

Fire: 18
Police: 17
Ambulance: 15

IMPORTANT!
A new code system for telephone and fax numbers in France came into effect in October, 1996. All the information that follows takes this change into account.
CALLING FRANCE FROM ABROAD
Dial the international prefix (00 from the UK and 011 from the US), then 33 for France, followed by a 9-digit number.

TELEPHONE

DIRECTORY INFORMATION
For numbers in France, dial 12. For international information, dial 00 33 12 followed by the prefix for the country concerned.
CALLING ABROAD FROM FRANCE
From France, dial 00, followed by the country prefix (44 for the UK; 1 for the US) and the number you wish to reach.
CALLS WITHIN FRANCE
For all local and inter-regional calls,

dial 0, followed by a 9-figure number.
TELEPHONE BOXES
To use these you will need telephone cards ("télécartes"), which are available in 50 or 120 units (costing 40.60F and 97.50F respectively) from "tabacs", metro stations and post offices.

FOREIGN-LANGUAGE GUIDES

The departmental tourist boards ♦ 314 can provide foreign-language guides for tourists on request.

THE COST OF A TELEPHONE CALL

LOIRE VALLEY   EUROPE

Midnight 8am   2pm 9.30pm

· ➤ Monday to
  RR   NR   RR   Friday

· ➤ Saturday
  RR   NR   RR

· ➤ Sunday and public holidays
            RR

NR: normal rate: 3.71F/min – RR : reduced rate: 3.08F/min

319

◆ Accommodation

Pleasant hotel rooms can be found for 250F and above: these are generally in two-star hotels (following the new system of classification). Out of season you can treat yourself to a night in one of the many châteaux and manor houses which have been converted into luxury hotels, for a price in the region of 600F. The Loire Valley also has many guest houses and "gîtes" which offer rooms at a reasonable price, often in opulent settings. Local tourist offices are often the best source of advice for reserving the type of accommodation that best suits your needs.

TOURIST OFFICES

ANGERS
Place Kennedy
Tel. 02 41 23 51 11
Open (summer)
Mon.–Sat. 9am–7pm;
Sun. 10am–1pm and
12–6pm
BLOIS
Pavillon Anne-de-Bretagne
3, av. du Docteur-Jean-Laigret
Tel. 02 54 74 06 49
Open (summer)
Mon.–Sat. 9.am–7pm; Sun. 10am–7pm

ORLÉANS
Place Albert 1er
Tel. 02 38 24 05 05
Open Mon.–Sat. 9.00-19.00; Sun. 10am–noon (and 3–6.30pm during July–August)
SAUMUR
Place de la Bilange
BP 241
Tel. 02 41 40 20 60
Open (summer)
Mon.–Sat. 9.15am–7pm; Sun. 10.30am–12.30pm and 3.30–6.30pm)
TOURS
78, rue Bernard-Palissy
Tel. 02 47 70 37 37
Open (summer)
Mon.–Sat. 8.30am–7pm; Sun. 10am–12.30pm and 3–6pm

HOLIDAY VILLAGES

These are village-style groups of holiday homes that offer tourists both relaxation and recreation in a rural setting. They are the ideal place to spend a relaxing holiday at a low price, in both summer and winter. There are around fifty holiday villages in the region as a whole.
◆ Fédération Française des

Stations Vertes de Vacances et des Villages de Neige
BP 598
21016 Dijon Cedex
Tel. 80 43 49 47

HOTELS

Hotels are classified in different categories, according to the new French system: from no stars to the luxury four-star category. Generally the price quoted is for the room and not per person. It is advisable to make advance reservations at Easter and during July and August. All the major hotel chains are represented in the Loire Valley.

SOME HOTEL ASSOCIATIONS

RELAIS ET CHÂTEAUX AND RELAIS DU SILENCE
Most of the châteaux-hotels in the Loire Valley belong to one of these two associations, whose members are high-quality establishments in exceptional settings.
◆ Relais et Châteaux
15, rue Galvani
75017 Paris
Tel. 01 45 72 90 00

◆ Relais du Silence
2, passage Du Guesclin
75015 Paris
Tel. 01 45 66 77 77
LOGIS DE FRANCE
These hotels, generally in the countryside, are traditional establishments with restaurants.
◆ Logis de France
83, av. d'Italie
75013 Paris
Tel. 01 45 84 70 00

CAMPING AND CARAVANNING

The Loire Valley has some 18,000 camping places in around 260 campsites; as regards classification, 50 percent of the sites have two stars, and 36 percent have three

or four stars. Many have lakes, bathing ponds or swimming pools, tennis courts or playing fields. CRTs publish free brochures listing all the campsites in the region.

GUEST HOUSES

CHAMBRES D'HÔTES
These private
houses in the town or
the country offer
accommodation to
travelers for one or
more nights. As well
as breakfast, guests
are sometimes
offered dinner at
the "table d'hôte"
(residents' table).
Prices for a room
in this type of
establishment vary
between 200F and
1,200F (for two
persons, including
breakfast).
  Bienvenu au
Château.
This association
includes châteaux,
manor houses and
other exceptional
establishments
offering
accommodation
in a spectacular
setting.

GÎTES
These are generally
traditional houses in
the countryside. The
prices vary between
1,000F and 3,000F per
week, for 4 to 6
people, depending on
classification (from
1 to 4 stars), the
locality and the time

of year. "Gîtes" are
often very popular
and can be reserved
from one year to
the next: it is
advisable to book
very early for the
summer period.

**GÎTES D'ÉTAPE
(HOSTELS)**
These gîtes are
designed for walkers
in particular, although
they are also open to
other travelers. They
cater for groups,
offering simple (and
increasingly
comfortable)
accommodation for
one or more nights,
often including
breakfast. Some
gîtes d'étape are in
troglodytic dwellings.
The average price
per night is 50F. For
information and
reservations contact
◆ Relais
départementaux
des Gîtes de France:
Indre-et-Loire
Tel. 02 47 27 56 10
Loire-et-Cher
Tel. 02 54 78 55 50
Loiret
Tel. 02 38 62 04 88
Maine-et-Loire
Tel. 02 41 23 51 23

EQUESTRIAN HOLIDAYS

The Loire Valley has
many equestrian
centers, and the
region offers
magnificent, varied
landscapes for horse-
lovers to explore. The
centers organize
courses and treks,
with hostel-type
accommodation.
◆ Centre de tourisme
équestre
49350 Trèves-
Cunault
Tel. 02 41 67 92 43
◆ Tourisme équestre
Le Sauvageot
49680 Vivy
Tel. 02 41 52 89 52

◆ Association
régionale de tourisme
équestre Val de
Loire-Centre
52, rue Alain-
Gerbault
41000 Blois
Tel. 02 54 42 95 60

The École nationale
d'équitation de
Saumur (National
Equestrian School at
Saumur) is open to
the public from April
to September.
Visitors can watch
demonstrations of
jumping, dressage
and display riding.
Tel. 02 41 53 50 66

CYCLING HOLIDAYS

The various
departmental
tourist boards
work together
with hotels and
campsites to
organize cycling
tours offering
accommodation
and a range of
related services,
such as bicycle
rental, luggage

transfer, maps
and documentation,
repair kits and
picnics on
request.
◆ Information on
cycling tours is
available from the
"Loisirs Accueil"
services of the
CDTs and from
most tourist
offices.

YOUTH HOSTELS

For the addresses
of youth hostels
(auberges de
jeunesse) in the
Loire Valley,
contact:

◆ Fédération des
Auberges de
Jeunesse
27, rue Pajol
75018 Paris
Tel. 01 44 89 87 27

◆ Wines of the Loire Valley

Coulée-de-serrant vines.

Troglodytic cellar cut into the rockface.

It is because of the Loire that vineyards have developed in this region: the warm west winds that blow along the river valley create a remarkably warm, sunny microclimate. The vineyards of the Loire Valley were established by the monks of the Cistercian and Benedictine abbeys in the Middle Ages. The Plantagenet and Valois kings enjoyed local wines and encouraged their development, while the proximity of the river furthered the growth of trade from the 12th century onward. For a long time the Loire wines were considered inferior to those of other regions, but over the last thirty years the local producers have achieved high quality standards, creating wines that are both robust and refined.

Wine Classification

The European denomination "Vin de qualité produit dans une région déterminée" (VQPRD) covers the two French categories "Appellation d'origine contrôlée" (AOC) and "Appellation d'origine vin délimité de qualité supérieure" (AOVDQS). The Ministry of Agriculture awards the "Appellation d'origine" classifications according to production standards laid down by the Institut National des Appellations d'Origine (INAO).

Appellations of the Loire

These wines can be produced in any of the vineyards of Anjou, Saumurois and Touraine ■ *30*.

Rosé de Loire

These are dry wines, crisp and fruity, produced from various types of grape (Cabernet-Franc, Cabernet-Sauvignon, Grolleau, Pineau d'Aunis and Gamay Noir).

Crémant-de-Loire

This type of wine is produced from a number of grape varieties grown on widely varying soils (mainly chalky). The fragrance of the wines can be grassy, floral or fruity, depending on where they are made.

The land of Chenin Blanc

Anjou is the land of the Chenin Blanc grape. A dozen appellations make use of it, for white wines that can be dry or sweet, including smooth dessert wines, and sparkling wines in Saumur. Chenin Blanc wines are generous and full-bodied in warm years; other vintages are drier (even sharp), and long-lived (up to half a century).

Anjou

Anjou is a traditional winegrowing area, famous for the sweet wines of Coteaux-du-Layon and Coteaux-de-l'Aubance.

A distinctive wine

◆ Le Savennières. This appellation, grown on 185 acres to the west of Angers, has a great tradition of dry Chenin Blanc wine for keeping. The vines flourish on four hillsides facing south–southeast, on soils of volcanic schist and red sandstone. As a young wine Savennières is austere and highly strung, with great vigor and a fragrance of ripe fruits and flowers. It has a distinctive, bitter taste. The wine needs five to ten years to develop from the floral to the mineral and to acquire more body. Two wines are distinguished from the rest of the appellation Coulée-de-Serrant (17 acres) and Roche-aux-Moines (82 acres).

Sweet wines

◆ Coteaux-du-Layon, Bonnezeaux and Quarts-de-Chaume. On the hillsides that border the Layon river, the Chenin Blanc vines produce famous sweet dessert wines. The morning mists allow the "noble rot" (*Botrytis cinerea*) to develop. The best wines are produced from very ripe grapes that have a high concentration of sugar, harvested selectively as the noble rot" appears. These wines have a very dense fragrance of candied fruits; when stored for several decades the flavors become more subtle and complex. The color is golden yellow when the wine is young, acquiring reddish and amber tints over time. The generic appellation is Coteaux-du-Layon (3,700 acres); six parishes and a village Chaume, which has specially well exposed soils) are allowed to use the appellation. Two vines have their own special appellations: Bonnezeaux (198 acres) and Quarts-de-Chaume (100 acres).

Coteaux-de-l'Aubance.
This appellation (250 acres) produces fruity, soft wines which are less sweet than their Layon counterparts.

EVERYDAY ANJOU WINES
The Anjou AOC covers the entire region, including the Saumurois (200 parishes in all).
The Anjou appellation is additionally associated with white wines. The wines produced entirely from Chenin Blanc grapes tend to be sweet.

Dry wines are obtained by combining Chenin Blanc with Chardonnay and Sauvignon. All the wines have citrus fragrances with floral notes.
◆ Rosé Anjou wines from Pineau d'Aunis and Grolleau grapes, are not sufficiently dry and are falling from favor.
◆ Red Anjou wines, which now account for the majority of production, are made from Cabernet-Franc and Cabernet-Sauvignon grapes. They are fresh, light wines which should be drunk while young.
◆ Anjou-Villages wines are fruity, expansive, strong and fleshy. Their high tannin content allows them to mature.
◆ Anjou-Gamay wines are thirst-quenchers which should be drunk within the year.
◆ Rosé d'Anjou, produced from Grolleau grapes, and Cabernet d'Anjou, made from the two Cabernet grape varieties, are soft, slightly sweet rosé wines.
◆ Anjou-Coteaux-de-la-Loire wines are white wines made from Chenin Blanc grapes, demi-sec or sweet.

◆ Red Saumur wine is produced on 1,850 acres of chalky and sandy-clay ground, using the two Cabernet varieties (Franc and Sauvignon). This is a very aromatic wine with elegant tannins, which matures well.
◆ Saumur Brut and Saumur Demi-Sec. The vines cover 3,200 acres on tufa limestone. The whites are made from Chenin Blanc grapes (with an authorized 20 percent addition of

Chardonnay and Sauvignon). They have fine, elegant bubbles and a pale-yellow color.
◆ Saumur-Champigny.
This vineyard of Cabernet-Franc and Cabernet-Sauvignon grows on chalky soils on the banks of the Loire and on more clayey soils on the banks of the Thouet. Only red wines are made, which are fruity and charming, or robust, spicy and full of character.

TOURAINE

This vineyard, covering 2,500 acres, goes back to Roman times. It was at its largest in the 19th century, just before the phylloxera crisis. Since the 1950's it has been expanding again, and producing wines of increasing quality.

THE GREAT RED APPELLATIONS
◆ Chinon
Vineyards of Cabernet-Franc vines grow on 4,700 acres on the left bank of the Loire, in the triangle formed by the confluence of the Vienne and the Loire. The vines grown on the gravelly areas are high-spirited and easy to drink. On the hillsides and on the plateaus, the clayey, siliceous soils produce finely structured wines. As for the great Chinons for keeping, they grow on the clayey, chalky soils of the Coteaux-de-Cravant and the Coteaux-de-Ligré.

◆ Bourgueil.
This appellation is grown on 3,000 acres, on the right bank of the Loire. The area is planted exclusively with Breton vines (Cabernet-Franc). Two-thirds of the vines stretch from the plain toward the terraces of sand and gravel, producing fruity, supple wines which should be drunk young. The remaining third grows on the chalky clay soils of the hillsides. Here, sheltered from the north winds, the vines produce full-bodied, tanninic wines which mature well (known as "vins de tuffeau").
◆ St-Nicolas-de-Bourgueil. The vines of this appellation are grown on terraces and on the clay soils of the hillsides. They are similar in character to Bourgueil wines, though even more supple.

SAUMUROIS

The Saumurois region is connected to Anjou by its history and to the Touraine by its soils: here, chalk gives way to schist and sandstone.
Saumur.
The area covered by this appellation

encompasses thirty-six parishes.
◆ White Saumur, a lively, floral and mineral wine, is produced from Chenin Blanc grapes, sometimes combined with Sauvignon and Chardonnay.

◆ WINES OF THE LOIRE VALLEY

VINTAGES			
	Red wines	White wines	Sweet white wines
1995	7	7	6
1994	6	6	6
1993	5	6	6
1992	6	6	6
1991	3	4	3
1990	9	9	10
1989	10	9	10
1988	7	8	7
1987	4	5	5
1986	6	7	7
1985	8	8	8
1984	5	6	5
1983	6	7	8
1982	7	7	7
1981	7	8	7
1980	6	6	6

Noteworthy older vintages include, for white wines and sweet wines, the excellent 1976, 1971, 1962 and 1959. The sweet wines from the great years of 1989 and 1990 will not achieve their peak until 2020.

WINES AND FOOD COMBINATIONS

HORS D'OEUVRE, COOKED/CURED MEATS:
Touraine, Anjou
FOIE GRAS: Quarts-de-Chaume
SHELLFISH: Saumur
OYSTERS: Savennières
CRAB, SHRIMPS, ETC.:
Anjou (white), Touraine (white).
LOBSTER, CRAYFISH:
Vouvray, Savennières.
FRESHWATER FISH:
Layon (dry), Touraine (white), Saumur.
SEA FISH: Vouvray, Savennières.
GRILLED FISH: Saumur-Champigny (red).
WHITE MEAT:
Anjou (red), St-Nicolas-de-Bourgueil.
RED MEAT: Chinon, Bourgueil.
GAME, POULTRY:
St-Nicolas-de-Bourgueil, Bourgueil.
GAME MEATS: Chinon, Bourgueil.
HARD CHEESES:
Touraine, Anjou (red or white).
SOFT CHEESES:
Anjou (red), St-Nicholas-de-Bourgueil.
GOAT'S CHEESES:
Anjou (white), Touraine (white).
DESSERTS:
Coteaux-du-Layon, Bonnezeaux.

◆ Touraine-Amboise. This vineyard covers 370 acres on either side of the Loire, producing light red wines made from Gamay grapes; they are more structured and age better when they include Cabernet and Côt grapes as well.

◆ Touraine-Azay-le-Rideau. Fine, dry white wines produced on 120 acres by the banks of the Indre; these wines mature well.

◆ Touraine-Mesland. These fruity and aromatic wines are produced in the east of Touraine.

◆ Cheverny. Fourteen different types of grapes are allowed in this appellation. The fruity red wines are made mainly from Gamay and Pinot Noir.

◆ Cour-Cheverny. This appellation is made from a single grape variety, the local Romorantin, which produces very distinctive white wines: delicate and highly strung.

OUTLYING VINEYARDS

◆ Coteaux-du-Loir. This small appellation produces white wines made from Chenin Blanc grapes and light, fruity red wines made from Pineau d'Aunis, Gamay and Cabernet as well as some rosé

◆ Jasnières. This white wine made from Chenin Blanc grapes is produced o a single hillside overlooking the Loir, facing due south. According to Curnonsky, "Prince o Gastronomes" ▲ 307 it is the best wine in the world three times each century. It is an exquisite, dry, minera wine, which needs te or so years to attain its full maturity.

◆ Valençay (VDQS). Fruity, aromatic wine best drunk young, produced from grape grown on the chalky, clay soils of the area

◆ Orléanais (VDQS). This vineyard was famous in the Middle Ages. Today, the Gris-Meunier grapes produce deep-rosé wines. The red wines are made from Pinot Noir grapes (known locally as "Auvernat"), while the whites are made from Chardonnay ("Auvernat Blanc").

◆ Coteaux-du Giennois (VDQS). A vineyard of 300 acres growing Sauvignon, Pinot and Gamay vines The wines ar light, crisp and fruity.

EXCURSION TO THE SANCERROIS

Not far from the Loire Valley are the famous vineyards of Sancerrois (some 5,000 acres in all), overlooking the river from their steep, east–southeast-facing hillsides. To the west, the pale soils produce vigorous, full-bodied wines. To the center the soils are stony and calcareous (called "caillottes"), producing wines tha are softer and fruitie To the east the soils are siliceous ("chailloux"), producing well-structured wines which develop more slowly. It is advisable to leave the red wines to mature for two to three years.

THE GREAT WHITE APPELLATIONS

◆ Vouvray. Vouvray wine comes in several different guises: dry, demi-sec or sweet, according to the year. It can be still, "pétillant" or sparkling according to the vinification process.

◆ Montlouis. This appellation covers 750 acres, between the Loire and the Cher, on a chalky plateau facing south. It is very similar to Vouvray in character.

EVERYDAY TOURAINE WINES

◆ Touraine. The regional appellation covers the whole of the Touraine region (12,000 acres). The soils are sandy and clay, sometimes with chalk.

he winegrowers of the Loire may appear rather rough and ready, ut this should not mislead you: they value quality more highly than e laws of the market. Some, inspired by their love of wine rather an financial motives, assemble collections of old vintages in their ellars, the like of which wine lovers dream about. Buying directly om producers is of course the best way of getting a bargain – but r real wine lovers it is the direct contact with winegrowers that ounts. If you intend to visit a vineyard, it is polite to telephone and t them know beforehand. However, there is no obligation to leave ith a case of wine that you do not really want to drink, merely on rounds of politeness.

cellar in Saumurois.

Troglodytic château in Anjou.

The letter and the figure given after each address refer to the maps of the area inside the covers of this guide.

ANJOU / BONNEZEAUX

OMAINE DE LA ANSONNIERE e owner of this tate learned his aft in the Sauternes gion. His very low tput is an indicator the quality of the ne. Noteworthy nes include a white jou, Christine 5F), a red Anjou OF) and a onnezeaux, athilde (160F). 49380 Thouarcé 7) l. 02 41 54 08 08
OMAINE DE AUTE-PERCHE is estate to the uth of Angers is e of the last oducers resisting e urban sprawl. nes produced on s 75-acre vineyard clude an Anjou- lage: the '93

vintage, which is ready to drink, sells for 32F; the '94 vintage sells for 30F.
◆ 9, chemin de la Godelière 49610 St-Melaine- sur-Aubance (B6) Tel. 02 41 57 75 65
DOMAINE DU FRESCHE Alain Boré owns the best soils of the hillside and produces a white Anjou wine of exceptional quality, for a very low price. The 1994 and 1995 vintages cost 23F.
◆ 49620 La Pommeraye (A6) Tel. 02 41 77 74 63
DOMAINE RICHOU This young winegrower has shown his determination to bring to the Loire winegrowing methods that have succeeded

elsewhere. His success is beyond question; choose from an Anjou- Gamay 94 at 23F and an Aubance from selected

COTEAUX-DU-LAYON

DOMAINE GAUDARD The white Anjou wines, including Paragères (25F for the '95 vintage), rival the Layons in terms of quality. Fans of sweet white wines will be tempted by the superb Or 1994, at 95F.
◆ Rte de St-Aubin 49290 Chaudefonds- dur-Layon (A6) Tel. 02 41 78 10 68
DOMAINE MICHEL ROBINEAU The prices here bear no relation to the quality of the wines

grapes, available from next winter at about 140F.
◆ Chauvigné 49610 Mozé-sur- Louet (B6) Tel. 02 41 78 72 13

and the effort devoted to producing them. Michel Robineau sorts the grapes again and again to select only the very best; the wines he makes are sold at ridiculously low prices. You will pay 36F to 72F, depending on quality, for wines which would cost twice this amount elsewhere.
◆ 16, rue Rabelais 49750 St-Lambert- du-Lattay (B7) Tel. 02 41 78 34 67

QUARTS-DE-CHAUME

CHÂTEAU BELLERIVE
The estate may have changed hands, but it has kept its outstanding winemaker, Jacques Lalanne. Lalanne's 1994 Quarts-de-Chaume, Quintessence, is one of the best Loire wines (120F).
◆ 49190 Rochefort-sur-Loire (B6)
Tel. 02 41 78 33 66

DOMAINE DES BAUMARD
Jean Baumard is just as well known for his Quarts-de-Chaume as he is for his Savennières. He has set himself up as a champion of good value for all his wines, and especially for his Quarts-de-Chaume estate acquired in 1954.
◆ 8, rue de l'Abbaye 49190 Rochefort-sur-Loire (B6)
Tel. 02 41 78 70 03

SAUMUR / SAUMUR-CHAMPIGNY

LANGLOIS-CHÂTEAU
Bollinger, the champagne producer, owns a controlling interest in this estate, which doubtless explains the meticulous production methods, which are carried out with a Champagne-like precision. The white Saumur from 1994 is well worth mentioning, at 52F. It is matured in casks from the outset.
◆ Rte de Gennes St-Hilaire-St-Florent 49400 Saumur (D7)
Tel. 02 41 40 21 40

LA CAVE DES VIGNERONS DE SAUMUR
This cooperative dispels once and for all the industrial image which is mistakenly associated with these French winemaking institutions. Its production methods are exemplary, and are given perfect expression in a red Saumur from '95 (costing 25F) and a sweet Coteaux-de-Saumur '95 at 80F.
◆ 49260 St-Cyr-en-Bourg (D7)
Tel. 02 41 53 06 08

BOURGUEIL AND ST-NICOLAS-DE-BOURGUEIL

DOMAINE DE LA CHEVALERIE
Pierre Caslot has a dozen or more vintages carefully arranged in cellars covering two and a half acres, cut into the tufa limestone. Four wines are represented, from the young vines of Peu-Muleau to the old stock of Les Busardières. The price difference between the different vintages is minimal, allowing visitors to select the best wines from the full range: Les Busardières 1993 and 1995 are recommended, at a price of 42F.
◆ 37140 Restigné (F7)
Tel. 02 47 97 37 18

DOMAINE DE LA LANDE
Marc Delaunay produces a number of wines grown in different types of soil. The Cuvée des Pins comes from vines planted in sandy, stony ground; Cuvée Prestige is grown in siliceous clay ground.

The former will suit those who like a fruity wine; the latter those who prefer a more full-bodied style. Prices range between 35F and 50F.
◆ La Lande 37140 Bourgueil (F7)
Tel. 02 47 97 80 73

DOMAINE DE LA COUDRAYE
How can a wine producer avoid loss of output in years with heavy rainfall? Yannick Amirault's estate has sand and gravel soils which drain the downpours very effectively. The result is wines that are the best of their appellation in wet years. For example, a Cuvée la Source 1993 of the appellation St-Nicolas-de-Bourgueil or the Graviers Vieilles Vignes 1994 at 35F.
◆ 37140 Bourgeuil (F7)
Tel. 02 47 97 78 07

DOMAINE DE CHAMPS-FLEURIS
In this part of the region, Chenin Blanc vines give way to the Cabernet grapes used to make Saumur-Champigny, which produce a more solid wine. You might prefer Patrice Rétif's two white Saumur wines at 23 and 26.50F: both are admirably balanced in two tonal ranges.
◆ 49730 Turquant (E7)
Tel. 02 41 38 10 92

DOMAINE DES ROCHES-NEUVES
Thierry Germain came from Bordeaux initially and has emigrated to Saumurois, where he makes wine with the technical precision which established the reputation of his home region. He has made a concession to modern trends with a wine from young vines (made by cold maceration); at the other extreme he produces a stunning wine fermented and matured entirely in the barrel.
◆ 56, bd St-Vincent 49400 Varrains (D7)
Tel. 02 41 52 94 02

CHINON

DOMAINE BAUDRY
…uying wine from …ernard Baudry …quires a degree … flexibiilty. You …ay still be able to …d some of the …4 vintage which …s decimated by … frost. Failing …s, you may have … fall back on the …uvée Domaine … around 37F), … the Grézeaux '95 …nnounced at 40F) … winter 1997, …d on the wine …m the old vines …er this.

◆ 13, coteau de
Sonnay
37500 Cravant (F8)
Tel. 02 47 93 15 79
CHARLES JOGUET
Charles Joguet is

synonymous with
quality in the region,
producing several
splendid wines,
including the Clos de
la Cure '95 at 41.50F
and the Varennes du
Grand Clos 1992 at
48F. The Clos de la
Dioterie, with its
seventy-year-old
vines, and the Clos
du Chêne Vert must
be considered among
the finest of the
region.
◆ 3, rue du Plaisir
37220 Sazilly (F8)
Tel. 02 47 58 55 53
OLGA RAFFAULT
The different

branches of the
Raffault family are
everywhere in the
Loire Valley.
However, Olga is
beginning to steal the
limelight from her
namesakes. When
women make wine
they are generally
better at it than men:
this is true in the
Loire as it is
elsewhere. Fabulous
Chinons: 34F for the
'94 vintage, 37.50F
for the '93.
◆ 1, rue des Caillis
37420 Savigny-en-
Véron (E7)
Tel. 02 47 58 42 16

VOUVRAY

…OS NAUDIN
…agnificent sweet
…nes around 90F,
…pending on
…ntage, from this
…e enthusiast who
…kes pride in
…atching his wines
…th culinary dishes.
…so worthy of note is
…dry white wine from
… at 47F, fragrant
…d full-bodied.
…4, rue de la Croix-
…isée

37210 Vouvray (I6)
Tel. 02 47 52 71 46
DOMAINE HUET
Sweet wines
produced by the
king of the
appellation: only
connoisseurs will be
able to make out the
subtle differences
between the Haut-
Lieu and the Clos
du Bourg. Prices
vary according to
whether the grapes

were from the first
selection, from 100F
to 170F.
Totally reliable.

◆ 11–13, rue de la
Croix-Buisée
37210 Vouvray (I6)
Tel. 02 47 52 78 87

TOURAINE

…OMAINE DE LA
…ARMOISE
…nry Marionnet's
…nes cost less than
…F, but surpass in
…ality most of the
…nes of the region.
…nong the whites,
…e Sauvignon
…. de Marionnet"
…quite sublime and
…nnot be too highly
…commended.
… for the reds,
…e Gamays are
…ade by carbonic
…aceration, which
…ves them a
…ique fruity flavor
…thout
…aptalization.
…41230 Soings-en-
…logne (N6)
…l. 02 54 98 70 73

DOMAINE DES ACACIAS
Charles Guerbois
exercises his wit and
his knowledge of
Latin in the names of
his wines: as in the
Vinovorax '93, at 35F
a bottle, which is
unusual for having
been harvested in
two stages to
combine both
liveliness and
maturity.
◆ Chémery
41700 Contres (M6)
Tel. 02 54 71 81 53

CHÂTEAU-GAILLARD
Vincent Girault has
abandoned
environmentally
unsound practices
and mechanical
harvesting in favor of
organic winemaking.
The result is excellent
white wines (27F) and

above all a Touraine-
Mesland (red) from
'95 at 28F, a subtle
blend of all the best
features of the estate.
◆ 41150 Mesland
(L5)
Tel. 02 54 70 27 14

This table follows the order of the itineraries as they appear in the guide. All towns and other places of interest are listed in alphabetical order in each itinerary. The letter and figure following the postal code refer to the co-ordinates on the main maps at the beginning and at the end of the guide. The numbers in the right-hand column give pages where you can find further information.

ORLÉANS	45000	O/P2	
CATHEDRAL	Open daily June 1–Sep. 15, 3–6.30pm except during services		▲ 114
CENTRE CHARLES-PÉGUY – HÔTEL EUVERTE-HATTE Rue du Tabour **Tel. 02 38 53 20 23**	Open Tue.–Fri. 2–6pm. Closed Jan. 1.		▲ 122
CENTRE JEANNE-D'ARC Pl. du Gal-de-Gaulle **Tel. 02 38 52 99 89**	Open daily except Mon., May–Oct., 10–11.30am and 2–5.30pm; Nov–Apr., 2–5.30pm. Guided tour (60 mins). Closed May 1, Dec 31, Jan 1 and Apr. 30.		▲ 118
HÔTEL CABU AND MUSÉE ARCHÉOLOGIQUE ET HISTORIQUE Pl. Abbé Desnoyers **Tel. 38 53 39 22**	Open daily except Tue. 10am–noon and 2–5.30pm. Guided tour (60 mins). Closed Jan.1, May 1 and 8, Nov. 1, Dec. 25.		▲ 119
HÔTEL GROSLOT Pl. de l'Étape **Tel. 02 38 79 22 30**	Open daily. June 16–Sep. 25, 9am–7pm; Sep. 26–Dec. 31, 10am–noon and 2–5pm; Jan. 1–June 15, 10am–noon and 2–6pm. Closed May 8 and during special events.		▲ 118
MUSÉE DES BEAUX-ARTS Pl. Ste-Croix **Tel. 02 38 53 39 22**	Open daily except Tue. 10am–noon and 2–5.30pm. Closed Jan. 1, May 1 and 8, Nov. 1, Dec. 25.		▲ 115
ORLÉANS-LA-SOURCE			
PARC FLORAL **Tel. 02 38 49 30 00**	Open daily June 16–Aug. 31, 9am–7pm; Apr. 1.–June 15 and Sep. 1—Nov. 12, 9am–5pm ; Nov. 13—Mar. 31, 2–4pm. Closed Dec. 25.		▲ 124
VAL D'ORLÉANS			
LA FERTÉ-ST-AUBIN	**45240**	**P4**	
CHÂTEAU **Tel. 02 38 76 52 72**	Open Mar. 17–Nov 11 daily, 10am–7pm; Nov. 12–Dec. 31 Wed., Sat., Sun., (daily during school holidays) 2–6pm; Jan. 1–Mar. 16 Wed., Sat., Sun. 2–6pm.		▲ 125
ORLÉANS TO GIEN			
BRIARE	**45250**	**T4**	
MUSÉE DE LA MOSAÏQUE ET DES ÉMAUX 1, bd Loreau **Tel. 02 38 31 20 51**	Open daily June–Sep., 10am–6.30pm; Oct.–Dec. and Apr.–May, 10am–12.30pm and 2–6pm. Closed Dec. 25,		▲ 137
CHÂTEAUNEUF-SUR-LOIRE	**45110**	**Q2**	
CHÂTEAU AND PARK **Tel. 02 38 58 41 18**	Visits to the grounds only, all year around.		▲ 127
MUSÉE DE LA MARINE DE LA LOIRE, DU VIEUX CHÂTEAUNEUF ET DE SA RÉGION 1, pl. Aristide Briand **Tel. 02 38 58 41 18**	Open daily except Tue, Jul.–Aug., 10am–noon and 2–5.30pm; Sep., 2–5.30pm; Oct. Sat.–Sun. 2–5.30pm; Nov.–Dec. and Jan.–Mar., Sun. 2–5.30pm; Apr.–May, Sat.–Sun. 10am–noon and 2–5.30pm; June, Mon., Wed.–Fri. 2–5.30pm, Sat.–Sun. 10am–noon and 2–5.30pm. Guided tour (60 mins). Closed May 1 and Dec. 25.		▲ 127
GERMIGNY-DES-PRÉS	**45110**	**Q3**	
CAROLINGIAN ORATORY **Tel. 02 38 58 27 03**	Open daily Mar. 16–Sep. 30, 8.30am–7pm; Oct. 1–Mar. 15, 9am–6pm.		▲ 128
GIEN	**45500**	**S4**	
CHÂTEAU AND MUSÉE DE LA CHASSE **Tel. 02 38 67 69 69**	Open daily. Apr. 29–Nov. 3, 9.30am–6.30pm; Nov. 4–Dec. 31 and Feb. 17–Apr. 28, Tue.–Sun. 10am–noon and 2–5pm. Guided tour (90 mins).		▲ 136
MUSÉE DE LA FAÏENCERIE, MANUFACTURE DE GIEN 78, pl. de la Victoire **Tel. 02 38 67 00 05**	Open all year around Sun. 10–11.30am and 2–5.30pm; Jun.–Oct., Mon.–Sat. 9–11.30am and 2–6pm; Nov.–Jan., 10–11.30am and 1.45–5.45pm; Feb.–May, 9–11.30am and 1.45–5.45pm. Closed Nov. 1 and 11, Dec. 25 and Jan. 1.		▲ 136
JARGEAU			
COLLEGIATE CHURCH OF ST-VRAIN	Open daily 9am–noon and 2–6pm (when closed, key available from the tourist office).		▲ 126

ST-BENOÎT-SUR-LOIRE	45730	R3	
ABBEY CHURCH Tel. 02 38 35 72 43	*Open daily except first Fri. of the month and during services, 10.30am–3pm. Guided tour (70 mins).*		▲ 130
ST-DENIS-DE-L'HÔTEL	45550	Q2	
MAISON MAURICE-GENEVOIX Pl. du Cloître Tel. 02 38 59 02 24	*Open daily. Sat.–Sun. 10am–noon and 2–6pm.*		▲ 126
ST-JEAN-DE-BRAYE	45800	P2	
MUSÉE CAMPANAIRE FONDERIE BOLLÉE 256, fbg de Bourgogne Tel. 02 38 86 29 47	*Open Apr.–Sep. daily except Tue. 10am–noon and 2–7.30pm; Jan.–Mar., Mon., Wed.–Fri., 2–5.30pm, Sat.– Sun. 10am–noon and 2–5.30pm; Sep.–Dec., 2– 5.30pm. Guided tour (2 hours). Closed Dec. 25 and Jan. 1.*		▲ 126
SULLY-SUR-LOIRE	45600	R3	
CHÂTEAU, RESIDENCE OF THE DUC DE SULLY Tél. 02 38 36 36 86	*Open daily June 1–Sep. 15, 10am–6pm; May 1–June 15 and Sep. 16–Oct. 31, 10am–noon and 2–6pm; Mar.–Apr. and Nov., 10am–noon and 2–5pm. Guided tour (50 min) and visits by candlelight in high season.*		▲ 132
COLLEGIATE CHURCH OF ST-YTHIER	*Open daily 10am–6pm.*		▲ 133

ORLÉANS TO BLOIS

BEAUGENCY	45190	N3	
CHÂTEAU DUNOIS AND MUSÉE RÉGIONAL DE L'ORLÉANAIS Tel. 02 38 44 55 23	*Open Apr.–Sep. daily except Tue., 10–11am and 2–6pm; Oct.–Mar., 10–11am and 2–6pm. Closed May 1 and Dec. 25. Guided tour (60 mins) in English.*		▲ 139
CHURCH OF NOTRE-DAME	*Open daily. 9.30am–6.30pm (5pm in winter)*		▲ 139
MEUNG-SUR-LOIRE	45130	N3	
CHÂTEAU Tel. 02 38 44 36 47	*Open daily. Jul. 1–Sep. 4, 9am–12.30pm and 1.30–6.30pm; Apr.–June, 10am–noon and 2–5.30pm; Sep. 5–Nov. 6, 10am–noon and 2–5pm; Jan.–Mar. and Nov., 7–Dec. 31. Sat.–Sun. 10am–noon and 2–5pm. Guided tour (60 mins) in English.*		▲ 138
ST-LAURENT-DES-EAUX	41220	N4	
NUCLEAR POWER STATION Tel. 02 54 44 84 09	*Visit by appointment. Two days' notice and proof of identity required. Children under 10 not admitted.*		▲ 139
TALCY	41170	M3	
CHÂTEAU OF THE SALVIATI Tel. 02 54 20 98 03	*Open daily Jul.–Aug., 9am–6pm, Apr.–June and Sep. 9.30am–noon and 2–6pm; Oct.–Mar. daily except Tue. 10am–noon and 2–4.30pm. Guided tour (45 mins). Closed May 1, Nov. 1 and 11, Dec. 25.*		▲ 140

BLOIS

BLOIS	41000	M4/5	
CHÂTEAU AND MUSÉE DES BEAUX-ARTS Tel. 02 54 74 16 06	*Open daily Jan. 2.–Mar. 14 and Oct. 14–Dec. 31, 9–11.45am and 2–4.45pm; Mar. 15–Jun. 14 and Sep. 1–Oct. 13, 9am–5.45pm; June 15–Aug. 31, 9am–7.15pm. Closed Dec. 25 and Jan. 1. Guided tours (60 mins) in English.*		▲ 148

AROUND BLOIS

CELLETTES	41120	M5	
CHÂTEAU AND PARC DE BEAUREGARD Tel. 02 54 70 40 05	*Open daily Jul.–Aug. 9.30am–6pm; Apr. and Sep., 9.30–11.30am and 2–6pm; Jan. 8–Mar. 31 and Oct.–Dec., 9.30–11.30am and 2–4.30pm. Guided tour (45 mins) in English.*		▲ 167
CHAMBORD	41250	N4	
CHÂTEAU AND NATIONAL PARK Tel. 02 54 50 40 00	*Open daily Jul.–Aug., 9.30am–6.45pm; Apr.–June and Sep., 9.30am–5.45pm; Jan.–Mar. and Oct.–Dec., 9.30–11.45am and 2–4.45pm. Closed Jan. 1, May 1, Nov. 1 and 11, Dec. 25. Guided tour (60 mins) in English.*		▲ 158

CHAUMONT-SUR-LOIRE	41150	**L5**	
CHÂTEAU, STABLES AND PARK Tel. 02 54 20 98 03	*Open daily Apr.–Sep., 9.30am–6pm; Oct.–Mar., 10am–4.30pm. Closed May 1, Nov. 1 and 11, Dec. 25. Guided tour (60 mins) in English.*	▲ 177	
FESTIVAL INTERNATIONAL DES JARDINS Tel. 02 54 20 99 22	*Open daily. June 15–Oct. 20, 9am–evening. Guided tour (50 mins) in English and Dutch.*		
CHEVERNY	41700	**M5**	
CHÂTEAU, TROPHIES ROOM AND KENNEL Tel. 02 54 79 96 29	*Open daily June 1–Sep. 15, 9.15am–6.45pm; Apr.–May, 9.15am–noon and 2.15–6.30pm; Sep. 16–Sep. 30, 9.30am–noon and 2.15–6pm; Oct. and Mar., 9.30am–noon and 2.15–5.30pm; Nov.–Feb., 9.30am–noon and 2.15–5pm. Guided tour in English, Dutch, Polish, Czech and Russian.* *Daily visit to the château and the park by hot-air balloon: June 1–Sep. 15, 9.15am–6.45pm; Sep.16–Sep. 30, 9.30am–noon and 2.15–6pm; Oct. 9.30am–noon and 2.15–5.30pm; Nov. 1–10, 9.30am–noon and 2.15–5pm; Apr. 15–May 31 9.15am–noon and 2.15–6.30pm.* *Feeding the dogs Apr. 1–Sep. 15, Mon.–Fri. at 5pm; Sep. 16–Dec. 31 and Jan.–Mar., Mon., Wed.–Fri. 3pm.*	▲ 170	
FOUGÈRES-SUR-BIÈVRE	41120	**L/M6**	
CHÂTEAU Tel. 02 54 20 98 03	*Open Apr.–Sep. daily, 9am–noon and 2–6pm; Oct.–Mar. daily except Tue., 10am–noon and 2–4.30pm. Closed May 1, Nov. 1 and 11, Dec. 25. Guided tour in English and Dutch.*	▲ 176	
FRESNES	41700	**M6**	
CHÂTEAU DE ROUJOUX AND MUSÉE HISTORIQUE ANIMÉ Tel. 02 54 79 53 55	*Open daily Mar. 25–Nov. 5, 11am–6pm.*	▲ 173	
TOUR-EN-SOLOGNE	41250	**N5**	
CHÂTEAU DE VILLESAVIN AND COLLECTION OF HORSE-DRAWN CARRIAGES Tel. 02 54 46 42 88	*Open daily May–Sep., 10am–7pm; Mar.–Apr. 10am–noon and 2–7pm; Oct. 1–Dec. 20, 2–5pm.* *Guided tour (55 mins) in English and Dutch.*	▲ 166	
TROUSSAY		**M5**	
CHÂTEAU AND MUSÉE SOLOGNOT (SOLOGNE LIFE) Tel. 02 54 44 29 07	*Open daily Jul. 1–Sep. 2, 10am–7pm; Sep. 3–30, 10am–1pm and 2–6pm; Oct. 1–Nov. 1, Sun. 10.30am–12.30pm and 2–5.30pm; Apr. 6–May 2, daily, 10.30am–12.30pm and 2–6.30pm; May 3–31, Sun. 10.30am–12.30pm and 2–6.30pm; June daily, 10am–1pm and 2–7pm.*	▲ 172	
AMBOISE	37400	**J6**	
ABBEY CHURCH OF ST-DENIS	*Open daily Jul.–Aug., 10am–noon and 3–7pm; Sep.–June, 8am–7pm*	▲ 188	
CHANTELOUP PAGODA Tel. 02 47 57 20 97	*Open daily Jul.–Aug., 9.30am–8pm; June–Sep., 10am–7pm; May, 10am–6pm; Apr. and Oct., 10am–noon and 2–5.30pm; Mar. 10am–noon and 2–5pm; Nov. and Feb. 15–28, Mon.–Fri. 2–5pm, Sat.–Sun. 10am–noon and 2–5pm.*	▲ 191	
CHÂTEAU Tel. 02 47 57 00 98	*Open daily Jul.–Aug., 9am–8pm; Apr.–June, 9am–6.30pm; Sep.–Oct., 9am–6pm; Nov. and Feb.–Mar., 9am–noon and 2–5.30pm; Dec.–Jan., 9am–noon and 2–5pm. Closed Dec. 25.* *Guided tour (45 mins), in English.*	▲ 184	
CLOS-LUCÉ MANOR HOUSE AND LEONARDO DA VINCI MUSEUM Tel. 02 47 57 62 88	*Open daily Jul.–Aug., 9am–8pm; Mar. 23–June 30 and Sep. 1–Nov. 12, 9am–7pm; Nov. 13–Dec. 31 and Feb. 1–Mar. 22, 9am–6pm.*	▲ 185	
MUSÉE DE LA POSTE 6, rue Joyeuse Tel. 02 47 57 00 11	*Open Apr.–Sep. daily except Mon. 9.30am–noon and 2–6.30pm; Oct.–Dec. and Feb.–Mar., 10am–noon and 2–5.30pm. Closed May 1, Nov. 1, Dec. 25 and at Easter.*	▲ 188	

AROUND AMBOISE

CHARGÉ	37530	J6
MUSÉE DE LA BATAILLE DE LA LOIRE ET DE LA RÉSISTANCE Tel. 02 47 57 05 24	Visit by appointment.	▲ 192

USSAULT-SUR-LOIRE	37400	I/J6
AQUARIUM DE TOURAINE AND PARC DES MINI-CHÂTEAUX Tel. 02 47 23 44 44	Open daily Jul.–Aug., 9am–midnight; Apr.–June and Sep., 9am–7pm; Oct.–Nov and Feb. 15–Mar. 31, 10am–6pm. Closed in Jan.	

TOURS

TOURS	37000	H6
ATELIER "HISTOIRE DE TOURS" LOGIS DU GOUVERNEUR 5 quai d'Orléans Tel. 02 47 64 90 52	Open Mar. 15–Dec. 15, Wed., Sat.–Sun. 3–6.30pm. Closed Easter, Ascension Day, Whit Sunday, Aug. 15, Nov. 1 and 11.	▲ 198
BASILICA OF ST-MARTIN rue Descartes	Open daily Easter–Sep,. 8am–7pm; Oct.–Easter, 8am–noon and 2–6.45pm.	▲ 204
CHÂTEAU DE TOURS Tropical aquarium Tel. 02 47 64 29 52	Open daily Jul.–Aug., 9.30am–7pm; Apr.–June and Sep. 1–Nov. 15, 9.30am–noon and 2–6pm, Sun. 2–6pm; Nov. 16–Mar. 31, daily 2–6pm.	▲ 198
Historial de Touraine (Musée Grévin) Tel. 02 47 61 02 95	Open daily Jul.–Aug., 9am–6.30pm; Sep.–Oct. and Mar. 16–June 30, 9am–noon and 2–6pm; Nov.–Mar. 15, 2–5.30pm	
CLOÎTRE DE LA PSALETTE (PSALETTE CLOISTERS) Tel. 02 47 45 42 04	Open daily Mar. 28–Sep. 30, 9am–noon and 2–6pm; Oct. 1–Mar. 27, 9am–noon and 2–5pm. Guided tour (45 mins). Closed May 1, Nov. 1 and 11, Dec. 25 and Jan. 1.	▲ 197
FLOWER MARKET	Wed. and Sat.	▲ 214
JARDIN DES PRÉBENDES D'OÉ AND JARDIN BOTANIQUE	Open daily 8am–evening.	▲ 215
MUSÉE ARCHÉOLOGIQUE HÔTEL GOUIN 5, rue du Commerce Tel. 02 47 66 22 32	Open daily May 15–Sep. 30, 10am–7pm ; Mar. 15–May 14, 10am–12.30pm and 2–6.30pm; Oct. and Feb. 1–Mar. 14, 10am–12.30pm and 2–5.30pm. Guided tour (30 mins)	▲ 208
MUSÉE DES BEAUX-ARTS 8, pl. François Sicard Tel. 02 47 05 68 73	Open daily except Tue., 9am–12.45pm and 2–6pm. Closed May 1, July 14, Nov. 1 and 11, Dec. 25.	▲ 198
MUSÉE DU COMPAGNONNAGE ST-JULIEN CLOISTER rue Nationale Tel. 02 47 61 07 93	Open daily June 16–Sep. 15, 9am–6pm; Apr. 1 –June 15, daily 9–11.30am and 2–5.30pm; Sep. 16–Mar. 31, daily except Tue. 9–11.30am and 2–4.30pm. Closed May 1, Jul. 14, Nov. 1 and 11 , Dec. 25	▲ 199
MUSÉE DU GEMMAIL AND UNDERGROUND CHAPEL rue du Mûrier Tel. 02 47 61 01 19	Open Mar. 15–Oct. 15, 10–11.30am and 2–6pm. Guided tour (60 mins). Closed Mon. except public holidays.	▲ 212
MUSÉE ST-MARTIN CHAPEL OF ST-JEAN rue Rapin Tel. 02 47 64 48 87	Open Mar. 15–Nov. 15, Wed.–Sun. 9.30am–12.30pm and 2–5.30pm. Closed May 1, Jul. 14.	▲ 205
MUSÉE DES VINS DE TOURAINE CELLIERS ST-JULIEN (CELLARS) 16, rue Nationale Tel. 02 47 61 07 93	Open daily except Tue., Apr. 1–Sep. 15, 9.30–11.30am and 2–5.30pm; Sep. 16–Dec. 31 and Mar. 9.30am–12.30pm and 2–4.30pm. Closed May 1, Jul. 14, Nov. 1 and 11, Dec. 25.	▲ 199
MUSÉUM D'HISTOIRE NATURELLE rue du Président-Merville Tel. 02 47 64 13 31	Open 10am–noon and 2–6pm. Closed Mon., May 1, Jul. 14 and Dec. 25.	▲ 212
ST-GATIEN CATHEDRAL	Open summer 8.30am–noon and 2–8pm; winter 8.30am–noon and 2–7.30pm.	▲ 196

TOURS TO VALENÇAY

CHENONCEAUX	37150	K7
CHÂTEAU, GARDENS AND MUSÉE DE CIRES (WAXWORKS) Tel. 02 47 23 90 07	Open daily Mar. 16–Sep. 15, 9am–7pm; Sep. 16–30, 9am–6.30pm; Oct. 1–15 and Mar. 1–15, 9am–6pm; Oct. 16–31 and Feb. 16–28, 9am–5.30pm; Nov. 1–15 and Feb. 1–15, 9am–5pm, Nov. 16–Jan. 31. 9am–4.30pm.	▲ 220

CHEMILLÉ-SUR-INDROIS	37460	L8
CHARTREUSE DU LIGET Tel. 02 47 92 60 02	*Open daily 9am–6pm.*	▲ 230

LOCHES	37600	K8
COLLEGIATE CHURCH OF ST-OURS	*Open daily, except during services: summer 9am–7pm;* *winter 9am–5pm.*	▲ 227
DONJON (KEEP) Tel. 02 47 59 07 86	*Open daily Jul. 1–Sep. 15, 9am–7pm ; Sep. 16–30 and* *Mar. 15–June 30, 9am–12.30pm and 2–6.30pm;* *Oct. 1–Mar. 14, 9am–12.30pm and 2–5.40pm.* *Closed Dec. 25 and Jan 1.*	▲ 228
LOGIS ROYAL Tel. 02 47 59 01 32	*Open daily Jul. 1 –Sep. 15, 9am–7pm; Sep. 16–30 and* *Mar. 15–June 30, 9am–noon and 2–6.30pm; Oct. 1–Mar.* *14, 9am–noon and 2–5pm. Closed Dec. 25 and Jan. 1.*	▲ 226
MUSÉE LANSYER AND MUSÉE DU TERROIR PORTE ROYALE 1, rue Lansyer Tel. 02 47 59 05 45	*Open Mar. 15–Oct. 15, daily 9am–noon and 2–5.30pm;* *Oct. 16–Dec.14, daily except Wed. 9–11.30am and* *2–3.30pm; Jan. 16–Mar. 14, daily except Wed.* *9–11.30am and 2–4.30pm.*	▲ 228

MONTRÉSOR	37460	L8
CHÂTEAU Tel. 02 47 92 60 04	*Open daily Apr.–Oct., 10am–noon and 2–6pm.*	▲ 231
COLLEGIATE CHURCH OF ST-JEAN- BAPTISTE	*Open daily 8.30am–7pm, except during services.*	▲ 231

NOUANS-LES-FONTAINES	37460	L/M8
CHURCH OF ST-MARTIN	*Open daily 8am–7pm, except during services*	▲ 231

VALENÇAY	36600	N8
CHÂTEAU AND MUSÉE DE VOITURES ANCIENNES Tel. 02 54 00 10 66	*Open daily June 16–Sep. 15, 9am–7pm; Sep. 16–Nov. 15* *and Mar. 16–June 15, 9am–noon and 2–7pm. Guided* *tour (50 mins).*	▲ 232

TOURS TO CHINON

AZAY-LE-RIDEAU	37190	G7
CHÂTEAU Tel. 02 47 45 42 04	*Open daily Jul.–Aug., 9am–6.30pm; Sep.–Oct. and* *Mar. 15–June 30, 9.30am–5.30pm; Nov. 1–Mar. 14,* *9.30am–noon and 2–5pm. Closed May 1, Nov. 1 and 11,* *Dec. 25, Jul–Aug. Guided tour (60 mins) in English.*	▲ 234

CHINON	37500	F9
CHÂTEAU Tel. 02 47 93 13 45	*Open daily Jul.–Aug., 9am–7pm; Sep.and Mar. 15–June* *30, 9am–6pm; Oct. 9am–5pm; Nov. 1–Mar. 14 9am–* *noon and 2–5pm. Closed Dec. 25. Guided tour (45 mins).*	▲ 244
CHAPEL OF STE-RADEGONDE AND MUSÉE DES ARTS ET TRADITIONS POPULAIRES Tel. 02 47 93 17 85 (O.T.)	*Visit by appointment with the tourist office.*	▲ 249
MAISON DES ÉTATS-GÉNÉRAUX AND MUSÉE DU VIEUX CHINON ET DE LA BATELLERIE 44, rue Haute St-Maurice Tel. 02 47 93 18 12	*Open daily Apr. 16–Sep. 30, 10.30am–12.30pm and* *3–6pm. Guided tour by apppointment.*	▲ 246

SACHÉ	37190	H7
CHÂTEAU AND MUSÉE BALZAC Tel. 02 47 26 86 50	*Open daily Jul.–Aug., 9.30am–6.30pm; Mar. 15–Apr. 30* *and Sep., 9am–noon and 2–6pm; Oct.–Nov. and Feb. 1–* *Mar. 14, 9am–noon and 2–5pm. Guided tour (45 mins).*	▲ 240
CHURCH OF ST-MARTIN-DE-VERTOU	*Open daily 9am–7pm.*	▲ 241

SEUILLY	37500	F8
LA DEVINIÈRE Tel. 02 47 95 91 18	*Open daily May–Sep. 10am–7pm; Mar. 15–Apr. 30,* *9am–noon and 2–6pm; Oct. 1–Mar. 14, 9am–noon and* *2–5pm.*	▲ 250

TAVANT	37220	G8
CHURCH OF ST-NICOLAS Tel. 02 47 58 58 06	*Open Mar.–Nov. daily except Tue.10am–noon and* *2.30–6pm*	▲ 251

TOURS TO FONTEVRAUD

AVOINE-CHINON — 37420 — F7

NUCLEAR POWER STATION
Museum and installations
Tel. 02 47 98 77 77

Visits by appointment. Phone 24 hours before intended visit. Proof of indentity required. Children under 13 are not admitted. ▲ 244

CANDES-ST-MARTIN — 37500 — E7

COLLEGIATE CHURCH OF ST-MARTIN

Open daily except during services. ▲ 271

FONTEVRAUD — 49590 — E8

ROYAL ABBEY
Tel. 02 41 51 71 41

Open daily June, 1–3rd Sun. in Sep., 9am–7pm; 3rd Sun. in Sep.–May 31, 9.30am–12.30pm and 2–6pm. Late evening visits by appointment. ▲ 272

LANGEAIS — 37130 — G7

CHÂTEAU
Tel. 02 47 96 72 60

Open daily Jul. 15–Aug. 31, 9am–9pm; Sep. and Apr. 1–Jul 14, 9am–6.30pm; Oct. 1–Nov. 2, 9am–12.30pm and 2–6.30pm; Nov. 3–Mar. 31, 9am–noon and 2–5pm. Closed Dec. 25. Guided tours (60 mins) in English. ▲ 268

MUSÉE DE L'ARTISANAT
24, rue de St-Laurent
Tel. 02 47 96 72 64

Open daily June 1–Sep. 15, 9am–7pm; Apr.–May and Sep. 16–Oct. 15, 10am–noon and 2–6pm; Oct. 16–Sep. 31 and Feb.–Mar., 2–6pm. Closed Dec. 25. ▲ 268

LUYNES — 37230 — H6

CHÂTEAU
Tel. 02 47 95 77 08

Open daily Apr.–Sep., 10am–6pm. Guided tours in English. ▲ 262

MONTSOREAU — 49730 — E7

CHÂTEAU AND MUSÉE DES GOUMS
Tel. 02 41 51 70 25

Open daily except Tue., May–Sep., 10am–noon and 2–6.30pm; Mar.–Apr. and Oct., 1.30–5.30pm. ▲ 276

RIGNY-USSÉ — 37420 — F7

CHÂTEAU AND WALL walk
Tel. 02 47 95 54 05

Open daily Jul. 14–Aug. 31, 9am–6.30pm; Apr. 7–Jul. 13 and Sep. 1–25, 9am–noon and 2–6pm ; Sep. 26–Nov. 11, and Feb. 12–Mar. 15, 10am–noon and 2–5.30pm. Guided tour (45 mins). ▲ 268

SAVONNIÈRES — 37510 — H6

GROTTES PÉTRIFIANTES
Tel. 02 47 50 00 09

Open daily Apr.–Sep. 9am–7pm; Oct. 1–Nov. 11 9am–noon and 2–6pm; Nov. 12–Dec. 15 and Feb. 5–Mar. 31 daily except Thur. 9am–noon and 2–6pm. ▲ 262

VILLANDRY — 37510 — G6

CHÂTEAU
Tel. 02 47 50 02 09

Open Jul.–Aug., 9am–6.30pm; Mar. 31–June 30 and Sep. 1–28, 9am–6pm; Sep. 29–Nov. 11, 9am–5pm; Feb. 17–Mar. 30, 9.30am–5pm. ▲ 263

GARDENS
Tel. 02 47 50 02 09

Open daily Jul.–Aug., 8.30am–8pm; May–June and Sep. 1–28, 9am–7.30pm; Mar. 1–30 and Sep. 29–Nov. 11, 9am–6pm; Mar. 31–Apr. 30 9am–7pm; Nov. 12–Feb 28, 9am–5pm. ▲ 264

SAUMUR — 49400 — D7

CHÂTEAU
Rue des Remparts
Tel. 02 41 51 30 46

Open daily June–Sep., 9am–6pm; Jul–Aug., Wed. and Sat. 8.30pm–10.30pm, late-night visits 10.30pm–midnight; Oct.–May daily except Tue., 9.30am–noon and 2–5.30pm. ▲ 280

CHURCH OF NOTRE-DAME DE NANTILLY
Pl. des Récollets

Open daily. ▲ 284

CHURCH OF ST-PIERRE

Open daily 8am–noon and 2–6pm. ▲ 280

MUSÉE DES ARTS DÉCORATIFS ET DU CHEVAL
Château
Tel. 02 41 51 30 46

Open June–Sep. daily 9am–6pm; Oct.–May daily except Tue., 9.30am–noon and 2–5.30pm. ▲ 280

MUSÉE DES BLINDÉS (CDEB) (ARMORED VEHICLES)
1043, route de Fontevraud
Tel. 02 41 53 06 99

Open daily 9am–noon and 2–6pm. ▲ 285

MUSÉE DE LA CAVALERIE Av. Foch **Tel. 02 41 83 93 06 (high season)** **02 41 83 93 17 (low season)**	*Open Tue., Thur. and Sun. 9am–noon and 2–5pm; Sat. before noon and 2–5pm.*	▲ 284
AROUND SAUMUR		**D7**
CHAPEL OF NOTRE-DAME DES ARDILLERS	*Open 9am–noon and 2–7pm.*	▲ 285
CHÂTEAU DE BOUMOIS	*Open Jul.–Aug., daily 9.30am–6.30pm; Palm Sunday and All Saints' Day, daily except Tue., 10am–noon and 2–6pm.*	▲ 285 ▲ 284
ÉCOLE NATIONALE D'ÉQUITATION (TERREFORT) **Tel. 02 41 53 50 66**	*Open June–Aug., daily except Sun and Mon. 9.30am–5pm; Apr.–May and Sep. 9.30am–5pm except Sat. before noon, Sun. and Mon. morning.*	▲ 289
GRAND DOLMEN (BAGNEUX) **Tel. 02 41 50 23 02**	*Open daily Mar. 16–Sep. 30, 9am–7pm; Oct. 1–Dec. 20 and Jan. 20–Mar. 15, 9am–6pm.*	▲ 292
MUSÉE DU CHAMPIGNON (ST-HILAIRE-ST-FLORENT) Rte de Gennes **Tel. 02 41 50 31 55**	*Open daily Feb.–Nov., 10am–7pm.*	

SAUMUR TO MONTREUIL-BELLAY		
DÉNÉZÉ-SOUS-DOUÉ	**49700**	**C7**
CARVED CAVERN **Tel. 02 41 59 15 40**	*Open Jul.–Aug., daily 10am–7pm; Apr.–June and Sep.–Oct., daily 2–7pm; Mar. and Nov., Sat. and Sun. 2.30am–6pm.*	▲ 288
DOUÉ-LA-FONTAINE	**49700**	**C7/8**
ARÈNES DE DOUCES Rue des Arènes **Tel. 02 41 59 22 28**	*Open Apr.–Oct., Tue.–Sun. 10am–noon and 2–6pm*	▲ 289
MOULIN DE LA FOURCHETTE (MOULIN CARTIER) **Tel. 02 41 59 20 49**	*Open Tue.–Sun. 10am–noon and 3–6pm.*	▲ 289
PARC ZOOLOGIQUE DES MINIÈRES Rue de Cholet **Tel. 02 41 59 18 58**	*Open daily Apr.–Sep., 9am–7pm; Oct.–Mar., 10am–noon and 2–6pm.*	▲ 289
LA SABLIÈRE **Tel. 02 41 59 28 23 (high season)** **and 02 41 59 03 59 (low season)**	*Open Jul.–Aug., daily 9.30am–noon and 2–7pm; Mar.–June and Sep.–Dec., Tue.–Sun. 9.30am–noon and 2–7pm*	▲ 289
FORGES	**49700**	**D7**
LA FOSSE (TROGLODYTIC HAMLET) **Tel. 02 41 59 00 32 (high season)** **and 02 41 52 27 60 (low season)**	*Open daily June–Sep., 9.30 am–7pm; Mar.–May and Oct., 9.30am–12.30pm and 2–6.30pm; Feb. 1–28 and Nov., Sat. and Sun. 2–6pm.*	▲ 288
LE COUDRAY-MACOUARD	**49260**	**D7**
MAGNANERIE Impasse Bel-Air **Tel. 02 41 67 91 24**	*Open May 15–Oct. 15, Tue.–Sun. 10am–6pm; Oct. 16–Dec. 24, Sat. and Sun. 2–6pm.*	▲ 289
LOURESSE-ROCHEMENIER	**49700**	**C7**
MUSÉE PAYSAN **Tel. 02 41 59 18 15**	*Open daily Apr. 1–Nov. 1, 9.30am–7pm; Nov. 2–30 and Feb.–Mar., Sat. and Sun. 2–6pm.*	▲ 288
LE PUY-NOTRE-DAME	**49260**	**D8**
COLLEGIATE CHURCH OF NOTRE-DAME	*Open daily June–Sep., 9.30am–7pm; Mar.–May and Oct., 9.30am–12.30pm and 2–6.30pm; Feb. and Nov., Sat. and Sun. 2–6pm.*	▲ 290
MONTREUIL-BELLAY	**49260**	**D8**
CHÂTEAU **Tel. 02 41 52 33 06**	*Open Apr. 1–Nov. 1, daily except Tue. 10am–noon and 2–5.30pm.*	▲ 291
TURQUANT	**49730**	**E7**
LA GRANDE VIGNOLE **Tel. 02 41 38 16 44 (high season)** **and 02 41 52 90 84 (low season)**	*Open daily May–Sep., 10am–7pm; Oct.–Apr. Wed.–Sun. 10am–7pm.*	▲ 287

| MOULIN CAVIER (CAVE MILL)
Tel. 02 41 51 75 22 | Open daily Jul.–Aug., 10am–8pm; May–June and
Sep.–Oct., 10am–noon and 2–6pm. | ▲ 286 |
| VAL-HULIN
SEMI-TROGLODYTIC HAMLET
Tel. 02 41 51 48 30 | Open Jul.–Aug., Tue.–Sun. 10am–noon and
2.30–6.30pm; Dec. 15–Feb. 15, Tue.–Sat. 10am–noon
and 2.30–6.30pm, Sun. 2.30–6.30pm. | ▲ 286 |

SAUMUR TO ANGERS

| **BRISSAC-QUINCÉ** | **49320** | **B/C6** | |
| CHÂTEAU
Tel. 02 41 91 22 21 | Open daily Jul. 1–Sep. 15, 10am–5.45pm; Apr.–June
and Sep. 16–Nov. 2, daily except Tue. 10am–noon and
2.15–5.15pm. | | ▲ 294 |

| **CUNAULT** | **49350** | **D6** | |
| CHURCH OF NOTRE-DAME
Tel. 02 41 67 92 44 | Open daily summer 8am–7.30pm, winter 8am–7pm. | | ▲ 292 |

GENNES-SUR-LOIRE	**49350**	**D6**	
CHURCH OF ST-VÉTÉRIN	Open daily 9am–7pm.		▲ 293
GALLO-ROMAN AMPHITHEATER Av. de l'amphithéâtre Tel. 02 41 59 22 28 (high season) 02 41 51 83 33 (low season)	Open Jul. 1–Aug. 31, daily 10am–noon and 2.30–6.30pm; Apr. 1–June 30 and Sep. 1–30, Sat. 3–5pm and Sun. 3–6pm.		▲ 293
WATER MILL OF SARRÉ	Open May–Sep., daily 10am–noon and 2–6pm; Oct.–Apr. by appointment.		▲ 293

| **GRÉZILLÉ** | **49320** | **C6** | |
| CHÂTEAU DE PIMPÉAN
Tel. 02 41 45 51 40 | Open May–Oct., 10am–7pm. | | ▲ 293 |

| **LES PONTS-DE-CÉ** | **49130** | **B6** | |
| MUSÉE DES COIFFES D'ANJOU
4, rue Charles-de-Gaulle
Tel. 02 41 44 68 64 (high season
and 02 41 79 75 75 (low season) | Open Jul.–Aug., daily 10am–12.30pm and 1.30–6pm;
June and Sep., Sat.–Sun. 2–6pm; Apr.–May and Oct.,
Sun. 2–6pm. | | ▲ 294 |

| **ST-GEORGES-DES-SEPT-VOIES** | **49350** | **C6** | |
| "HÉLICE TERRESTRE DE L'ORBIÈRE"
Tel. 02 41 57 95 92 | Open daily May–Sep., 11am–8pm; Oct.–Apr., 2–6pm and
by appointment. Evening visits by appointment. | | ▲ 293 |

| **TRÈVES** | **49350** | **D7** | |
| CHURCH OF ST-AUBIN | Open daily except during services. | | ▲ 292 |

ANGERS

ANGERS	**49000**	**B5/6**	
CHÂTEAU AND TAPESTRY OF THE APOCALYPSE Tel. 02 41 87 43 47	Open daily June 1–Sep. 15, 9am–7pm; Sep. 16–Mar. 26, 9.30am–12.30pm and 2–6pm; Mar. 27–May 31, 9am–12.30pm and 2–6.30pm. Guided tour (1½ hours)		▲ 297
CHURCH OF ST-SERGE	Open Jul., 1–3rd Sun. in Sep., Mon.–Sat. 9am–7pm, Sun. 2.30–6pm; Oct.–June, daily 9am–7pm except Sun. am.		▲ 307
GALERIE DAVID-D'ANGERS 33 bis, rue Toussaint Tel. 02 41 87 21 03	Open June 12–Sep. 17, daily 9am–6.30pm; Sep. 18–June 11, daily except Mon. 9am–noon and 2–6pm.		▲ 305
HÔTEL PINCÉ AND MUSÉE TURPIN DE CRISSÉ 32 bis, rue Lenepveu Tel. 02 41 88 94 27	Open June 12–Sep. 17, daily 9am–6.30pm; Sep. 18–June 11, daily 10am–noon and 2–6pm.		▲ 306
BOTANICAL GARDENS Rue Boreau	Open daily 7am (summer), 8am (winter)–evening.		▲ 307
LOGIS DE L'ESTAIGNIER AND MUSÉE DE L'ÉTAIN (PEWTER) Tel. 02 41 88 67 41	Open Jul. 16–Aug. 31, daily except Sun.–Mon. 9.30am–noon and 2–7pm; Sep. 1–Jul. 15, daily except Sun. 9.30am–noon and 2–7pm.		▲ 302
MUSÉE DES BEAUX-ARTS 10, rue du Musée Tel. 02 41 88 64 65	Open June 12–Sep. 17, daily 9am–6.30pm; Sep. 18–June 11, daily except Mon. 10am–noon and 2–6pm.		▲ 304
NATURAL HISTORY MUSEUM 43, rue Jules-Guitton Tel. 02 41 86 05 84	Open daily except Mon. 2–5pm.		▲ 307

MUSÉE JEAN-LURÇAT Hôpital St-Jean **Tel. 02 41 24 18 45**	*Open Jul. 1–Sep. 15, daily 9am–6.30pm;* *Sep. 16–June 30, daily except Mon. 10am–noon and* *2–6pm. Closed Jan. 1, Jul. 14, Nov. 1 and 11, Dec. 25.*	▲ 308
ST-MAURICE CATHEDRAL Rue St-Christophe	*Open daily summer 8am–7pm; winter 9am–5pm.*	▲ 297

AROUND ANGERS

ST-GEORGES-SUR-LOIRE	**49170** **A6**	
CHÂTEAU DE SERRANT **Tel. 02 41 39 13 01**	*Open Jul.–Aug. daily, 10–11.30am and 2–5.30pm;* *Sep.–Oct. and Apr.–June, daily except Tue. 10–11.30am* *and 2–5.30pm.*	▲ 310
ÉCUILLÉ	**49460** **B4**	
CHÂTEAU DU PLESSIS-BOURRÉ **TEL. 02 41 32 06 01**	*Open Jul.–Aug., daily 10am–5.45pm; Sep.–Oct. and* *Mar.–June, daily except Wed. and Thur. 10am–noon and* *2–5.45pm; Nov. and Feb., daily except Wed. 2–5.45pm.*	▲ 311
LE PLESSIS-MACÉ	**49770** **A5**	
CHÂTEAU **Tel. 02 41 32 67 93**	*Open Jul.–Aug., daily 10am–noon and 2–6.30pm;* *June and Sep., daily except Tue. 10am–noon and* *2–6.30pm; Oct–Nov. and Mar.–Apr., daily except Tue.* *1.30–5.30pm; May, daily except Tue. 1.30–6pm.*	▲ 310
BAUGÉ	**49150** **D5**	
CHÂTEAU AND MUSÉE D'ART **POPULAIRE** **Tel. 02 41 89 18 07**	*Open Jul.–Aug., daily except Sun. am 10am–noon and* *2.30–5.30pm; Sep. 1–15, June 15–30, daily except Tue.* *and Sun. am 10am–noon and 2.30–5.30pm.*	▲ 312
MAZÉ	**49630** **C5**	
CHÂTEAU DE MONTGEOFFROY **Tel. 02 41 80 60 02**	*Open June 15–Sep. 15, daily 9.30am–6.30pm;* *Sep. 16–Nov. 1 and Mar. 23–June 14, daily 9.30am–noon* *and 2.30–6.30pm. Guided tour by appointment in English.*	▲ 312

USEFUL ADDRESSES

ORLÉANS, *338*
ORLÉANS TO GIEN, *338*
ORLÉANS TO BLOIS, *339*
IN AND AROUND BLOIS, *340*
IN AND AROUND AMBOISE, *341*
IN AND AROUND TOURS, *342*
TOURS TO VALENÇAY, *343*
TOURS TO CHINON, *343*
TOURS TO FONTEVRAUD, *345*
SAUMUR, *345*
SAUMUR TO
MONTREUIL-BELLAY, *346*
SAUMUR TO ANGERS, *346*
IN AND AROUND ANGERS, *346*

We have selected the following as good representatives of their various categories. The list covers a range of establishments, including traditional "auberges", gastronomic landmarks that gourmets should not miss, hotels that are friendly and good value. They are all close to the historical sites and châteaux.

ORLÉANS

Postal code 45000 (O/P2)

RESTAURANTS

LA POUTRIÈRE
8, rue de la Brèche
Tel. 02 38 66 02 30
This traditional vine-worker's house has been converted into a luxury "auberge" with a garden and swimming pool. Simon Le Bras is especially fond of shellfish and fish, which he skilfully combines with the vegetables of Orléans and the fruit of the Loire Valley. His cuisine reveals a perfect mastery of the produce, seasonings and garnishes.
Menus 150F (lunch, wine included), 250–350F
À la carte 300–380F

LES ANTIQUAIRES
2–4, rue au Lin
Tel. 02 38 53 52 35
Poultry cooked in the contemporary style, but in Orléans vinegar, which is a condiment dating from the 14th century. Michel Pipet is well-versed in traditional cuisine. The "salade tiède" of calf sweetbreads with foie gras, the sea bass "paupiettes", and the "tarte aux pommes", all demonstrate the same high standards. A highly sophisticated menu, just like the décor.
Menus 155F (midweek), 190–390F
À la carte 280–320F

GIEN

Postal code 45500 (S4)

HOTEL-RESTAURANT

★ **HÔTEL DU RIVAGE**
1, quai de Nice
Tel. 02 38 37 79 00
Fax 02 38 38 10 21
Taste roast pike-perch in a garden by the banks of the Loire. Chef Thierry Renou's cuisine is steeped in the traditional Loire virtues of simplicity and harmony; it would be greatly appreciated if the titles of the dishes were inspired by the same principles. Notable dishes include the stuffed pig's trotters, mushrooms with truffle sauce and "Paris-Gien", a gâteau with raspberries and praline ice-cream. Christian Gaillard, the manager,

is in charge of reception and service.
Menus 140–380F
À la carte 250–400F
16 rooms, 3 suites 300–520F

ORLÉANS TO GIEN

CHÂTEAUNEUF-SUR-LOIRE

Postal code 45110 (Q2)

HOTEL-RESTAURANT

AUBERGE DU PORT
Tel. 02 38 58 43 07
Closed Wed. and Dec.
A simple "auberge" in the town of Maurice Genevoix, the local writer. The menu includes dishes you will find in Genevoix's novel "Raboliot": fried fish, matelotes, game, and simple veal fricassée with wild mushrooms. The rooms overlook the river and the bridge. Perfect for a walk along the banks of the Loire.
Menus: 75–170F
4 rooms with shower, 165F

CHÉCY

Postal code 45430 (P2)

RESTAURANT

LE WEEK-END
1, pl. du Cloître
Tel. 02 38 86 84 93
Traditional Orléans cuisine presented in a simple rustic setting by a chef with a distinguished background. Fillet of pike-perch and beef "forestière", ragoût of pheasant and jugged hare in the fall. Service and wine list of comparable quality.
Menus: 78 (midweek), 130–200F
À la carte: 180–300F

GERMIGNY-DES-PRÉS

Postal code 45110 (Q3)

HOTEL-RESTAURANT

HÔTEL DE LA PLACE
Tel. 02 38 58 20 14
Fax 02 38 58 21 33
Cordon-bleu cuisine which goes perfectly with the simple Carolingian church and its famous mosaic. This village hotel is a delightful place to stay or eat. Some of the rooms are very basic, others have a full range of facilities.
Menus: 59F (midweek), 89–130F
À la carte: 120–220F
11 rooms, 160–220F

JARGEAU

Postal code 45150 (Q2)

RESTAURANT

AUX QUAIS DE LOIRE
23, rue du 71e B.C.P.
Tel. 02 38 59 92 18
Closed Sun. eve and Mon.
Mme Chansard is the manageress of this restaurant, which has a panoramic view over the Loire. Jargeau is the capital of the "andouillette": beyond this, the restaurant also serves "salade solognote", pike-perch and salmon, as well as local poultry. The setting is pleasant and the cuisine is impressive: the chef

HOW TO USE THIS SECTION

The addresses are presented following the order of itineraries in the guide. Within each itinerary, towns and establishments are listed in alphabetical order. The map reference following the postal code refers to the general maps at the front and back of this guide. The telephone and fax numbers incorporate the new system of numbering which came into use in France in October 1996.

...as formerly at the 'egresco.
Menus: 90–220F
À la carte: 200–300F

ST-BENOÎT-SUR-LOIRE

Postal code 45110 (R3)

HOTEL

HÔTEL DU LABRADOR
pl. de l'Abbaye
Tel. 02 38 35 74 38
Fax 02 38 35 72 99
A quiet, partially renovated hotel: some rooms have exposed beams and all conveniences. A lovely setting at the foot of the abbey of St-Benoît, where you can enjoy the peaceful atmosphere of the river valley with a thought for Max Jacob, who lived here before leaving for Drancy.
45 rooms, 180–360F

ST-JEAN-DE-BRAYE

Postal code 45800
(P2)

RESTAURANT

LA GRANGE
205, fg de Bourgogne
Tel. 02 38 86 43 36
Closed Sun., Mon., and Aug.
There were lots of "mauviettes" (weaklings) about during the reign of Charles IX, when Pithiviers was granted the royal privilege for lark pâté. Here, François Chapot offers classical French cuisine, with plenty of game in season, venison, and wild boar. A good cellar of Orléans wines.
Menus: 100–280F
À la carte: 250–320F

SULLY-SUR-LOIRE

Postal code 45600
(R3)

HOTEL-RESTAURANT

HOSTELLERIE DU GRAND-SULLY
10, bd du Champ-de-Foire
Tel. 02 38 36 27 56
Fax 02 38 36 44 54
Closed Sun. evening.
A summer terrace where you can taste chicken "Bon Roy Henri", pike-perch with baby vegetables cooked in a "papillote", or fillet of perch with beurre blanc and crayfish. The cuisine is steeped in the gentle harmonies of the majestic river valley. Comfortable rooms. Traditional house renovated by Philippe Calciat.
Menus: 150–210F
À la carte: 250–350F
10 rooms, 270F

ORLÉANS TO BLOIS

BEAUGENCY

Postal code 45190
(N3)

HOTEL-RESTAURANT

HOSTELLERIE DE L'ÉCU DE BRETAGNE
Pl. du Martroi
Tel. 02 38 44 67 60
Fax 02 38 44 68 07
The rooms of this old coaching inn (preferable to those in the annex) are completely in character with the town, where you can see fish swimming by from the bridge in summer. A sparkling cuisine, with unusual combinations of flavors: rabbit with gingerbread, pork with honey.
Menus: 90F (lunch),
130–200F
25 rooms, 265–365F

CLÉRY-ST-ANDRÉ

Postal code 45370 (O3)

HOTEL-RESTAURANT

LES BORDES
9, rue des Bordes
Tel. 02 38 45 71 25
Fax 02 38 45 96 95
"Orléans, Beaugency, Notre-Dame de Cléry, Vendôme . . .": these are the words of an old song commemorating the fact that in the days of Villon and Louis XI this was a place of pilgrimage, a famous stopping point on the road to Compostela. Huge traditional building in its own grounds. A variety of rooms.
Menus: 60–180F
21 rooms, 80–290F
1 apartment, 450F

LA FERTÉ-ST-AUBIN

Postal code 45240 (P4)

RESTAURANT

LA FERME DE LA LANDE
Rte de Macilly
Tel. 02 38 76 64 37
Closed Sun. eve. and Mon.
The restaurant is housed in a former farmhouse of the Château de La Ferté-St-Aubin, which has been carefully restored. The manager is friendly and the chef offers both the pike-perch of the Loire and Gâtinais duckling sweetmeats. In the hunting season you can try Lièvre à la Royale (hare) – a recipe invented by Carême – and tarte Tatin.
8 menus: 138–370F
À la carte: 250–300F

MER

Postal code 41500 (N4)

RESTAURANT

LES CALANQUES
21, rue Saint-Hême
Tel. 02 58 81 00 55
This large 16th-century house, with its

traditional fireplace and exposed beams, has been converted into a fish restaurant. Local fish are served (pike-perch, pike, salmon) alongside Coquilles St-Jacques, sea bass, and shellfish: all prepared with great precision by Philippe Colombet.
Menus: 100–170F
À la carte: 250–300F

MEUNG-SUR-LOIRE

Postal code 45130 (N3)

HOTEL-RESTAURANT

AUBERGE SAINT-JACQUES
80, rue du Général-de-Gaulle
Tel. 02 38 44 30 39
Fax 02 38 45 17 02
You will not find here the fish that Rabelais served his guests at St-Ay, very close by. The parfait of pike and the young rabbit with onions created by chef Le Gall (winner of the Trophée de la cuisine et de la pâtisserie) exemplify his excellent, simple cuisine.
Menus: 90F (midweek)–220F
À la carte: 250F
12 rooms, 190–260F

OLIVET

Postal code 45160 (O2)

HOTEL-RESTAURANT

LE RIVAGE
635, rue de la Reine-Blanche
Tel. 02 38 66 02 93
The fish of the great river itself, and of the Loiret and the nearby lakes of the Sologne, make a major contribution to the elegant cuisine of François Tassain. This idyllic refuge, situated on an island, also serves Sologne pigeon, calf sweetbreads with crayfish and morel, and the "cendré d'Olivet" praised by Balzac.
Menus: 155–300F
À la carte: 250–350F
18 rooms 370–590F

SAINT DYÉ-SUR-LOIRE

Postal code 41500 (M/N4)

HOTEL-RESTAURANT

MANOIR DE BEL-AIR
(3 miles north of Chambord)
Tel. 02 54 81 60 10
Fax 02 54 81 65 34
Closed Jan. 20–Feb. 20
An old ivy-covered building where you will find both traditional Loir-et-Cher cuisine and dishes from Beauce: the Loire connects these distinct gastronomic regions, which overlap only at harvest time (Sologne quail) and grape-picking (game). By the riverside.
Menus: 118–218F
40 rooms, 240–400F

TAVERS

Postal code 45190 (N3)

HOTEL-RESTAURANT

LA TONNELLERIE
12, rue des Eaux-Bleues
(near the church, approach from Beaugency on the N152)
Tel. 02 38 44 68 15
Fax 02 38 44 10 01
"My hoops on my back, my tools in my hand, I preserve for the people's pleasure". This is the motto of the "tonnelier" (cooper) – and also of Alain Pouey, who serves part-smoked pike-perch and "rillons" of Touraine flavored with herbs, in an elegant, tastefully decorated setting.
Menus: 125–230F
À la carte: 280–450F
12 rooms, 700–880F
8 suites, 800–1,235F

VILLENY

Postal code 41220 (O4)

HOTEL-RESTAURANT

LES CHÊNES-ROUGES
Tel. 02 54 98 23 94
Fax 02 54 98 23 99
Closed Sun. eve. and Mon. (exc. June–Aug.) and Feb.
A hunting lodge by the side of a lake in the forest. The rooms look out over the reeds, which hide the cross-shaped sluice gate. A landscape of birch trees. Serves seasonal cuisine: game in winter, fish from the lakes in summer (bleak, dace, tench and sometimes rainbow perch).
Menus: 170–185F
9 rooms, 600–800F

◆

BLOIS

Postal code 41000 (M4/5)

RESTAURANTS

L'ORANGERIE DU CHÂTEAU
1, av. du Docteur-Jean-Laigret
Tel. 02 54 78 05 36
Facing the royal

BRACIEUX

Postal code 41250 (N5)

RESTAURANT

★ LE RELAIS DE BRACIEUX
1, av. de Chambord
Tel. 02 54 46 41 22
Closed Tue. eve. and Wed.
This former coaching inn first became the Café de la Gare, and then was converted into a substantial restaurant sixty years ago. Today the restaurant is decorated in a tasteful contemporary style. Bernard Robin

château. Jean-Marc Molveaux presents the full range of Loir-et-Cher cuisine, combining dishes from Vendômois, Touraine, Beauce and Sologne. Molveaux comes from Savoie himself, which makes his achievement all the more notable. He uses top-quality local produce (game, fish, fresh vegetables).
Menus: 125–320F
À la carte: 270–360F

AU RENDEZ-VOUS DES PÊCHEURS
27, rue du Foix
Tel. 02 54 74 67 48
Closed Sun. and Mon. lunchtime.
Fresh and salt-water fish are a specialty in this restaurant which was once a grocery store in the old town, a favorite haunt of locals. Éric Reithler creates his dishes opportunistically, making use of what is freshly available: cold lobster soup, oysters, Dublin Bay prawns. The desserts must also be mentioned: Blois "pistoles", Vendôme pralines.
Menu: 145F
À la carte: 250–310F

has served his own version of classical cuisine here since 1975, without forgetting local specialties: carp "à la Chambord", pike mousseline, and the delicious Sologne-

AROUND BLOIS

CANDÉ-SUR-BEUVRON

Postal code 41120 (L

HOTEL-RESTAURANT

HOSTELLERIE DE LA CAILLÈRE
36, rte des Montils
Tel. 02 54 44 03 08
Fax 02 54 44 00 95
Closed Jan. 2–Feb. 28
Jacky Guidon creates a high-quality cuisine in his peaceful, pleasant establishment, set amidst trees and fields. Classical cuisine with a new twist: pike-perch with citrus fruits and ginger, duck breast in honey, cinnamon and almonds. A wide selection of Loire wines. Tasteful rooms.
Menus:
88F (midweek)–278F
À la carte: 220–280F
14 rooms, 330–360F

CHAMBORD

Postal code 41250 (N4)

HOTEL-RESTAURANT

HÔTEL DU GRAND-SAINT-MICHEL
Tel. 02 54 20 31 31
Fax 02 54 20 36 40
Closed Nov. 12–Dec. 2

style "pâté de pommes de terre". An unforgettable experience, with exceptional wines; the game is unrivalled.
Menus: 200–550F
À la carte: 330–640F

*opposite the château,
...fairytale spectacle
...raight out of
...Cinderella" or "Beauty
...d the Beast". Once
...e tourists have left,
...ke a stroll in the
...ounds in the evening,
...hile the chefs prepare
...e grilled salmon with
...urre blanc, or the wild
...ar stew. Touraine
...nes a specialty.
...enus: 130F
... la carte: 200F
... rooms, 260–420F*

CHAUMONT-SUR-LOIRE

...stal code 41150
...5)

...ESTAURANT

A CHANCELIÈRE
... rue de Bellevue
... 02 54 20 96 95
...small, rustic
...stablishment which
...s already gained a
...putation, in the
...ounds of the famous
...âteau. Poultry from
...cal smallholdings
...th morel, "poulet au
...ng" following the
...cipe from Berry, the
...mous Sologne duck
...uffed the day before
...d cooked slowly).
...uality, good prices and
...urteous
...rvice.
...enus: 79–205F

CONTRES

...stal code 41700
...6)

...ESTAURANT

SAINT-VINCENT
...sly (4 miles away, on
... D675 and D21)
... 02 54 79 50 04
...osed Sun. eve. and
...on.
... unpretentious
...çade at the heart
... the village, but an
...cellent menu and an
...egant rustic setting.
...e friendly chef
...esents an original,
...ried cuisine, with
...expected
...mbinations: pork
...nfit with rhubarb
...uce, guinea-fowl
...th spiced wine, etc.
...good selection of
...cal wines.
...enus: 90–220F

ONZAIN-EN-TOURAINE

Postal code 41150 (L5)

HOTEL-RESTAURANT

★ **DOMAINE DES HAUTS-DE-LOIRE**
Route d'Herbault
(take the D1)
Tel. 02 54 20 72 57
Fax 02 54 20 77 32
The Bonnigal family has
turned this old hunting
lodge into a delightful
hotel. The cuisine of
chef Rémy Giraud, a
native of Vendôme, is
both expert and
approachable, drawing
on local traditions. The
entrées are light and
delicious: caramelized
foie gras of duck with
rhubarb, shellfish ravioli
with broad beans. The
Vendôme pigeon
cooked with
mushrooms is full of
flavor. The Vouvray
wines go perfectly with
the "crème
chocolatée", flavored
with tea and blackberry.
High-quality setting and
service.
Menus: 290–475F
À la carte: 380–500F
10 suites, 1,600–1,800F

COUR-CHEVERNY

Postal code 41700 (M5)

HOTEL-RESTAURANT

CHÂTEAU DU BREUIL
(2 miles away, on the
D52)
Tel. 02 54 44 20 20
Fax 02 54 44 30 40
Closed Jan. 2–Feb. 20,
Sun. eve. (out of
season) and Mon.
lunchtime.
All the splendor of an
18th-century residence
in its own grounds, and
serving top-quality food.
Patrick Léonce creates
exquisite combinations:
artichoke and lobster
medallions in
"barigoule" sauce, bass
in a pastry crust with
cèpes. Delightful setting
and good service.
Menus: 195–375F
À la carte: 400–450F
16 rooms, 530–890F

MONT-PRÈS-CHAMBORD

Postal code 41250 (M5)

HOTEL-RESTAURANT

LE SAINT-FLORENT
(6 miles south of
Chambord, on the
D923)
Tel. 02 54 70 81 00
Fax 02 54 70 78 53
A pretty, simple hotel
in the heart of château
country. The menu
features traditional
Sologne dishes such
as pig's trotters, carp
with Chinon. The
game terrine is
delicious.
Menus: 81–210F
18 rooms, 200–265F

◆

AROUND AMBOISE

NOIZAY

Postal code 37210 (I6)

HOTEL-RESTAURANT

CHÂTEAU DE NOIZAY
Rte de Chançay
(5 miles to the east on
the D46)
Tel. 02 47 52 11 01
Fax 02 47 52 04 64
Closed Nov. 12–Mar. 15
A château dating from
the 16th century, set
amid ancient trees, with

AMBOISE

Postal code 37400
(J6)

HOTEL-RESTAURANT

★ **LE CHOISEUL**
36, quai Charles-Guinot
Tel. 02 47 30 45 45
Fax 02 47 30 46 10
Closed Nov. 26–Jan. 20
The elegant, austere
building of the Choiseul
stands at the foot of
the château, on the
quayside – by the side
of the "moving road",
as the Loire used to
be called when it was
used for shipping. The
chef Pascal Bouvier
deftly combines a
modern repertoire
of flavors and tastes,
as in his "nonette de
foie gras de canard",
celery and balsamic
caramel with wild
herbs, or the fondant
of oysters with green
lentils from Berry. The
roast loin of lamb with
bacon sauce and
young peas goes
perfectly with a
Touraine-Amboise wine.
Lovely rooms and very
attentive service.
Menus: 200–400F
À la carte: 300–420F
28 rooms, 540–990F
4 suites, 1,200–1,600F

extremely elegant rooms. The chef, Didier Frebout, uses local produce and adapts his cuisine to the changing seasons, displaying a mastery of flavors: "petits-gris" (snails) and "rillons de Touraine", foie gras in Vouvray wine, pike-perch in Chinon.
Menus: 145–340F
À la carte: 240–360F
14 rooms, 950–1,300F

ST-OUEN-LES-VIGNES

Postal code 37530 (J5)

RESTAURANT

L'AUBINIÈRE
Rue J.-Gauthier
Tel. 02 47 30 15 29
Closed Mon. eve. and Wed. (except July and Aug.)
The cuisine of Jacques Arrayet is seasonal, with exquisite, intense flavors: tomatoes in warm oxtail vinegar, red mullet steak with red peppers, lobster with coriander. In summer

★ **JEAN BARDET**
57, rue Groison
Tours
Tel. 02 47 41 41 11
Fax 02 47 51 68 72
Closed Mon. lunchtime Apr.–Oct., Sun. eve. and Mon. Nov.–Mar..
Jean Bardet is a cook, a gardener and a poet, who is able to share his passions with others. "Pike with beurre blanc tastes best in rainy weather," he declares, while uncorking a bottle of chilled wine. A Montlouis 1989 (Domaine Delétang), for example, to match the flavors of turbot

you can eat on the terrace, at the heart of this village near Amboise.
Menu: 110F (midweek), 190–340F
À la carte: 300–400F

◆

TOURS

Postal code 37000 (H6)

RESTAURANTS

CHARLES BARRIER
101, av. Tranchée
Tel. 02 47 54 20 39
Closed Sun. eve
Charles Barrier is a long-established chef in the classical tradition: he is one of the great French chefs of the last thirty years. The elegant setting matches the culinary pleasures: lobster terrine with tomato in the Breton style, and young-guinea fowl with foie gras and fondant potatoes. Often imitated, rarely equalled.
Menus: 230–470F
À la carte: 370–500F

LA ROCHE LE ROY
57, rte Saint-Avertin
Tel. 02 47 27 22 00
Closed Sat. lunchtime, Sun. eve. and Mon.

poached with asparagus. The hazel grouse of the Racan area, a rare bird with dense, tasty flesh, goes best with a Bourgueil (Domaine de la Chevalerie) by Pierre Caslot (1986). The best

In an old manor house in Tours, Alain Couturier excels in the preparation of local, seasonal dishes: pike-perch with beurre blanc, matelote of eels with Chinon wine, fricassée of hazel grouse with morel mushrooms. The wine is kept in a cellar hollowed out of the rock.
Menus: 160F (lunch), 200–350F
À la carte: 240–400F

AROUND TOURS

ROCHECORBON

Postal code 37210 (H6)

HOTEL-RESTAURANT

LES HAUTES-ROCHES
86, quai de Loire
Tel. 02 47 52 88 88
Fax 02 47 52 81 30
Hotel closed mid-Jan.–mid-Mar. Panoramic view over the Loire and troglodytic caves, in an extraordinary location. Chef Didier Edon has a predilection for seafood dishes (burbot, smoked duck, turbot supreme, "persillade" of squid with pickled tomato), but he also cooks pigeon with exceptional skill.
Menus: 150F (lunch), 270–355F
8 rooms, 3 suites, 995–1,200F

restaurant in the area. Very comfortable rooms, lovely gardens. Warm welcome and service.
Menus 270–720F
À la carte 500–700F
16 rooms, 650–1 200F
5 suites, 1,400–1 800F

RESTAURANT

L'OUBLIETTE
34, rue des Clouets
Tel. 02 47 52 50 49
Closed Sun. eve and Mon.
This restaurant has a troglodytic dining room hollowed out of the tufa rockface: a natural setting for the creations of Thierry Duhamel, which vary according to the season and availability of local produce. Lobster with Vouvray and baby vegetables, pan-fried Dublin Bay prawn with asparagus. Good Vouvray wines at very reasonable prices.
Menus: 948–290F
À la carte: 280–320F

SEMBLANÇAY

Postal code 37360 (H5)

HOTEL-RESTAURANT

HOSTELLERIE DE LA MÈRE-HAMARD
Pl. de l'Église
Tel. 02 47 56 62 04
Fax 02 47 56 53 61
Closed Sun. eve. and Mon. (except Apr. 15–Oct. 15).
An old house set in a garden, with simple, comfortable rooms. The dining room is just as traditional as the cuisine, which uses exclusively fresh produce (pike-perch, salmon, game in season). Friendly welcome and service.
Menus: 99–250F
9 rooms, 200–255F

VALLIÈRES (PAR FONDETTES

Postal code 37230 (H6)

RESTAURANT

AUBERGE DE PORT-VALLIÈRES
Tel. 02 47 42 24 04
Closed Sun. eve. and Mon.
Jean-Jacques Thomas considers that "terrine

e couenne" (pork
rrine) brings out the
vor of the local wines.
od is served from
ne in the morning:
sparagus, pig's
tters, roast venison
d fried fish. Small
election of excellent
nes.
enu: 85F

◆

TOURS TO VALENÇAY

CHENONCEAUX

ostal code 37150 (J6/7)

OTEL-RESTAURANT

ÔTEL DU ON-LABOUREUR CHÂTEAU
rue du Docteur-
retonneau
l. 02 47 23 90 02
ax 02 47 23 82 01
osed Nov. 13–Dec. 16
d Jan. 3–Feb. 15
*his "auberge" in the
llage, close to the
hâteau, serves
aditional local food.
e rooms are
xtremely comfortable,
d the dining room
ens onto a lovely
atio. Antoine Jeudi
es to use local
roduce: eels marinière
n matelote", "magret
e canard" with Chinon.*
enus: 150–300F
la carte: 280–320F
3 rooms, 320–700F
suites, 800–1,000F

LE GRAND-PRESSIGNY

ostal code 37350 (I9)

OTEL-RESTAURANT

ESPÉRANCE
el. 02 47 94 90 12
osed Mon. and
n.6–Feb.3.
*aulette and Bernard
orset run this
stablishment, in a
aditional, opulent-
oking house.
aditional dishes made*

ROMORANTIN

Postal code 41200 (O6)

HOTEL-RESTAURANT

★ GRAND HÔTEL DU LION-D'OR
69, rue Georges-Clemenceau
Closed Fe. 19–Mar. 21
One of France's great restaurants. This house near Valençay once belonged to a friend of François I; today it is an elegant hotel with a patio at the heart of the small town, run by two generations of the Clément family. Didier Clément, the chef, uses

from locally grown produce: pan-fried foie gras with apples, turbot with vermouth-flavored "mousse de St-Pierre", Touraine pigeon cooked with spices. Pleasant rooms at the heart of the village.
Menus: 100–195F
À la carte: 280–320F
10 rooms, 150–200F

LE PETIT-PRESSIGNY

Postal code 37350 (I9)

RESTAURANT

LA PROMENADE
Tel. 02 47 94 93 52
Closed Sun. eve and Mon.
Jacky Dallais learned the art of creating unusual dishes from Jacques Manière. He demonstrates his skill with "pain brûlé" accompanying "parmentier de foie gras et artichaut", white asparagus and veal with "gribiche" sauce. The comfortable setting and attractive décor of this village restaurant and the friendly service make this a must for all gourmets.
Menus: 120–350F
À la carte: 350–400F

---

the best produce (Dublin Bay prawns, lobsters, eels), with a mastery of cooking methods and spices (stuffed pigeon, calf sweetbreads), and close attention to the

MONTRICHARD

Postal code 41400 (L6)

RESTAURANT

GRILL DU PASSEUR "CHEZ SUZANNE"
Pont de Montrichard
(at Faverolles-sur-Cher)
Tel. 02 54 32 06 80
A pleasant restaurant on the Cher, with superb red meats roasted on a spit in the fireplace, and good local wines. By night the view over the old town is stunning: the waters of the Cher flow under the bridge at the foot of the 12th-century keep, which once protected the town from invaders.
À la carte: around 150F

◆

TOURS TO CHINON

BEAUMONT-EN-VERON

Postal code 37420 (F8)

HOTEL-RESTAURANTS

CHÂTEAU DE DANZAY
Tel. 02 47 58 46 86
Fax 02 47 58 84 35
An elegant 15th-century château set in the heart

---

fine details. Impeccable service, and the best wines of the Loire.
Menus: 420F (lunch)-600F
À la carte: 520F
6 suites, 1,500–2,100

of the famous vineyard of Véron. Excellent rooms with four-poster beds and medieval-style wooden furniture, in keeping with the château's historical past. The restaurant, open only in the evening, offers a range of regional dishes, which are skilfully prepared.
Menus: 290–350F
10 rooms, 650–1,500F

LA GIRAUDIÈRE
Tel. 02 47 58 40 36
Fax 02 47 58 46 06
Restaurant closed Tue., Wed. lunchtime and Nov. 15–Mar. 15; hotel open all year
17th-century manor house with dovecote, set in its own grounds. A peaceful, delightful setting, with tasteful, opulent rooms. The restaurant is open daily, with a modest range of dishes: braised ox-tongue with truffle sauce, "civet de canard" (duck stew). Some very good local wines.
Menus: 110–300F
20 rooms, 200–395F
5 suites, 320–480F

L'ÎLE-BOUCHARD

Postal code 37220 (G8)

RESTAURANT

★ AUBERGE DE L'ÎLE
3, pl. Bouchard
Tel. 02 47 58 51 07
Closed Sun. eve, Mon.
and Jan. 2–Feb. 20
The terrace of this modest auberge overlooks the bridge on the Vienne; the setting has a timeless quality. The menu offers a range of typical Loire dishes, including: asparagus in puff pastry with lamb sweetbreads, and roast pike-perch with a "ragoût de grenouilles et de morilles" (ragoût of frog and morel). *Chinon wine goes splendidly with the pig's trotters with potatoes and mushrooms, in a "sauce diable". The local goat's cheese, Sainte-Maure, goes with the white wines of the region: Cheverny, Amboise, Azay-le-Rideau . . . names shared by famous châteaux and excellent wines.*
Menus: 95–260F
À la carte: 260–300F

★ AU PLAISIR GOURMAND
2, rue Parmentier
Chinon
Tel. 02 47 93 20 48
The cuisine of chef Jean-Claude Rigollet is inspired by regional traditions, with his "fouée à l'ancienne", "mousseline de brochet" (pike mousse), leek terrine with rillons, and tart of calf sweetbreads. The pike-perch in Chinon wine is equally traditional. By contrast, Rigollet shows his inventiveness with the Dublin Bay prawns with courgettes and vanilla, best accompanied by a Coteaux-du-Layon wine. This lovely Renaissance building in the heart of old Chinon is beautifully decorated: it is a must for visitors to the land of Rabelais. Extensive list of local wines. The restaurant is managed by Danielle Rigollet.
Menus: 175–340F
À la carte: 280–320F

CHINON

Postal code 37600 (F8)

RESTAURANT

L'OCÉANIC
13, rue Rabelais
Tel. 02 47 93 44 55
Closed June 8–16
Chinon stretches alongside the waters of the Vienne, where fishers catch the pike-perch which feature prominently in the region's cuisine. This restaurant in the old town has achieved a well-deserved reputation. It serves excellent seawater and freshwater fish, presented very simply and accompanied by local wines, at reasonable prices.
Menus: 98–155F

HOTEL

LE DIDEROT
4, rue Bufon
Tel. 02 47 93 18 87
Fax 02 47 93 37 10

MARÇAY

Postal code 37500 (F8)

HOTEL-RESTAURANT

★ CHÂTEAU DE MARÇAY
Tel. 02 47 93 03 47
Fax 02 47 93 45 33
Closed Sun. eve and Mon. out of season and Jan. 28–Mar. 16
This magnificent château built of tufa limestone and slate, dating from the late Middle Ages, stands in landscaped gardens which symbolize the "Garden of France", with vineyards all around. The rooms is peaceful hotel near to the Place Jeanne-d'Arc occupies an 18th-century building of tufa limestone with a lovely half-timbered staircase. The service is excellent and the prices are reasonable. All the rooms are different. Homemade jellies are served at breakfast, beside an old fireplace.
28 rooms, 250–400F

MONTBAZON

Postal code 37250 (H7)

HOTEL-RESTAURANT

CHÂTEAU D'ARTIGNY
Rte d'Azay-le-Rideau
Tel. 02 47 26 24 24
Fax 02 47 65 92 79
Closed Jan. 1–13.
When François Coty, the perfumer, was unable to buy Chambord, he resigned himself to reproducing an in the château and its outbuildings are furnished very tastefully, with top-level facilities. The chef, Pascal Boudin, presents a range of classical dishes which draw inspiration from local produce and traditions: poached eggs with cream of wild mushrooms, sole soufflé with herbs from the garden, and exquisite desserts. Guests can eat on the terrace in summer. Extensive wine list, very attentive service.
Menus: 145–385F
À la carte: 340–420F
34 rooms, 495–1,350F
6 suites, 1,420–1,680F

...8th-century château.
...ow this building has
...een converted into
...luxury hotel, offering
...e best in service
...nd facilities. An
...tensive menu is
...erved in the round
...ning room: fish dishes,
...sparagus, hazel
...ouse with truffles.
...agnificent wine list.
...enus: 250–440F
... la carte: 380–450F
... rooms, 520–1,640F
...suites, 2,300–2,680F

◆

TOURS TO FONTEVRAUD

BOURGUEIL

...ostal code 37140
...7)

...ESTAURANTS

...UBERGE DE TOUVOIS
...te de Gizeux
... miles to the north,
... the D 749)
...l. 02 47 97 88 81
...ouraine is the
...reen heart" of the

Loire Valley, the land
of "primeurs" (early
wines), good cheeses,
and an abundance
of fruit. This auberge
by the forest is run
by Pascal Calmettes:
it is an idyllic place,
serving traditional
cuisine (millefeuille
d'escargots, kidneys
with three types of
mustard) and
Bourgueil wines.
Menus: 85–125F
À la carte: 240–280F

GERMAIN
Rue A.-Charier
Tel. 02 47 97 72 22
A reliable restaurant.
Charcuterie (cooked/
cured meats) plays
a vital role in
the gastronomy of
this region: the pâtés,
sausages, rillettes
and rillons are best
accompanied by
a straightforward
Sauvignon or a
delicate Vouvray.
Menus: 90–180F

FONTEVRAUD-L'ABBAYE

Postal code 49590
(E8)

RESTAURANT

LA LICORNE
Allée Ste-Catherine
Tel. 02 41 51 72 49
This restaurant, set
in the gardens of an
18th-century residence,
offers a classical style
of cuisine, which
changes throughout
the year depending
what is in season
and the local produce
that is available.

GUEST HOUSE

★ DOMAINE
DE MESTRÉ
Fontevraud-l'Abbaye
Tel. 02 41 51 75 87
Fax 02 41 51 71 90

A delightful farm, which
has been run by the
same family since the
18th century, set in a
landscape of hills and
trees near to the

Salmon with anchovy
sauce, aubergines
gratin, roasted calf
sweetbreads with
Layon wine: any of
these provides a
perfect accompaniment
to the local wines.
Menus: 110–280F
À la carte: 300–380F

LUYNES

Postal code 37230
(H6)

HOTEL-RESTAURANT

DOMAINE
DE BEAUVOIS
Rte de Cléré
(2½ miles to the
northwest, on the
D49)
Closed Jan. 11–Mar. 9
A magnificent house in
a verdant setting, with
its own swimming pool
at the end of the lawn.
Stéphane Pineau offers
"classic wines of the
estate, with traditional
dishes", including the
sole roulade with
Vouvray and the pigeon
in a salted pastry crust.
Menus: 200–360F
À la carte: 340–380F
36 rooms, 920–1,400F

MONTSOREAU

Postal code 49730
(E7)

HOTEL-RESTAURANT

HÔTEL DE LA LOIRE
Tel. 02 41 51 70 06
Fax 02 41 38 15 08
A unique setting at the
confluence of the Loire
and the Vienne, which

confluence of the
Loire and the Vienne
are offered at an
attractive price.
Guests can taste
produce from the farm
itself, including chicken,
veal, and cheese from
the dairy. An old-
fashioned farm with a
warm, traditional
atmosphere; it
welcomes many
visitors from outside
France.
Dinner: 135F
12 rooms, 230–380F

meet amid valleys
and forests. A
reliable, family-run
establishment, and a
good base for exploring
Candes and the Basilica
of St-Martin. Simple
rooms and good-quality
local cuisine.
Menus: 79–160F
14 rooms, 160–265F

◆

SAUMUR

Postal code 49400
(D7)

RESTAURANTS

L'ESCARGOT
30, rue du Maréchal-
Leclerc
Tel. 02 41 51 20 88
Closed Wed. out of
season
The restaurant serves
snails, of course, but
also the "rillons"
described by Balzac
as a "piece of pork
fried in its own fat,
which looks like
a cooked truffle".
Saumur wines a
specialty. The menu
includes traditional
dishes, like a tasty
"boudin de brochet"
(pike sausage) with
Dublin Bay prawns.
Menus: 73–165F
À la carte: 200–150F

LES DÉLICES
DU CHÂTEAU
Courtyard of the
château
Tel. 02 41 67 65 60
Pierre Millon runs
this restaurant in the
former chapel of the
Château de Saumur,
dating from the 14th
century, looking down
over the town and the
river. It is a unique
place, especially in
summer when guests
can eat on the shady
terrace. An imaginative
menu, featuring fish,
local vegetables and
fruits, and game in
season.
Menus: 175–285F
À la carte: 290–390F

SAUMUR TO MONTREUIL-BELLAY

OIRON

Postal code 79100
(E9)

HOTEL-RESTAURANT

RELAIS DU CHÂTEAU
Tel. 02 49 96 54 96
Fax 02 49 96 54 45
The young chef
Éric Bernier is highly
skilled at combining
different flavors and
textures in a very
original way. His
dishes bear the
hallmark of culinary
genius: the "verdurette
de gésiers confits"
(gizzard), the pike-perch
with oyster
sauce, and the noisettes
of lamb with port and
cinnamon.
Menus: 75–158F
À la carte: 240 280F
15 rooms, 130–230F

THOUARS

Postal code 79100
(D9)

HOTEL-RESTAURANT

LE CLOS SAINT-MÉDARD
Tel. 02 49 66 66 00
Fax 02 49 96 15 01
Pierre Aracil's
restaurant, with its
austere style of décor, is
set in a robust medieval
building. The cuisine is
full of flavor and rustic in
style: eels in flaky
pastry with horseradish,
"pot au feu de St-
Jacques" with Massais
butter, and beef and
ragoût of pig's trotters.
Menus: 98–320F
4 rooms, 230–280

SAUMUR TO ANGERS

CHÊNEHUTTE-LES-TUFEAUX

Postal code 49350
(D7)

HOTEL-RESTAURANT

LE PRIEURÉ
(4½ northwest of
Saumur, on the D751)
Tel. 02 41 67 90 14
Fax 02 41 67 92 24
Taste the atmosphere
of Anjou in this
delightful Renaissance
manor house set in
extensive grounds,
overlooking the Loire.
The luxury rooms and
the dining hall have
views over the river.
Jean-Noël Lumineau
highlights local
products in a typically
Angevin menu. A
good selection of
Loire wines.
Menus: 230–400F
À la carte: 350–400F
20 rooms, 2 suites,
500–1,350F

LES ROSIERS-SUR-LOIRE

Postal code 49350
(D6)

RESTAURANT

JEANNE-DE-LAVAL
54, rue Nationale
Tel. 02 41 51 80 17
A large auberge by
the river. Michel
Augereau, employed
by his father Albert,
is establishing himself
as a chef of
considerable skill,
after training with
Joël Robuchon. His
typically Angevin
cuisine features
variations on local
themes: crayfish,
Loire fish with beurre
blanc, ballottine of
pigeon with truffles.
A good list of Loire
wines.

Menus: 180–420F
À la carte: 380–470F
8 rooms, 300–550F
(at the Hôtel des Ducs
d'Anjou)

ANGERS

Postal code 49000
(B5/6)

HOTEL-RESTAURANTS

PAVILLON PAUL-LE-QUÉRÉ
3, bd Foch
Tel. 02 41 20 00 20
Fax 02 41 20 06 20
Closed Sun. eve.
Paul Le Quéré makes
skilful use of local
produce, as it becomes
available on the market:
artichoke and
asparagus combined
with Dublin Bay prawns
(cooked with pepper)
and burbot cooked with
herbs in a rustic sauce.
A lovely classical
building.
Menus: 150–470F
6 rooms, 500–800F

**HÔTEL D'ANJOU
RESTAURANT
"LA SALAMANDRE"**
1, bd Foch
Tel. 02 41 88 99 55
Fax 02 41 87 22 21
Closed Sun.
This is the main hotel in
the town for receptions
and celebrations. The
restaurant features the
classical cuisine of
Daniel Louboutin: grilled
bass with basil cream
sauce, pigeon rissole
with truffle sauce.
A perfect prelude to
visiting the Tapestry of
the Apocalypse.
Menus: 120–195F
À la carte: around 300F
53 rooms, 355–580F

AROUND ANGERS

BÉHUARD

Postal code 49170 (B

RESTAURANT

NOTRE-DAME
12, pl. de l'Église
Tel. 02 41 72 20 17
Upriver from the
remarkable confluence
of the Maine and the
Loire is a church (whic
has survived repeated
flooding) and this
magnificent village
restaurant, which
serves specialties of
Anjou: mussels, fried
Loire fish, smoked
goose, eels, duck.
Accompanied by a
crisp Anjou wine.
Menus: 85–185F

ST-GEORGES-SUR-LOIRE

Postal code 49170
(A6)

RESTAURANT

RELAIS D'ANJOU
Tel. 02 41 39 13 18
The old press-house,
opposite the abbey, ha
a barrel standing on th
terrace. The cuisine is
classical and local at
once: terrine of pike
with crayfish, boudin of
lobster with cabbage,
Anjou pigeon with
garlic cloves.
Menus: 105–280F

ST-SYLVAIN-D'ANJOU

Postal code 49480 (B

RESTAURANT

AUBERGE D'ÉVENTAR
(Rte de Paris N 23)
Tel. 02 41 43 74 25
Good, classical cuisine
from Jean-Pierre
Maussion, a native of
the Loire. All the local
specialties are here:
andouillette with
shallots, farm-raised
chicken, Anjou pigeon
with Savennières. One
of the best places to
sample traditional
Angevin cuisine.
Menus: 135–365F

APPENDICES

BIBLIOGRAPHY, *348*
LIST OF ILLUSTRATIONS, *350*
INDEX, *356*

◆ BIBLIOGRAPHY

ESSENTIAL ◆ READING ◆

◆ BENTLEY (J.): *The Loire*, Philip, London, 1986
◆ GOUVION (C.): *Châteaux of the Loire*, Thames & Hudson, London, 1986
◆ LONGNON (J.) and GAZELLES (R.) (introduction): *Les Très Riches Heures du Duc de Berri*, Thames & Hudson, London, 1969/ Abrams, US, 1984
◆ MYHILL (H.): *The Loire Valley – Plantagenet and Valois*, Faber and Faber, London, 1978
◆ SEYDOUX (P.): *Châteaux of the Loire*, Thames & Hudson, London, 1992
◆ WALDEN (H.): *Loire Gastronomique*, Conran Octopus, London, 1992

GENERAL ◆ READING ◆

◆ ARDAGH (J.) and JONES (C.): *Cultural Atlas of France*, Facts on File, New York/Oxford, 1991
◆ AUDEBERT (B.) and TOURNAIR (J.): *La Châtre et la Vallée Noire*, Editions Souny, Limoges, 1985
◆ BAILEY (A.) et al: *The Taste of France*, Webb and Bower (Publishers) Ltd., Exeter, 1983
◆ BAROLI (M.): *La Vie Quotidienne en Berry au temps de George Sand*, Hachette, Paris, 1982
◆ BAZIN (R.): *Paysages et Pays d'Anjou*, Calmann-Lévy, Paris, 1926
◆ BEDEL (M.): *La Touraine, gens et pays de chez nous*, De Gigord, Paris, 1935
◆ BOYLESVE (R.): *Portrait de la France*, Vol. IV, Émile-Paul Frères, Paris, 1926
◆ BURY (J.P.T.): *France 1814–1900*, Methuen, London, 1949
◆ BURNAND (R.): *La Vie Quotidienne en France 1870–1900*, Hachette, Paris, 1943
◆ CHAMBERLAIN (S.): *Bouquet de France – an epicurean tour of the French provinces*,

Hamish Hamilton, London
◆ CHIROL (S.) et SEYDOUX (P.): *Le Val de Loire. Des châteaux et des manoirs*, Le Chêne, 1991
◆ CLÉMENT (M-Ch. & D.): *La Sologne gourmande*, Albin Michel, Paris, 1993
◆ COLLAS (R.): *Heurs et malheurs des soieries tourangelles*, Le Clairmirouère, Blois, 1987
◆ COURTE (L.), GATEAUD (P) and STEPHAN (B.): *La Loire en sursis. Croisade pour le dernier fleuve sauvage d'Europe*, Sang de la Terre, Paris, 1990
◆ DYER (C.): *Population and Society in Twentieth-Century France*, Hodder & Stoughton, London, 1978
◆ GENEVOIX (M.): *Images du val de Loire*, Imprimerie Nationale, Paris, 1900
◆ GUERLIN (H.): *La Touraine, Le Blésois, Le Vendômois: Choix de Textes précédés d'une étude*, H. Laurens, Paris, 1911
◆ HALÉVY (D.): *Visites aux Paysans du Centre (1907–1934)*, Grasset, Paris, 1935
◆ MASTROJANNI (M.): *Le Grand Livre des vins de Loire*, Solar, Paris, 1991
◆ MENDRAS (H.) AND COLE (A.): *Social Change in Modern France: Towards a Cultural Anthropology of the Fifth Republic*, Cambridge University Press, Cambridge, 1991
◆ ROUGÉ (J.M.): *Le Folklore de la Touraine*, C.L.D., Chambray-lès Tours 1975
◆ ROWE (V.): *Châteaux of the Loire*, Putnam, London, 1958
◆ ROWE (V.): *The Loire*, Eyre Methuen, London, 1974
◆ PARIS (T.): *The River Yonne and the Canal du Nivernais from the Seine to the Loire*, Enterpris, Bideford, c. 1992
◆ WALDEN (H.): *Régions gourmandes. Le Pays de Loire*, Hatier, Paris, 1993

◆ *Walking in the Loire Valley*, trans WILSON (A.): Robertson McCarta, London 1990
◆ WEBER (E.): *Peasants into Frenchmen: the Modernization of Rural France, 1870–1914*, Chatto & Windus, London, 1977
◆ ZELDIN (T.): *Histoire des Passions Françaises* (5 vols.), Éditions du Seuil, Paris, 1980–1

◆ HISTORY ◆

◆ BOUSSARD (J.): *Le Comté d'Anjou sous Henri II Plantagenêt et ses fils (1151–1204)*, Slatkine, Paris, 1977
◆ DALLAS (E.), *The Imperfect Peasant Economy, the Loire Country, 1800–1914*, Cambridge University Press, Cambridge, 1990
◆ DAVID-DARNAC (M.): *The True Story of the Maid of Orleans*, trans. De Polnay (P.), W.H. Allen, London, 1969
◆ DUBY (G.) and MANDROU (R.): *A History of French Civilisation*, Weidenfeld & Nicolson, London, 1964/Random House, New York, 1975
◆ FARMER (S.): *Communities of St Martin – Legend and Ritual in Medieval Tours*, Cornell University Press, Ithaca and London, 1991
◆ FRANCE (A.): *The Life of Joan of Arc*, trans. Stephens (W.), John Lane, The Bodley Head, London, 1909
◆ GAULTIER (J.): *Histoire de la Châtre et Berry*, Éditions de vagabond, Paris, 1982
◆ GOUBERT (P.): *The Ancien Régime*, Weidenfeld and Nicolson, London, 1973/ Harper and Row, US, 1970
◆ GOUBERT (P.): *French Peasantry in the Seventeenth Century*, Cambridge University Press, Cambridge, 1982, US, 1986
◆ KEEN (M.): *The Pelican History of Medieval Europe*,

Penguin, Harmondsworth, 1968
◆ McLEOD (E.): *Charles of Orleans, Prince and Poet*, Chatto & Windus, London, 1969
◆ MAUROIS (H.): *A history of France*, Jonathan Cape, London, 1949

◆ ARCHITECTURE ◆

◆ BABELON (J. -P.): *Les Châteaux de France au siècle de Renaissance*, Picard Paris, 1990
◆ BILLY-CHRISTIAN (F.) RAULIN (H.): *L'Architecture rurale française*, Paris, Berger-Levrault, 198●
◆ BINNY (M.): *Châteaux of the Loire*, Penguin Books, London, 1993
◆ DEFARGES (B.) and BERLAND (J.-M.): *Val de Loire roman*, Zodiaque, La Pierre-qui-Vire, 1965
◆ DUTTON (R.): *The Châteaux of France*, B.T. Batsford, London 1969
◆ GASCAR (P.): *Chambord*, Delpire Éditeur, Switzerland, 1962
◆ GUILLAUME (J.): *Léonard de Vinci et l'architecture française: la villa de Charles d'Amboise e le château de Romorantin, Revue d l'Art*, no. 25, 1974
◆ HALL (M.): *Château de Blois, Loire, Country Life*, April 11 1996
◆ JEANSON (D.): *La Basilique Saint-Martin de Tours*, C.L.D., Chambray-lès Tours, 1988
◆ LELONG (C.): *La Touraine romane*, Zodiaque, La Pierre-qui-Vire, 1977
◆ LEVRON (J.): *Châteaux of the Loire* trans. Coburn (O.), Nicolson Eyre, London, 1963
◆ LESUEUR (F. and P.) *Le Château de Blois*, Picard, Paris, 1970
◆ LESUEUR (F. and P.): *Léonard da Vinci et Chambord, Études d'art nos. 8, 9 and 10* Paris-Alger, 1953–4
◆ MARTIN-DEMÉZIL (J.): *Chambord*, Société Française

archéologue, Paris, 86
NICOLAY-MAZERY and AUDIN (J.-B): *The French Château: Life, Style, Tradition,* Thames & Hudson, London, 1991
◆ PORCHER (J.): *Anjou roman,* Zodiaque, Pierre-qui-Vire, 87
SARRAZIN (A.): *Maisons rurales du Val de Loire: Touraine, Blésois, Orléanais, Sologne,* Vincent Real, 1976
SEYDOUX (P.): *Châteaux et manoirs du Blésois,* Paris, Morande, 1990
SULLAM (J.) and AITE (C.): *Villages of France,* Weidenfeld & Nicolson, London, 88

◆ FINE ARTS ◆

BLUNT (SIR A.): *Art and Architecture in France 1500–1700,* Pelican History of Art, Penguin Books, Harmondsworth, 1970
DEMANGE (F.): *Images de la Révolution. L'imagerie populaire orléanaise à l'époque révolutionnaire,* Musée des Beaux-Arts d'Orléans, 1989

◆ LITERATURE ◆

ALAIN-FOURNIER: *Le Grand Meaulnes (The Lost Domain),* trans. Davison (F.) Oxford University Press, Oxford/New York, 1986
BALZAC (H. DE): *Droll Stories,* Garden City Publishing Company Inc., Garden City, New York, 1928
BALZAC (H. DE): *Le Curé de Tours,* Pléiade/Gallimard, Paris, 1971
BALZAC (H. DE): *Eugénie Grandet,* trans. Ellen Marriage, Everyman's Library, London, Alfred Knopf, New York, 1992
BALZAC (H. DE): *La Grenadière,* Pléiade/Gallimard, Paris, 1971
BALZAC (H. DE): *Le Lys dans la Vallée (The Lily of the Valley),* trans Waring, (J.),

J.M. Dent & Co., London/New York, 1987
◆ BALZAC (H. DE): *La Rabouilleuse,* Pléiade/Gallimard, Paris, 1971
◆ BAZIN (R.): *La Terre qui meurt,* Calman-Lévy, Paris, 1978
◆ BETHAM-EDWARDS: *East of Paris,* Hurst and Blackett, London, 1902
◆ DU BELLAY (J.): *Poète du XVIe Siècle,* Pléiade, Gallimard, Paris, 1953
◆ BENJAMIN (R.): *L'Homme à la recherche de son âme,* La Palatine, Geneva, 1943
◆ COLETTE: *Claudine à l'École,* Livre de Poche, Paris 1973
◆ COLETTE: *Looking Backwards,* trans. David Levay, Peter Owen, London, 1975
◆ DUMAS (A.): *La Reine Margot,* Dutton, New York/Dent, London, 1968
◆ FLAUBERT (G.): *Par les champs et les grèves,* Encre, Castillon-en-Couserans, 1984
◆ DE LA FONTAINE (J.): *Relation d'un Voyage de Paris en Limousin,* 1663
◆ GENEVOIX (M.): *Raboliot,* Éditions du Seuil, Paris, 1980
◆ GENEVOIX (M.): *Solognots de Sologne,* Chêne, Paris, 1977
◆ HUXLEY (A.): *The Devils of Loudun,* Penguin, Harmondsworth, 1971
◆ HUGO (V.): *Œuvres Complètes: Voyages,* Robert Laffont/Bouquins, Paris, 1987
◆ JAMES (H.): *A Little Tour in France,* from *Collected Travel Writings: the Continent,* The Libraries of America, New York, 1993
◆ PÉGUY (C.): *Œuvres Poétiques Complètes,* La Pléiade, Gallimard, Paris, 1957
◆ PROUST (M.): *À la recherche du temps perdu,* La Pléiade, Gallimard, Paris, 1954
◆ QUIGNARD (P.): *Les Escaliers de Chambord,* Gallimard, Paris, 1989
◆ RABELAIS (F.): *Gargantua and Pantagruel,* trans. Sir Thomas Urquhark

and Pierre le Motteux, Everyman's Library, London, Alfred A. Knopf, New York 1994
◆ RABELAIS (F.): *The Complete Works of François Rabelais,* trans. Frame (D.M.), University of California Press, Berkeley, 1991
◆ RONSARD (P.): *Œuvres complètes,* Pléiade, Gallimard, Paris, 1950
◆ SAND (G.): *François le champi,* Michel Lévy Frères, Paris, 1858
◆ SAND (G.): *Les Maîtres sonneurs,* Calmann-Lévy, Paris
◆ SAND (G.): *La Mare au Diable,* Calmann-Lévy, Paris
◆ SAND (G.): *The Miller of Angibault,* Weldon & Co., London, 1848
◆ SAND (G.): *Mémoires du'un touriste,* Albatros, Paris
◆ STENDHAL: *Mémoires d'un touriste,* Paris, Albatros, 1986
◆ TINDALL (G.): *Célestine, Voices from a French Village,* Sinclair-Stevenson, London, 1995
◆ DE VIGNEY (A.): *Cina-Mars, ou une Conjuration sous Louis XIII,* Folio/Gallimard, Paris, 1980
◆ VIVIER (R.), ROUGÉ (J.-M.) and MILLET (E.): *Contes et Légendes de Touraine,* Arrault, Tours, 1945
◆ WAUGH (E.): *The Diaries of Evelyn Waugh,* Michael Davie, Book Club Associates, London, 1976
◆ WORDSWORTH (W.): *The Prelude – or growth of a poet's mind,* ed. de Selincourt, OUP, London/New York 1970
◆ WORDSWORTH (W.): *Residence in France,* Oxford University Press, Oxford/New York, 1970
◆ ZOLA (E.): *La Terre,* G. Charpentier et Cie, Paris, 1887

**TRAVELERS'
◆ TALES ◆**

◆ EVELYN (J.): *The Diary of John Evelyn,* ed. de Beer (E.S.), 1955

◆ GERNHARD (C.G.): *Through France with Berzelius: Live Scholars and Dead Volcanoes,* Pergamon Press, Oxford, 1989
◆ LEE (V.): *Genius Loci – notes on places,* John Lane, The Bodley Head/John Lane Company, New York, 1908
◆ LOCKE (J.): *Locke's Travels in France, 1675–1679,* ed. Lough (J.), Cambridge University Press, Cambridge, 1953
◆ MORRIS (J.) ed: *Travels with Virginia Woolf,* The Hogarth Press, London, 1993
◆ TAINE (H.): *Journeys through France – being impressions of the provinces,* T. Fisher, Unwin, London, 1897
◆ WHARTON (E.): *Abroad – Selected Travel Writings 1888–1920,* Robert Hale, London, 1995
◆ WRAXALL (N.): *A Tour through the Western, Southern and Interior Provinces of France,* 1784
◆ YOUNG (A.): *Travels in France during the years 1787, 1788 and 1789,* Cambridge University Press, Cambridge, 1950

. ◆ GUIDES ◆

◆ DUIJKER (H.): *Loire, a wine-lover's touring guide,* Het Spectrum, Utrecht, 1994
◆ EPERON (J.): *The Loire,* Pan, London, 1992
◆ SEELY (J.): *The Loire Valley and its wines,* Lennard, London, 1989
◆ WADE (R.): *The companion guide to the Loire,* Collins, London, 1979

Abbreviations:
Bibl. Dép.: Bibliothèque
Départementale
Bibl. Mun.: Bibliothèque
Municipale
Bibl. Nat.: Bibliothèque
Nationale
RMN: Réunion des Musées
Nationaux, Paris
1 *Savonnières, Cher River*,
postcard, Bibl. Dép.
d'Indre-et-Loire.
2–3 *Blois, Sand sifter*,
postcard, Musée des
Beaux-Arts, Blois.
4 *Pont de Ruan, Drinking
trough*, postcard, Bibl. Dép.
d'Indre-et-Loire.
4–5 *Tours, The Frozen
Loire*, anon. photo, 1880,
Bibl. Mun. de Tours.
6 *Barrel-making workshop
in Touraine*, postcard, Bibl.
Dép. d'Indre-et-Loire.
6–7 *Chinon, Grape
harvest*, postcard, Bibl.
Dép. d'Indre-et-Loire.
9 *The Loire at Tours*,
autochrome, © Musée
Albert Kahn.
12/13 *The Loire near
Orléans*, © A. Grenet/Diaf.
The Loire at Gien,
© Jacques Guillard/Scope.
The Loire at Blois, © Éric
Guillemot/Gallimard.
Old windmill at Thouard,
© Jacques Guillard/Scope.
*St-Laurent des Eaux
nuclear power station*,
© Éric Guillemot/Gallimard.
33 *Consecration of David
and Coronation of Louis XII*,
diptych, 1521, Musée de
Cluny, Paris, © Giraudon.
34–5 *Emblems*, ill. by
Jean-Claude Sénée. *Book
of Hours of Anne de
Bretagne*, illumination,
16th century, Bibl. Nat.,
Paris. *Henri III handing
over the power insignia to
Henri IV*, tapestry, Château
d'Écouen, © Giraudon
36 *Huisseau Dolmen*, in
Album Launay, 19th
century, Bibl. Mun. de
Vendôme. *Aqueduc de
Luynes*, Claret-Martineau,
litho, 19th century, Bibl.
Dép. d'Indre-et-Loire.
37 *Éloge de la croix*,
Raban Maur,
Manuscript 145,
10th century, Bibl. Mun.
d'Orléans. *Anjou Cross*,
© Inventaire général des
Pays de Loire.
38 *Richard the Lionheart*,
engraving, 18th century,
© Roger Viollet. *Henri II
Plantagenet*, engraving,
idem.
39 *Battle of Agincourt*,
miniature in Vigiles de
Charles VII, Bibl. Nat.,
Paris. *Joan of Arc as a peasant girl*,
miniature from a
manuscript of her trial, Bibl.
Nat., Paris.
40 *The Royal Château of
Plessis-lès-Tours in 1480*,
A. Pernot, coll., La Riche,
Château du Plessis-lès-
Tours. *François I*, Jean
Clouet, 16th century,
Musée du Louvre, Paris,
© RMN. *Henri III and the*

Duc de Guise, Charles
Durupt, detail, oil on
canvas, Musée des Beaux-
Arts, Blois.
41 *Virgin and Child
Surrounded by Angels*,
Jean Fouquet, oil on
canvas, 16th century,
Musée d'Art, Anvers,
© Giraudon.
Louis XIV, H. Rigaud, oil on
canvas, 1701, Musée de
Versailles, © RMN.
Leonardo da Vinci, self-
portrait, oil on canvas, 16th
century, Musée des Offices,
Florence, © Giraudon.
42 *To the Sans-Culottes of
Orléans*, revolutionary
poster by Jean-Baptiste
Letourmy, Musée
historique, Orléans.
Napoléon III, H. Flandrin,
1863, oil on canvas, Musée
de Versailles, © RMN.
43 *St-Pierre-des-Corps
station*, postcard, Bibl. Dép.
d'Indre-et-Loire. *The
Prussians at Tours*, litho,
19th century, Musée des
Beaux-Arts de Tours.
Steam ship, detail from a
poster, 1840, priv. coll.
44 *Jean Royer inaugurates
the works along the Cher
River, 1967*, coll. Arch. de
la Nouvelle République,
coll. G. Proust. *Château
d'Ussé*, poster, Constant
Duval, © La Vie du Rail.
The TGV at Vendôme,
© Photothèque SNCF.
45 *The Loire between
Bréhemont and St-Michel*,
postcard, Bibl. Dép.
d'Indre-et-Loire.
46 *The "Fram"*, photo,
1898, Musée des Beaux-
Arts de Blois. *The Canal of
the Loire and the Cher*,
J. M. W. Turner, watercolor
and gouache, 1830,
Ashmolean Museum,
Oxford. Illustrations by
Maurice Pommier.
47 *Steam ship 21*, litho,
19th century, Musée du
Château des Ducs, Nantes.
View of Amboise, detail,
J. Ouvrié, oil on canvas,
1847, Musée de l'Hôtel de
Ville, Amboise. Illustrations
by Maurice Pommier.
48–9 *Flûtrau Port-Ligny on
the Vienne River, 1988*, coll.
Philippe Véteau.
Illustrations by Maurice
Pommier.
50–1 *Charles Langlais-
Riou, Bargeman at
Morannes*, oil on canvas,
1859, priv. coll.
Thanksgiving plaque,
Maquette de gabare,
Eugène Archambault,
polychrome wood, 1852,
coll. Church of St-Georges-
sur-Cher. Ellébéore.
Illustrations by Maurice
Pommier.
52 *Le Défaut*, Karl Reille,
watercolor, 1960, coll.
Galerie La Cymaise, Paris,
coll. Pierre Pitrou/Gallimard,
© ADAGP. *Le Pigache*,
card game © Christian de
la Terveille. *Untitled*, Henri
Koehler, oil on canvas,
1991, idem.

53 *Hunting "Buttons"*,
coll. Gallimard. *Chapel of
St-Hubert, Amboise*, litho.,
Bibl. Mun. de Tours. *Boar
Hunting Cry*, René
Princeteau, oil on canvas,
Galerie La Cymaise, Paris.
*Touraine Hunt, Chaudenay
Equipage, Forest of
Lancosme, Honors to the
Count of Amaury de
Louvencourt, 28 Dec.,
1982*, idem.
54–55 *Fishing on the Loire*,
postcard, Bibl. Dép.
d'Indre-et-Loire. *Loire
"terrine" recipe*, coll. Éric
Guillemot/Gallimard.
56 *Typical produce*,
coll. Gallimard.
58–9 *St-Benoît Chevet*,
color J. S. Roveri, Bibl.
du Patrimoine, Paris.
*Elevation of the Church
of St-Aignan*, Bibl. du
Patrimoine, Paris. *Ground
plan of the Abbey Church
of Fontevrault*, by J.S.
Roveri. *Detail from the
Tavant wall paintings and
ground plan of the crypt*,
© Serge Chirol. *Elevation
of the Porch of the Church
of Chênehute-les-Tuffeaux*,
ill. by J. S. Roveri. *Elevation
of the bell tower of Notre-
Dame de Cunault*, Bibl. du
Patrimoine, Paris.
60–1 *Elevation of the
Chapel of St-Hubert de
Blois and of St-Gatien
Cathedral*, ill. Gallimard.
*Elevation of Orléans
Cathedral*, Cross section of
the choir, Bibl. du
Patrimoine, Paris. *Detail
from the frescos at the
Château de Pimpéan*,
© Jean-Paul Gislard.
Diagram of Angevin vaults,
ill. by Bruno Lenormand.
62–3 *Elevation and detail
of the door of the Collegiate
Church of Montrésor*, Bibl.
du Patrimoine, Paris.
*Ground plan and façade of
the Church of St-Vincent de
Paul*, ill. Gallimard.
*Elevation of the porch of
the Church of the Minimes*,
Tours, idem. *Elevation of
the Church of Notre-Dame-
des-Ardilliers*, Saumur, ill.
by Philippe Candé.
64–5 *Elevation of the
Château d'Angers*, ill. by
Philippe Candé. *View from
horseback of the Château
de Sully*, Bibl. du
Patrimoine, Paris.
*Detail of the
machicolations, Porte
des Cordeliers, Loches*,
ill. by Jean-Marie Guillou.
*Elevation and ground plan
of the Château de Chinon*,
idem. *Diagram of the
Loches keep*, ill. Gallimard.
*Ground plan of the
Beaugency keep*, Bibl. du
Patrimoine, Paris.
66–7 *Elevation of the
Château de Langeais*,
*Elevation of the Château
de Chaumont-sur-Loire*,
*Elevation of the Louis XII
Wing at Blois*, *Elevation of
the Château de Gien*,
Elevation of the Château

d'Amboise, Bibl. du
Patrimoine, Paris.
68–9 *Detail of a
monogram of François I*,
Elevation of the staircase
at Blois, Elevation of the
balconies at Blois,
Elevation and plan of the
façade at Villesavin, Bibl.
du Patrimoine, Paris.
*Detail of the fireplace at
Chambord*, ill. by Claude
Quiec.
70–1 *Elevation of the
Gaston d'Orléans Wing*,
Bibl. du Patrimoine, Paris
*Detail of a window at the
Château de Cheverny*,
*Elevation of the Château
de Valençay*, ill. by Philip
Candé. *Elevation of the
Château de Cheverny* an
of the Château de Ménar.
ill. Gallimard.
72–3 *Cross section of the
Maison Rouge at Chinon*,
Detail of building process
ill. by Maurice Pommier.
*Detail of the Maison
d'Adam, Angers*, coll.
Éric Guillemot/Gallimard.
*Construction of the
Maison d'Adam*, *Detail
of a Renaissance window*
Angers, ill. by Philippe
Candé. *Detail of
noggings*, ill. Gallimard.
*Construction of a house
at Tours*, Bibl. du
Patrimoine, Paris.
74–5 *Construction and
ground plan of the Maiso
Pierre-du-Duy at Tours*,
*Construction of the Hôtel
Pincé at Angers*,
*Construction of the façad
of the Hôtel Cabu at
Orléans*, Bibl. du
Patrimoine, Paris.
*Construction of hôtels
in the Rue d'Escures at
Orléans*, ill. by Phillipe
Candé. *Construction of th
Évêché de Blois and of th
Hôtel Lefebvre at Tours*, il
Gallimard.
76–7 *Troglodyte dwelling
and details*, ill. by Philippe
Candé. *House in Sologne*
ill. Gallimard.
78–9 *Watermill with a
vertical wheel*, *Brickyards*
ill. Gallimard. *Tower
windmill*, *Pivot windmill*,
Cave windmill, ill. by
Maurice Pommier.
80 *The Well*, ill. by Bruno
Lenormand. *Dovecote*,
Loge de Gâtine,
Winegrower's Cottage,
ill. by Philippe Candé.
81 *View of the Mill and the
Côte de St-Avertin*, Antoine
Rougeot, oil on canvas,
19th century Musée des
Beaux-Arts, Tours.
82 *Ocre léger à la tache
violette*, Olivier Debré,
Oil on canvas, Musée des
Beaux-Arts, Tours. *Jardin
de la France*, Max Ernst,
oil on canvas, 1962,
Musée d'Art moderne,
Centre Georges Pompidou
Paris.
83 *Gris-bleu de Loire à la
Tache verte*, Olivier Debré,
oil on canvas, 1977, Musée
des Beaux-Arts, Tours.

4–5 *Fishermen on the banks of the Loire at Tours*, detail, Gabriel Firmin Bogier, oil on canvas, 19th century, Musée des Beaux-Arts de Rouen. *Loire Landscape*, Édouard Debat-Ponsan, oil on wood, Musée des Beaux-Arts, Tours. *Pasture by the Loire*, Rodeau, oil on canvas, idem. *Clouds*, Paul Fachet, idem.
6–7 *The Château de Chambord*, E. Dupuis, oil on wood, 1853, Musée des Beaux-Arts, Orléans. *Courtyard of the Château de Blois*, Crace, watercolor drawing, 1847, © The British Architectural Library, RIBA, London. *Château de Blois, Galerie des Loges, entrance of the Château*, woodcarvings, Grace, drawings, idem.
8 *La Chute de Jéricho, Jours landscape*, illumination in *Antiquités judaïques*, 16th century, Bibl. Nat., Giraudon.
9 *View of Tours*, after Turner, litho., priv. coll., coll. Gallimard.
10 *View of Amboise*, litho., priv. coll., coll. Gallimard.
12 *View of Chaumont*, litho., priv. coll., coll. Gallimard.
15 *Amboise Forest, Rémeaux marsh*, postcard, Bibl. Dép. d'Indre-et-Loire.
17 *View of Angers*, litho., priv. coll., coll. Gallimard.
18–9 *View of Luynes*, litho., priv. coll., coll. Gallimard.
11 *View of Chambord*, litho., priv. coll.
11 Gallimard.
12 *View of Loches*, litho., priv. coll., coll. Gallimard.
13 *Winegrower at work*, postcard, Bibl. Dép. Indre-et-Loire.
14 *Tasting*, postcard, Bibl. Dép. d'Indre-et-Loire. *The Wine Press*, miniature, detail, Bibl. Mun. de Tours.
15 *View of Chaumont*, lemon, oil on canvas, 1909, Musée des Beaux-Arts de Blois.
16–7 *Aerial views of the Loire*, coll. Éric Guillemot/Gallimard.
18 *Château de Chaumont, Chanteloup Pagoda, Château d'Azay-le-Rideau*, coll. Éric Guillemot/Gallimard.
19 *Château de Fougères-sur-Bièvre*, © Michel Guillard/Scope. *Château de Cheverny*, coll. Éric Guillemot/Gallimard. *Château de Beauregard*, © Serge Chirol.
10 *The Loire*, coll. Patrick Vaud/Gallimard. *The Loire at Menars*, © Michel Guillard/Scope. *The Loire in winter*, coll. Éric Guillemot/Gallimard.
11 *View of Orléans*, Pratt-Pries/Diaf.
12 *Philippe VI*, illumination, 1306, French Manuscript 2258,

Folio 4, verso, Bibl. Nat., Paris.
113 *Orléans*, stamp, priv. coll. *View of the Cathedral*, © Benoît Voisin.
114 *The Cathedral, Choir, Woodcarvings in the choir*, © Serge Chirol. *Charles d'Orléans*, tapestry, detail, 15th century, Musée des Arts Déco, Paris, DR. *Chevet of the Cathedral*, litho., Charles Pensée, 1848, priv. coll.
115 *Portrait of the "Bastard of Orléans", Comte de Dunois*, Tours School of painting, c. 1450, coll. Hengel. *La Fête Gloanec*, P Gauguin, oil on canvas, 1889, © Musée des Beaux-Arts d'Orléans. *La Liberté*, Revolutionary print, Jean-Baptiste Le Tourny, 1792, Musée Historique, Orléans.
116 *Signature of Joan of Arc*, © Louis Falquet. *Siege of Orléans by the English*, miniature, in *Les Chroniques abrégées des Rois de France*, 15th century, Bibl. Nat., Paris. *Joan of Arc in Armour*, miniature, 15th century, Archives Nationales, Paris, © Louis Falquet. *"Battle of the Herrings"*, miniature, in *Vigiles de Charles VII*, Bibl. Nat., Paris.
117 *Joan of Arc Entering Orléans*, Jean-Jacques Sherrer, oil on canvas, 19th century, © Musée des Beaux-Arts d'Orléans. *Bombardes, couleuvrines et boulets*, © Louis Falquet. *The Maid, The Battle, The Battle of Patay*, Franck Craig, oil on canvas, 1907, Musée d'Orsay, Paris, © RMN.
118 *Hôtel Groslot*, © Benoît Voisin. *Town Hall*, © Michel Guillard/Scope. *Hôtel Groslot, Statue of Joan of Arc and detail of window*, coll. Patrick Léger/Gallimard.
118–19 *The Dancer*, bronze, Treasure of Neuvy-en-Sullias, Musée historique et archéologique, Orléans, coll. Musée des Beaux-Arts, Orléans.
119 *Hôtel Cabu*, watercolor, Bibl. du Patrimoine, Paris, coll. Gallimard. *Hôtel Cabu*, coll. Patrick Léger/Gallimard. *Treasure of Neuvy-en-Sullias*, stamp, priv. coll.
120 *Georges V Bridge*, © Jean-Paul Gislard. *Hôtel du Cerceau*, watercolor, Bibl. du Patrimoine, Paris, coll. Gallimard. *Portrait of Étienne Dolet*, engraving, Bibl. Nat., Paris. *The Préfecture*, litho., priv. coll.
121 *Rue Royale*, © Michel Guillard/Scope. *Maison de la Coquille*, © Benoît Voisin.
122 *Hôtel Toutin*, © Benoît Voisin. *Hôtel Hatte*, L. Vaudoyer, watercolor, 1851, Bibl. du Patrimoine,

Paris, coll. Gallimard. *Charles Péguy*, © Roger Viollet.
122–3 *Place du Martroi, Statue of Joan of Arc*, coll. Patrick Léger/Gallimard.
123 *Place du Martroi*, coll. Patrick Léger/Gallimard.
124 *Portrait of Jean Zay*, all rights reserved. *Château de la Source*, © Jean-Paul Gislard.
125 *Parc Floral de la Source*, © Jean-Paul Gislard. *Château de la Ferté-St-Aubin*, © Alain Beignet. *Scene from the movie "La Règle du Jeu"*, Jean Renoir, 1939, all rights reserved.
126 *Combleux*, © Jean-Paul Gislard. *Combleux*, © Michel Guillard/Scope. *St-Jean-de-Braye, Fonderie Bollée*, coll. Patrick Léger/Gallimard. *Maurice Genevoix*, photo, 1960, © Roger Viollet.
127 *Château de Châteauneuf-sur-Loire*, © Bernard Régent/Diaf. *The Seed-sower*, stamp, priv. coll.
128 *Germigny Oratory*, watercolor, Bibl. du Patrimoine, Paris, coll. Gallimard. *Germigny, interior and exterior of the Church*, © Serge Chirol.
129 *Germigny, mosaic*, © Serge Chirol. *Abbey of St-Benoît-sur-Loire, phevet*, © Serge Chirol.
130 *St-Benoît-sur-Loire, porch*, © Jacques Guillard/Scope. *St-Benoît-sur-Loire, porch*, © Serge Chirol. *Chapiteau*, © Jacques Guillard/Scope. *Chapiteau*, © Serge Chirol
131 *House of Max Jacob*, coll. Patrick Léger/Gallimard. *Detail of the paving*, © Serge Chirol. *Max-Jacob*, © Roger Viollet
132 *Château de Sully*, © Serge Chirol. *Château de Sully, structure*, © Bernard Régent/Diaf
132–3 *The 1836 Bridge at Sully*, Charles Pensée, litho., priv. coll.
133 *Portrait of the Duc de Sully*, Norblain de la Courdaine, oil on canvas, 19th century, Musée de Versailles, © Popovitch/ RMN. *Courtyard of Château de Sully*, © Serge Chirol. *View of Gien*, © Xavier Richer/Hoa-Qui.
134–5 *Gien earthenware*, Musée de la Faïence, Gien, all rights reserved.
136 *Anne de Beaujeu*, detail from the Bourbons Reredos, Maître de Moulins, late 15th century, Moulins Cathedral, © Giraudon. *Château de Gien*, © Musée de la Chasse, Gien. *Gien, Musée de la Chasse, François Desportes Room*.
137 *Bridge-Canal at Briare*, ill. by P. Biard,

© Gallimard. *Bridge-Canal at Briare*, © Voies Navigables de France.
138 *Le Roman de la Rose*, miniature, 15th century, Bibl. Nat., Paris.
139 *View of Beaugency*, © Michel Guillard/Scope. *Courtyard of the Château Dunois*, Jourdain Pellieux, oil on canvas, 1839, Musée Dunois, Beaugency. *Beaugency, Town Hall*, L. Vaudoyer, watercolor, 1845, Bibl. du Patrimoine, Paris.
140 *Plan de Talcy*, ADLC. *Courtyard of the Château de Talcy*, © Jacques Guillard/Scope. *Château de Menars, detail from the Eleven Views and of the Parc de Menars*, Emmanuel Lansyer, 1879, Musée des Beaux-Arts de Tours. *Marquise de Pompadour*, F. Boucher, 18th century, Musée du Louvre, Paris, © RMN.
141 *Ermine*, stained-glass window, Château de Blois, Musée des Beaux-Arts, Blois.
142–3 *Map of Blois*, © Atelier de Bayonne.
144 *Coat of arms*, detail, Mangier, litho., 1675, Musée des Beaux-Arts, Blois. *Stone bust*, sculpture found at Blois, 1st century, Musée archéologique, Blois. *Ball at the Court of the Valois*, detail, oil on canvas, 16th century, Musée des Beaux-Arts, Blois. © Giraudon. *Blois*, watercolor, litho., 16th century, Archives Départementales de Loir-et-Cher. *Portrait of Gaston d'Orléans on Horseback*, Claude Denuet, oil on slate, 1630, Musée des Beaux-Arts, Blois. *Louis XII's signature*, 16th century coll. Xavier Anquetin-Coréav. *Blois, Poulain Chocolate Factory*, photo, 1875. Musée des Beaux-Arts, Blois.
145 *View of Blois*, coll. Daniel Castets. *Ball at the Court of the Valois*, detail, oil on canvas, 16th century, Musée des Beaux-Arts, Blois. © Giraudon. *Watch*, Font-Laurier, c. 1650, Musée des Beaux-Arts, Blois.
146 *Allegoric Portrait of Henri III*, drawing, 16th century, Bibl. Nat., Paris. *Meeting of the États Généraux at the Château de Blois in 1588*, drawing, 15th century, idem. *Assassination of the Duc de Guise*, after P. Delaroche, oil on canvas, 1834, Musée des Beaux-Arts, Blois. *Henri III and the Duc de Guise*, Pierre-Charles Comte,oil on canvas, 1855, Musée des Beaux-Arts, Blois.
147 *Henri III*, attr. to François Quesnel, oil on

canvas, 16th century, Musée du Louvre, Paris, © RMN. *The Three Guises*, detail, oil on wood, 16th century, Musée des Beaux-Arts, Blois, © Lauros-Giraudon. *Henri III handing over the insignia of power to Henri IV*, tapestry, late 16th century, Château d'Écouen, Musée nat. de la Renaissance, © Giraudon.

148 *François I Staircase*, Félix Duban, watercolor, 19th century, Bibl. du Patrimoine. *Seal of Louis II, Comte de Blois et de Chastillon*, Blois, Archives Départementales de Loir-et-Cher. *The Queen's Escape From the Château de Blois, 1619*, Rubens, Galerie Médicis, © RMN. *The Chapel of the Château de Blois*, Albert Robida, drawing in *La Vieille France, la Touraine*, priv. coll.

149 *Cul-de-lampe*, Château de Blois, coll. Éric Guillemot/Gallimard. *Porcupine*, stained-glass window, Château de Blois, coll. Château de Blois. *Sculptures of the Château de Blois*, details, in *Mémoires* de A. Félibien, 1681. coll. Château de Blois. *Joan of Arc*, stained-glass window, 20th century, coll. Château de Blois.

150 *Catherine de Médicis*, earthenware, coll. Château de Blois. *Mark of Ulysse on earthenware*, 19th century, coll. Château de Blois. *Galerie des Loges*, autochrome, early 20th century, © Musée Albert-Kahn.

151 *Emblem of Claude de France*, Margaret Aulton, drawing, 1925, priv. coll. *Fireplace in the great hall*, coll. Château de Blois. *Earthenware by Ulysse*, coll. Château de Blois. *Salle des États*, 1588, coll. Château de Blois.

152 *Madeleine of Scotland*, attr. to Corneille de Lyon, 16th century, Musée des Beaux-Arts, Blois. *Virgin and Child With Musicians*, Marco d'Oggiono, oil on wood, early 16th century, idem.

153 *Anne de Bretagne Oratory*, Albert Robida, drawing, in *La Vieille France, La Touraine*, priv. coll. *Portrait of Robert-Houdin*, Bibl. Mun. de Blois. *Church of St-Nicolas*, elevation of the northern side, Bibl. du Patrimoine, Paris.

154 *Blois, Rue du Palais*, knocker, Musée des Beaux-Arts, Blois. *Blois, Rue du Palais*, knocker, idem. *Façade over the*

Courtyard of the Hôtel d'Alluye, ill. by Jean-Claude Sénée. *Views of Blois* (detail), *Degrés Denis Papin*, steps, Eugène Gervais, 1865, Musée des Beaux-Arts de Blois. *Blois, Garden of the Episcopal Palace*, coll. Jean-Noël Thibault. *Fountain of the Place Louis XII*, Albert Robida, drawing, in *La Vieille France, la Touraine*, priv. coll.

155 *Jacques-Gabriel Bridge, Blois*, aerial view, coll. Éric Guillemot/Gallimard. *Cloisters of St-Saturnin*, H. Sauvage, oil on canvas, Musée des Beaux-Arts, Châteauroux.

156 *Hunting Scene in the Parc de Chambord*, detail, tapestry, Château de Chambord, © Ed. Gaud.

157 *Map of the Park and of the Château de Chambord*, after Toussaint Dubreuil, Château de Chambord, © Ed. Gaud. *St-Dyé-sur Loire, Ramparts along the Loire*, postcard, early 20th century, Archives Départementales de Loir-et-Cher.

158 *The Staircase*, watercolor, Bibl. du Patrimoine, Paris. *Chambord Staircase*, engraving, Archives Départementales de Loir-et-Cher. *Chambord Staircase*, Albert Robida, drawing in *La Vieille France, la Touraine*, priv. coll. *Chateaubriand*, A. L. Girodet-Trioson, oil on canvas, 19th century, Musée de Versailles, © RMN. *Château de Chambord*, northwestern façade, watercolor, Bibl. du Patrimoine, Paris.

159 *Salamander*, bas-relief, Château de Chambord, © Ed. Gaud. *François I*, Titian, oil on canvas, 16th century, Musée du Louvre, Paris, © RMN. *Chambord Terraces*, detail, coll. Serge Chirol.

162 *Charles V*, Van Orley, oil on canvas, Museum of Capodimonte, Naples, © Alinari-Giraudon. *Château de Chambord*, Leonardo da Vinci, 16th century, sketch in *Codex Atlanticus*, Bibl. Ambrosia, Milan. *Château de Chambord*, detail, coll. Éric Guillemot/Gallimard. *The Hunt*, tapestry, © Ed. Gaud.

163 *Château de Chambord*, aerial view, coll. Éric Guillemot/Gallimard. *Leonardo da Vinci*, self-portrait, © Scope. *The Lantern*, litho, 19th century, Archives Départementales de Loir-et-Cher.

164 *Château de Chambord*, P.D. Martin, oil on canvas, Musée de Versailles, © RMN. *Le Bourgeois Gentilhomme*, Briffard et Fauvé, engraving, Musée de la Comédie-Française. *M. Jourdain's Fencing Lesson*, Fesh and Whirsker, gouache, idem.

165 *Le Maréchal de Saxe*, M. Q. de La Tour, pastels, Musée Carnavalet, © Giraudon. *The Comte de Chambord, Baron de Schwiter*, oil on canvas, 19th century, Château de Chambord, Constant Duval, poster, © La Vie du Rail. *Peau d'Âne*, Jacques Demy, 1969, priv. coll.

166 *Château de Villesavin, Medallion, Moat*, coll. Jean-Noël Thibault. *Château de Villesavin, Structure*, coll. Gallimard. *Bust of François I*, idem. *Château de Villesavin*, © Daniel Sudres/ Scope.

167 *Château de Beauregard, Cabinet des Grelots*, © Ed. Gaud. *Château de Beauregard*, aerial view, coll. Éric Guillemot/Gallimard. *Château de Beauregard, Animated clock*, 16th and 17th century, © Castelet.

168 *Château de Beauregard, Galerie des Illustres*, © Ed. Gaud. *Restoration stages*, coll. Marc Philippe. *Three portraits at various stages of restoration*, idem.

169 *Portrait of Sébastien du Portugal ("French" appearance)*, coll. Marc Philippe. *Original Portrait of Sébastien du Portugal*, idem. *Tiled floor of the Galerie des Illustres*, Delft, 17th century, © Castelet.

170 *Cheverny*, poster, © La Vie du Rail. *Main staircase of the Château de Cheverny*, coll. Serge Chirol. *Ceiling of the Château de Cheverny*, coll. idem.

171 *Château de la Loire*, stamp, Musée de la Poste. *Tintin*, Hergé, four frames from *Red Rackham's Treasure* and *The Castafiore Emerald*, © Casterman.

172 *Château de Troussay, stone carvings*, coll. Jean-Noël Thibault. *Château de Cheverny, interior views*, idem. *The Cheverny Hunt*, postcard, early 20th century, Archives Départementales de Loir-et-Cher. *Château de Cheverny*, tapestry, detail, coll. Jean-Noël Thibault. *Cheverny vineyard*, © Jean Daniel Sudres/Scope. *Bottle of wine from Cheverny vineyards*, coll. Gallimard.

173 *Sign*, coll. Gallimard. *Château de Troussay*, coll. Jean-Noël Thibault. *Château de Troussay*, interior and exterior déco, coll. Jean-Noël Thibault.

174 *Marcilly-en Gault, Traditional Houses*, coll. Alain Beignet. *Large leaf reedmace*, idem. *Orléanais government map*, detail, Musée de Sologne, Romorantin-Lanthenay. *Napoleon III Visiting the Coudray Farm*, Raymond Esbrac, oil on canvas, 1851, Musée des Beaux-Arts, Orléans.

175 *Rush in flower, Heather, Broom, Villeherviers, St-Viâtre, Grande Corboie Marsh, Silver birches, Sologne mutton*, coll. Alain Beignet.

176 *Fougères-sur-Bièvre*, postcard, Archives Départementales de Loir-et-Cher. *Château de Fougères, Renaissance Door*, ill. by Jean-Claude Sénée. *Château de Fougère*, ill. by Jean-Marc Lanusse.

177 *Chaumont*, Constant Duval, poster, 1921, © La Vie du Rail. *Diane de Poitiers*, oil on canvas, coll. Château de Chaumont.

178 *Well of the Château de Chaumont*, coll. Gallimard. *Château de Chaumont*, Margaret Aulton, litho., 1925, priv. coll. *Château de Chaumont*, aerial view, coll. Éric Guillemot/Gallimard.

179 *Château d'Amboise* first representation, miniature, coll. Musée de l'Hôtel de Ville, Amboise.

182 *Charles VII*, after Charles VII's master painter, oil on wood, Musée Condé, Chantilly, © Lauros-Giraudon. *Château d'Amboise*, wood carving, © Jean Daniel Sudres/Scope.

183 *Execution of the Amboise Conspirators*, engraving, 19th century, Bibl. Mun. de Tours. *François I*, drawing, 1569, Musée Condé, Chantilly, © Giraudon. *Louis-Napoleon Bonaparte releases Abdel Kader*, Ange Tissier, oil on canvas, 1861, Musée de Versailles, © RMN.

184 *Leonard da Vinci*, stamp, Musée de la Poste, Paris. *Amboise*, litho, 19th century, Bibl. Mun. de Tours. *Terraces of the Château*, litho, 19th century, idem. *Château d'Amboise*, © Ed. Gaud. *Plan of the Château d'Amboise*, Du Cerceau, Bibl. Nat., Paris.

185 *Le Clos-Lucé at Amboise*, stamp, Musée de la Poste, Paris.

86 Multiple-Opening rearm, Leonardo da nci, drawing, 16th entury, © Jean-Daniel uldres/Scope. Plane, odel IBM, © idem. arachute, Leonardo da nci, 16th century, idem. Parachute, model IBM, © idem. Death of eonardo da Vinci, oil on anvas, 19th century, Vincent Godeau.
87 Leonardo da Vinci, elf-portrait. © Scope. elicopter, model IBM, Serge Chirol.
88 Mary Magdalene, the Church of St-Denis, oll. François Joly. locktower and Church St-Denis, © Scope. he Drowned Woman, hurch of St-Denis, oll. François Joly. View the Château d'Amboise rom the Road Between lois andTours, Dagnan, ho., 19th century, rchives épartementales d'Indre Loire.
89 Church of St-Denis, p, detail, coll. François oly. Façade of the Town all, watercolor, 1881, ibl. du Patrimoine, Paris. olychrome Virgin, wood, 5th century, Musée de Hôtel de Ville, Amboise.
90 Max-Ernst Fountain, oll. François Joly. View Amboise from Île d'Or, oll. idem. Le Grenier de ésar, idem. The Duc e Choiseul, Van Loo Vorkshop, 18th century, usée de l'Hôtel de Ville, mboise.
91 Île d'Or, oll. François Joly. hanteloup Pagoda, abriel Bouret, oil on anvas, 19th century, oll, Association des mis de Chanteloup, usée des Beaux-Arts , ours.
92 Chanteloup Pagoda, etails, coll. François Joly. océ, Church, postcard, arly 20th century Bibl. lun. de Tours.
93 Panoramic View of ours, P.A. Demachy, l on canvas, 19th entury, Musée des eaux-Arts, Tours.
94-5 Map of Tours, Atelier de Bayonne.
96 Tours coat of arms, uot, gouache, 19th century, Musée des Beaux-rts, Grégoire de Tours, amp, Musée de La Poste, aris. omb of the Children of harles VII and Anne de retagne, coll. Gallimard. ours Cathedral, Monthelier, ho., 19th century, rchives épartementales d'Indre Loire.
97 Psalette Cloisters, atercolor, 1891, rchives épartementales d'Indre Loire. St-Gatien

Cathedral, stained-glass windows, coll. Éric Guillemot/Gallimard.
198 Taste, Abraham Bosse, oil on canvas, 17th century, Musée des Beaux-Arts, Tours. Christ in the Garden of Olives, Andrea Mantegna, 15th century, idem.
199 St-Symphorien footbridge at Tours, postcard, early 20th century, Bibl. Dép. d'Indre et Loire. Church of St-Julien, detail, Éric Guillemot/Gallimard. Musée du Compagnonnage, sign, coll. Éric Guillemot/ Gallimard.
200 Colors of Devoirant and their travel boxes, 1880, coll. François Icher. Compagnon Maréchal-Ferrant du Devoir Dressed in Full Regalia, in Le Compagnonnage illustré, Agricol Perdiguier, 1860. Masterpiece, Musée du Compagnonnage, Tours, coll. Valoire, Blois.
201 Colors of Premier Compagnon, coll. François Icher. Grand chef-d'œuvre des compagnons cordiers exécuté, Barthès, © Roger Viollet. Champ de conduite de Tours, Auguste Lemoine, 1838, Musée du Compagnonnage, Tours, coll. Valoire, Blois. Pommel of the Staff, coll. François Icher. Journeymen's mother, idem.
202 Porte Place Foire-le-Roi, detail, coll. Éric Guillemot/Gallimard. Bibl. Mun., elevation of the main façade, Bibl. Mun. de Tours. Hôtel du Commerce, coll. Éric Guillemot/ Gallimard.
203 Tours, Rue Nationale, postcard, early 20th century, Bibl. Dép. d'Indre-et-Loire. The Fountain of the Americans, coll. Éric Guillemot/ Gallimard. The Collapse of Wilson Bridge, ADIL, Fonds Arsicaud.
204 The Collapse of the Abbey of St-Martin, litho., Bibl. Mun. de Tours. St-Martin Basilica, Charlemagne Tower, coll. François Joly. The Clocktower, idem. Charlemagne Tower, litho, 19th century, Bibl. Dép. d'Indre-et-Loire.
205 Charlemagne Tower and St-Martin Basilica, coll. Patrick Lavaud. St-Martin, bas-relief, idem. St-Martin Cloister, idem.
206 Death of Saint Martin at Candes, illumination, Bibl. Mun. de Tours. Saint Martin, illumination, idem.
207 Death of Saint Martin, illumination, Bibl. Mun. de Tours. Hours of Saint Étienne,

Knight of St-Martin, drawing, Musée du Louvre, Paris, © Giraudon. Saint Martin preaching in the Forests of Touraine, André Bachant, oil of canvas, 1949, Musée des Beaux-Arts de Tours. St-Martin Basilica, Tours, coll. Patrick Lavaud. St-Martin Basilica, Tours, idem. Church of Marmoutier, litho., 19th century, Bibl. Mun. de Tours.
208 Hôtel Gouin, coll. Éric Guillemot/ Gallimard. Place Plumereau, © C.L.D. Hôtel Gouin, bas-relief, coll. Éric Guillemot/ Gallimard.
209 Street signs, Staircase, coll. Gallimard. Garden of St-Pierre le Puillier, coll. Éric Guillemot/Gallimard. Door of the House of Tristan, Albert Robida, drawing in La Vielle France, la Touraine, priv. coll.
210-1 Houses at Place Pumereau, ill. by Maurice Pommier.
212 Market, Place du Grand Marché, postcard, early 20th century, Bibl. Dép. d'Indre-et-Loire. Homage to Kandisky, Musée du Gemmail, Tours, © Michel Guilllard/Scope. The Tournois Pound, coll. Gallimard. Place de Châteauneuf, postcard, early 20th century Bibl. Dép. d'Indre-et-Loire.
213 The Basil Fair, © CLD. Street signs, coll. Éric Guillemot/ Gallimard.
214 Tours, Palace of Justice and Town Hall, postcard, early 20th century, Bibl. Mun. de Tours. Victor Laloux, oil on canvas, 1883, Musée des Beaux-Arts de Tours. Tours, Boulevard Béranger, coll. Éric Guillemot/Gallimard.
215 Tours, Palais des Congrès, coll. Vinci, Centre international de congrès de Tours. Alfred Mame, engraving, 19th century, Bibl. Mun. de Tours. Rue Léonard-de-Vinci, coll. Éric Guillemot/ Gallimard. Jardin des Prébendes d'Oé, Delpeire, oil on canvas, Musée des Beaux-Arts de Tours.
216 The Cher River, coll. Gallimard.Château de Montpoupon, ill.
217 View of the Collegiate Church of the Château de St-Aignan, © Jean-Daniel Sudres/ Scope. Collegiate Church of St-Aignan, frescos of the crypt, © Serge Chirol. Parc de Beauval, coll. Jean-Noël Thibault.
218-9 Château de Chenonceau, © Serge

Chirol. View of the Château de Chenonceau with detailed sections, ill. by Philippe Biard.
220 Diana's Bath, François Clouet, oil on canvas, Musée des Beaux-Arts, Rouen. Louise de Lorraine, drawing, 16th century, Bibl. Nat., Paris. Diane de Poitiers, drawing, 16th century, Musée Condé, Chantilly, © Giraudon. Catherine de Médicis, oil on canvas, 16th century, Galleria degli Uffizi, Florence, © Giraudon.
221 Château de Chenonceau, litho, 19th century, Bibl. Mun. de Tours. Chenonceau, Constant Duval, poster, © La Vie du Rail. Jean-Jacques Rousseau in the open air, engraving, 17th century, © Roger Viollet. Madame Dupin, Nattier, oil on canvas, 18th century, Château de Chenonceau, © Pix.
222 View of the Château de Chenonceau, litho, 19th century, Bibl. Mun. de Tours. Allée de Chenonceau, © Michel Gaillard/Scope. Thomas Bohier, profile and coat of arms, engraving, Bibl. Nat., Paris. Touraine, Mereno, poster, 1902, © La Vie du Rail.
223 Château de Chenonceau, wine label, priv. coll. La Tour des Marques, coll. Gallimard. Chapel of the Château de Chenonceau, litho., 19th century, Bibl. Mun. de Tours. The Gallery, coll. Serge Chirol. Chenonceau, view from the town, postcard, early 20th century, Bibl. Dép. d'Indre-et-Loire.
224 Tour St-Antoine and Porte des Cordeliers, coll. Serge Chirol. Town of Loches, litho, 19th century, Bibl. Mun. de Tours.
225 Loches Keep Whitehead, litho, 19th century, Archives Départementales d'Indre-et-Loire., coll. Patrick Lavaud/Gallimard.
226 Château de Loches, E. Bruneau, watercolor, Bibl. du Patrimoine, Paris. Stained-glass window of the royal residence, coll. Patrick Lavaud/Gallimard. Iron cage, litho, 19th century, Bibl. Dép. d'Indre-et-Loire.
227 The Royal City, E. Bruneau, watercolor, Bibl. du Patrimoine, Paris. Stained-glass window of the royal residence, coll. Patrick Lavaud/ Gallimard. Virgin and Child Surrounded by Angels, Jean Fouquet, oil on canvas, Musée d'Art, Anvers, © Giraudon. Loches, Oratory of Anne

de Bretagne, coll. Patrick Lavaud/Gallimard.
228 Vigny, Nadar, photo, © Roger Viollet. *Loches, Rue Picois*, postcard, late 19th century, Bibl. Dép. d'Indre-et-Loire. *Loches, Church of St-Ours*, detail of the portal, coll. Patrick Lavaud/Gallimard. *Loches, the Collegiate Church*, postcard, early 20th century, coll. Bibl. Mun. de Tours.
229 *Loches, Maison du Centaure*, bas-relief, coll. Patrick Lavaud/Gallimard. *View of Loches*, Emmanuel Lansyer, oil on canvas, 19th century, Musée Lansyer, Loches. *Japanese armour*, idem. *Loches*, coll. Patrick Lavaud/Gallimard.
230 *Bell Tower of the Trinité*, Hevrion, wash drawing, Bibl. du Patrimoine, Paris. *Chartreuse du Liget, portal*, © CLD. *Chapelle du Liget*, watercolor, 19th century, Bibl. du Patrimoine, Paris.
231 *Château de Montrésor*, © Jean Daniel Sudres/Scope. *Descent from the Cross*, Jean Fouquet, oil on canvas, coll. Church of Nouans-les-Fontaines, coll. Serge Chirol.
232 *Cheese and wine*, coll. Serge Chirol.
232–3 *Exterior and interior views of the Château de Valençay*, © Serge Chirol.
234 *Rue de la Mairie*, coll. Patrick Lavaud/Gallimard. *Azay-le-Rideau, the Château*, Victor Petit, litho, 19th century, Bibl. Mun. de Tours.
235 *Château d'Azay-le-Rideau*, Constant Duval, poster, 20th century, © La Vie du Rail. *Sculpted ermine*, coll. Patrick Lavaud/Gallimard.
236–7 *Château d'Azay-le-Rideau*, Jacques Hardion, 1904, Bibl. du Patrimoine, Paris, coll. Gallimard.
238 *Façade and staircase of Azay-le-Rideau*, litho, 19th century, Bibl. Dép. d'Indre-et-Loire. *Sculpted salamander*, coll. Patrick Lavaud/Gallimard. *Engraved wood panels*, idem. *Azay-le-Rideau*, aerial view, coll. Éric Guillemot/Gallimard.
239 *Château d'Azay-le-Rideau*, © Serge Chirol.
240 *Décor of the Church of Azay-le-Rideau*, © Serge Chirol. *Saché*, © CLD. *Saché, outside view of the Château*, Balzac's bedroom, © CLD. *Balzac's*

Bedroom, Maxime Dastugue, after Louis Boulanger, oil on canvas, 19th century, Musée de Versailles, © RMN.
241 *Saché, 15th-century houses*, postcard, Bibl. Dép. d'Indre-et-Loire. *Saché, the Church*, postcard, idem. *Saché, Calder's stabile*, coll. Patrick Lavaud.
242 *Charles VII*, Jean Fouquet, oil on canvas, 15th century, Musée du Louvre, Paris, © RMN.
243 *Joan of Arc goes to Chinon to see the King*, after *Les Vigiles de Charles VII*, 1484, Bibl. Nat., Paris, © Roger-Viollet. *Bas-relief, Chinon*, coll. Patrick Lavaud/Gallimard.
244 *Château de Chinon (view from the south)*, H. Deverni, watercolor, 1882, Bibl. du Patrimoine, Paris. *Château de Chinon, Statue of Joan of Arc*, coll. Patrick Lavaud/Gallimard. *Château de Chinon (view from the north)*, H. Deverni, watercolor, 1882, Bibl. du Patrimoine, Paris.
245 *Château de Chinon, Clock tower*, coll. Patrick Lavaud/Gallimard. *Wine label*, Chinon vineyards priv. coll.
246 *Chinon, Rue Haute-St-Maurice street sign*, coll. Patrick Lavaud/Gallimard. *Chinon, bas-relief*, idem. *Chapitre de la confrérie des Bons Entonneurs rabelaisiens*, © Serge Chirol.
247 *Chinon, bas-relief*, coll. Patrick Lavaud/Gallimard. *Chinon, houses in Rue Voltaire*, idem.
248 *Chinon, Hôtel des Eaux-et-Forêts*, coll. Patrick Lavaud/Gallimard. *Chinon market place*, Clarey Martineau, litho, 20th century, Bibl. Dép. d'Indre-et-Loire. *Chinon, Chapel of Ste-Radegonde*, coll. Patrick Lavaud/Gallimard.
249 *View of the Abbey of Chinon*, litho, 1810, Archives Départementales d'Indre-et-Loire, idem. *Chinon, Ste-Radegonde bas-relief*, idem. *Aliénor d'Aquitaine and her Daughter*, wall painting, Chapel of Ste-Radegonde, © Serge Chirol.
250 *Rabelais*, anon., oil on canvas, coll. Les amis de Rabelais, La Devinière. *Signature of Rabelais*, idem. *Rabelais*, after Gustave Doré, poster, coll. idem. *Portrait idéal de Rabelais*, Matisse, pencil, 1951, idem, © Succession H. Matisse. *Lémeré, Château du Rivau*, © Serge Chirol.

251 Title page of *Pantagruel*, Bibl. Nat., Paris. *Lerné, the Marson caves*, coll. Gallimard. *Lerné, view from the church*, postcard, Bibl. Mun. de Tours.
252–3 *Church of Tavant, crypt wall paintings*, 12th century, © Zodiaque.
254 *Church of Tavant, wall painting, Christ in Majesty*, © Tegarci Giraudon. *Church of Tavant, crypt wall paintings*, 12th century, © Zodiaque.
255 *Crypt of the Church of Tavant*, © Serge Chirol. *Church of Tavant, crypt wall painting*, 12th century, © Zodiaque.
256–7 *Fresco and wall painting*, ill., © Gallimard.
258–9 *Ronsard*, engraving, Bibl. Nat., est. Paris. *Plessis-lès-Tours, Priory of St-Cosme, Tomb of Ronsard*, © Michel Guillard/Scope.
260 *Emblem of the House of Georges Le Manach*, priv. coll. *Louis XI*, anon., oil on canvas, Musée des Beaux-arts, Tours. *The Weaver*, tile, 18th century, Bibl. Forney, Paris.
261 *Brocade*, 19th century, Musée des Beaux-Arts, Tours. *Louis XI having mulberry trees planted near Tours*, André Bauchant, 1943, Musée nat. d'Art moderne, Paris. *Jacquard Loom*, © Serge Chirol.
262 *Château de Luynes*, drawing, priv. coll. *Château du Plessis-lès-Tours*, aerial view, coll. Éric Guillemot/Gallimard. *Château du Plessis-lès-Tours*, © Michel Guillard/Scope. *Savonnières, Cher river banks*, postcard, Bibl. Mun. de Tours.
263 *Savonnières, angler by the Cher dam*, postcard, Bibl. Dép. d'Indre-et-Loire. *Château de Villandry*, aerial view, coll. Éric Guillemot/Gallimard. *Château de Villandry*, stamp, Musée de la Poste. *Savonnières, the Cher river banks*, detail, postcard, Bibl. Mun. de Tours.
264–5 *Gardens of Villandry under the snow*, coll. Patrick Lavaud. *Quince*, idem. *Château and garden of Villandry in the 19th century*, drawing, Musée des Beaux-Arts de Tours. *Joachim Carvallo*, coll. Château de Villandry. *View of the Château de Villandry and of the gardens*, coll. Patrick Lavaud.
266–7 *View of the Villandry gardens*, coll. Patrick Lavaud.
268 *Château de Langais*, poster, © La Vie du Rail.

Louis XII and Anne de Bretagne, engraving, Bibl. Nat., Paris. *Langeai earthenware*, vase, coll. Alain Doron.
269 *Langeais, the suspension bridge*, postcard, Archives Départementales d'Indre-et-Loire. *Views of the Loire near Langeais*, coll. Patrick Lavaud/Gallimard.
270 *Château d'Ussé*, poster, Constant Duval, © La Vie du Rail. *Dormer window of the Château d'Ussé*, Albert Robida, in *La Vieille France, La Touraine*, priv. coll. *Candes, the church*, postcard, Bibl. Dép. d'Indre-et-Loire.
271 *Portal of the Collegiate Church of St-Martin*, detail from litho Bibl. Mun. de Tours. *Death of Saint Martin*, stained-glass window, detail, © Ed. Gaud.
272 *Fontevraud Cloister*, © Éd. Gaud. *Robert d'Arbrissel preaching*, engraving, 19th century © Roger Viollet. *Marie-Gabrielle de Rochechouart*, oil on canvas, coll. Centre Culturel de l'Ouest. *Fontevraud, kitchen*, © Éd. Gaud. *Fontevraud, chevet of the Abbey Church*, idem.
273 *Escape from Fontevraud*, page from a journal, coll. Centre Culturel de l'Ouest.
274 *Fontevraud, detail*, © Éd. Gaud. *Fontevraud, staircase*, idem. *Fontevraud, wall painting Christ on the Cross*, idem.
275 *Fontevraud, recumbent statues*, idem. *Abbey of Fontevraud*, stamp, coll. Centre Culturel de l'Ouest.
276 *View of the Château de Montsoreau*, by Wismes, litho, priv. coll. *Portrait of Alexandre Dumas*, att. to Daumier, Association des Amis d'Alexandre Dumas, Marly-le-Roi. *Montsoreau*, © Michel Guillard/Scope.
277 *Château de Saumur*, illumination, in the *Très Riches Heures du Duc de Berry*, Musée Condé, Chantilly, © Giraudon.
278 *Saumur*, litho, 19th century, priv. coll. coll. Gallimard.
279 *Croupade*, bronze, D. Conte, Musée du Cheval, Saumur, © Pratt Priess/Diaf.
280 *Portrait of King René*, detail from Matheron diptych, 15th century, Musée du Louvre, Paris, © RMN. *Le bal sauvage*, detail from a tapestry, 15th century, Musée des Arts Décoratifs, Saumur, © Pratt-Pries/Diaf. *Salle des faïences*, © Serge

hirol. *Sainte Catherine*, statue from Ateliers des ords de Loire, 15th entury, © Pratt-Pries/Diaf. **81** *Aerial view of the hâteau de Saumur*, oll. Éric Guillemot/ allimard. *Portrait of uplessis-Mornay*, ngraving, priv. coll. **82–3** *Cadre Noir inserts* Alain Laurioux/ cole nationale équitation, Saumur. *arrousel*, 1993, © Noël autemanière/Scope. **84** *César Bridge*, Jean-Paul Gislard. *ademoiselle Florence La ram*, © Alain Le Bot/ af. Church of Nantilly, e Wismes, litho, priv. oll., coll. Gallimard. **85** *Notre-Dame- es-Ardilliers*, © Noël autemanière/Scope. *hâteau de Boumois*, etails, © Éric Guillemot/ allimard. **86** *Le Val-Hulin*, © Éric uillemot/Gallimard. a *Grande Vignole*, Yann Arthus ertrand/Altitude. **87** *Shark's tooth*, François Joly. *arson caves* © Éric uillemot/Gallimard. **88** *Dénezé sous Doué*, Jean-Paul Gislard. oué La Fontaine, *ue des Perrières*, idem. oué la Fontaine, *detail of e Musée des Anciens ommerces*, © Éric uillemot/Gallimard. oué La Fontaine, Parc *ologique des Minières*, em. *Dolmen de la adeleine*, idem. **90** *Le Puy-Notre-Dame, e Ceinture*, © Inventaire énéral des Pays de ire. *Montreuil Bellay, the alled town*, © Jean-Paul slard. **91** *Montreuil Bellay*, e Wismes, litho, priv. oll., coll. Gallimard. *-Hilaire*, © Éric uillemot/Gallimard. **92** *Château de mpéan*, © Jean-Paul slard. *Cunault, elevation the main façade*, 1880, oll. Bibl. du Patrimoine, aris, coll. Gallimard. **93** *"Hélice terrestre e l'Orbière"*, © Éric uillemot/Gallimard. *hâteau de Pimpéan, apel frescos*, © Jean- aul Gislard. **94** *Château de Brissac*, Wojtek Buss/Hoa-Qui. avé windmill near *rissac, aerial view of onts de Cé*, © Éric uillemot/Gallimard. **95** *Angers, Pont de eilles*, J. V. de Fleury, on canvas, c. 1840, usée des Beaux-Arts, gers. **96** *Saint Louis, ained-glass window in ezières-en-Brenne*, Guy Fleury/Artéphot. *hâteau d'Angers*,

© Éric Guillemot/ Gallimard. **297** *Coin minted in Angers by Foulques Nerra*, c. 1030, © Ohanna, all rights reserved. *View of the Château d'Angers*, litho., 19th century, all rights reserved. **298** *Château tower*, © Éric Guillemot/ Gallimard. *King René, detail from a stained-glass window in the Abbey of Loroux*, © Inventaire général des Pays de Loire. *Donadieu de Puycharic, funerary statue from the Church of the Jacobins*, idem. *Château gardens*, © Éric Guillemot/ Gallimard. **299** *Angers, deer in the moat*, © Michel Gotin/ Scope. *The Château*, © Jean-Paul Gislard. *Moat*, © Éric Guillemot/ Gallimard. *The Châtelet*, idem. *The Château, fire escape holes*, © Serge Chirol. *View of the Galerie de l'Apocalypse*, © Inventaire général des Pays de Loire. **300–1** *Tapestry of the Apocalypse*, © Inventaire général des Pays de Loire. **302** *Cathedral, Southern Rosace, High altar*, © Eric Guillemot/Gallimard. *Cathedral, wall painting, The Life of Saint Maurille*, 14th century, © Inventaire général des Pays de Loire. *Treasury, arm reliquary*, 15th century, idem. **303** *The Cathedral*, © Pratt-Pries/Diaf.*René Bazin*, © Roger Viollet. *Maison d'Adam, sculpted wood*, © Jean-Paul Gislard. *Maison d'Adam*, idem. **304** *Former Abbey of St-Aubin*, © Jean-Paul Gislard. *Female mask in gilded copper*, coll. Musée d'Anjou, Angers. *Portrait of David d'Angers*, photo, 1845, © Roger Viollet. *Le Logis Barrault*, by Wismes, litho, priv. coll., coll. Gallimard. **305** *David d'Angers*, stamp, coll. Musée de la Poste. *Francesca da Rimini*, Ingres, oil on canvas, 1819, © Musée des Beaux-Arts d'Angers. *Hervé Bazin*, 1981, © Roger Viollet. *Galerie David d'Angers*, © Olivier Martel/Hoa-Qui. *Galerie David D'Angers*, © Jean-Paul Gislard. **306** *Watercolor of the façade of the theater*, Auguste-Joseph Magne, 1870, coll. Musée d'Angers. *The Theater*, © Jean-Paul Gislard. *Hôtel Pincé*, watercolor, Auguste-Joseph Magne, 1976, coll. Bibl. du Patrimoine, Paris, coll. Gallimard.

307 *"La Boule de fort"*, © Jean-Paul Gislard. *Watercolor plates*, Pierre-Joseph Redouté, late 18th century, coll. Musée botanique, Angers, © Pratt-Prie/Diaf. *Curnonsky*, © Roger Viollet. *Church of St-Serge, Angers*, © Serge Chirol. **308** *Pont de Verdun over the Maine*, © Pratt-Pries/ Diaf. *"Signe y materia"*, José Grau-Garrga, tapestry, 1968, coll. Musée Jean Lurçat, Angers. *Angels Bearing the Instruments of the Passion, detail from tapestry*, coll. Musée du château d'Angers. *Hôpital St-Jean*, © Éric Guillemot/Gallimard. **309** *Jean Lurçat*, © Roger Viollet.*Liberté, detail from tapestry, Jean Lurçat*, 1943, coll. Musée Jean Lurçat, Angers. *Mai, Mario Prassinos, tapestry*, 1960, idem. *Champagne, Atelier Tabard, Aubusson*, 1959, idem. **310** *Library of the Château de Serrant*, © A. Février/Diaf. *Château de Serrant*, © Wojteck Buss. **311** *Balcony of the Château du Plessis-Macé*, © Pratt-Pries/Diaf. *Le Plessis-Macé*, © Michel Gotin/Scope. *Le Plessis Bourré, painted ceiling*, © Alain Le Bot/Diaf. *Le Plessis-Bourré*, © Jean-Paul Gislard. **312** *Baugé, Pharmacy of St-Joseph Hospital*, © Pratt-Pries/Diaf. *The Blue Mine*, © Olivier Martell/Hoa-Qui. **314** *Château de Montsoreau*, © Éric Guillemot/Gallimard. **317** *TGV Atlantique*, © Kid/Kervella/Hoa-Qui **322–3** *Coulée de Serrant*, © Jean-Paul Gislard. *Troglodytic dwelling*, Saumur, © Julien Quideau/Hoa-Qui. *Wine bottles*, © Éric Guillemot/Gallimard. **325** *Cave in St-Cyr-en-Bourg*, © N. Thibaut/ Hoa-Qui. *Soussay, Troglodytic château*, © Richard Manin/ Hoa-Qui.

We would like to thank the following people and institutions for their help:

M. Patrick Boyer
M. Carvallo
Mme Florence Dauge
M. Dontenwille
M. Dupavillon
Mme Favard
M. Giquel
Mme Godefroy Durand-Ruel
M. Pierre Huteau
Mme Le Platre
M. Yves Maufra
M. Perraguin
M. Jean Poulain
Mme Muguette Rigaud
M. Steinberg
Mlle Claudine Varin
Mme Barbara Wright
Les Archives Départementales du Loir-et-Cher
La Bibl. du Patrimoine, Paris,
La Bibl. Dép. d'Indre-et-Loire à Tours
La Bibl. Mun., Tours
La Bibl. Mun., Vendôme
La Documentation de l'Inventaire, Orléans
La Photothèque de la Ville-de-Tours
Le Musée de l'Hôtel de Ville à Amboise
Le musée régional de l'Orléanais à Beaugency
Le Musée archéologique de Blois
Le Musée des Beaux-Arts de Blois
Le Musée des Amis du Vieux Chinon
Le Musée de Sologne, Romorantin-Lanthenay
Le Musée de Sologne, Romorantin-Lanthenay
Le Musée Lansyer, Loches
Le Musée des Beaux-Arts, Tours
Le Musée du Compagnonnage, Tours
Le musée municipal, Vendôme
Les Amis de Rabelais et de La Devinière
La Galerie La Cymaise, Paris
Pierre Aucante
Anne and Alain Beignet
Anne and Serge Chirol
Martine and Alain Doron
Jean-Paul Grossin
François Joly
Patrick Lavaud
Jean-Pierre Moreau
Jean-Luc Péchinot
Pierre Pitrou
Jean-Noël Thibault
Les Éditions CLD, Tours
Les Éditions du Zodiaque

◆ INDEX

Page numbers in bold refer to the
Practical information section.

◆ A ◆

Abbate, Niccolo dell' 167
Abd-el-Kader 183
Ackerman, Jean 292
Adam, Michel 233
Agincourt, battle of 39,
114, 117
Agriculture 26
Aignan, Saint 114
Alain-Fournier 92–3
Alaric II, King of the
Visigoths 37, 190
Alcuin 37, 196, 205
Amboise 18, 40, 162, 163,
180–82
– Chanteloup Pagoda 330
– Chapel of St-Hubert 60
– Chapel of St-Jean 190
– Château 66, 87, 93, 100,
101, 264, 330
– Château-Gaillard 185
– Church of Notre-Dame-
du-Bout-des-Ponts 190–91
– Church of St-Denis
188–9, 191, 330
– Church of St-Florentin
182, 185, 189
– Clos-Lucé 185, 330
– Conspiracy 38
– Éperon des Châtelliers
36, 182
– Greniers de César 190
– Hôtel de Ville 189
– Île d'Or 184, 190–1
– Leonardo da Vinci
Museum 185, 330
– Maison des Pages de
Charles VII 190
– Maison Enchantée 188
– Max Ernst Fountain 190
– Musée de la Poste 188,
189, 330
– Musée de l'Hôtel de Ville
188
– Tour de l'Horloge 188
Amboise Conspiracy 40,
183
Amboise family 177
Andes 36
Androuet Du Cerceau,
Jacques 75, 87, 118, 119,
221, 264
Androuet du Cerceau,
Jean 184
Angers 12, 16, 37, 40–44,
296–7, 310
– Abbaye du Ronceray 309
– Ancien Évêché 303
– Cathedral of St-Maurice
302–3, 336
– Catholic University 302
– Centre International de la
Tapisserie 297
– Chapel of Ste-Geneviève-
St-Laud 299, 308
– Château 65, 182–5,
297–9, 300, 311
– Church of St-Serge 60,
307, 335
– Église de la Trinité 309
– Festival d'Anjou 306
– Former Abbey of St-
Aubin 304, 305
– Former Abbey of St-
Nicolas 309
– Former Collegiate Church
of St-Martin 304
– Galerie David d'Angers
305, 335
– Hôpital St-Jean 308
– Hospital Chapel 308–9
– Hôtel Ayrault-de-St-Hénis
306
– Hôtel Bardoul de la
Bigottière 306
– Hôtel Chemellier 306
– Hôtel de Coulanges 302
– Hôtel de la Godeline 303

– Hôtel de Lancreau-de-
Bellefonds 307
– Hôtel de Maquillé 306
– Hôtel Pincé 335
– Hôtel de Richeteau 309
– Hôtel de Thévalle 303
– Hôtel de Ville 307
– Hotel des Pénitentes 309
– Hôtel du Guesclin 309
– Hôtel du Roi-de-Pologne
305
– Hôtel Ménage 306
– Hôtel Pincé 74, 306
– Hôtel St-Martial 302
– Jardin des Plantes 307,
335
– Jardin du Mail 307
– Logis Barrault 304–5
– Logis de l'Estaignier 302,
335
– Lycée Joachim-du-Bellay
307
– Maison d'Adam 72, 73,
303–4
– Maison de la "Belle
Angevine" 306
– Maison des Vins 303
– Montée St-Maurice 302
– Musée des Beaux-Arts
304–5, 335
– Musée de l'Étain (Pewter
Museum) 302, 335
– Musée Jean-Lurçat 308,
336
– Musée de la Tapisserie
Contemporaine 306
– Musée Turpin-de-Crissé
306, 336
– Museum of Paleontology
307
– Natural History Museum
307, 335
– Place de la Paix 309
– Place du Ralliement 306
– Place Louis-Imbach 306
– Place Ste-Croix 303
– Promenade du Vout-du-
Monde 302
– Rue de l'Oisellerie 303
– Rue des Arènes 304
– Rue Donadieu-de-
Puycharic 302
– Rue du Cornet 306
– Rue St-Aubin 304
– Rue St-Laud 73, 306
– Rue Toussaint 305
– Tour des Anglais 308
– Tour St-Aubin 304
– Ursuline Chapel 306
Angers, David d' 314
Animal farming and
breeding 28–9
Anjou 12, 13, 26, 37, 38,
42, 325
Anjou Cross 37
Annaud, Jean-Jacques 217
Anne de Beaujeu 136, 229
Anne de Bretagne 34, 40,
155, 185, 196, 227, 243,
268
Anne de Montmorency
238, 239
Anne of Austria 290
Arbrissel, Robert d' 272,
274, 275
Archambault, Albert 213
Ardier, Paul 167, 168
Arp, Jean 241
Asnières, Abbey of 290
Attila 114, 126
Aubigné, Agrippa d' 140,
183
Aurelianum (later Orléans)
112
Avoine-Chinon nuclear
power station 13, 244, 333
Ayrault, Pierre 306
Azay-le-Rideau 38, 234,
240

– Château de 68, 100, 108,
170, 234–9, 240, 332
– Manoir de la Rémonnière
239

◆ B ◆

Babou, Marie 188
Bagneux 289
– dolmens 36, 289, 334
Balue, Cardinal 226
Balzac, Honoré de 90–1,
101–2, 103, 208, 212, 235,
240–1, 250
Barault, Olivier 304
Barré, Nicolas 312
"Bastard of Orléans" (Jean,
Comte de Dunois) 115,
116, 139
Bastarnay, Imbert de 231
Bastarnay family 231
Bauchant, André 207, 261
Baudricourt, Robert de
243
Baugé 297
– Chapelle de la
Girouardière 312
– Château 312, 336
– Hôpital St-Joseph 312
– Musée d'Art Populaire
336
Bayeux, Mathieu 203
Bazin, Hervé 305, 314
Bazin, René 303, 305, 310,
314
The Bear 217
Beauce 13, 112
Beaugency 43, 117, 139
– Château Dunois 65, 109,
139, 329
– Church of Notre-Dame
139, 329
– Hôtel de Ville 139
– Keep 65
– Musée Régional de
l'Orléans 329
Beaulieu-lès-Loches 230
– Abbey of Ste-Trinité 230,
297
Beaune-Semblançay,
Jacques de 202, 238
Beauregard, Château de
167–8, 329
Beauval, Parc de 217
Beauvau, Bernard de 293
Becket, Thomas à 230
Bedel, Maurice 208, 247
Bellay, Joachim du 16, 41,
314
Benedict, Saint 130, 131
Bernard, Samuel 221
Berthelot, Gilles 235, 238,
239
Berthier, Maréchal 165
Berzelius, John Jacob 104
Besnard, Ulysse 150
Betham-Edwards, Matilda
94
Biardeau 285
Biencourt, Armand de 238,
239
Blacas, Duke of 270
Black Death 39
Blésois 12, 13, 26
Blois 13, 16, 40, 41, 43, 44,
144–5, 173
– Ancien Évêché 75, 154
– Cathedral of St-Louis 154
– Chapel of St-Calais 148,
149
– Château de 67, 68, 69,
71, 87, 91, 95, 99, 100,
148–53, 197, 236, 329
– Church of St-Nicolas 143,
153
– Church of St-Saturnin 155
– Church of St-Vincent 63

– Cloisters of St-Saturnin
155
– earthenware 150
– Escalier Denis Papin 154
– Hôtel d'Alluye 142, 154
– Jardin du Roi 153
– Lapidary Museum 155
– Louis XII Fountain 155
– Maison des Acrobates
154
– Musée des Beaux-Arts
152, 329
– Musée d'Histoire
Naturelle 155
– Musée Diocésain d'Art
Religieux 155
– Place Louis XII 154, 155
– Place St-Louis 154
– Pont Jacques-Gabriel
145, 155
– Rue du Palais 154
– Rue St-Honoré 154
– Tour du Floix 149
Boats 45–6
Bobeau 84
Bodinier, Guillaume 306
Bohier, Thomas 220, 222,
235
Boissimont, Charles de 267
Bonheur, Gabrielle
(Coco Chanel) 284
Bonnecamp, Nicolas de
265
Bonnezeaux 325
Borgia, César 243
Bosse, Abraham 198
Bottling wine 32
Boucher, François 152
Boucher, Jacques 115,
117, 118
"Boule de Fort" 307
Boumois, Château de 285,
334
Bourbon, Henri de 165
Bourdichon, Jean 41, 213,
227, 314
Bourgueil 325
Bourgueil, St-Nicholas-de-
326
Bourré, Jean 268, 311
Boutinière, La 288
Boyer, architect-sculptor
170
Boylesve, René 106–7, 241
Braniçki, Count 231
Brezé, Pierre de 294
Briare 137
– Musée de la Mosaïque et
des Émaux 328
Brickyards 78, 79
Briçonnet, Jean 209, 212
Briçonnet, Katherine 220,
222, 223
Brissac-Quincé, Château
294, 335
Broglie, Amédée de 178
Brunet, Pierre 305
Bueil, Antoine de 268
Buhler brothers 215
Burges, William 87
Burgunds 37
Bussy d'Amboise, Louis de
276
Byron, Lord 265

◆ C ◆

Cabu, Philippe 119
Caccia, Pietro 161, 162
Cadre Noir see Saumur
Caesar, Julius 36
Caesarodunum (later
Tours) 196
Calder, Alexander 241
Calvin, John 40, 121
Candes-St-Martin 270–2
– Archbishop's Residence
272
– Castle 272

Collegiate Church of
-Martin 271, **333**
Maison-Dieu 272
angey (Church of
-Martin) 192
apet, Hughes 37, 112
apetians 296, 298
arnutes 36, 112, 133
aron, Antoine 152
arvallo, Dr Joachim 263,
64, 265
assandra 41, 140
astellane, Marquis de
3
atherine de Médicis 35,
, 99, 150, 168, 177, 183,
0, 221, 223
enabum (later
urelianum; then Orléans)
, 112
halands 46, 48, 49, 51
hamberlain, Samuel 98–9
hambord, Château de 13,
, 44, 68, 87, 95, 156,
8–65, 166, 182, 233,
5, **314**, **329**
hampaigne, Philippe de
5, 231, 305
hanel, Coco 284
hanteloup, Château de
, 108, 189, 191–2
hargé 192
Musée de la Bataille de
ire et de la Résistance
2, **331**
harlemagne 37, 128, 205,
9
harles, Duke of Orléans
, 114, 144, 280
harles IV 38
harles V 34, 38, 123, 160,
0
harles VI 34, 38, 39
harles VII 34, 39, 40, 88,
4, 242, 243, 244, 246,
8, 268, 271
harles VIII 34, 40, 66,
6, 154, 163, 182, 184,
5, 188, 196, 268, 271
harles IX 34, 168
harles the Bald 224, 271
harles the Bold 112, 177
harles le Simple 37
harron, Guillaume 140
hateaubriand 161, 270
hâteauneuf-sur-Loire 127
Balade des Mariniers 127
Château 127, **328**
Church of St-Martial 127
Halle St-Pierre 127
Musée de la Marine de la
ire 127, **328**
Park **328**
hâtre, La 103
haumont-sur-Loire 100
Château de 67, 108,
7–8, **330**
Garden Festival 178, **330**
hauvigny, Charles de 161
hemillé-sur-Indrois
hartreuse du Liget, **332**
hênehutte-les-Tuffeaux
2
Church of Notre-Dame
, 292
henonceaux 100, 216
Château de 69, 87, 170,
7, 217, 218–23, 233,
5, **314**, **331**
heverny
Château de 13, 53, 70,
9, 170–1, 172, **330**
Church of St-Étienne 172
hinon 38, 40, 116, 242–4,
7
Abbey of St-Pierre-de-
uilly 251
Chapel of

Ste-Radegonde 248, 249,
332
– "La Chasse Royale"
mural 249
– Château 64, 96, 100,
242–3, 244–6, **332**
– Château de Milieu 64,
244–5
– Château de la Roche-
Clermault 251
– Château du Rivau 250–1
– Church of St-Étienne 243,
248
– Church of St-Maurice 248
– Collegiate Church of
St-Mexme 242, 249
– La Devinière 250
– Fort du Coudray 64,
244–5
– Fort St-Georges 64, 244
– Grand-Carroi 246, 247
– Hôtel des Eaux et Forêts
248
– Hôtel du Baillage 248
– Hôtel du Gouverneur 248
– Hôtel Torterue de
Langardière 246
– Maison des États-
Généraux 246, 248, **332**
– Maison Rouge 72, 246
– Musée des Arts et
Traditions Populaires **332**
– Musée du Vin et de la
Tonnellerie 246
– nuclear power station 139
– Place du Général-de-
Gaulle 248
– Priory of Ste-Mélanie 64
– Rue de la Lamproie 247,
248
– Rue Jeanne d'Arc 246
– Rue Voltaire 246, 248
– wine of 244, 245, 246
– Waxwork museum,
331
Choiseul, Duc de 189–92,
209, 282
Christianity
– arrival of 36
– spread of 37
Cicindela 21
Claude de France 34, 35,
148, 235, 239
Clément, Jacques 40
Clermont, Comte de 116
Cléry-St-André 138
Clotet, treasurer 160
Clotilda, Saint 209
Clouet, François 41, 220,
314
Clovis 37, 112, 190, 212
Colette 102
Combleux 128
Corbeau, Renée 306
Corbineau, Pierre 306
Corder, M. 282
Cormorant 19
Corneille de Lyon 152
Corniche angevine 310
Cortona, Dominico da 163
Cosmas, Saint 259
Cossé, René de 294
Coteaux-du-Layon 309
Coudray-Macouard 289
– Church 289
– Magnanerie 289, **334**
Coulée-de-Serrant, La
311
Cousin, Jean 152
Coustou, Guillaume 155
Coysevox, Antoine 310
Craft guilds (*compagnons*)
199, 200–1
Craig, Frank 117
Culant, Louis de 116
Cunault, Notre-Dame
church 59, 292–3, **335**
Curnonsky (Maurice-
Edmond Sailland) 54, 307

◆ D ◆

D'Albert, Charles 262
Damian, Saint 259
Dampierre-en-Burly
nuclear power station 13
David d'Angers 294, 304,
305, 306
David-Darnac, Maurice 96
Debat-Ponsan, Edouard 84
Debré, Michel 190
Debré, Oliver 83
Delacroix, Eugène 248
Delaporte, Louis 228
Delft, Coppin 293
Delorme, Philibert 310
Demy, Jacques 165
Deneuve, Catherine 165
Dénezé-sur-Doué 288
– Carved cavern **334**
Descartes, René 203, 250
Desportes, François 136
Deverni, Henri 244
Diane de Poitiers 40, 119,
168, 177, 220, 221, 223
Dindault, Émile 124
Dolet, Étienne 120
Dolmens 36, 289, 290, 291
Donadieu de Puycharic,
Pierre 298
Dorian, Jean and Charles
203
Doué-la-Fontaine 286, 287,
288–9
– Arènes de Douces 289,
334
– Maison Carolingienne
289
– Moulin de la Fourchette
289, **334**
– Parc Zoologique des
Minières 289, **334**
– Roseraie du Parc Foulon
289
– Rue des Perrières 288,
289
– La Sablière 289, **334**
Doulcet, Françoise 140
Dovecotes 80
Du Thier, Jean 167
Dubray, Vital-Gabriel 122
Ducos, Pierre-Roger 183
Dumas, Alexandre, *père*
150, 276
Dupanloup, Félix 115
Dupin, Claude 221
Dupin, Madame 220, 221
Duplessis-Mornay, Philippe
278–9, 280, 281, 282
Dupuy, Étienne 87
Duras, Duchesse de 270
Duthoit, Louis 124

◆ E ◆

Écueillé 311
Edict of Nantes 40, 41,
226, 260, 279
Eduens 133
Edward III, King of England
38
Edward the Black Prince
38
Eel-pot fishing 22
Eiffel, Gustave 137
Elbène, Alphonse 115
Eleanor of Aquitaine 38,
249, 275
Éluard, Paul 309
Ermine, as an emblem 235,
237, 239
Ernst, Max 83, 190
Espine, Jean de L' 74
Estampes, Jacques d'
232
Estampes, Louis d' 232
Euverte, Saint 114

◆ F ◆

Fachet, Paul 84
Falun 76, 286, 287, 289
Ferté-St-Aubin 125
– Château **328**
Festivals **315**
Firmin-Rogier, Gabriel 84
Fish and fishing 22–3
Fish terrine 54–5
Flandrin, Suzanne 253
Flaubert, Gustave 151,
188, 222
Focillon, Henri 253
Fonderie Bollée 126
Fontevraud abbey 30, 59,
227, 272–5, **333**
Food 50–5
Forests 24–5, 216
Fosse, La 288, **334**
Fossils 287
Fouaces (pancakes) 251
Fougères-sur-Bièvre,
Château de 109, 176,
330
Fougeu d'Escures, Pierre
123
Foulon, Joseph-François
288
Foulques V le Jeune 37
Foulques le Roux 224
Foulques Nerra 37, 182,
224, 230, 231, 268, 278,
288, 290, 291, 294, 296,
297, 298, 304, 309, 312
Fouquet, Jean 41, 88, 227,
231, 242, **314**
Fouquet, Nicolas 183
Foyatier, Denis 122
Fram 47
France, Anatole 203
François, Bastien 205
François I 34, 35, 40, 68,
99, 123, 130, 148, 154,
156, 158, 160–63, 166,
182, 183, 185, 186, 189,
202, 220, 223, 229, 235,
239
François II 34, 40, 168,
183, 220
François II of Brittany 268
Franks 36, 37
Freppel, Bishop 302
Fresco painting 256–7
Fresnes
– Château de Roujous **330**
– Musée Historique Animé
330
Fûtreau 47, 48

◆ G ◆

Gabare 48
Gabriel, Ange-Jacques
140
Gabriel, Jacques V 145,
154, 155
Galembert, Comte de 253
Gambetta, Léon 43
Garlande, Manassès de
138
Gaston d'Orléans 144, 145,
148, 149, 163, 170, 183
Gauguin, Paul 115
Gauls 36
Gauzlin, Abbot 130, 131
Gemmail (stained glass)
212
Genet, Jean 273
Genevoix, Maurice 91–2,
125, 126
Gennes 293
– Amphitheater, Gallo-
Roman 293, **335**
– Church of St-Vétérin 293,
335
– Dolmen de la Madeleine
289

◆ INDEX

– Water Mill of Sarré 293, **335**
Geoffroi Plantagenet 37
Germans 37
Germigny-des-Prés 128–9
– Carolingian oratory **328**
Gervais, Antoine-Denis 303
Gien 12, 13, 43, 133
– Bridge 133, 134, 136
– Château of 67, 133, 136, **328**
– Church of Ste-Jeanne-d'Arc 133, 136
– earthenware 133, 134–5
– Musée de la Chasse 136, **328**
– Musée de la Faïencerie 136, **328**
Gildin de Saumur 268
Gilles, Saint 249
Giocondo, Fra Giovanni 188
Glasdale, William of 116
Gleb, Thomas 308
Goat's cheese 29, 54
"Gomphe serpentin" 21
Gondoin 285
Grace, John Gregory 87
Grande Vignole 287, **334**
Grandin 202
Grape picking 31, 32
Gregory of Tours 37, 182, 196, 199, **314**
Groslot, Jacques 118
Grottes Pétrifiantes 262–3
Guérinière, La 282
Guesclin, Bertrand du 38
Guidi, Dominico 127
Guillaume IX of Aquitaine 290
Guillaume de Lorris 138
Guise, Henri, Duc de 40, 146, 147, 148, 152, 183, 198
Guise family 40
Guyenne 38

♦ H ♦

Hallays, André 227
Hardouin-Mansard (Mansart), Jules 70, 71, 164, 310
Hébert, Émile 248
Henri II 35, 40, 168, 177, 183, 220, 229
Henri II Plantagenet 37, 38, 230, 242, 244, 275
Henri III 34, 40, 146, 147, 148, 150, 221, 276, 298, 305
Henri IV (Henri de Navarre) 35, 40, 114, 132, 137, 146, 147, 168, 170, 262, 281
Henry II, King of England 64, 231
Henry V, King of England 39
Hergé 171
Hilaire, Saint 206
Hire, La 116, 117
Holy Girdle of the Virgin 290
Hoplia, Blue 19
Horticulture 26–7, 124
Hôtel Lefebvre de Montifray 75
Hotte, Général L' 282
Huguenots 40, 114, 139, 144, 146, 183, 279, 281
Hundred Years War 38–9, 66, 72, 73
Huns 37, 114
Hunting 52–3
Hurault, Henri 170
Hurault family 172

♦ I ♦

Indre-et-Loire 12, 43
Ingrand, Max 149, 240
Isabelle d'Angoulême 249, 275

♦ J ♦

Jacob, Max 115, 129, 131
James, Henry 93–4, 150, 172
Jarente, Monseigneur de 118
Jargeau 36, 117, 126
– Collegiate Church of St-Vrain 126, **328**
– Musée de la Fondation Oscar Roty 127
Jean II le Bon 38, 199
Jean de Cambes 276
Jean sans Peur 39
Jehan de Bondolf 300
Joan of Arc 39, 96, 112, 114, 116–17, 118, 120, 136, 138, 149, 153, 157, 227, 242–8, 291
John the Recluse 248, 249
Joly-Leterme (architect) 284

♦ K ♦

Kingfisher 20
Koehler, Henry 52

♦ L ♦

La Fontaine, Jean de 150
La Morandière, Jules de 173, 178
La Saussaye, Louis de 173
La Tour, Georges de 115
Lackland, John (King John) 230, 242, 249, 275
Lair, Count Charles 280
Laloux, Victor 205, 207, 214
Lamprey River 23
Langeais 40, 97, 268, 297
– Bridge 269
– Château de 66, 100, 268, **333**
– Church of St-Jean-Baptiste 268
– Church of St-Laurent 268
– earthenware 268
– Keep 268
– Musée de l'Artisanat 268, **333**
Langres, Château de 100
Languet, Hubert 281
Lansyer, Emmanuel 228, 229
Lauzun, Duc de 183
Law, John 232
Le Breton, Jean 166, 263
Le Camus 191
Le Ray, Jacques Donatien 177
Lee, Vernon 96–7
Lefèvre, Théodore 125
Legendre de Villemorien, Charles 232, 233
Lemaitre, Jules 83
Lenepveu, Jules-Ernest 306
Leonardo da Vinci 40, 162–3, 185–7, 190, 225, **314**
Lerné 251
Leroux, Philippe 200
Lesbahy, Philippe 235, 238, 239
Leszczynski, Stanislas 165
Liget, Chartreuse du 217, 227, 230
Lighters 46, 48
Limeray 192
Limoges boat 49

♦ M ♦

McMahon, Alfred 217
Maczon (Maçon), Robert le 292

Lisch, Juste 128, **314**
Livre Tournois 213
Lobin, Léon 248
Loches 40, 64, 216, 217, 224, 297
– Château 65, 226
– Collegiate Church of St-Ours 227–8, 229, **332**
– Donjon **332**
– Fortifications 228
– Hôtel de Ville 229
– Keep 224–5, 228
– Logis Royal 226–7, **332**
– Maison d'Agnès Sorel 229
– Maison de la Chancellerie 229
– Maison de l'Argentier du Roi 229–30
– Maison de l'Écuyer du Roi 229
– Maison du Centaure 229
– Musée du Terroir 228, **332**
– Musée Lansyer 228, **332**
– Place du Marché-aux-Légumes 229
– Porte des Cordeliers 224, 229
– Porte Picois 229
– Porte Royale 226, 228
– Rue du Château 229
– Tour St-Antoine 224, 229
Locke, John 100
Loges 80
Loir River 44
Loir-et-Cher 12, 13, 16, 43
Loire River, source of 18, 126
Loiret River 44
Louis, Duke of Orléans 35, 39, 114
Louis I of Anjou 37, 280, 300
Louis II of Anjou 280, 298, 299
Louis VII 38
Louis IX (St Louis) 38, 65, 225, 280, 296, 298, 308
Louis XI 34, 40, 88, 138, 154, 177, 182, 184, 196, 202, 204, 208, 225–6, 258–62, 268, 271, 284, 311
Louis XII (Louis II d'Orléans) 34, 35, 40, 41, 136, 144, 148, 154, 177, 198, 209, 225, 243
Louis XIII 35, 138, 168, 183, 223, 298
Louis XIV 35, 41, 136, 154, 163–4, 165, 183, 198, 226, 290
Louis XV 35, 165, 273, 282, 312
Louis XVI 35, 42
Louis XVIII 312
Louis the Pious 288
Louis-Napoleon 42
Louis-Philippe 118, 183
Louise de Lorraine 220, 221, 223
Louresse-Rochemenier
– Musée Paysan **334**
Lully, Giovanni Battista 163
Lurçat, Jean 308, 309
Lurçat, Mme Simone 308
Lussault-sur-Loire
– Aquarium de Touraine **314**, **331**
Luther, Martin 40
Luynes 36, 262
– Château **333**

Maillé family 259
Maine 37, 38
Maine River 44
Maine-et-Loire 12, 42, 43, 44
Mame, Alfred 215
Mansard, François 148, 151
Marguerite d'Anjou 287, 303
Margueron, Jean-Anthym 215
Marie de Bretagne 291
Marie de Médicis 148
Marie d'Orléans 118
Marigny, Marquis de 140
Markets **319**
Marmoutier abbey 30, 36, 196, 206
Marques, Jean 220
Marques, Pierre 220
Marsay, Étienne de 308
Marson
– Château 288
– Troglodytic farm 287
Martel, Geoffroy 230
Martin, Saint 36, 188, 196, 204–7, 210, 213, 215, 270, 271
Martin, Sand 21
Matisse, Henri 250
Mayenne River 44
Menars, Château de 71, 110, 140
Menhirs 36, 293
Menier, Gaston 223
Menier family 221
Mercogliano, Pacello de 182, 185, 188
Mérimée, Prosper 178
Meung, Jean de (Jean Chopinel) 138
Meung-sur-Loire 117, 138
– Château **329**
– Church of St-Lyphard 1
Mexme, Saint (Maxime) 242, 248, 249
Mignard, Nicolas 171
Mills 13, 78–9, 125, 138, 176, 220, 222, 240, 286, 289, 290, 293, 294, 312, **314**, **335**
Mitterrand, François 305
Molière 163, 164, 202
Montgeoffroy, Château de 312, **336**
Montils-lès-Tours
– château 260
Montpoupon, Château de 216, 217
Montrésor 216, 217, 231, **332**
– Collegiate Church of St-Jean-Baptiste 62, 231, **332**
Montreuil-Bellay 290, 291, 297
– Château-Neuf 291, **334**
– Château-Vieux 291, **334**
– Logis des Chanoines de la Collégiale 291
– Tour St-Jean 290
Montrichard 217
Montsoreau 276
– Château **333**
– Musée des Goums **333**
Morel, Philippe 307
Mosnier, Jean 170, 171
Moulins 104
Mousseaux 288
Mushrooms 26, 56, 286, 292
– Musée du Champignon **334**

♦ N ♦

Napoleon I 42, 165, 183, 198, 232, 273, 312

apoleon III 42, 174, 183
et fishing 22
euvy-en-Sullias 119
evers 104
ini, Jean-Baptiste 152, 77
ouans-les-Fontaines 216, 31, **332**
ouvel, Jean 214

◆ O ◆

do 128
ggiono, Marco d' 152
livet 124–5
rder of Saint Michel 184
rléanais 12, 13, 26
rléans 13, 16, 36, 37, 39, 4, 43, 44, 56
Ancien Couvent des inimes 123
Ancien Évêché 115
Campo-Santo 115
Cathédrale Ste-Croix 61, 14–15, **328**
Centre Charles-Péguy 22, **328**
Centre Jeanne d'Arc 118, **28**
Chambre de Commerce 23
Chancellerie 123
Chapel of St-Jacques 18
Chapelle Notre-Dame-es-Miracles 121
Church of Notre-Dame-a-Recouvrance 122
Church of St-Pierre-du-lartroi 123
Collegiate Church of St-ignan 121
Collegiate Church of St-erre-le-Puellier 121
Hôtel Cabu 75, 118, 119, **28**
Hôtel de la Préfecture 20
Hôtel des Créneaux 115, 19
Hôtel Euverte-Hatte 22, **328**
Hôtel Groslot 118, **328**
Hôtel Hector-de-Sauxerre 20, 139
Hôtel Moderne 124
Hôtel Pommeret 124
Hotel Toutin 122
Jardin Jacques-Boucher 22
Maison de Jean Dallibert 21
Maison de Jeanne d'Arc 18
Maison "de la Coquille" 21
Maison de la Pomme 119
Maison des Chevaliers u Guet 120
Maison "Du Cerceau" 19–20
Maison du Sancier 119
Musée Archéologique et istorique de l'Orléanais 19, **328**
Musée des Beaux-Arts 5, **328**
Pavillon Colas-des-ancs 122
Pavillons d'Escures 75, 23
Place Abbé-Desnoyers 18–19
Place Albert Ier 124
Place de l'Étape 123
Place du Châtelet 118, 21
Place du Général de aulle 118

– Place du Martroi 121, 122, 123, 124
– Place Ste-Croix 115
– Pont George-V 121
– Porte Bannier 122
– Rue Alsace-Lorraine 124
– Rue de Bourgogne 120
– Rue de la République 124
– Rue d'Escures 123
– Rue du Bourdon-Blanc 115, 120
– Rue Étienne-Dolet 120
– Rue Jeanne-d'Arc 115, 118
– Rue Notre-Dame-de-Recouvrance 122
– Rue Royale 124
– Rue Ste-Catherine 118–19
– Salle des Thèses 120–21
– statue of Joan of Arc 118, 122
– Tour Blanche 121
Orléans Canal 120
Orléans-la-Source 113
– Chateau de la Source 124
– Parc Floral 124, **328**
– Sources du Loiret 124
Osier, Red 19
Oudry, Jean-Baptiste 136

◆ P ◆

Pagot, François 118
Palissy, Bernard 262
Paludina 21
Pasteur, Louis 123
Patay, battle of 117
Patout, Pierre 203
Patton, General George 43
Pays de la Loire region 12, 44
Peau d'Âne 165
Péguy, Charles 106–7, 122
Pelouze, Madame 221
Pépin III le Bref 37
Perche hills 13, 16
Perrault, Charles 121, 270
Perronet, Jean 121
Phélipeaux de la Vrillière, Louis 127
Philip the Fair 242–3
Philip the Tall 243
Philippe I 130
Philippe II Auguste 38, 133, 225, 231, 242, 244, 271, 275, 278
Philippe IV le Bel 38
Philippe VI de Valois 38, 112, 168
Philippe d'Orléans 132, 145
Philippe de Commynes 243, 244, 248
Philippe le Hardi, Duke of Bourgogne 38
Pimpéan, Château de 60, 292, 293, **335**
Pirogues 48, 49
Plessis-Bourré, Château du 311, **336**
Plessis-lès-Tours 40, 196, 209, 259, 262
Plessis-Macé, Château du 310–11, **336**
Plumereau, Charles 208
Pluvinel 282
Pocé-sur-Cisse 192
Pompadour, Madame de 140, 190
Pontbriant, François de 160
Ponts-de-Cé, les 294
– Church of St-Aubin 294
– Church of St-Maurille 294
– Keeps 294
– Musée des Coiffes d'Anjou 294, **335**

Pot, Thomas 274
Pouilly-sur-Loire 98–9
Poulain, Auguste (chocolate manufacturer) 43, 47, 56, 145
Prassinos, Mario 309
Princeteau, René 53
Proust, Marcel **314**
Provinces 12–13
Puy-Notre-Dame 290
– Collegiate Church of Notre-Dame 290, **334**

◆ Q ◆

Quarts-de-Chaume **326**

◆ R ◆

Rabbits 20
Rabelais, François 41, 97–8, 121, 203, 242, 243, 246, 247, 248, 250–51, 268, 276, 289, **314**
Radegund, Saint 248, 249
Raffin, Antoine 238
Raffin, Antoinette 240
Raymond du Temple 132
Redshank 20
Refuge, Pierre de 176
Regions 12–13
Règle du jeu, La 125
Reille, Karl 52
Renaudie, La 183
René I of Anjou, Duke 37, 280, 281, 284, 287, 296, 298, 299, 312
Renoir, Jean 125
Restout, Jean 123
Richard II, King of England 38
Richard the Lionheart 38, 246, 275
Richelieu, Cardinal de 130, 244, 261
Richet, Professor Charles 264
Ridel, Hughes 234
Rigny-Ussé
– Château **333**
– Wall walk **333**
Robert I, Count of Anjou 289
Robert the Pious 112
Robert-Houdin 153
Robertet, Florimond 154
Robin, André 302–3
Roche-aux-Moines, La 311
Rochechouart, Gabrielle de 273
Rochechouart, Louise Françoise de 273
Rochemenier 288
Roguet, Félix 221
Rollon 37
Ronsard, Pierre de 41, 140, 167, 202, 250, 258–9
Roty, Oscar 127
Rou Marson 288
Rougé, Jacques-Marie 228
Roujoux, Château de 173
Rousseau, Étienne 235
Rousseau, Jean-Jacques 221
Rousseau, Théodore 87
Rousset, Louis-Edmé 145
Rouxellé, Marguerite de 241
Rowe, Vivian 99–100
Rubens, Peter Paul 148
Ruprich-Robert, Victor and Gabriel 183, 184

◆ S ◆

Saché 240–41
– Château 240, **332**
– Church of St-Martin-de-Vertou 241, **332**

– Church of St-Symphorien 240
– Musée Balzac 240–1, **332**
Sailland, Maurice-Edmond *see* Curnonsky
Saint Bartholomew's Day Massacre 40, 146
St-Aignan Collegiate Church 59, 217
St-Avry, Château de 97
S-Benoît-sur-Loire Abbey 30, 58, 128, 129–31, **329**
Saint-Cosmé 258–9
– Priory of 258
St-Denis-de-l'Hôtel 126
– Maison Maurice Genevoix 126, **329**
St-Dyé 156–7
St-Florent, Abbey of 291, 292
St-Hilaire-St-Florent 291
– Church of St-Barthélemy 291
– Troglodyte caves 292
St-Jean-de-Braye 126
– Musée Campanaire Fonderie Bollée **329**
St-Laurent-des-Eaux nuclear power station 13, 139, **329**
St-Martin de Tours basilica 37
Saint-Nectaire, François de 125
Ste-Maure 29
Salamander 24
– emblem 182, 235, 237, 239
Salviati, Bernardo 99, 100, 140
Sand, George 102–4
Sanson, Paul-Ernest 178
Sapine 46
Sarrazin, Jacques 298
Sarthe River 44
Saugré 288
Saumur 13, 41, 42, 96, 101–2, 278–9, 297, **326**
– Cadre Noir 279, 281, 282–3, 284
– Château 280, 281, **333**
– Church of Notre-Dame-des-Ardilliers 41, 63, 285, **334**
– Church of St-Pierre 280–81, **333**
– École d'Application de l'Armé Blindée et de la Cavalerie 281
– École de Cavalerie 279, 281
– École Nationale d'Équitation 282, 284, **334**
– Hôtel de Ville 281
– L'Île d'Offard 284
– Maison de la Reine de Sicile 284
– Manège des Écuyers 281
– Montée du Fort 280
– Montée du Petit Genève 280
– Musée de la Cavalerie 284, **334**
– Musée des Arts Décoratifs 280, **333**
– Musée du Cheval 280
– Museum of Armored Vehicles 285, **333**
– Notre-Dame de Nantilly 284
– pilgrimages 279
– Place du Chardonnet 281, 282
– Quai Mayaud 281
– wine 278
Saumurois 12, 286
Sauxerre, Hector de 120
Savonnières 262, 263
– Grottes Pétrifiantes **333**

Saxe, Maréchal de 165
Saxons 36, 37
Say, Marie-Charlotte 178
Scott, Sir Walter 262
Sebastian of Portugal 169
Sedan, battle of 43
Segré 310
Selles-sur-Cher 29
Serrant, Château of 310, **336**
Seuilly
– La Devinière **332**
Sforza, Ludovico 225
Sheep 231
Sicard, François 205, 214, 240
Silk industry 260–61, 289
Slate quarrying 312
Snowdrop 19
Sologne 13, 16, 24, 112, 138, 174–5
Sorel, Agnès 88, 227, 268
Soufflot, Germain 140
Soufflot, Jacques Germain 71
Sourdeau, Jacques 160, 161
Spires 312
Staël, Germaine de 233
Steamboats 45
Suffolk, Earl of 116
Sully, Duc de (Maximilien de Béthune) 132, 133
Sully-sur-Loire 65, 132–3
– Château, Residence of the Duc de Sully **329**
– Collegiate Church of St-Ythier **329**

◆ T ◆

Taine, Hippolyte 90
Talbot, Lord 116, 117
Talcy 140
– Château of the Salviati 99–100, 140, **329**
Talleyrand-Périgord, Charles Maurice de 232, 233
Tapestry of the Apocalypse 297, 299, 300–1, 308, 309, **314**, **335**
Tavant
– Church of St-Nicholas 58, 251, **332**
– wall-paintings 252–5
Theodulf 37, 112, 114, 128, 129, 130
Thévalle family 303
Thibault le Tricheur, Count of Blois 242, 278
Thiron, Bernard 290
Thory, René de 285
Thouard 13
Tiger Beetle 21
Tindall, Gillian 103
Tools (boat-building) 48, 49
Toue 46, 48
Tour-en-Sologne
– Château de Villesavin **330**
– Collection of horse-drawn carriages **330**
Touraine **327**
Tours 12, 16, 36, 37, 40, 41, 43, 44, 93, 100, 116, 194–6, 270
– Archeological Museum 208
– Basilica of St-Martin 196, 204–5, 207, **330**
– Bibliothèque Municipale 203
– Brasserie de l'Univers 214
– Cathédrale St-Gatien 196–7, 271
– Cayenne des

Compagnons du Devoir 208–9
– Chapel of St-Jean 205, **331**
– Château 198, **330**
– Church of St-Denis 212, 213
– Church of St-Julien 199, 203
– Church of St-Saturnin 209
– Cité Alfred-Mame 215
– Cloître de la Psalette **331**
– Cloister of St-Martin 205
– Convent Church of the Minimes 63
– Flower market 214, **331**
– Garlic and Basil fair 213
– Hôtel Babou de la Bourdaisière 202
– Hôtel Binet 209
– Hôtel Choiseul 209
– Hôtel de Beaune-Semblançay 202
– Hôtel de Juste 209
– Hôtel de la Croix Blanche 212–13
– Hôtel de Ville 214
– Hôtel du Commerce 202
– Hôtel Gouin 208, 259, **331**
– Hôtel Lefebvre de Montifray 75, 214
– Hôtel Mame 214
– Hôtel Pierre du Puy (Maison de Tristan) 74, 209
– Hôtel Robin-Quantin 209
– Jardin Botanique 215
– Jardin de St-Pierre-le-Puellier 209
– Jardin des Chanoines 209
– Jardin des Prébendes d'Oé 215, **331**
– Logis de Mars 198
– Logis du Gouverneur 198, **330**
– Maison de la Pucelle Armée 199
– Maison de Tristan (Hôtel Pierre du Puy) 74, 209
– "Le Molière" café 202
– Musée Archéologique **331**
– Musée des Beaux-Arts 198, **331**
– Musée du Compagnonnage 199, **331**
– Musée du Gemmail 212, **331**
– Musée Grevin **331**
– Musée d'Histoire Naturelle 212, **331**
– Musée St-Martin 205, **331**
– Musée des Vins de Touraine 199, **331**
– Palais de Justice 214
– Palais des Congres Léonard-de-Vinci 214
– Passage des Jacobins 202
– Passage du Coeur-Navré 199
– Place Anatole-France 203
– Place de Châteauneuf 204, 212–13
– Place du Grand-Marché 212, 213
– Place Foire-le-Roi 199, 202
– Place Henri-de-Segogne 209
– Place Jean-Jaures 214
– Place Plumereau 208, 209, 210–11
– "Pont de Fil" 199
– Pont Wilson 203
– Priory of St-Éloi 214–15
– Quai d'Orléans 36
– Railway station 214

– Rue Bretonneau 213
– Rue Briçonnet 209, 212
– Rue Colbert 199
– Rue Constantine 208
– Rue de Châteauneuf 213
– Rue de la Grosse-Tour 213
– Rue de la Monaie 73
– Rue de la Paix 209
– Rue de la Rôtisserie 213
– Rue de la Scellerie 212
– Rue des Cerisiers 212
– Rue des Orfèvres 212
– Rue du Change 212, 213
– Rue du Cygne 202
– Rue du Mûrier 212
– Rue du Petit-St-Martin 213
– Rue du Poirier 212
– Rue du Président-Merville 212
– Rue Jules-Favre 202
– Rue Littré 209
– Rue Nationale 203
– Rue Paul-Louis-Courier 208–9
– silk industry 260–1
– St-Gatien Cathedral 61, **331**
– St-Julien Cloister **331**
– St-Julien cellars **331**
– Theater 202
– Tomb of the Children of Anne de Bretagne and Charles VIII 204
– Tour Charlemagne 204
– Tour l'Horloge 204, 205
– Tropical aquarium **331**
– Underground cloister, **331**
Trélazé 312
Trémoille, Guy VI de 133
Trèves 292
– Church of St-Aubin 292, **335**
– Logis de la Cour-Condé 292
Trinqueau, Pierre 161
Troglodyte dwellings 12, 76, 80, 250, 251, 286–9, 291, 292, 293, **315**
Troussay
– Château de 172–3, **330**
– Museum of Sologne country life 173, **330**
"Trousse-culotte" fishing 23 ·
Troyes, Antoine de 161, 165
Turner, J.M.W. 87
Turons 36, 182, 196
Turpin de Crissé 306

◆ U ◆

Ulger de Douai, Bishop 302, 303
Ussé, Château de 100, 268, 270

◆ V ◆

Val-Hulin 286, **335**
Valençay 216, 232
– Château de 67, 70, 217, 232–3, **332**
– Musée de Voitures Anciennes **332**
– *pyramide* 29
Vigée-Lebrun, Élisabeth 191, 231
Vignole, Jean de 287
Vignon, Claude 189
Vigny, Alfred de 178, 228
Vikings 37, 48, 196
Villandry
– Château 263–7, **333**
– Church of St-Étienne 263

– Gardens 263, 264–7, **314**, **333**
Villesavin, Château de 69, 166, 263
Villon, François 138
Vinegar 56, 123
Vineyards 30–2, 56, 98, 293, **314**, **322–7**
Visigoths 37
Vitry, Bernard 299
Voglie, Jean de 203
Voltaire 125, 132
Vouvray **327**

◆ W ◆

Walsh, Viscount 178
Warminski, Jacques 293
Wars of Religion 40, 113, 146, 281, 298
Watteau, Antoine 115
Waugh, Evelyn 100
Weasel 20
Webber, Melville 253
Wharton, Edith 91
Wilde, Oscar 95
Willow, Gray 20
Windmills/Water mills see Mills
Wine Council of Anjou and Saumur 303
Winegrowers' cottages 77, 80
Wines 30–2, 172, 311, **314**, **322–7**
Winterhalter, Franz 231
Woodland 24–5
Woolf, Virginia 96
Wordsworth, William 94–5
World War Two 43, 133

◆ X ◆

Xaintrailles 116

◆ Y ◆

Yolande d'Aragon 280, 284, 298, 312
Young, Arthur 191, 197

◆ Z ◆

Zay, Jean 124